M. Shane O'Guin

P9-DTR-764

The Gospel of

JOHN

Also by James Montgomery Boice

Witness and Revelation in the Gospel of John
Philippians: An Expositional Commentary
The Sermon on the Mount
How to Live the Christian Life (originally, *How to Live It Up*)
Ordinary Men Called by God (originally, *How God Can Use Nobodies*)
The Last and Future World
John: An Expositional Commentary (5 volumes)
"Galatians" in the *Expositor's Bible Commentary*
Can You Run Away from God?
Our Sovereign God, editor
Our Savior God: Studies on Man, Christ and the Atonement, editor
Does Inerrancy Matter?
The Foundation of Biblical Authority, editor
Making God's Word Plain, editor
The Epistles of John
Genesis: An Expositional Commentary (3 volumes)
The Parables of Jesus
The Christ of Christmas
The Minor Prophets: An Expositional Commentary (2 volumes)
Standing on the Rock
The Christ of the Open Tomb
Foundations of the Christian Faith (4 volumes in one)
Christ's Call to Discipleship
Transforming Our World: A Call to Action, editor
Ephesians: An Expositional Commentary
Daniel: An Expositional Commentary
Joshua: We Will Serve the Lord
Nehemiah: Learning to Lead
The King Has Come
Romans: An Expositional Commentary (4 volumes)
Mind Renewal in a Mindless Age
Amazing Grace
Psalms: An Expositional Commentary (3 volumes)
Sure I Believe, So What!
Hearing God When It Hurts
Two Cities, Two Loves
Here We Stand: A Call from Confessing Evangelicals, editor
  with Benjamin E. Sasse
Living by the Book
Acts: An Expositional Commentary
The Heart of the Cross, with Philip G. Ryken
What Makes a Church Evangelical?

The Gospel of

JOHN

Volume 2

Christ and Judaism

John 5–8

JAMES
MONTGOMERY
BOICE

 Baker Books

A Division of Baker Book House Co
Grand Rapids, Michigan 49516

© 1985, 1999 by James Montgomery Boice

Published by Baker Books
a division of Baker Book House Company
P.O. Box 6287, Grand Rapids, MI 49516-6287

Previously published by Zondervan Publishing House

Third, printing, October 2002

Printed in the United States of America

Library of Congress Cataloging-in-Publication Data

Boice, James Montgomery, 1938–
    [Gospel of John]
    The Gospel of John / James Montgomery Boice.
       p.   cm.
    Includes bibliographical references and indexes.
    Contents: v. 2. Christ and Judaism, John 5–8.
    ISBN 0-8010-1073-X (hardcover)
    1. Bible. N.T. John Commentaries. I. Title.
BS2615.3.B55   1999
226.5'077—dc21   99-22764

For current information about all releases from Baker Book House, visit our web site:
http://www.bakerbooks.com

To him who is indeed that Christ,
the Son of the living God

Contents

Preface   ix

57. Christ and Judaism (5:1)   349

58. The Third Miracle (5:2–9)   355

59. Lord of the Sabbath (5:9–16)   361

60. The History of the Sabbath (5:9–16)   367

61. The Day of the Resurrection (5:9–16)   373

62. How to Celebrate Sunday (5:9–16)   379

63. Is God Silent? (5:17–23)   385

64. Possessing Eternity in Time (5:24–27)   391

65. A Matter of Life or Death (5:28–30)   397

66. The Witnesses to Christ (5:31–47)   403

67. Why Miracles? (5:36)   409

68. The Witness of the Scriptures (5:37–38)   415

69. The Purpose of the Scriptures (5:39)   421

70. The Misuse of the Scriptures (5:39–44)   427

71. The Accusation of the Scriptures (5:45–47)   433

72. The Fourth Miracle (6:1–4)   439

73. Three and the Master (6:5–9)   445

74. Who's in Charge? (6:10–15)   451

75. The Fifth Miracle (6:16–21)   457

76. The Search (6:22–27)   463

77. A Golden Sentence (6:28–29)   469

78. "I Am the Bread of Life" (6:30–35)   475

79. Those Who Shall Come (6:36–37)   481

80. The Certainty of Divine Grace (6:37)   487

81. No One Driven Away (6:37)   493

82. The Keeping Power of God (6:38–39)   499

83. God's Will Confirmed by Jesus (6:40)   505

84. Murmurs of Disbelief (6:41–47)   511

85. The Two Mannas (6:48–51)   517

86. Food Indeed and Drink Indeed (6:52–59)   523

87. Discipleship Tested by Doctrine (6:60–65)   529

88. Nowhere to Go but Forward (6:66–68)   535

89. A Disturbing Revelation (6:69–71)   541

90. What Time Is It? (7:1–10)   547

91. What Do You Think of Jesus? (7:11–13)   553

92. Man's Doctrine, God's Doctrine (7:14–18)   559

93. Judging by Right Judgment (7:19–24)   565

94. Who Has Done More Than Jesus? (7:25–31)   571

95. "Where I Am, You Cannot Come" (7:32–36)   577

96. An Invitation and a Promise (7:37–39)   583

97. Christ, a Divider of Men (7:40–44)   589

98. None like Jesus (7:45–52)   595

99. The Woman Taken in Adultery (7:53–8:11)   601

100. Never a "Thing" (7:53–8:11)   607

101. "I Am the Light of the World" (8:12)   613

102. The Witnesses Agree (8:13–18)   619

103. Three Questions (8:19–27)   625

104. The Uplifted Christ (8:28–29)   631

105. Believing on Jesus (8:30–32)   637

106. Free Indeed! (8:33–36)   643

107. Sons of Abraham (8:37–40)   649

108. That Other Family (8:41–50)   655

109. The Last Enemy (8:51)   661

110. Christ and Abraham (8:52–56)   667

111. Is Jesus God? (8:57–59)   673

Notes   679

Subject Index   684

Scripture Index   692

Preface

 It has been more than thirty years since I began to study the Gospel of John in a serious way and nearly twenty-five years since my studies of the Gospel began to appear in print. They have been out of print for some time. So it was with much gratitude that I learned of Baker's interest in reissuing them in this revised and attractive version.

When I first preached on John, I was often asked whether I ever found myself running out of ideas as I progressed at such a slow pace. (My exposition of the entire Gospel took eight years.) I answered such questions with the reply that the opposite was actually the case. Rather than running low on ideas or growing stale as a result of the week-by-week exposition, I found myself increasingly stimulated by John's narrative and regretful that in spite of every effort on my part I was still unable to penetrate all the deep truths of the book or to express adequately what I saw. In my studies for this volume, particularly for the comments on chapter 6, I found myself delving deeper into the doctrines of grace as summarized under the five distinguishing points of the Reformed faith (or Calvinism) and was greatly blessed as a result. There is a sense in which the founding of the Philadelphia Conference on Reformed Theology (1974) and later my involvement in the work of the Alliance of Confessing Evangelicals (founded 1994) had its origin in my work on this chapter.

There have been related blessings too. In the course of preparing this volume I discovered the sermons of Charles Haddon Spurgeon as I had not done previously, and I came to love his ability to handle even the most difficult doctrines pastorally. Consequently, a debt to Spurgeon shows up increasingly from these pages forward.

At times, as in the first volume, I deviate from a straightforward exposition of the text to deal in somewhat greater detail with themes suggested by it. In the previous volume I did this in reference to witnessing and baptism, which I discussed for a total of eight chapters (chapters 16–23). In this volume, eight more chapters are similarly spent, first, in regard to the questions of sabbath observance versus the celebration of Sunday as the day of Christian worship (chapters 59–62) and, second, in regard to the doctrine of the Scriptures (chapters 68–71).

The outline of John's Gospel, which I introduced in volume 1 as the basis of the five-volume division of my exposition, is still being followed. Volume 1 deals with the coming of the light of the Lord Jesus Christ into this world (chapters 1–4). Volume 2 deals with the growth of hostility toward him on the part of the religious leaders (chapters 5–8). This is linked to the sabbath question, hence the lengthy discussion of that subject. Volume 3 shows Jesus beginning to call out a people to himself from among Israel, beginning with the calling of the man who had been born blind (chapters 9–12). Volume 4 examines the final discourses (chapters 13–17). Volume 5 contains an exposition of the last events of Christ's earthly life, culminating in his resurrection (chapters 18–21).

The writing of these studies is the most difficult work I do, far more difficult, for example, than counseling, preaching, traveling, or any of the other normal activities that make up the bulk of an active ministry. Yet this is important work. I trust that it will be greatly blessed to many students of God's Word. Others have worked on this volume, particularly Miss Caecilie Foelster, who carefully edited all my early manuscripts and saw them through the various stages of production. May God richly bless their efforts in thus helping to make the divine Word more widely and fully known. I earnestly pray that what is of the human author only may be quickly forgotten. May that which is of God bear much fruit unto life eternal.

To him who is indeed "that Christ, the Son of the living God" be all glory forever. Amen and amen.

James Montgomery Boice
Philadelphia, Pennsylvania

Christ and Judaism

57

Christ and Judaism

John 5:1

Some time later, Jesus went up to Jerusalem for a feast of the Jews.

The fifth chapter of John's Gospel begins a new section of the book. Like the first major section of the Gospel, this next section extends over four chapters, beginning with chapter 5 and ending with chapter 8. It deals as a whole with the development of opposition to the Lord Jesus Christ on the part of the Jewish leaders in Jerusalem and with Christ's response to their opposition. The fact that this is a new section is important; for if we recognize the differences between this section of the Gospel and the first four chapters, we will have a lesson for ourselves about how we are to persevere in God's service.[1]

Little is ever accomplished in this life without a firm purpose. Caesar would never have conquered Gaul; Einstein would never have discovered relativity; the United States of America would never have landed men on the moon; nor would many thousands of other great accomplishments ever have been achieved without a firm purpose. Moreover, just as this is true in secular matters, so is it true spiritually. The only difficulty is that many Christians seem to live more by whim than by a firm determination to pursue the will of the Lord; consequently, many lack a firm purpose. We know what this means per-

349

sonally when we begin a work but soon drop it, when we determine to study the Bible every day but end up doing so only for about a week, when we get fired up to witness for Jesus Christ but then stop when we notice the first real sign of hostility.

Why do so many Christians seem to live like this? Why do we lack perseverance? There may be many answers, of course, but there are two main reasons—hostility and the danger of success. It is my conviction that these two dangers faced the Lord Jesus Christ in his determination to fulfill the will of his Father in his life and that we can be helped by studying his reactions to them. Simply put, the first of these dangers emerges in the fifth chapter of John in the opposition of the Jewish rulers to Christ and his teachings and is dealt with there, while the second danger—the danger of success—emerges in chapter 6.

At the end of these chapters, chapters 5 and 6, we find Jesus firmly following the path that God had set before him; namely, the path of the cross.

The Jewish Elite

The fifth chapter of the Gospel begins with a sentence that immediately shifts our attention to a new class of people. John writes, "Some time later, Jesus went up to Jerusalem for a feast of the Jews."

The new class of people is "the Jews," but we must not understand this to mean all of the Jewish people; that is, the term is not meant ethnically. When John says "the Jews" he means the Jewish rulers who had their headquarters in Jerusalem, and it is these primarily with whom Jesus now comes into conflict.

The expression "the Jews" is not at all common in the other three Gospels— Matthew, Mark, and Luke. These Gospels use the phrase occasionally, most often in the expression "the King of the Jews." But at the most this is only half a dozen times or so. In John the case is quite different. In the fourth Gospel the phrase occurs some seventy times. It is true that in some instances out of this great number of occurrences the term is neutral, or even praiseworthy, as in Christ's statement, "Salvation is from the Jews" (4:22). But generally the term is used critically of those religious leaders who opposed Christ and the gospel. Thus John clearly distinguishes between the Galileans, who were Jewish in the ethnic sense, but whom he does not call Jews, and the Jews of Jerusalem. Moreover, even in regard to Jerusalem he distinguishes between the leaders, whom he terms "Jews," and others. For instance, the parents of the man born blind were certainly Jewish, but they are not called Jews. Instead, they are said to have reacted in certain ways because "they were afraid of the Jews" (9:22), meaning the religious leaders.

It is these jealous and hostile leaders of the Judaism of Christ's day who are now brought into the picture. According to the first four chapters of John's Gospel most of the major groupings of the nation had already responded to Christ favorably—the disciples of John the Baptist and other Judeans, the Samaritans, the people of Galilee, even (according to the previous chapter) some who were in the service of Herod. The only exception has been the Jewish rulers.

There is probably a historical reason why the Gospel shifts to the conflict between Christ and these men at this point, and this is simply that a number of important historical events had taken place between Christ's last visit to Jerusalem and the visit recorded in the fifth chapter. There is a lapse of time here that John indicates generally by the phrase "some time later." It was during this lapse of time that the events in question took place.

What happened during this period? First, there had been a shift in the policy of Rome toward the Jewish nation that had greatly sharpened the danger of insurrections and war. The anti-Semite Roman commander Sejanus, working through Pilate, deprived the Sanhedrin of its jurisdiction over capital crimes, with the result that the Sanhedrin had to abandon the Great Hall of Hewn Stone in the temple court and move as a body to the market of Annas on the temple mount. We see the results of this change a year or so later when the Sanhedrin was compelled to come to Pilate seeking the death penalty in the case of Jesus Christ. Second, there was an increase, partly as a result of the Roman action, of Zealot activity leading the more pessimistic among the rulers to predict a time of persecution and suffering. Thus, Rabbi Johanan ben Zakkai prophesied the future destruction of the temple, and Rabbi Zadok began a forty-year partial fast for the preservation of Jerusalem that ended only when the city was overrun by the Roman legions under Titus and destroyed by them. From the biblical point of view the most significant event was the arrest and eventual execution of John the Baptist, who was Christ's forerunner. We notice this by comparing John 3:24, where we are told that "This was before John was put in prison," with 5:33–35, which speaks of the ministry of John in the past tense.

In such a tumultuous period of history it is no wonder that the leaders of Judaism reacted to the emergence of Jesus as a new and potentially dangerous figure. It is understandable that their hostility intensified when he revealed himself to be above their personal interpretation of the law and actually defended his actions by identifying himself with God the Father. Here is a great hostility. Yet Jesus did not allow this hostility to deter him from following the path the Father had set before him.

Do you allow hostility to deter you? If you determine to live for God in the midst of this sinful world or speak a word for Jesus Christ to those who do not yet know him, you can be sure that hostility in some form will come. Perhaps you have already experienced it. Have you allowed it to get you off the track of Christian living and witnessing? If so, you need to get back on the track by following the example of Jesus.

No Bitterness

Jesus Christ did not allow the hostility of the Jewish leaders to deter him from the path that God had placed before him. But, on the other hand, neither did he allow it to produce a bitterness in his outlook on his ministry. Unfortunately, this bitterness has often happened to Christ's disciples, perhaps to you. I have known Christians who have not allowed hostility to get them off course, but unfortunately they have become so bitter that they have greatly limited their opportunities for service and it has darkened their lives.

It is interesting to note, precisely at this point, that this is what some scholars have claimed happened in the early church in reference to Judaism, and that we even have a reflection of what happened in references such as those in which John critically mentions "the Jews." In other words, some scholars are saying that Christian anti-Semitism has its origins in the New Testament Scriptures and can be eliminated only when today's Christians repudiate their error at its source.

Let me give you some references that will made this clear. In a recent book a well-known Jewish rabbi, Rabbi Ben Zion Bokser, argues that "the historic roots of Christian anti-Semitism go back to the basic teachings of the New Testament."[2] In another book Rabbi Samuel Sandmel argues similarly, "We Jews figure as villains, all of us or some of us, in much of your Bible. Only very lately has this bothered you extensively and intensively, and the reality has to be faced that some of you are not bothered by this at all."[3]

It is not just rabbis that have been making this point. Actually, the same accusation has been leveled—only in even more forceful language—by Protestants. A. Roy Eckhardt, editor of the *Journal of the American Academy of Religion,* states that "all the learned exegesis in the world cannot negate the truth that there are elements not only of anti-Judaism but of anti-Semitism in the New Testament." He calls for a denunciation by Christians of "anti-Semitic allegations" in John, in Paul, and elsewhere.[4] On other fronts Noel Freedman of the San Francisco Theological Seminary has claimed that the New Testament "is simply an anti-Semitic book."[5] In the foreword to *Judaism and the Christian Predicament,* Union Theological Seminary's Frederick C. Grant has expressed the hope that the reversal of traditional attitudes toward the Jews that he detects in our age "will in time . . . involve more than just a formal repudiation of anti-Semitism. It will also include a repudiation of impossible literalism and legalism in the interpretation of the Bible, or the refusal to interpret it at all."[6]

Is this true? Is the New Testament anti-Semitic? One cannot help admiring the vigor with which these writers—both Christians and Jews—are attempting to purge the world of anti-Jewish prejudice. And there can be little doubt that the defeat of anti-Semitism is long overdue. Nevertheless, at the same time, one must question whether this approach properly represents the biblical view and whether the cure prescribed is adequate. Actually, it is more likely that the cavalier way in which some Protestant exegetes handle Scripture actually breeds an insensitivity to it and consequently sets aside the one sure hope of a cure.

In the first place, it simply is not true that the New Testament is anti-Semitic. It is true that the New Testament contains statements that sound anti-Semitic to modern ears, conditioned as they are by centuries of prejudice. The New Testament speaks of a general failure of the Jewish people in the time of the apostles to believe in Jesus as their Messiah and Savior, and it laments this unbelief. Still, if this is to be judged anti-Semitic, then statements about the failure of Gentiles to believe must be considered anti-Gentile. Actually, the New Testament writers show great anguish because those of their own nation had failed to embrace what was for them the "Good News" of God's action in Christ for man's salvation. At no point in any of the nonbiblical literature of the times does any writer claim, as Paul does (Rom. 9:3), that he would be content to see himself accursed if that would bring about the salvation of the Jewish people.

Critics have imagined an anti-Semitic element in John's references to "the Jews" as those who crucified Jesus. But, as we have seen, this was a political designation for John rather than an ethnic one. He himself was a Jew and was proud, as were the other disciples, of his heritage.

Second, the current judgment against certain biblical strains seems to overlook entirely the positive things said about the Jews in the New Testament, even by those writers who are judged to be most anti-Semitic in their statements. Paul is considered a prime offender because of his sharp polemic, particularly against the Judaisers who were subverting his hard-won churches. But it is Paul who most clearly spells out the advantages of Judaism. "What advantage, then, is there in being a Jew, or what value is there in circumcision?" he asks. "Much in every way! First of all they have been entrusted with the very words of God" (Rom. 3:1–2). "Theirs is the adoption as sons; theirs the divine glory, the covenants, the receiving of the law, the temple worship and the promises. Theirs are the patriarchs, and from them is traced the human ancestry of Christ" (Rom. 9:4–5). This certainly is not anti-Semitism. On the contrary, it shows an unusual sensitivity to God's dealings with the Jews in history and great appreciation for the spiritual inheritance available to all men through them.

Moreover, if the Jews as a whole have refused to believe in Jesus, this is remarkable to the New Testament writers precisely because of the way God worked through the Jews in the past. It is this that gives rise to extensive comment. In Paul's mind, the fact that God seems now to be working through the Gentiles, calling out another people, the church, is so unexpected and so astonishing that he properly calls it a "mystery" kept secret since the world began.

Finally, the New Testament also points to great future privileges for Israel, when Israel as a whole will receive her Messiah, even as many individual Jews receive him now. Eckhardt argues that Jesus is not the Messiah of Israel because he is not the kind of Messiah Israel was and is expecting. But this is faulty logic. One might as well say that he is not the Savior of the Gentiles because most Gentiles do not want a Savior. The Christian must argue against both these conclusions, maintaining that Jesus is indeed the Messiah and Sav-

ior in spite of people's rejection of him, and that it is precisely people's un-
awareness of this need that most reveals it. Moreover, it would even be a correct reading of Paul (Romans 9–11) and John (Revelation) to claim that God
has preserved the Jewish people throughout history so that they can bear a
great witness to him in the end days.

Our Example

The conclusion of all this is that Jesus Christ did not respond to the hostility of the leaders of Israel toward himself with bitterness any more than he
allowed their criticism to deter him from his path to the cross. In his reaction we have a pattern for our own.

How are we to avoid these two dangers? There is only one answer. It is by
keeping our eyes upon the Lord Jesus. John Bunyan pictured it graphically
in *Pilgrim's Progress* in a scene in which Pilgrim escapes death from two fe-
rocious beasts who are chained to either side of a path. He escapes by walking directly toward a light that is held before him. Christ is our light. His
light shines on the path we are to follow. The Bible admonishes us to lay aside
everything that might hinder us in our purpose and to run life's race "fix[ing]
our eyes on Jesus, the author and perfecter of our faith, who for the joy set
before him endured the cross, scorning its shame, and sat down at the right
hand of the throne of God" (Heb. 12:2).

58

The Third Miracle

John 5:2–9

Now there is in Jerusalem near the Sheep Gate a pool, which in Aramaic is called Bethesda and which is surrounded by five covered colonnades. Here a great number of disabled people used to lie—the blind, the lame, the paralyzed. One who was there had been an invalid for thirty-eight years. When Jesus saw him lying there and learned that he had been in this condition for a long time, he asked him, "Do you want to get well?"

"Sir," the invalid replied, "I have no one to help me into the pool when the water is stirred. While I am trying to get in, someone else goes down ahead of me."

Then Jesus said to him, "Get up! Pick up your mat and walk." At once the man was cured; he picked up his mat and walked.

The day on which this took place was a Sabbath.

It is almost commonplace today to observe that the "system" often seems to help those who need it least while it is hardest on the destitute. We speak of this economically when we say that the rich get richer while the poor get poorer. Those who are well educated often get better educations. Those on the treadmill of unemployment and relief often sink deeper and deeper into the welfare morass. In one sense, some people even apply the principle in the area of religion when they say—wrongly, of course—that "God helps those who help themselves." So deeply is this ingrained in the modern mind that people try to tell me that the last statement—"God helps those who help themselves"—is in the Bible.

Actually, the opposite is true. For one of the great principles of the Word of God is that God, the Almighty, helps the helpless. The gospel is for everyone. But that only means that it is to you and me, who cannot help ourselves spiritually, that the offer of salvation comes.

The Need of Humanity

The fifth chapter of John contains one of the great biblical expressions of this principle. It is the third miracle that John records in his Gospel, specifically the miracle in which Jesus Christ enables a lame man to walk. There are probably two reasons why John records it. First, it was this miracle that marked the beginning of angry disbelief and hostility toward Jesus on the part of the Jewish leaders. It is to this theme that the Gospel now turns. Second, there is the fact that the story illustrates how Jesus came to the weak and helpless, and saved them. This aspect of the story is particularly apparent at the beginning of the account of the hostility that developed between Jesus and the Jewish leaders; for the leaders were the ones who should have accepted him and among whom we would have thought he should have done his most extensive work. But they were insensitive, and Christ moved instead among the masses.

John tells us that all this happened when Jesus returned to Jerusalem for a feast. This would have been one of the great religious feasts of Israel, though we do not know which one. Apparently he was alone, for none of the disciples is mentioned as having been with him. While in Jerusalem Jesus passed by the pool of Bethesda, which John tells us was distinguished by five collonades, where he saw the lame man.

It is interesting to stop at this point to note that the pool of Bethesda, mentioned here by John, is now known to archaeologists. There was a time when critics of the Gospel were giving the book a very late dating and were arguing in part on the basis of this reference that the author of the Gospel did not really know what Jerusalem was like in Christ's time. They said no one had ever heard of a pool by this name and, besides, no one has ever even uncovered a five-sided pool from antiquity. Now, however, the name "Beth Eshatain" has emerged from the copper scroll found among the Dead Sea Scrolls. It gives us the name Bethesda. And what is even more important, the pool itself has been found. Actually, the pool of Bethesda (now known as the pool of St. Anne) is two twin pools each surrounded by colonnades. Thus, there are five collonades—four of which surround the pools and one that divides them. This is the pool of which the apostle John was writing when he recorded that in Christ's day sick people gathered there believing that an angel intermittently stirred up the water, and that whenever this happened the next person to step into the water would be cured.

It is a pitiful picture, as John relays it. But it is far more pitiful when we realize that he is including the description to dramatize the helpless and woefully hopeless condition of the human race.

"Now there is in Jerusalem near the Sheep Gate a pool, which in Aramaic is called Bethesda and which is surrounded by five covered colonnades. Here a great number of disabled people used to lie—the blind, the lame, the paralyzed" (5:2–3). What a comprehensive description that is! It is really a twofold description. First, the people are called disabled; that is, they are said to be without strength to help themselves. Then, their disability is spelled out by three more terms. John calls them blind, lame, and paralyzed.

This is the human race as it stands apart from the grace of God through Jesus Christ. How does God view people before that act in which he places new life within them? One answer is in Romans 5:6, which tells us that it was when we were "still powerless" that Christ died for the "ungodly." The American Standard Version of the Bible and the Roman Catholic Confraternity translation both translate this verse to say that it was when we were "weak" that the love of God was shown to us. The Williams and Goodspeed translations say "helpless." Phillips uses the English word "powerless." Beyond this, the lexicons tell us that the Greek word means "infirm, feeble, unable to achieve anything great, destitute of power among men, sluggish in doing right." In other words, God tells us that it was when we found it impossible to do anything for ourselves spiritually that Christ died for us.

When we use the word "impossible," we must be careful to indicate in what sense the word is meant. For instance, there are cases of conditional impossibility in which we mean that something is impossible unless something else should happen. I might say that it is impossible for me to pay all this month's bills, but that is a conditional impossibility since it might happen that I would receive an unexpected check that would cover them. I would be using the word in the same way if I should say that it is impossible for me to take on an extra job, *unless* I drop one that I am already doing; or that it is impossible for me to work with this noise, *unless* I wear earmuffs. I could extend this list indefinitely, for there will always be an infinite number of things that are impossible, *unless* something else should happen.

In quite another category, however, are those impossibilities that will remain impossibilities because they can never be affected by circumstances. It is impossible for a thing to be true and false at the same time and in the same relationship. It is impossible for black to be white. It is impossible for something to exist and not exist at the same time. God places disabled man in this category of impossibilities when he declares that it is impossible for man to do anything by himself that will satisfy God.

We find these truths summarized in the many verses that tell us what man cannot do spiritually. We read, "The man without the Spirit does not accept the things that come from the Spirit of God, for they are foolishness to him, and he *cannot* understand them, because they are spiritually discerned" (1 Cor. 2:14). Jesus asked the people of his day, "Why is my language not clear to you?" then answered, "Because you are *unable* to hear what I say" (John 8:43). Peter wrote that, unaided by God, a person *cannot* cease from sin (2 Peter 2:14).

Blind, Lame, Paralyzed

In case any should question the full import of what John is teaching at this point, he goes on to three additional terms to characterize the great multitude at the pool of Bethesda. They also characterize us. The first term is "blind." Jesus spoke of this blindness in chapter 3 when he told Nicodemus, "No one can see the kingdom of God unless he is born again" (3:3). He spoke of it again when he said to the religious leaders (after he had healed a man who had been born blind), "If you were blind [i.e., like the man who had been born blind but who, nevertheless, had believed], you would not be guilty of sin; but now that you claim you can see [which they could not do], your guilt remains" (9:41). The religious leaders thought they could see, but they were actually blind about spiritual things, as they proved by their refusal to believe on Jesus. The man who had been born blind knew he was blind, but Jesus gave him spiritual as well as physical sight, which he proved by confessing Jesus as his Lord and by worshiping him (9:38).

The second word is "lame." It follows the other, for how can a person walk the narrow way that leads to life if he is blind? The story of the paralytic man who was brought to Jesus by his friends who lowered him into Jesus' presence on a mat through an opening in the ceiling illustrates our spiritual lameness (Matt. 9:1-2; Mark 2:1-5; Luke 5:17-21). The man could not come on his own. He needed someone to bring him to Jesus. Jesus spoke of man's inability to walk in a spiritual sense when he declared, "No one can come to me unless the Father who sent me draws him" (6:44).

Finally, John also tells us that humanity is "paralyzed." Have you never heard someone say, "Oh, I ought to get up and do so and so, but I feel so tired I can't raise my arms. I feel paralyzed"? Well, that is precisely the case in spiritual terms. The difficulty is not with knowing that there is a job to be done. We should be righteous. We should be like Jesus Christ. It is just that when we think about such a standard we seem paralyzed. Certainly, we could say with the apostle Paul as he writes of himself apart from the power of God at work in his life, "For I have the desire to do what is good, but I cannot carry it out" (Rom. 7:18).

Grace

It is a desperate picture if we take it seriously. Yet it is the glorious prelude to the gospel of God's grace, for it is to such people—blind, lame, and paralyzed—that Christ came.

We read that the Lord Jesus Christ walked into that vast collection of sick people and saw there a man who had been disabled for thirty-eight years. No one recognized Christ as he moved among them, for they were blind spiritually. Besides, they had their hopes set on the superstition about the moving of the water. No one rose to meet him, for they were lame. No one reached out a hopeful hand; they were paralyzed. Yet Jesus moved among them and healed this most helpless of sinners.

"Do you want to get well?" Jesus asked him.

The lame man answered, "Sir, I have no one to help me into the pool when the water is stirred. While I am trying to get in, someone else goes down ahead of me."

Jesus commanded, "Get up, pick up your mat and walk." At once the man was made well and did as Jesus commanded.

That is how God saves sinners today. If our salvation depended upon our recognizing him or reaching out a hand toward him, who would be saved? The answer is: No one. Yet instead of waiting for us to come—instead of waiting to "help those who help themselves"—Christ comes to us and speaks the words that give life.

In Harry Ironside's commentary on this passage, the well-known Bible teacher tells a story from the early days of his ministry. He was in San Francisco at the time, and it was his custom then to take some of the Sunday school children down to the beach on Washington's birthday. On one particular morning, as he did this, he found the beach covered with all sorts of wreckage. At first no one knew where it had come from. But later, when they had returned to the city, they learned that it had come from a great liner called the *Rio de Janeiro,* which had been on its way to America from China. Trying to make the San Francisco harbor in the fog the previous evening, the ship had run upon a rock and been broken in pieces. Although hundreds of people were drowned in this accident, some escaped. The newspaper told this story about one of them. A young American journalist on board ship had both his legs broken. He lost consciousness, and while in that condition had been thrown into the water. The water probably brought him back to consciousness and he began to float. He floated for hours. Finally that utterly helpless man was drawn out of the water by a rescue party. As Ironside read that, he saw in the story a marvelous picture of God's grace to sinners. Some swam for hours before they were picked up, strong and hearty men. Others were drowned. But this man had no ability to swim; he was helpless. Yet he was saved. No wonder Jesus told us that "the Son of Man came to seek and to save what was lost" (Luke 19:10).

No Argument

He came to find you. Will you argue that you are not helpless, that you are not blind, lame, or paralyzed? If you will argue God's verdict upon your spiritual capabilities, you will not be saved. The Bible teaches that God will not debate his verdict upon the spiritual condition of the human race. God declares that the creature is not the Creator. You are not as perfect as the Lord Jesus Christ, and that makes you a spiritual paralytic or any other name for a handicap that you may wish to apply to it. Yet—this is the glory of the gospel—it is for such that Christ died.

In the seventeenth century, an English bishop named William Beveridge wrote these words: "I cannot pray, except I sin; I cannot preach, but I sin; I cannot administer, nor receive the holy sacrament, but I sin. My very repentance needs to be repented of; and the tears I shed need washing in the blood of Christ." Bishop Beveridge was right. But as soon as I am able to accept the fact that I am ungodly man by nature and therefore completely unable to rise to meet God by any inborn effort, then I can also know that my sins have been dealt with in Christ and that he gives new life to all who trust him for their salvation.

59

Lord of the Sabbath

John 5:9-16

The day on which this took place was a Sabbath, and so the Jews said to the man who had been healed, "It is the Sabbath; the law forbids you to carry your mat."

But he replied, "The man who made me well said to me, 'Pick up your mat and walk.'"

So they asked him, "Who is this fellow who told you to pick it up and walk?"

The man who was healed had no idea who it was, for Jesus had slipped away into the crowd that was there.

Later Jesus found him at the temple and said to him, "See, you are well again. Stop sinning or something worse may happen to you." The man went away and told the Jews that it was Jesus who had made him well.

So, because Jesus was doing these things on the Sabbath, the Jews persecuted him.

The ninth verse of chapter 5 has brought us to an ominous note. The story of the healing of the disabled man at the pool of Bethesda has just been told, but at this point we read: "The day on which this took place was a Sabbath."

This does not sound too serious to us because the observance or nonobservance of the sabbath is not too big an issue in our time. Nevertheless, the issue was serious in Christ's time and, what is more, actually loomed larger and larger as Christ's ministry unfolded. On the grounds of this issue the Jerusalem authorities eventually plotted to destroy him. It is also true, however, that in another sense the issues are serious in our time too, even though, strictly speaking, most persons are not struggling with the question of how to worship God on Saturday. The importance of the issue emerges when we ask these questions: Why is it that Christians generally worship on the first day of the week, on Sunday, rather than on the Jewish sabbath, which is Sat-

361

urday? Is God displeased with worship on either one of these days? Why do we not observe both? Or even, why observe either? Does worship on a given day of the week have anything to do with true religion?

These questions lie behind the subject matter of the next four studies, each of which deals with the sabbath-Sunday question. More specifically, the chapters deal with the problem that arose between Jesus and the Jewish authorities, the purpose and history of the Jewish sabbath, the significance of the Christian observance of the first day of the week, and the question of how we as Christians should celebrate it.

Grace or Regulations?

We must begin, however, with the real significance of the sabbath question, and that is: Is the Christian to be ruled by grace or is he to be under regulations? The special gravity of this problem is set forth in a quotation that shows Dr. Lewis Sperry Chafer's view of the sabbath question.

"The distinction between the reign of law and the reign of grace is at no point more sharply drawn than in the question of the observance of the seventh day of the week or the first day of the week; for these two days are symbolical of the dispensations to which they are related. Likewise, at no point is personal religious prejudice, which is born of early training and sentiment, more assertive than on the sabbath question. It was His liberal teaching on the observance of the sabbath which, more than aught else, provoked the wrath of the Jewish leaders against Christ, and, it may be observed, there is no religious subject today which so draws out personal convictions and opinions. The reason is evident. Few have really comprehended the exact character and principle of grace. To many, Christianity is a system of human works and character building from which merit accrues. And the observance of a sabbath day presents extraordinary opportunities for the exercise of meritorious works."[1]

This, of course, was precisely the situation in Christ's day, as also in ours. God had commanded a sabbath for the Jewish people, but the leaders had perverted it by transforming it into a system by which they thought they were earning grace by good works.

The need to observe the sabbath is found in the Ten Commandments. God said, "Remember the Sabbath day by keeping it holy. Six days you shall labor and do all your work, but the seventh day is a Sabbath to the LORD your God. On it you shall not do any work, neither you, nor your son or daughter, nor your manservant or maidservant, nor your animals, nor the alien within your gates" (Exod. 20:8–10). This basic principle was further developed in other Old Testament books and was applied to all areas of Jewish life, even to the way the fields were treated. Thus, Jeremiah warns that the failure of the people of his day to properly observe the sabbath would result in the fall of Jerusalem to the Babylonians: "Be careful not to carry a load on the Sabbath day or bring it through the gates of Jerusalem. Do not bring a load out of your houses or do any work on the Sabbath, but keep the Sabbath day holy, as I commanded your forefathers. . . . But if you do not obey me to keep the Sabbath day holy by not carrying any load as you come through the gates of Jerusalem on the Sabbath day, then I will kindle an unquenchable fire in the gates of Jerusalem that will consume her fortresses" (Jer. 17:21–22, 27).

This was God's teaching for Israel concerning the sabbath. Moreover, it was taken so seriously by him that we even read that the people remained captive in Babylon for seventy years so that all the broken sabbaths on the land might be paid for (2 Chron. 36:21).

The difficulty lay in the fact that the leaders of Israel had added man's regulations to God's law, and this had reduced the observance of the sabbath to the worst forms of legalism. For instance, the law said that a man was not to travel on the sabbath day (Exod. 16:29). "But what is traveling?" asked the scribes. "What constitutes a journey?" In answering this question they then developed the concept of a sabbath day's journey, which was roughly a thousand yards. So a man could walk that far on the sabbath, but to walk more than that was sin. If, however, a rope was tied across the end of a street, then the whole street technically became one house; and a man could walk a thousand yards beyond the rope. Or if he deposited enough food for a meal at any given place on Friday night, on the next day he could walk to it, eat his meal (thereby technically establishing a home), and then walk a thousand yards more. If he were clever enough at this, I suppose that a determined man could walk halfway across Palestine.

Or, take the matter of carrying a burden. The text in Jeremiah prohibits this. But what is a burden? Is a handkerchief a burden? The answer was yes if it was carried, but no if it was worn as an article of clothing. So, obviously, the way to get a handkerchief out of an upstairs drawer and into a downstairs drawer was to take it out of the one, tie it around your neck, go downstairs, and then place it in the new location.

The same logic also worked in this way. Take a man who is out walking. He spits. Is that work? It depends on what happens to the saliva. If it goes into the dirt and makes a slight furrow, then that is plowing and it is work. But if it hits a rock, no work is done. So, under this system, being religious on Saturday more or less depended on which direction you spit.

All this was abhorrent to the Lord Jesus Christ. So he determined to rescue Israel from her enslavement to these man-made sabbath regulations and to restore a proper balance by showing that the sabbath was made for man rather than man for the sabbath. In this way he paved the way for a fuller revelation of God's grace in his coming death and resurrection.

The Example of King David

We want to come back to the discussion of this theme in John's Gospel, but before we do we need to turn to the parallel discussion of the same issue in Matthew. The reason is that Matthew's Gospel, more than John's, was written to Jews and therefore develops this subject in a fuller form.

Jesus had been walking through the grain fields with his disciples on the sabbath, and his disciples were hungry. The disciples leaned over and gathered a few heads of grain. They rubbed it in their hands, releasing the chaff, and then ate the ripe grain. Unfortunately, nearby Pharisees saw it and objected that it was not lawful for the disciples to do this on the sabbath; for, according to their view, this was harvesting. Jesus answered, "Haven't you read what David did when he and his companions were hungry? He entered the house of God, and he and his companions ate the consecrated bread—which was not lawful for them to do, but only for the priests. Or haven't you read in the Law that on the Sabbath the priests in the temple desecrate the day and yet are innocent? I tell you that one greater than the temple is here. If you had known what these words mean, 'I desire mercy, not sacrifice,' you would not have condemned the innocent. For the Son of Man is Lord of the Sabbath" (Matt. 12:3–8).

In this reply there are three principles. The first is contained in Jesus' remarks concerning King David. Every Jew knew the story to which he referred. David had been anointed by God to be king over the people, but they had rejected this anointed king in order to follow Absalom, David's rebellious son. David was forced to flee from Jerusalem for his life. He had no food. Being without food, he and his followers entered the tabernacle and took the "consecrated" that was always there and ate it. Every Jew knew that only the priests were allowed to enter the temple. Only priests could eat this bread. Nevertheless, God did not strike David dead for doing it. Why? The explanation is that God considered the anointing of David to be more important than the law about the bread. And it was useless and hypocritical for the people to be pretending to serve God through the minute laws of the tabernacle worship when they were rejecting God's king. It is insulting to God to act out ritual if the heart is far from him.

This clearly applied to the situation in Christ's day. For it was also useless and hypocritical for the scribes and Pharisees to be insisting upon their little sabbath rules while they were actually turning their back on God's anointed Messiah, the Lord Jesus. There he was! He was greater than the temple! So if they rejected him, even the sabbath, backed by all the Old Testament laws, was meaningless.

Formalism

The second principle in Christ's reply is that the formalism practiced by the Jewish authorities actually blinds one to real need. In other words, it hardens people in their relationship to others. Jesus noted this when he remarked that they did not know the meaning of the statement, "I will have mercy and not sacrifice."

Here were men who were being punctilious in the observance of their interpretation of God's law, and yet we read that because Jesus was not obeying their regulations they were determining to kill him. Moreover, they would even try to keep their own regulations while they did it. The arrest of Jesus came at the time of the Passover, the most holy week and day in Israel's calendar. The difficulty these men faced was that they wanted to dispose of Jesus without defiling themselves for the Passover. So they held a conference to see how they could fit it all in. They concluded that it could be done if they could follow this order. There would be a trial by night (which was illegal—but not so illegal, they argued, as failing to keep the Passover). Next there would be an official trial by day, in the early morning hours. There would be an approach to Pilate (they needed to make sure that no one actually went into his quarters, for that would defile any Jew and prohibit him from eating the Passover). Finally there would be the execution. The whole thing would be over by noontime, and everyone involved could then go and worship Jehovah. So they marched along the little path of their own regulations. When it was necessary they stepped out just enough to murder God. Then they stepped back in and went on with their formalism.

Let this horror teach us how terrible it is to have a religion of rules and ceremonies when the heart is far from the Savior. No horror is so great that it has not been practiced by someone at some time in the name of religion. And nothing is so bad as the tendency of the human heart to seize on some outward, useless, and hypocritical ceremony and follow it to the letter without turning at all to God.

In contrast to this deadly effect of formalism on the lives of the Jewish leaders, Jesus simply showed by his actions that people were far more important than rules and that the showing of mercy is a far higher obligation upon a follower of God than regulations. Thus, in Matthew, after Jesus' discussion with the leaders, he simply healed a man with a withered hand (Matt. 12:9–13), while in John he provoked the same issue by curing the disabled man (John 5:1–16). The Pharisees wanted to use these men to trap Jesus. Jesus, out of his great compassion, wanted to heal them.

These verses from Matthew also show a third principle. It brings us back to the account of the conflict in John. The third principle Jesus states is that whatever their little rules and regulations might be, he, rather than they, was the Lord of the sabbath. He established the sabbath. He was God. This was his claim. Thus, he could alter the sabbath, suspend it, or even remove it as the case would be. In the same way today, Jesus makes a claim to be the Lord of your sabbaths, your habits, your aspirations, your abilities, your life. We are faced with the same fact of human nature that the Pharisees faced; namely, that it is so much nicer to try to pile up a collection of human credits than to allow Jesus to manifest his lordship in our lives. The lordship of Jesus Christ? That is Christianity. The other is only religion.

The Committee

At this point the story in John's Gospel ends with a very dark sentence. It had begun on an ominous note—"the day on which this took place was a sabbath"—but by now the skies that were threatening had become so black with clouds that they contained murder. We are told, "So, because Jesus was doing these things on the Sabbath day, the Jews persecuted him" (v. 16).

What does this mean? Well, it means that the Jews of Christ's day did what organized religion often does. They formed a committee. The purpose of this committee was to find a way to trap Jesus. We would call it a lynching committee. We do not know exactly what was said, of course, for the hearings of this committee were conducted behind closed doors. Nevertheless, we have a pretty good idea from what happened afterward. One of the rabbis must have said, "Let's get him on the question of taxes. We'll ask if he considers it right to pay taxes to the Roman government. If he says yes, we'll laugh him to scorn. For we'll say, 'What kind of a Messiah is this who tells us to knuckle under to the Romans?' But if he says no, we'll have him then too. For we'll simply go to the Romans and say, 'You have an insurrectionist on your hands.'" They put the question to Jesus. But Jesus destroyed their arguments by replying, "Give to Caesar what is Caesar's, and to God what is God's" (Matt. 22:21).

The Pharisees went back to their meeting. Someone else said, "Let's get Jesus on a moral issue. Let's find a woman who is committing adultery and then drag her off to Jesus. We'll say, 'What are you going to do about it?' If he says, 'Let her go free,' we'll accuse him of disregarding the law, for Moses said that an adulteress should be killed by stoning. But if he says, 'Do what Moses commanded; kill her,' then we will laugh in his face: 'Come unto me, all ye that labor and are heavy laden, and I will give you a brick.'"

"Why all this viciousness?" one commentator asks. "Why this desire to destroy the meek and lowly Jesus? Why this murderous attempt to do away with God? The answer is here in the sabbath question. They wanted rules, they did not want God's grace. They wanted human merit. They did not want the simplicity of divine pardon. They wanted to do something for themselves. They had it all worked out. They would make a show of keeping a day as sacred, while their hearts wallowed in lust and their minds conceived schemes of greed. Their avarice could swell to outrageous proportions, but the sabbath would be their cloak. Keeping a day would be their mask."[2]

The Pharisees and scribes saw that Jesus was destroying this dream castle they had built. So they devised means to do him in. In a sense, of course, they succeeded. At least they put him to death. They killed him. But he rose from the dead and—think how ironic and significant this is—not on their useless sabbath of death, but on the first day of the week, soon to become the new day of joyous Christian celebration.

60

The History of the Sabbath

John 5:9–16

The day on which this took place was a Sabbath, and so the Jews said to the man who had been healed, "It is the Sabbath; the law forbids you to carry your mat."

But he replied, "The man who made me well said to me, 'Pick up your mat and walk.'"

So they asked him, "Who is this fellow who told you to pick it up and walk?"

The man who was healed had no idea who it was, for Jesus had slipped away into the crowd that was there.

Later Jesus found him at the temple and said to him, "See, you are well again. Stop sinning or something worse may happen to you." The man went away and told the Jews that it was Jesus who had made him well.

So, because Jesus was doing these things on the Sabbath, the Jews persecuted him.

Many devout Christians would agree with everything I have said up to this point about the Jewish perversion of the sabbath in the time of Jesus Christ, but they would still insist that the seventh day of the week rather than the first day of the week is the proper day for Christian worship. In fact, whole denominations teach this doctrine. And in addition to those who belong to these denominations and believe this teaching, there are undoubtedly others who observe Sunday but who are nevertheless confused about the issue and sometimes wonder why they worship on Sunday.

This study will be far-ranging. For some it may appear too complex or detailed. I believe, however, that if we study these themes, we will profit immensely both in understanding the unique dealings of God with the Jewish people and in appreciating the special and God-given character of the Christian's Sunday.

No Sabbath before Moses

The earliest mention of any sabbath, either in the Bible or in secular writings, occurs early in Genesis. It is found there even before the fall of Adam. We are told that "by the seventh day God had finished the work he had been doing; so on the seventh day he rested from all his work. And God blessed the seventh day and made it holy, because on it he rested from all the work of creating that he had done" (Gen. 2:2–3). Obviously, this verse appeals to those who believe that everyone should worship on the seventh day, and I must admit frankly that this is a possible support for their argument. Certainly, if we had no other references to the sabbath in Scripture and found that men as a whole observed it, that would be a reasonable explanation for the practice and a basis for it. On the assumption that this basis exists, Sabbatarians claim that the setting apart of the sabbath day by God in the Garden of Eden established a law that is binding on every member of the human race.

The difficulty, however, is that Genesis 2:2–3 does not exactly say this and, what is more, there is ample evidence to the contrary both in secular records and in Scripture. What these verses say is that God blessed the seventh day because on it he ceased from the work of creation. But it does not say when he sanctified it; that could have occurred later. Nor is there any record either here or elsewhere of any actual sabbath observance by anyone before the time of Moses. There is evidence of the offering of sacrifices, of prayer, of circumcision by Jewish people before Moses' day—but not of sabbath keeping. Besides, there is no evidence that any nation other than Israel ever kept the sabbath at any time—either before Moses' day, after his day, or currently.

This argument from silence has its limitations, of course. An argument from silence always does. Nevertheless, we cannot overlook the fact that the sabbath is not even mentioned in the Book of Job in spite of the fact that the whole discussion throughout the better part of forty-two chapters turns on the many details of human obligation toward God. Job is concerned with a historical period several hundred years before the exodus and thus throws additional light on our discussion relating to this period.

For Jews Only

Having looked at the major text cited in support of Sabbatarianism from the early history of the race, we must now turn to passages that tell us when the sabbath *was* instituted and for whom.

The first is in Nehemiah. Nehemiah had been instrumental in furthering a great revival among the Jews who had returned to Jerusalem after the Babylonian captivity, and in connection with this revival he had been active in encouraging a special service of worship and rededication. In this service the priests led the people in praising God. They said about God's relationship to Israel, "You came down on Mount Sinai; you spoke to them from heaven. You gave them regulations and laws that are just and right, and decrees and commands that are good. You made known to them your holy Sabbath and gave them commands, decrees and laws through your servant Moses" (Neh. 9:13–14). Here the establishing of the sabbath is linked to the giving of the law at Sinai. It is implied that the sabbath itself was not known or observed before that time.

The second passage is from Exodus, which takes us back to the time at which the law concerning the sabbath was first revealed to Israel. Exodus says: "Then the LORD said to Moses, 'Say to the Israelites, "You must observe my Sabbaths. This will be a sign between me and you for the generations to come, so you may know that I am the LORD, who makes you holy. Observe the Sabbath, because it is holy to you. Anyone who desecrates it must be put to death; whoever does any work on that day must be cut off from his people. For six days, work is to be done, but the seventh day is a Sabbath of rest, holy to the LORD. Whoever does any work on the Sabbath day must be put to death. The Israelites are to observe the Sabbath, celebrating it for the generations to come as a lasting covenant. It will be a sign between me and the Israelites forever, for in six days the LORD made the heavens and the earth, and on the seventh day he abstained from work and rested"'" (Exod. 31:12–17).

In these verses the sabbath is described as a sign between God and Israel. The fact that it is between God and Israel is important; it is mentioned twice. Moreover, a direct address to Israel either by name or by second person pronouns occurs nine times. It is difficult to see how anything other than prejudice could apply these words to any nation other than Israel or miss the fact that the sabbath was a part of the law and as such was intended to distinguish the nation of Israel from others.

The third passage makes the same point. In Ezekiel God tells us of his special dealings with the Jewish people: "Therefore I led them out of Egypt and brought them into the desert. I gave them my decrees and made known to them my laws, for the man who obeys them will live by them. Also I gave them my Sabbaths as a sign between us, so they would know that I the LORD made them holy" (Ezek. 20:10–12). Once again the verses reiterate that the sabbath was made known by God at Sinai and that it was exclusively a sign for Israel.

We might add at this point that only a sabbath applied to Israel living within the fairly fixed geographical bounds of Palestine either makes sense or is possible. Why? Because the sabbath obviously begins at different times in different parts of the world due to the different time zones. Thus, it is impossible for people all over the earth to observe it simultaneously, as Sabbatarian theory would seem to require.

Perhaps the final and most conclusive evidence for this special giving of the law of sabbath observance to Israel lies in the interesting fact that the sabbath, if known, was not observed even by Israel before God's special revelation concerning it. The evidence for this is in the fact that on the way to Sinai God gave Israel a preview of what was coming concerning the sabbath by means of his instructions concerning the gathering of manna. It was the fifteenth day of the second month after their departure from Egypt, and the people were hungry. They complained to Moses. God told Moses that he would send bread from heaven in a form that was later called manna. They would receive it each day for six days; but then on the sixth day, they were to gather double, for on the next day, the seventh, there would be no provision. The people did this, not knowing precisely why there would be no bread on the seventh day. On the sixth day, therefore, after they had gathered double manna, Moses explained in full, saying, "This is what the LORD commanded: 'Tomorrow is to be a day of rest, a holy Sabbath to the Lord. So bake what you want to bake and boil what you want to boil. Save whatever is left and keep it until morning.' . . . Bear in mind the the LORD has given you the Sabbath; that is why on the sixth day he gives you bread for two days. Everyone is to stay where he is on the seventh day; no one is to go out." We read, "So the people rested on the seventh day" (Exod. 16:23, 29, 30).

The point of all this is that the events of this chapter, which I have just summarized, cover eight days, ending with the first observance of the sabbath in history. And if someone should argue that the first day was also a sabbath, a close examination of the chapter will show that this was not so. For on that day, according to verse 1, the people journeyed from Elim to the wilderness of Sin, a distance of over twenty miles. Clearly this was a far cry from the sabbath day of rest that was given to the people a week later.

Perhaps it is also worth noting here that Lewis Sperry Chafer, who writes on the sabbath question in his book entitled *Grace*, wisely points out that even in Israel the sabbath was not always celebrated on the seventh day of the week and that, because of the Jewish calendar, it was often the case that certain kinds of work were done on all days, even on Saturdays. He writes: "The sabbath, but for necessary exceptions, was the seventh in a series of seven, whether of days or years. Of necessity it often fell on other days of the week as well as on Saturday. There were at least fifteen sabbaths which were fixed dates in their given month, and these sabbaths fell on those particular dates regardless of the day of the week. . . . Again, certain working days were established days. The lamb must be taken on the tenth day of the first month and be killed, roasted with fire, and eaten on the fourteenth day of the month. Likewise, Abid sixteenth could in no wise have been a sabbath for that date was appointed as the beginning of harvest (Deut. 16:9; cf. Lev. 23:15). All these labors would have been direct violations of the sabbath law; yet these ceremonies were appointed for certain predetermined dates, and from time to time must inevitably have been in conflict with the predetermined sabbath."[1]

We conclude that the sabbath was for Israel alone, that it was neither instituted nor observed before the exodus and the giving of the law at Sinai, and that even in Israel the sabbath itself was not always observed on the seventh day of the week. Even in Israel, God was not interested in the seventh day as an inflexibly recurring seven. For it was true then, as now, even though in that day Israel was under law and the sabbath was a divine regulation, it is useless to worship God by rules if the heart is far from him.

End of the Sabbath

Finally, I want you to see how completely and abruptly the practice of sabbath observance changed with the coming of the gospel of Christ. Some have objected that Jesus himself observed the sabbath, which is true. But the attempt to insist on the observance of Saturday because Jesus observed it comes from the failure to realize that the reign of law gave way to the reign of grace at his death. Jesus was born a Jew, born "under the law." During his lifetime he kept the sabbath, although, of course, in the way God intended it to be kept rather than in the way the scribes and Pharisees dictated. He was a Jew. Yet at his death law as a system binding upon God's people passed away. Paul declares that through his death God blotted out "the written code, with its regulations against us and that stood opposed to us; he took it away, nailing it to the cross" (Col. 2:14).

Did you know that in Acts the word "sabbath" is found only nine times and that not once is it spoken of as a day observed by Christians? The first chapter speaks of it in the phrase "a Sabbath day's walk" (v. 12). In chapter 13 the word occurs four times in describing how Paul used the sabbath day for his evangelistic ends, going into the synagogue to preach to the Jews who were assembled there (vv. 14, 27, 42, 44). Later chapters give similar references (15:21; 16:13; 17:2; 18:4). Nowhere is it even suggested that God's people met on the seventh day or even regarded it with any special affection or attention.

Finally, in the epistles we are told explicitly that believers in the Lord Jesus Christ are freed from all such observances. Thus, we find Paul writing, "Therefore do not let anyone judge you by what you eat or drink, or with regard to a religious festival, a New Moon celebration or a Sabbath day. These are a shadow of the things that were to come; the reality, however, is found in Christ" (Col. 2:16–17). Or again, writing to the Galatians, "But now that you know God—or rather are known by God—how is it that you are turning back to those weak and miserable principles? Do you wish to be enslaved by them all over again? You are observing special days and months and seasons and years! I fear for you, that somehow I have wasted my efforts on you" (Gal. 4:9–11).

"It is significant, then, that in all the Epistles, wherein the believer's obligation under grace is set forth," as Chafer says, "the only use of the word *sabbath* is under absolute prohibition concerning observance, and that it is there held to be in conflict with the most vital and superseding elements of grace."[2]

God's Grace

We need to stop at this point. In the next chapter we are going to move in a freer and much more positive way to a discussion of why Christians worship on Sunday instead of on Saturday and what associations this day has for them. But before we do that we need to say one thing in reference to those who insist that God still requires a sabbath-day observance. It is true that we are told in Scripture that we are not to be bound by days. But it is also true that we are not to judge those who are so bound. Paul writes to the Romans, therefore, that although it is wrong to be bound by days, nevertheless, it is possible for an uninformed Christian to observe them even, from his point of view, to God's glory (Rom. 14:5–6). In dealing with our Christian brothers in such matters we are to deal in great love.

At the same time and without the least pride, we will be able to profit from our knowledge and so flee with horror from a legalism that would bind us to days. "When we are thus free," one writes, "the Lord will possess our Mondays and Tuesdays, our Wednesdays and Thursdays, our Fridays, Saturdays and Sundays, and all our days and weeks and months and years because he has bought us and possesses our hearts in simple grace."[3]

61

The Day of the Resurrection

John 5:9–16

The day on which this took place was a Sabbath, and so the Jews said to the man who had been healed, "It is the Sabbath; the law forbids you to carry your mat."

But he replied, "The man who made me well said to me, 'Pick up your mat and walk.'"

So they asked him, "Who is this fellow who told you to pick it up and walk?"

The man who was healed had no idea who it was, for Jesus had slipped away into the crowd that was there.

Later Jesus found him at the temple and said to him, "See, you are well again. Stop sinning or something worse may happen to you." The man went away and told the Jews that it was Jesus who had made him well.

So, because Jesus was doing these things on the Sabbath, the Jews persecuted him.

In my study at Tenth Presbyterian Church in Philadelphia I have a volume called *The American Book of Days*. It is a compendium of information about America's holidays, festivals, and anniversaries arranged like a volume of daily readings—several anniversaries or holidays for each day of the year. It is hard to read it without getting the point that, no matter what the day of the year may be, that day is important

373

for someone. We all have our special days—a birthday, the day we became engaged, our wedding day, the day of our promotion, even the anniversary of the death of some special friend.

In this chapter we want to deal with the most important day of all. It is a great day, and the best thing about it is that it does not occur merely once each year; it occurs weekly. That day is Sunday. It is important because it is the weekly remembrance of the resurrection of the Lord Jesus Christ and because, for those who will have it so, it marks a new relationship between the Father of the Lord Jesus Christ and those who believe in him.

A New Day

I make the point that Sunday is a new and joyous day because there are some within the Christian church who try to make Sunday into something somber and serious, which it was never intended to be. They try to make it into a Christian duplication of the Jewish sabbath. In some cases these persons even go so far as to abandon the *celebration* of Sunday altogether and instead *observe* Saturday. This, according to the New Testament, is to fall from grace into law, which means falling into bondage to the observance of "days and months and seasons and years" (Gal. 4:10).

In speaking about this subject I have found that many persons are helped to see the difference between Saturday worship and Sunday worship by realizing that God never intended the observance of the Jewish sabbath to go on indefinitely. In fact, in the heart of the Old Testament, in the Book of Psalms, there is a prophecy concerning the time at which the sabbath observance would end and actually give way to the entirely different Christian celebration. In Psalm 118 we are told: "The stone the builders rejected has become the capstone; the LORD has done this, and it is marvelous in our eyes. This is the day the LORD has made; let us rejoice and be glad in it" (vv. 22–24).

There is nothing in the Bible itself to explain the image—"the stone the builders rejected"—but there is an explanation of it in Jewish tradition. At the time of the building of Solomon's temple all the stones for the temple were cut to shape at the quarry and were then transported to the temple site where they were assembled without the sound of metallic tools. The achievement of this goal required great care in the cutting of the stones, and the architect's plans were closely followed. One day a stone that did not seem to fit the building arrived at the construction site. The builders laid it aside, and it was soon forgotten. Some time later the builders came to a place in the building where a special stone, a keystone or cornerstone, was required. They sent down to request it from the stonecutters in the quarry, but they were told that the stone they requested had already been sent up. After a while the old, rejected stone was found. This was the one that was missing. So the proverb, "The stone the builders rejected became the capstone," passed into the language.

In Psalm 118 this proverb is quoted, but it is quoted with a prophetic cast. It is used as an image to picture Christ's coming death and resurrection. Jesus is the stone that the leaders of Israel refused. Yet he has become the cornerstone of God's righteous dealings with mankind. The day of the recovery of the stone is the day of the resurrection. Thus, this day, the day of the resurrection, is the new day that the Lord made and in which all who know him as Savior shall be glad.

We know that this is a proper interpretation of Psalm 118:22–24 because it was the interpretation given to it by Peter when he spoke before the Sanhedrin in Jerusalem after the Lord's resurrection. He said of Jesus: "He is 'the stone you builders rejected, which has become the capstone.' Salvation is found in no one else, for there is no other name under heaven given to men by which we must be saved" (Acts 4:11–12).

The conclusion is that the Christian Sunday, the Lord's Day, has no relationship whatever to the Jewish sabbath. We do not celebrate Sunday because God once set aside the seventh-day observance for Israel. We celebrate Sunday because on that day God did a marvelous new thing in raising the Lord Jesus Christ from the dead.

Eleven Important Events

I wonder if you have ever noticed that beginning with the resurrection, every event recorded in the New Testament that had important religious significance fell on the first day of the week, the Lord's Day. This has been pointed out by Lewis Sperry Chafer in his book *Grace*. There are eleven events.

1. The first and most important of these eleven events is that on the first day of the week *Jesus Christ arose from the dead*. This great fact is mentioned in all the Gospels and is referred to constantly throughout the rest of the New Testament.

I often have said in speaking about the resurrection of Christ that the celebration of the first day of the week by the earliest Christians, rather than the observance of the Jewish sabbath, is itself one of the great proofs that the resurrection occurred. It is a remarkable fact that although most of the early believers were Jews and although they had long been in the habit of worshiping on Saturday, nevertheless another day was chosen as the day of Christian gathering. This could not come about either by whim or by chance. Only the actual, historical resurrection of Jesus Christ can account for it. It is one of the great evidences for the resurrection. On the other hand, the fact that there was a Sunday resurrection is in its turn evidence of the new character of the age in which we live. Thus, we pattern our lives on the resurrection life of Christ and not on the principles of Mosaic legislation.

Chafer writes, "When Christ arose from the dead, Christianity was born, and the new creation was brought into existence. There is nothing in the old order for the believer. He stands on resurrection ground. He belongs only to the new creation. God is faithful to all that He has wrought in Christ and He, according to His Word, will not suffer the child of the new creation to go back and celebrate the beginning of the old and fallen creation from which

His child has been saved through infinite riches of grace. If the children of grace persist in relating themselves to the old creation by the observance of the sabbath, it is evidence of their limitations in the knowledge of the Word and will of God; it is to fall from grace."[1]

2. On the first day of the week *the Lord Jesus Christ ascended into heaven for the first time* after his earthly life. We find a record of this in John 20:17, in which Jesus says to Mary Magdalene, "Go . . . to my brothers and tell them 'I am returning to my Father and your Father, to my God and your God.'"

Where did Jesus spend the forty days between the events of this Easter morning and his final ascension into heaven nearly seven weeks later? We must not think of him as darting around the countryside trying to hide behind rocks or trees and then appearing suddenly for a few moments in what are the recorded appearances of the Lord to his disciples. During those days Jesus passed freely between earth and heaven, the first time being early on the first Easter morning. Do you remember how he said to Mary, "Do not hold on to me, for I have not yet returned to the Father," but then a very short time later allowed the other women to touch him and that evening invited the disciples to do so also (Matt. 28:9; Luke 24:39)? It is an apparent contradiction, but the answer that seems right to me is that between the two occurrences Jesus did ascend to the Father. This was the fulfillment of the Old Testament illustration of the wavesheaf that was brought to the Lord before the harvest. Jesus had to ascend to present the value of his atoning death before the Father in fulfillment of Leviticus 16 (cf. Hebrews 9). Thus, the announcement of a completed atonement is also a part of the resurrection day's significance.

3. On the first day of the week *Jesus appeared to the disciples for the first time while they were in the upper room and there bestowed peace upon them.* Peace is one of the three results of justification that are listed by the apostle Paul in the fifth chapter of Romans. He speaks of peace, access to God, and rejoicing. All these Christ gave to the disciples. They had not been at peace. They were not aware of God's presence. They certainly were not rejoicing, for we are told that they were gathered together in secret for fear of the Jews. Jesus changed each one of these states of mind by his presence.

4. On the first day of the week *Jesus Christ first broke bread with the disciples.* This happened twice, once in the presence of the two disciples, whom he had overtaken on the road to Emmaus, and once in the upper room with all the disciples at the end of the first Lord's Day. These were the first postresurrection observances of the communion service.

5. On the first day of the week *Jesus opened the understanding of his disciples* so that they might understand all that the Scriptures had taught concerning him.

We read in that magnificent twenty-fourth chapter of Luke that on that first resurrection day, when the Lord met the Emmaus disciples who were on the way home, he began to "open the scriptures." Later, when they were eating together and he began to break bread, they understood who he was. Finally, in the upper room Jesus "opened their minds so they could understand the Scriptures." He told them, "This is what is written: 'The Christ will suffer and rise from the dead on the third day, and repentance and forgiveness of sins will be preached in his name to all nations, beginning at Jerusalem'" (Luke 24:45–47). We follow Christ's lead when we read and interpret the Scripture on Sunday.

6. On the first day of the week *Jesus commissioned the disciples to the task of world evangelism.* He said in John 20:21, "As the Father sends me, I am sending you." We read in Luke 24:48 that he said, "You are witnesses of these things." We are commissioned to go into this world with the gospel, even as Jesus was commissioned.

7. On the first day of the week *Jesus breathed on the disciples, imparting the Holy Spirit to them* (John 20:22).

8. On the first day of the week, seven weeks after the resurrection, *the Holy Spirit descended from heaven at Pentecost* and began his ministry for the entire age of the Christian church. Today we look to the Spirit for the imparting of spiritual gifts and skills and for the work of correction, reproof, and conversion as he works through the preaching and teaching of the Bible.

9. On the first day of the week *the Holy Spirit directed Paul to gather the believers together and preach to them.* The account is found in Acts 20 and concerns a period of Paul's life when Paul was pursuing missionary work at Troas. It is an interesting chapter. In the sixth verse of the chapter we are told that Paul spent seven days in the city; that is, he was there for each of the seven days of the week, including a seventh day and a first day (this is, a Saturday and a Sunday). There was obviously an opportunity to choose between either of the two days, but we are told, "On the first day of the week we came together to break bread. Paul spoke to the people" (v. 7). This is another indication of the normal pattern of the early Christian observance.

10. *The first day of the week was established by Paul as the day on which the Corinthian believers were to "set aside . . . in keeping with [their] income"* (1 Cor. 16:2). In other words, it was the day on which offerings were to be taken and dedicated to the Lord's work.

11. Finally, on the first day of the week *the Lord Jesus Christ appeared to the apostle John on the island of Patmos* and gave him that great revelation of himself in all his present heavenly glory. The same revelation also outlined his plans for the future, for the church age and for that which will follow his coming again.

A Present Pattern

These eleven important events, all of which occurred on the Lord's Day rather than on the Jewish sabbath, show us the importance of the day of the resurrection for the church in this age. Not only do they show us the importance of this day and indicate that this is the proper day for Christian worship, but they also give us our pattern for the present Christian celebration. Everything that we do in church on this day is based on these eleven great events. These are: the gathering of ourselves together, the reading and interpretation of the Scriptures, the preaching and teaching of the Word of God, the collecting of offerings, the observance of communion, and above all the remembrance and worship of the One who died for us and rose again. We do not do these things by accident or by whim. This is God's pattern. We follow it out of thanksgiving for what God has done for us through the Lord Jesus Christ, our Savior.

Finally, we observe the Lord's Day as God's great weekly reminder that we are not under law in our relationship to the Lord. We are under grace. When a Christian falls from grace, what happens to the Christian? He does not lose his salvation. That is not what the phrase means. To fall from grace is to fall into law. To fall from grace is to fall into bondage to man-made regulations.

Let us live in the full sunshine of God's grace, which is our right as members of God's new creation. We have been called by grace. We have been redeemed by grace. We are justified by grace. We are sanctified by grace. God operates constantly by grace. He is our gracious God.

62

How to Celebrate Sunday

John 5:9-16

The day on which this took place was a Sabbath, and so the Jews said to the man who had been healed, "It is the Sabbath; the law forbids you to carry your mat."

But he replied, "The man who made me well said to me, 'Pick up your mat and walk.'"

So they asked him, "Who is this fellow who told you to pick it up and walk?"

The man who was healed had no idea who it was, for Jesus had slipped away into the crowd that was there.

Later Jesus found him at the temple and said to him, "See, you are well again. Stop sinning or something worse may happen to you." The man went away and told the Jews that it was Jesus who had made him well.

So, because Jesus was doing these things on the Sabbath, the Jews persecuted him.

How should a Christian celebrate Sunday? This is the question to which the three preceding studies on the sabbath and the Lord's Day have been heading and for which we have now laid sufficient groundwork. How should a Christian celebrate Sunday? The simplest answer to that question is indicated in the very name that is given to it in the Bible. It is the Lord's Day. Hence, it is to be lived in whatever manner will most honor and glorify the Lord Jesus Christ.

379

One commentator has written, "The conscious effort to promote God's honor is more important than the forms by which we try to do so. Some will use one method, some another; but in either case it is the Godward intention that matters. And whatever means we adopt, the test of our genuineness will be the measure in which gratitude and praise are the distinguishing marks of our lives. . . . We may not all confess our faith in the same terms, or worship according to the same rites, or govern ourselves according to the same discipline; we may not find it easy to cooperate in common tasks: but age after age men who could not agree in other things have united to praise God with a single voice. Our hymnbooks are still the greatest manuals of Christian unity."[1]

It does not follow from this, however, that all forms of worship or all attitudes toward the Lord's Day are equally valid or even equally useful in promoting God's honor. Consequently, it is worthwhile asking in a slightly more specific way: Just how can a Christian best and properly celebrate the Lord's Day? The answers to this question obviously must be far from any form of rules or legalism and must clearly recognize that in any individual case the Christian is ultimately answerable to God alone for how he or she celebrates it.

Only for Christians

First, however, we must make it clear that the day of the resurrection, no matter how it is celebrated, is for believers only. As the sabbath under the law belonged to the nation Israel and not to any other of the gentile nations, so, in the same way, the new day of the resurrection belongs in grace only to those who are regenerated by the Holy Spirit. We must not force those who are not yet Christians to observe it.

I am aware as I say this that this principle cuts across an attitude that has long prevailed in English-speaking countries and that many will wish to defend it. But I want to say as kindly as I can that in my opinion the desire of many Christians to force non-Christians to keep Sunday is misdirected and in some cases quite harmful. From my own selfish point of view I am quite glad that there are Sunday "bluelaws" in some parts of America. In fact, when I see the harm that is done in some areas of Philadelphia as the result of the liquor traffic, I could wish that the bars were closed permanently and that the money wasted in drinking was used for the family involved or in the education of young children. Still, this does not have anything to do with the Christian Sunday, and any attempt to force non-Christians to observe it in a Christian way is unbiblical and harmful.

Why? Lewis Sperry Chafer, whom I have quoted frequently in these studies, provides the explanation in these words: "The unsaved sustain no relation to the Lord's Day, since that day belongs only to the new creation, and therefore the pressing of the observance of a religious day upon the individual who is unsaved, is misleading in the extreme; for it tends to the utter confusion of the gospel of grace. God is not calling on the unsaved to keep a day to which they could in no way be related. The issue between God and the sinner is the one issue which the new gospel of grace has raised and imposed. It is a question as to whether he will believe on the Lord Jesus Christ unto forgiveness and eternal life. The person who observes a day while rejecting Christ as Savior, is no nearer salvation or acceptance with God than he would be otherwise. That supposed merit, gained by keeping a day, may be the one thing that hinders him from discovering Christ as the Savior for a meritless sinner. Men are not saved by any works whatsoever, and any teaching which misdirects them at this point is 'another gospel' and subject to the anathema of God (Gal. 1:8)."[2]

None of us would think of forcing baptism or communion upon a person who has not trusted in the Lord Jesus Christ for salvation. In the same way, the celebration of the first day of the week is given to help a person remember the resurrection of the Lord Jesus Christ from the dead, and the only person who can keep that day in a way acceptable to God is the person who believes that Jesus died for his sin and that he has been raised from the death of his old self into newness of life through Christ Jesus.

Joy

How then should a *Christian* observe Sunday? Or, more correctly, how should a Christian *celebrate* Sunday? The first answer comes in one form from that famous first question of the Westminister Shorter Catechism. The question asks: "What is the chief end of man?" The answer given to it by the Old Scotch Covenanters was this: "Man's chief end is to glorify God and to enjoy him forever." *Joy* is to be the first characteristic of the Lord's Day.

Like everything else associated with the Lord's Day this too has a foundation in the events of that first resurrection Sunday. In Matthew's Gospel, in its account of Christ's resurrection appearances, the first word on the lips of the risen Lord as he greeted the women who were returning from the tomb was, "Greetings" (28:9). The word is *chairo,* which literally means "Rejoice!" Jesus told the women to be glad. They were to be happy. This was the day that the Lord had made and they were to rejoice and be glad in it.

If this is so—and it is—then let us be done with the long faces and solemn demeanors that so often characterize the people of God on the Lord's Day. And let us be done also with the type of worshiper who comes to church only to go home. Do not come if you do not enjoy the preaching of the Word and the response of the congregation in word and in song. In the early days of the church the apostles did not have to go around ringing doorbells to get people to come out to the service. They did not have to maintain every-member visitation plans to renew flagging interest in the worship. In fact, the opposite was true. We read in the second chapter of Acts that at this period at least all the Christians "devoted themselves to the apostles' teaching and to the fellowship, the breaking of bread and to prayer. . . . Every day they continued to meet together in the temple courts. They broke bread in their homes and ate together with glad and sincere hearts, praising God and enjoying the favor of all the people. And the Lord added to their number daily those who were being saved" (Act 2:42, 46–47).

These were happy Christians. Other people liked to be with them, perhaps most of all because they were happy. Friendships developed. Then, on the basis of these friendships, the Lord moved and added to the church daily such as should be saved.

Have you ever thought that your attendance at church on Sunday and your conduct while there are important in the conversion of non-Christians? Look at it like this. Imagine a man—or woman—who is alone in the city and who drops by your church some morning or evening. He has a problem and it seems that there is no one to help him. Suppose he goes in out of desperation and finds only a handful of miserable people who mumble the hymns and then begin to look at their watches as the minister preaches. What will he think? He will think that there is nothing to interest him there. There is no life, no answer to problems. He will conclude, rightly, that those who are present are present only out of a sense of duty or routine. On the other hand, if he enters to find the church packed with people who obviously enjoy the worship, who sing as well as they can and take notes on the sermon, he will conclude that even if he may not understand what it is all about, still there is something to it. He begins to pay attention. And God uses his heightened awareness to lead him to the conviction of sin and conversion. This has happened many times, and there are people in my own church today for whom this is a testimony.[3]

May I suggest that you are not really celebrating Sunday at all if you do not enjoy it.

Activity

The second important characteristic of the Lord's Day should be *activity*. Think of the first Lord's Day. It was clearly a day of activity: the women on the way to the tomb, the appearances of Jesus, the return to Jerusalem of the Emmaus disciples, the sharing of experiences, communion, the Lord's commission. It is possible, if you have been working hard for the other six days of the week, that Sunday might have to have the characteristic of a "day of rest" for you. But this is not an integral part of the Lord's Day. The sabbath was the day of rest. If you need to rest, try resting on Saturday. The Lord's Day should rightly be a day of activity.

Note what Chafer says: "The Lord's Day is not a day for selfish entertainment or amusement. It is not a day for idleness and rest. Its privileges should be, and will be, preserved by all who delight to do His will. It becomes an opportunity for many who are held by secular work during the days of the week, to offer the fullest service of prayer, worship, and testimony which belongs to their Lord. The instructed Christian no longer labors to be accepted of God, which was the obligation under the law; but he, being accepted in grace, labors to glorify his Lord who saves him. He has ceased from his own works, and though ceaselessly active, is working in the power and energy of the Spirit."[4]

This does not mean, of course, that any old activity will reflect the fullest significance of the day. You may mow your grass, if you wish. You are not under law. But this does not have very much to do with Christ, nor does it help to express your joy in his resurrection. Other types of activity are significant.

The first is worship. I know it may strike some persons as strange to speak of worship as an activity; for many people conceive of worship in a passive sense, that is, sitting in a pew and letting the words of the day run through one's head like water. But this is a travesty of real worship. Jesus Christ said that real worship is done "in spirit and in truth" (John 4:24). Truth involves content. Thus, worship is above all else an active, rational activity. It must engage the mind.

Why do we have Scripture readings in the speech of the people instead of in Hebrew, Greek, or Latin? Why are the words of the music in common speech? Why does a sermon stand at the heart of each service? The answer is, to engage our minds.

"We must therefore beware of all forms of emotional, aesthetic or ecstatic worship in which the mind is not fully engaged, and especially of those which even claim that they are superior forms of worship," writes John R. W. Stott. "The only worship pleasing to God is heart-worship, and heart-worship is rational worship. It is the worship of a rational God who has made us rational beings and given us a rational revelation so that we may worship him rationally, even 'with all our mind.'"[5]

The second highly significant activity that ought to characterize the Lord's Day is our witness. Jesus Christ revealed this characteristic of the day when he instructed the women, "Go to my brothers," and later informed the disciples that they were to carry the good news of his life, death, and resurrection into all the world. Do you do that on Sunday? You can do it on any day, of course. It is of the essence of our day that anything done on Sunday can also be done (and should be done) on other days also. But do you at least bear a witness on Sunday? This is a day to invite your friends to go with you to hear God's Word proclaimed. At the least it is a day on which you should teach your children what you know about Christ.

Expectation

I have already said a good bit about the proper Christian celebration of the Lord's Day. It is for Christians only. It is to be characterized by joy. It is to be filled with activity. There is one thing more: it also should be characterized by a great spiritual *expectation*.

I love Sunday. And one of the reasons why I love Sunday is that I never know in advance what will happen. As I leave my house on the way to the church I never know precisely whom I will meet or what will take place. I do not know who will be present or who will respond to the preaching. I never plan messages to preach at problems that I imagine to be present in the congregation, and yet it is often the case that what I say is used of the Lord to speak precisely to some problem. Lives are changed. What is more, not infrequently that day is the turning point in someone's entire spiritual experience.

Do you go to the company of God's people with such expectation? If you do, it will increase your joy and cause you to work even harder. You will thrill to God's grace. And you will know in a personal way the burden of these words that summarize most of our Sunday activity: "So whether you eat or drink or whatever you do, do it all for the glory of God" (1 Cor. 10:31); "be prepared in season and out of season; correct, rebuke and encourage—with great patience and careful instruction" (2 Tim. 4:2); "pray continually" (1 Thess. 5:17); "be joyful always" (1 Thess. 5:16); "stand firm. Let nothing move you. Always give yourselves fully to the work of the Lord, because you know that your labor in the Lord is not in vain" (1 Cor. 15:58).

63

Is God Silent?

John 5:17–23

Jesus said to them, "My Father is always at his work to this very day, and I, too, am working." For this reason the Jews tried all the harder to kill him; not only was he breaking the Sabbath, but he was even calling God his own Father, making himself equal with God.

Jesus gave them this answer: "I tell you the truth, the Son can do nothing by himself; he can do only what he sees his Father doing, because whatever the Father does the Son also does. For the Father loves the Son and shows him all he does. Yes, to your amazement he will show him even greater things than these. For just as the Father raises the dead and gives them life, even so the Son gives life to whom he is pleased to give it. Moreover, the Father judges no one, but has entrusted all judgment to the Son, that all may honor the Son just as they honor the Father. He who does not honor the Son does not honor the Father, who sent him.

Ⅰn our study of John's Gospel, we come to the first of a series of discourses by Jesus, recorded in John 5:17–47. It is rightly first, for it deals with that problem in religious thought that is itself rightly first in theological thinking. How can a person know God? And, supposing that it is possible to know him, how can the things said about God by those who claim to possess such knowledge be verified?

385

A Contemporary Question

These are very important questions, particularly in the intellectual climate of the twentieth century. In our century many thinkers are saying that the questions of how one can know God and how that which is said about him can be verified have no answer.

Some maintain that there is no answer because God himself never speaks to answer them. This is the position of a man like Ingmar Bergman, the filmmaker, for instance. Sometime ago I heard this story about him told by Os Guinness, a brilliant young intellectual formerly associated with the work of L'Abri Fellowship in Switzerland. According to Guinness, Bergman had been listening to some music by Stravinsky and while listening to it had a vision. He imagined that he was in a great nineteenth-century cathedral. He was wandering around and came to a portrait of Christ. Suddenly Bergman realized the importance of this painting. So he went up to it and shouted, "Speak to me! I will not leave this cathedral until you speak to me!" There was no answer, of course. Christ said nothing. So the film that Bergman produced that same year, in which a number of characters despair of ever finding God, is called *The Silence.*

The silence of God is a problem, however, even for committed Christians. Take the example of suffering. The world is filled with suffering, but generally God does not seem to hear men's cries in suffering or alleviate their anguish. Thus, one writer who addresses the problem from a Christian perspective writes questioningly, "Earnest and thoughtful men face these realities, and have ears to hear that cry; and their indignant wonder finds utterance at times in some such words as those of the old Hebrew prophet and bard, 'Doth God know? And is there knowledge in the Most High?'"[1]

The other way in which our contemporaries argue that the questions about knowing God have no answers is in the view that religious language is mere symbolism. It is "God Talk," as they say in many of our seminaries today. It is meaningless. This attitude differs from the first one in that, while the first says that God is present or may be present but is *silent,* the second attitude affirms that even the idea of *God* is meaningless. God is not there, and so religious terms have no rational value.

We can illustrate what this means by the ways in which a little phrase such as "God bless you" is used by non-Christians. On the lips of a Christian the sentence has meaning. It is a prayer that the God who created the world and the individual and who died to redeem him in Christ will keep and enrich his life. But what meaning can the phrase possibly have on the lips of a non-Christian newscaster, for instance, a man who merely ends his program with the quip, "Well, good night, everybody. See you tomorrow night at 6:00 p.m., and God bless"? In this form the phrase does not have rational content. It is used only for its emotional or psychological value. In other words, it is used only because it creates a good feeling in the listener. Many are claiming that this is all that is accomplished by any religious talk. It has manipulative value, but there is no real meaning to it.

Another way of expressing this same thought is in the words of Edward Gibbon, author of *The Decline and Fall of the Roman Empire*. Gibbon wrote of the first Christian century that all the religions of the world were regarded by the common people as "equally true," by the philosophers as "equally false," and by the magistrates as "equally useful." In this system, a system that, incidentally, seems to be reproduced in our day, all truth is relative and religious statements in particular are meaningless.

Against these views Christianity holds a unique position. Christians believe that God has spoken, that he has spoken clearly, and that what he has said is true. This is the point of Christ's first discourse in John's Gospel. It has two main parts. In the first part (vv. 17–30) Jesus teaches that a man can know God because God the Father is revealed in God the Son. In the second part of the discourse (vv. 31–47) Jesus gives evidence for this claim, pointing out that his testimony is substantiated by a series of other God-given witnesses. We want to begin to look at the opening part of the discourse in this study.

Father and Son

The first statement that Jesus makes is that he is one with the Father in all the Father's actions. He says it negatively and then positively. First, "I tell you the truth, the Son can do nothing by himself; he can only do what he sees his Father doing" then, "because whatever the Father does the Son also does" (v. 19). This is a claim to divinity, to identity with God. It is an assertion that everything God the Father does, Jesus does; and everything Jesus does is also done by the Father. The conclusion of the matter is that Jesus is God.

But there is more to the statement than this. For when Jesus began his discourse with the claim "My Father is always at his work to this very day, and I, too, am working," he was not only suggesting that the Father was working with him in all the actions performed during his earthly life, he was also saying that the Father had been working with him and he with the Father in all their actions previously. In other words, Jesus was turning the minds of his Jewish listeners back to God's work from the beginning of creation, and he was claiming to have been a part of that work also.

This is an important point in our understanding of who Jesus is, for it is not just enough to think of him in the particular time period in which he lived on this earth. In one of my earlier writings I told a story that illustrates what we need to do if we are to understand him properly. In the summer of 1962, a friend and I made a trip around the Mediterranean Sea that eventually brought us to Luxor, in upper Egypt. We were there to see several of the ruins, particularly the great temple of Luxor, built more than 3,000 years ago by Amenophis III. There are great columns in this temple, all about a dozen feet in diameter and reaching sixty to eighty feet into the sky. Our attention was attracted to one column near the edge of the excavations on the top of which there was a small house. We asked our guide how it got there. The old man answered that before the excavations had reached this area, there was a farmer living on the outskirts of the modern city of Luxor who had been looking for a solid foundation on which to build his house. He scratched about in the sand and eventually came upon what he believed was bedrock. He built his house there. In time, as the wind began to blow around the sides of the house and push the sand away, which it does in the desert, the farmer found that he had built his house not upon bedrock, as he had supposed, but upon a piece of hand-hewn rock. Later he realized that the rock was part of a column, and still later he discovered that it was a standing column. By this time the excavations had reached his area, the ground was taken away, and eventually his house was left standing on the top of the column where we saw it.

This is an illustration of some people's misunderstanding of the Lord Jesus Christ. They will acknowledge that he was a great man and will even claim that their lives are built upon him to some degree. To them he is a great teacher. This is true, of course. But although it is true, by itself this view is as misleading as the view of the Egyptian farmer who thought that he was building his house on bedrock. To have a true understanding of Jesus Christ a person must push aside the thousands of years of human history and catch a picture of him existing with God the Father and working with God the Father from eternity.

Obedience

The second point that Jesus makes concerning his relationship to the Father is that his identity with the Father also involves obedience. It is a matter of the will, which means that the mind of the Father and the mind of the Son are united. We must not think that when Jesus claimed to be able to do nothing, except what he saw the Father doing, he was saying that he was something like a robot, a zombi, who carried out the directives of the Father without thinking. This is not at all what he was saying. Christ is a person. He has a personality, including an intellect and feelings. He faced temptations, real temptations. There were discouragements. Nevertheless, in nothing did he ever disobey his Father. He obeyed him, and he obeyed willingly.

This is what he wants you to do, in one sense, or rather what he enables you to do when he saves you. The trouble with us is that we are the opposite of Jesus Christ at this point. We are not interested in obeying God. We are interested in doing our own thing. We want to run our own lives. We want to be "god" to ourselves. Jesus was not like that, for everything he did he did out of love for God and out of obedience to him.

Christ's third claim was that he was one with the Father in love. Jesus had said that everything he did he did in unity with the Father. He showed that this unity of action was based on obedience. But then, as a third claim, he also went on to show that this was a unity based on love: "For the Father loves the Son and shows him all he does" (v. 20).

Is it not wonderful to know that at the heart of God's nature there is love? How do we know that the nature of God is love? I know that the Bible teaches this. It says so explicitly in 1 John 4:8, 16. But how do we know, apart from the Bible? The answer is: We know that God is love only because of the nature and actions of the Lord Jesus Christ who is both God and love. Someone will point to the beauty of creation. But if you do that, you are only proving that God is a God of order. The creation reveals nothing about love. If you argue that some of the things God has created are useful to men and, therefore, reveal God's concern for them, I will point out that other parts of creation are not useful and are even destructive. Love has to do with a personality. It is a characteristic of persons. So how do we know that God has a personality and that his personality is characterized by love? Only through Christ. Jesus Christ loved us and gave himself for us.

Life and Judgment

Finally, there are two more statements that Jesus makes regarding his relationship to the Father. He says in verse 20, "For the Father loves the Son and shows him all he does. Yes, to your amazement he will show him even greater things than these." The "greater things" are those that are described in the next verses. They are, first, that the Son gives life to whom he pleases and, second, that the Son will be the judge of men on the Father's behalf. He states the first claim by saying, "For just as the Father raises the dead and gives them life, even so the Son gives life to whom he is pleased to give it" (v. 21).

This was an appeal to the Old Testament that any knowledgeable Jew would have recognized. The Old Testament taught that only God could give life or raise the dead to new life. In Deuteronomy 32:39 God says, "I myself am He! There is no god beside me. I put to death and I bring to life." First Samuel 2:6 says, "The LORD brings death and makes alive; he brings down to the grave and raises up." When the Syrian general Naaman came to the king of Israel seeking a cure for his leprosy because he had heard that Elijah could cure him, the king of Israel thought that Naaman was seeking cause for a quarrel and replied in despair, "Am I God? Can I kill and bring back to life?" (2 Kings 5:7). Throughout the Old Testament it is the same. The giving of life—whether life in physical birth, spiritual life, or the life of the resurrection—is God's prerogative. Consequently, when Jesus claimed to be able to give life he was also clearly claiming to be God.

The same thing is true about judgment. Every Jew knew that one day God would unleash his final judgment. Deuteronomy 1:17 declares that "judgment belongs to God." This too was God's prerogative. So when Jesus claimed to be the One who would actually carry out the judgment of the Father, he was claiming (no less certainly than in his other statements) that he was God.

Put together, these statements set forth Christ's claim that Jesus is God and acts with God from the beginning of all things to the end, from creation to the final judgment, from eternity to eternity.

The Way

The final verse in this section tells us that God the Father has committed judgment to Jesus so "that all may honor the Son just as they honor the Father" (v. 23). How do we honor the Son? Above all by acknowledging that he is who he says he is and submitting to him and to his teaching. John R. W. Stott has written on this point, "If Jesus who thus taught with authority was the Son of God made flesh, we must bow to his authority and accept his teaching. We must allow our opinions to be moulded by his opinions, our views to be conditioned by his views. And this includes his uncomfortable and unfashionable teaching."[2]

This also includes Jesus' teaching about salvation. Sometime after the events recorded in John 5, Jesus said that he was going to the cross in order to give his life "a ransom for many" (Mark 10:45). He said toward the end of his life, "I am the way and the truth and the life. No one comes to the Father except through me" (John 14:6). Are these things true? They are if Jesus is who he said he is. If he is God, they have to be true. He is the way, the only way, to the Father. Do you believe it? Do you honor him in his teaching about salvation?

Finally, do you honor him in his teaching about the Christian life? He taught you how to live. The Bible is full of his teaching. Do you attempt to follow it? It is not only your duty if you are a Christian; it is the only sensible course for any man or woman.

64

Possessing Eternity in Time

John 5:24–27

"I tell you the truth, whoever hears my word and believes him who sent me has eternal life and will not be condemned; he has crossed over from death to life. I tell you the truth, a time is coming and has now come when the dead will hear the voice of the Son of God and those who hear will live. For as the Father has life in himself, so he has granted the Son to have life in himself. And he has given him authority to judge because he is the Son of Man."

If we are to judge by television shows today—which, incidentally, is not a bad way of judging what is on most people's minds most of the time—then certainly many people are concerned about life. One of the most popular programs ever to appear on television is *This Is Your Life*. One of the great afternoon moneymakers is *Love of Life*. Even the commercials get into the act when they argue, "You've got a lot to live," and then offer something to help you live it better.

A concern with life and its qualities is basic to men. Unfortunately, the promises being offered in our day for an abundance of life are inadequate, and even the best of these solutions fades into insignificance when compared to the great offer of life that is presented to us by the Lord Jesus Christ.

391

Apparently matters were not so different in the past either, for men and women were just as concerned with life then as now. This state of affairs undoubtedly led John, the author of the fourth Gospel, to speak of life and of Jesus as the source of life many times. For instance, in the opening verses of the letter he wrote, "In him was life, and that life was the light of men" (1:4). In the third chapter he records the conversation with Nicodemus about the new birth. This is a discussion of life. In speaking to the Samaritan woman Jesus offers "living water." The theme occurs again and again in each of the great discourses. Finally, in the first of the two conclusions to John's Gospel, occurring in chapter 20, the author of the Gospel writes, "Jesus did many other miraculous signs in the presence of his disciples, which are not recorded in this book. But these are written that you may believe that Jesus is the Christ, the Son of God, and that by believing you may have life in his name" (vv. 30–31). According to this last verse, the desire to see all men enter into the life of God was one of John's main purposes in writing. It is also one aspect— and from one point of view even the major aspect—of Christ's coming to earth to save men.

This theme is discussed at some length in the verses that are now before us, verses 24–29 from the fifth chapter of John. In discussing life these verses take us through the entire scope of the believer's experience with the Lord. First, in verse 24, Jesus is quoted as saying that God gives life initially; that is, God acts first in placing spiritual life within the individual whom he is drawing to himself. Second, verses 25 and 26 say that in this present time, after we have become Christians, God gives abundance of life through Christ Jesus. Third, verses 28 and 29 speak of a special manifestation of that life in the resurrection of our bodies. These verses deal with a divine life that God gives freely, and they teach that it is possible to live that life now.

The Gift of Life

The first point of these verses, then, is that the possession of divine life begins with God's action rather than man's. In other words, life is not a reward for believing. It is the other way around. Life comes first; a person believes afterward. He believes because God has first placed his life within him. The verse says, "I tell you the truth, whoever hears my word and believes him who sent me has eternal life and will not be condemned; he has crossed over from death to life" (v. 24).

I must admit, of course, that many preachers have taken this verse in the other sense. They have taught that the phrases represent a temporal sequence so that a person must first hear and believe, then, as a result of his believing, come into the possession of life. This is not right. In the first place, no sequence is involved at all. In John's vocabulary "hearing" is the same thing as "believing." It means to hear with the heart. The point of these two phrases is that hearing the words of *Christ* and believing *God* are identical. This is even the main point of the discourse.

Second, the tense of the verb "have" is present rather than future. If the possession of eternal life were the result of believing, then the verse should have a future verb. It should say, "Whoever hears my word and believes him who sent me *will have* eternal life." Actually, the present tense of the verb is used to indicate that the one who believes does so because he already has the life of God within him.

A chapter later Jesus expresses precisely the same teaching negatively when he says, "No one can come to me unless the Father who sent me draws him" (6:44).

The third and conclusive reason for taking John 5:24 in the sense I have been indicating is that this is the teaching of the Word of God as a whole. Take the case of Abraham, as an example. What did God do when he called Abraham? Did he look down from heaven and say, "Let's see now, perhaps I can find a man who has a little bit of goodness in him, perhaps a little bit of faith. Can I find something to work with? Ah, yes, there's a person who has something. Abraham! He has faith. I'll start with him." Not at all! The Word of God tells us that Abraham was no different from the rest of his contemporaries (Josh. 24:2). They were devil worshipers. So it was an act of pure grace when God called one man out of the rest. Not one of the people then living in Ur of the Chaldees knew anything about the true God. But God came to Abraham in such a blaze of glory, as Stephen relates (Acts 7:2), that Abraham immediately obeyed the divine call. God always comes first, and when he comes to a person, that person follows.

Abraham's Descendants

Unfortunately, while it is true that many persons will admit this in the case of others, there will always be some who will seek an exception for themselves. This was true in Jesus' day, as in ours. In Jesus' day the argument went like this. "Granted," his opponents would say, "that Abraham was called when he was a devil worshiper and had nothing in himself to commend him to God! Granted that truth. But how does it follow from this that the same is true for those of us who are Abraham's descendants? Certainly our descent counts for something." When this objection was raised, Jesus answered it by pointing out that God is concerned with spiritual rather than physical descent. Thus, while it is true that those who argued this way may have been descendants of Abraham physically, it was just as obvious that they had not descended from him spiritually, for all of Abraham's spiritual children would believe in Jesus. He concluded, "If God were your Father, you would love me, for I came from God and now am here. . . . You belong to your father, the devil" (8:42, 44). Where does spiritual descent come from? The only answer is that it comes directly from God.

We see this in the case of Abraham's immediate descendants. The Jews were claiming to have a special position with God because they were descended from Abraham, but they had overlooked the fact that Abraham had given life to more than one son. Isaac was the child of promise. But before Isaac there had been Ishmael. What about him? Clearly God had chosen Isaac, thereby demonstrating that he is the sole source of life and that he does not choose to impart that life to everyone.

There might have been some—there undoubtedly were in Paul's day—who would have argued that God made his choice on the basis of the worthiness or unworthiness of the mother. They would have pointed out with great glee that although both Isaac and Ishmael were sons of Abraham, only Isaac was Abraham's son by Sarah. The other—they would have said it with contempt—was the son of the Egyptian slave girl Hagar.

Is that the reason for God's choice? We have only to pass down to the next generation to see the answer, for when God makes his next choice he makes it between two brothers, born of the same Jewish mother. And, lest anyone try to introduce the question of age as a factor, he sees to it that the two boys are twins. Moreover, just to make sure that no one can argue that the choice was made on the basis of the moral character of the sons, God announces his choice when they are still in the womb; in other words, before either Esau or Jacob had a chance to do anything that was good or evil.

Once again the choice lay entirely in the heart of God. God gives blessing to whom he chooses. He gives life to whom he chooses. There is just no possible human way of accounting for his ways.

Here is the way Paul presents the argument in Romans 9:

> It is not as though God's word had failed. For not all who are descended from Israel are Israel. Nor because they are his descendants are they all Abraham's children. On the contrary, "It is through Isaac that your offspring will be reckoned." In other words, it is not the natural children who are God's children, but it is the children of the promise who are regarded as Abraham's offspring. For this was how the promise was stated: "At the appointed time I will return, and Sarah will have a son."
>
> Not only that, but Rebekah's children had one and the same father, our father Isaac. Yet, before the twins were born or had done anything good or bad—in order that God's purpose in election might stand: not by works but by him who calls—she was told, "The older will serve the younger." Just as it is written: "Jacob I loved, but Esau I hated."
>
> verses 6–13

Moreover, this is the way God always works. When did God call Moses? The answer is, when Moses was merely a baby floating in a basket on the waters of the Nile. When did God choose John the Baptist to have faith in himself and eventually to be the forerunner of the Messiah? The answer is, before he was born, as was announced both to his mother Elizabeth and to Mary, the mother of the Lord. When did Christ call most of his disciples? When they had first come seeking him? No, rather when they were fishermen practicing their trade. That is the way he calls you. God calls through different means, of course. It is often through preaching. Sometimes it is through the life or witness of a Christian friend. Sometimes he uses a radio program or a book. But whatever the means, the point is that God calls first. What is more, he places the new spiritual life within the individual so that, being awakened to the call of eternity, the one who is the object of that call can hear him and respond, believing.

Life Abundant

We must not think, of course, that this initial call of God is the whole story. There is also the present life of the believer and the life of the resurrection, which is future. Jesus goes on to speak of these two further aspects of life in the verse following the one we have been studying.

Verses 25 and 26 declare, "I tell you the truth, a time is coming and has now come when the dead will hear the voice of the Son of God and those who hear will live. For as the Father has life in himself, so he has granted the Son to have life in himself." Here the reference to the "dead" is to those who are spiritually dead, as in the verse that goes before. But the verb that introduces the word "life" is future, rather than present. This means that in this verse Jesus has in view the increasingly abundant present life of the one who believes in him. The order is this. First, God plants his life within the one whom he desires to become his child. Second, because of the new life within, the child now hears the Word of God and believes. Third, the child increasingly enters into the experience of that life by believing. So Jesus is saying, "The one whom I have called is to live now in an abundant way."

Is your life abundant? It is possible to be a Christian and miss the abundant life; many do. Still, it is your privilege to enter into it increasingly as you permit Jesus to change your life daily.

Resurrection Life

Finally, in verses that we are going to return to more extensively in our next study, Jesus also speaks of future life, referring to the resurrection. He has spoken of the initial gift of life, in which a person becomes a believer. He has spoken of life in the present. Now he turns to the future. "Marvel not at this; for the hour is coming, in which all that are in the graves shall hear his voice, and shall come forth: they that have done good, unto the resurrection of life; and they that have done evil, unto the resurrection of damnation" (vv. 28–29). According to these verses, the life that is given in the moment of spiritual regeneration will have its true end only in the total entrance into life through the resurrection.

What is the life that we who believe in the Lord Jesus Christ possess? It is the life of God himself. Peter tells us that we may "participate in the divine nature" (2 Peter 1:4). Therefore, that life is as eternal and indestructible as God himself. It will go on forever; and it will not be an eternally wretched and debased

existence, as our lives would be if we were left to ourselves, but rather the continually entering into that life that possesses all the qualities of God.

Some have imagined that this life is not everlasting. Some have imagined
that it is not eternal. But if that can be so, then words have no meaning and
the Word of God is meaningless. If eternal life can be lost, it is not eternal.
If it can be taken from us, it is not eternal. If we can renounce it so that it
no longer belongs to us, it is not eternal. Is God changeable? Certainly not!
Then his gifts cannot be withdrawn. The Bible says, "God's gifts and his call
are irrevocable" (Rom. 11:29). If God had given us ten years' life, then that
life could not be lost before the end of the ten years. If he had given us one
thousand years' life, then that life could not be lost before the end of the
one thousand years. In the same way, if he has given us eternal life, then that
life is eternal life. We can be certain that it will lead straight on to the moment
of our own physical resurrection . . . and beyond.

65

A Matter of Life or Death

John 5:28–30

"Do not be amazed at this, for a time is coming when all who are in their graves will hear his voice and come out—those who have done good will rise to live, and those who have done evil will rise to be condemned. By myself I can do nothing; I judge only as I hear, and my judgment is just, for I seek not to please myself but him who sent me."

Do you know the difference between "temporary" and "permanent"? Temporary refers to something that can be changed; permanent refers to something that cannot be changed. This is important for understanding our present subject. For the subject is God's judgment, and the central point is that God's judgment will establish a permanent distinction between men, some entering into the fullness of life and some into what the Bible calls death or damnation.

The day of God's judgment is spoken of in many places in the Bible. For instance, to the Romans Paul wrote of "the day when God will judge men's secrets through Jesus Christ, as my gospel declares" (Rom. 2:16). He preached to the Greeks in Athens, saying that the times of their ignorance God had formerly overlooked "but now he commands all people everywhere to repent. For he has set a day when he will judge the world with justice" (Acts 17:30–31). The Book of Revelation describes this judgment in the twentieth chapter. Jesus also spoke of this judgment, saying, "Do not be amazed at this, for a time is coming when all who are in their graves will hear his voice [he meant his own] and come out—those who have done good will rise to live, and those who have done evil will rise to be condemned. By myself I can do

397

nothing; I judge only as I hear, and my judgment is just, for I seek not to please myself but him who sent me" (John 5:28–30).

These verses present three doctrines. First, death is not the end of existence. Second, there are two forms of existence beyond the grave, one good and one terrible. Third, the particular kind of existence to be entered into depends upon the individual's relationship to the Lord Jesus Christ. The obvious conclusion is that each person ought to examine himself in regard to this relationship.

More Beyond

The first point of Christ's teaching is that physical death is not the end of existence. It was not the end, either for himself or for others. Quite clearly he expected to die. He once said that he was going to give his life as a ransom for many. He told his disciples that he was going up to Jerusalem where he would be arrested, beaten, and then killed because of the hatred of the religious leaders toward him. All this happened. Yet Jesus also spoke of the fact that he would rise again after three days and return to the disciples.

We see from this text that Jesus expected others, both good and evil persons, to live on. Life is not the proper word to describe it, of course. Existence is a better term. Nevertheless, whatever term we use, it is obvious that according to Jesus the grave is not the end for anyone.

In this he was at one with Old Testament teaching. It often is said that ideas of the afterlife are not fully developed in the Old Testament, and this is true to a degree. Still, the great assumption of the Old Testament is that life does continue beyond the grave. For instance, it lies behind the descriptions of the death of the patriarchs that tell us that they were gathered in death to those who had gone before. Abraham is said to have "breathed his last and died at a good old age, an old man and full of years; and he was gathered to his people" (Gen. 25:8). We are told that Isaac "died and was gathered to his people" (Gen. 35:29). Jacob nourished the same expectation when he was told of the apparent death of his favorite son, Joseph. We read that "he refused to be comforted. 'No,' he said, 'in mourning will I go down to the grave to my son'" (Gen. 37:35).

The King James Version uses the word "sheol" in this last verse as another indication of the Old Testament faith in a life to come. "Sheol" has been translated as "hell" or "death" as well as the "grave" in other versions of the Old Testament. But we should never exclude the fact that in the Old Testament Sheol is a place name. It is the name of the place to which the dead go, much as "hades" or "limbo" designated the abode of the dead for the Greeks. On the one hand, those who die in faith go there. This is proved by Jacob's statement. On the other hand, it also is the destination of adulterers, sinners, and the heathen (Num. 16:33; Prov. 7:27; Isa. 14:9–15).

The existence of Sheol is a great testimony to the fact of life after death, and Jesus in his turn endorsed it. One commentator has written, "While opinions may well differ on the interpretation of what the Old Testament tells about the *nature* of life in Sheol, there can be no disputing its insistence on the *fact* of life in Sheol. Life here on earth is not the complete span for man; beyond it there is another and different existence which he cannot avoid, for 'what man is he that shall live and not see death, that shall deliver his soul from the power of Sheol?'"[1]

It is possible that in the years before Christ's coming, devout men and women might have disputed whether these things were actually so. But whatever the case then, there can be no doubt of the truth that there is life beyond the grave now. Why can there be no doubt? There can be no doubt because of Christ's resurrection. Before 1492 Spanish coins often showed the Straits of Gibraltar with the Latin inscription *ne plus ultra.* It meant "no more beyond." So far as men knew, the western end of the Mediterranean Sea, marked by the Straits of Gibraltar, was the end of land. In that year, however, Columbus discovered the coast of America across the great sea. When he returned from his voyages the coins that had been in circulation were reissued, but now they bore the inscription *plus ultra,* "more beyond." This became the motto of the Spanish crown. In the same way, the Lord Jesus Christ once passed through the straits of death and returned, bringing abundant evidence that the Old Testament hope was well grounded.

Two Destinies

Likewise, we must note that Jesus did not merely reinforce what the Old Testament characters believed. He went on to show that beyond the grave there was to be a resurrection, that there would be a resurrection unto life for believers and a resurrection unto condemnation for unbelievers, and finally that these resurrections would forever establish the different destinies for these two groups.

It is true, of course, that in a few instances there may have been partial anticipation of this hope in the Old Testament also. Job was testifying of this faith when he said, "I know that my Redeemer lives, and that in the end he will stand upon the earth. And after my skin has been destroyed, yet in my flesh I will see God" (Job 19:25–26). David was certainly expressing this hope when he declared, "But God will redeem my life from the grave; he will surely take me to himself" (Ps. 49:15). Still it is true that the full doctrine regarding a resurrection of the just to life and a resurrection of the wicked to punishment came in its fullness only through Christ's teaching. In fact, our text (from the early public ministry of Jesus) may be the earliest complete statement of this truth in history.

It is a glorious statement, at least for believers. Why? Because it refers to the consummation of our great salvation.

Perhaps I can best explain what this means by pointing out that when God determines to save a man he determines to save all of him. When man was created he was created a trinity, possessing a body, soul, and spirit. Man sinned;

when he sinned each part of his being came under the curse of sin and God's wrath. God had said to Adam in regard to the tree of knowledge, "When you eat of it you will surely die" (Gen. 2:17). When man sinned he died. His spirit died immediately—which he demonstrated by hiding from God. His soul began to die. His body died eventually and returned to the ground. Now, what happens when God saves a man? When God saves a man he replaces each part of man's being with a new part and, what is more, he does so in the order in which they were lost. First, he gives the person a new spirit. This is the life of God within him. During this life God begins to form a new soul as the individual is transformed after the image of Christ. This soul is called the "new man," which is placed in the individual by God and which exists there alongside the old man that is destined to perish. Finally, God creates a new body that will be united to the soul and spirit at the resurrection.

It is this uniting of our new souls and spirits with our new body for which we long. Now we have our old bodies. In death they will be gone, and our souls and spirits (which are the Lord's) will go to be with Jesus. When he returns we will receive our new bodies, and our salvation will be complete. Those who believe in Jesus wait expectantly for that day.

Damnation

On the other hand, in all honesty we must point out that, according to these same words, Jesus spoke of a resurrection not only unto life, as I have just described it, but also unto condemnation. At this point the King James Version reads "damnation," but the word is the same one that occurs in John 3:18: "He that believeth on him is not condemned; but he that believeth not is condemned already" (KJV). It means that he is condemned to an eternity without God. God is the source of all good. Consequently, this existence is bad and is therefore properly described as being filled with terrors, woes, misery, wailing, and deep cries.

Let this thought grip your mind. God has appointed a day in which all men and women who have ever lived will be brought before him and judged. Death is not the end. Therefore you and I—whoever we may be—must stand before him. Will your judgment be "unto life" because of your relationship to Jesus Christ? Or will your judgment be "unto condemnation"? Will the judgment unite you to God or be the means of your separation from him forever?

Mercy or God's Justice?

If you are asking yourself this question and are concerned about the answer, I now have the privilege of showing you that you can know the answer and can know it beyond any questioning. It all depends upon your relationship to Jesus Christ. If you come to the point of standing before God just as you are—without ever having benefited from Christ's death on your behalf or from his offer of righteousness and new life—then God will have no alternative but to banish you from his sight. You are sinful, no matter how good you may seem in your own eyes, and God cannot condone sin. What is more, you will find yourself the object of his fierce wrath. You are his creature. He has made you. Yet, you have rejected his way and spurned his Son, who came to earth and suffered to save people from their sin.

On the other hand, if you will come as one who has believed on the Lord Jesus Christ and in what he has done for you, then God promises to receive you as he receives Jesus. In fact, since Jesus is himself the Judge, it is Jesus who will receive you; and he will take you into heaven as one whose sin has already been punished and who now stands, not in his own soiled character but in that new life of the body, soul, and spirit that is given by God. How then can he fail to receive you? How can he reject you when you come not as the old creation, ruined by sin, but as his new creation made perfect in the life of the Savior?

It has always been my experience that those who have not yet believed in Christ react in one of two ways at the thought of God's judgment. Some simply refuse to believe it. They think quite wrongly, I believe, that judgment is inconsistent with God's character. "God is love," they argue; "how can a loving God condemn anyone?" The answer to this view is that God's love is not inconsistent with his judgment and that, whatever we may think about the matter, the Bible quite obviously speaks of these two themes as compatible.

The other objection is more dangerous. These persons believe that it is somehow ignoble of themselves to receive salvation through Christ. To receive salvation in this way is to depend on God's mercy or grace, and they would far rather deal with God's justice. "I don't want mercy from God," they will say. "All I want is a fair shake. I just want justice."

I pity the person who wants nothing from God but justice. The justice of God? The justice of God will send a person to hell; the justice of God will never save him. Justice condemns! It is only the grace of God in Jesus Christ that pardons and makes alive.

The result of seeking nothing from God but justice is illustrated vividly by an incident from the life of the patriarch Abraham. Abraham had separated from his nephew Lot and had gone to live in the hill country of Palestine, while Lot had gone to live in the cities of Sodom and Gomorrah. The sin of the cities called for judgment, and God came to Abraham to tell him that he was about to destroy them. Immediately Abraham began to think of his nephew. He, too, would be destroyed if God acted as he had said. So Abraham began to reason with God. "If you destroy Sodom and Gomorrah as they are," he argued, "You will end up destroying the righteous along with the wicked. Suppose there are fifty righteous persons in the city? Won't you preserve the city for the sake of the fifty righteous? Shall not the Judge of all the earth do right?"

"I will not destroy Sodom if fifty righteous persons can be found there," said God.

At this point Abraham began to worry that there might, in fact, not be fifty righteous people in Sodom. He could think only of four himself—Lot, Lot's wife, and Lot's two daughters. Besides, Lot might not have been very much of an evangelist. So Abraham continued, "Suppose five of those fifty persons are lacking. Will you destroy the city for the lack of the five?"

"No," said God. "I will not destroy it if forty-five righteous persons are found there."

"Suppose there are only forty," said Abraham. "Shall not the Judge of all the earth do right?" God said that he would not destroy it for forty.

"Suppose there are thirty?"

"No, not for thirty."

"Twenty?"

"No, not for twenty." Finally Abraham reduced the number of righteous persons required for the salvation of the city to ten, and God promised not to destroy the city for ten. But even then Abraham had not reduced the number far enough. So, after God had removed the reluctant Lot, his wife, and his daughters from the city, judgment fell and the cities of the Dead Sea plain were eradicated.

That is what happens when the Judge of all the earth does right. Men are condemned by God's rightness. God's justice sends sinners to hell. Do you want justice? How foolish! On the other hand, how wonderful that the one who has been given new life in Christ need never confront that justice but instead will enter by the portal of physical death and resurrection into the fullness of life eternal! Do you trust the Lord Jesus Christ for your salvation? You must decide. The decisions of this life affect the issues of eternity.

66

The Witnesses to Christ

John 5:31–47

"If I testify about myself, my testimony is not valid. There is another who testifies in my favor, and I know that his testimony about me is valid.

"You have sent to John and he has testified to the truth. Not that I accept human testimony; but I mention it that you may be saved. John was a lamp that burned and gave light, and you chose for a time to enjoy his light.

"I have testimony weightier than that of John. For the very work that the Father has given me to finish, and which I am doing, testifies that the Father has sent me. And the Father who sent me has himself testified concerning me. You have never heard his voice nor seen his form, nor does his word dwell in you, for you do not believe the one he sent. You diligently study the Scriptures because you think that by them you possess eternal life. These are the Scriptures that testify about me, yet you refuse to come to me to have life.

"I do not accept praise from men, but I know you. I know that you do not have the love of God in your hearts. I have come in my Father's name, and you do not accept me; but if someone else comes in his own name, you will accept him. How can you believe if you accept praise from one another, yet make no effort to obtain the praise that comes from the only God?

"But do not think I will accuse you before the Father. Your accuser is Moses, on whom your hopes are set. If you believed Moses, you would believe me, for he wrote about me. But since you do not believe what he wrote, how are you going to believe what I say?"

The fifth chapter of John is concerned almost entirely with the question of how an individual can know God. In the language of theology this is the question of epistemology, and it has two parts.

403

The first part deals with means. By what means can we know God? What is the channel by which God reveals himself? The second part deals with verification. Once we are aware of the channel by which we can know God, by what means can the channel itself be verified? In other words, how can we know that this means of knowing God can be trusted?

Fortunately, both parts of this question are discussed in John 5. We have looked at the first part already. The chapter has now brought us to the second part. In the first part of the speech recorded here, Jesus has declared himself to be equal with God and, consequently, the only one through whom God can be known. He has claimed to be the giver of life as well as the one who is entrusted with the final judgment. Put in the terms I have just used, this means that Jesus is himself the channel by which we can know God and that this is true because he is God. At this point one might naturally raise the second part of the question. "You say that Jesus is God. Well, then, upon what evidence is such a claim grounded?" In the context of Christ's speech itself one might ask, "Why should Christ's hearers, the Jews, believe such testimony? Why should they consider Jesus reliable?"

In answer to these questions and in deference to the procedure of Jewish law, which required two or three witnesses for the establishment of any fact, Jesus now cites three independent testimonies that reinforce and corroborate his own. They are the testimony of John the Baptist, the witness of Jesus' miracles, and the witness of the Old Testament Scriptures. These supportive witnesses are important for us simply because they are still valid. They require belief in Christ's claims.

The Father's Testimony

Before we begin to look at the witness of John the Baptist, the miracles, and the Scriptures in detail, we need to see something about their nature and therefore why Jesus appeals to them.

The central point is simply that when Jesus appeals to these supplementary witnesses to his claims, he does not appeal just to facts or circumstances, even less to what just might happen to be the opinion of some person concerning himself. He actually appeals to the witness of the Father that is made on his behalf. In other words, just as Jesus is content to seek the will of God in all his acts and sayings (vv. 19–20), so is he content to let God bear witness to his claims. This is why the testimonies of John the Baptist, Jesus' miracles, and the Old Testament Scriptures are important.

We can see this principle clearly by imagining that a person has come to see us at our home with the news that our boss has given us a big promotion to that of a vice president in the firm. It is good news, of course, but it is meaningless unless the messenger has really come from the boss. If we call the firm and find that they have never heard of this person, then we can dismiss the visit as some strange practical joke. However, if the messenger really was sent by the boss, then we know that his offer is genuine. In the same way, the question of whether the supplementary witnesses to Jesus are really from God or not is important.

This is the point of the verses that begin this section of Christ's teaching. These verses say, "If I testify about myself, my testimony is not valid [that is, my witness does not meet the requirements of the law regarding the two or three witnesses]. There is another who testifies in my favor, and I know that his testimony about me is valid" (vv. 31–32).

Who is the "other" witness? Some scholars have thought that this person is John the Baptist, primarily because a discussion of his witness follows immediately. This is possible, of course. Yet everything in the context points to a different conclusion. In the first place, the witness of this verse is described in the present tense—"There is another who *testifies* in my favor"—while the witness of John the Baptist is described as being past. Second, the full form of the expression—"testimony about me"—has the effect of setting the first testimony aside for special notice, while in this passage John's testimony is actually placed on a lesser footing. Third, the first two verses seem to be introductory. For these reasons, it seems wise to view the "other witness" as God the Father and to find the witness of the Father expressed in the testimony of John, in the miracles, and in Scripture. The witness of the Father is referred to explicitly in the citation of each one (vv. 36–38).

The point of this is simply that the value of such testimony is to be traced precisely to the fact that it is the testimony of God. In other words, God the Father has not only sent God the Son, through whom he may be known. He has, in addition and at the same time, provided other supplemental witnesses so that people may both know that he has spoken in Christ and have no excuse for neglecting to put their trust in him.

John the Baptist

The first of the supplemental witnesses cited by Jesus in John 5 is John the Baptist. We have already looked at John in some detail in previous studies, particularly in relation to his character as a witness. John was a great witness. He is a pattern for our own witness. Yet he is brought forward here not simply because he is a witness (in the same way that Christians today might be witnesses) but because he is a particular type of witness, a prophet.

It might be assumed from John's rejection of any claim to be identified with the Messiah, with Elijah, or with "the prophet" mentioned in John 1:20–21 that John the Baptist was also rejecting the prophetic role itself. But this is unwarranted. It is true that John refused to claim that he was "*the* prophet" of Deuteronomy 18:15, but this is not the same thing as rejecting a prophetic function entirely. In these denials John was denying any importance of his own. However, it is precisely in pointing away from himself and to Christ that he emerges most strongly in the prophetic role.

We should note in the first place that as a priest and a Nazarite John was the perfect figure of the prophet. He was a priest by descent from Zacharias, his father; and he was a Nazarite by choice, as Samson, Samuel, and many others had been before him (cf. Luke 1:15). It is against the background of a common recognition of John as a prophet that one can understand the questions of the delegation that came to him from Jerusalem.

The prophetic nature of John's mission is indicated also by the statement that John did not speak on his own accord but rather as one who had been sent by God. This statement is repeated twice in the fourth Gospel. It is found first in the prologue, where we are told, "There was a man who was sent from God; his name was John" (1:6). Later it is found on the lips of John himself in the statement, "I am not the Christ but am sent ahead of him" (3:28). This latter statement has its origins in the Old Testament in the words of Malachi: "See, I will send my messenger, who will prepare the way before me" (Mal. 3:1; cf. Matt. 11:10; Mark 1:2; and Luke 7:27).

A third indication of John's prophetic role is found in Jesus' reference to John as a "lamp that burned and gave light" (v. 35). This lamp is not a light that shines in its own right (like the sun) but a lamp that has been kindled from a source outside itself, a "kindled light." John is not the light. Only Jesus is the light. Nevertheless, John is important because he has been kindled by that light. Having been set on fire by God, he bears witness to Jesus.

What should we make of John the Baptist? He lived long ago. He was just one man. Still, Jesus says that John lived to verify his claim to be God, that this was his message. Was John right? Is Jesus God? In answering this question Jesus himself asks you to reckon with John's testimony.

Miracles

The second supplemental witness appealed to by Jesus is that of his signs or miracles. He calls them his "work." He says, "I have a testimony weightier than that of John. For the very work that the Father has given me to finish, and which I am doing testifies that the Father has sent me" (v. 36).

What is this work? How are we to think of it as a witness to Jesus Christ? The best answer to these questions, which we will see in greater detail in the next study, is found in the term that John most characteristically uses in speaking of Christ's miracles. He calls them "signs." A sign is a symbol, a pointer to something signified. It is apparent that a miracle may be a sign by pointing to the presence of God or to a prophetic figure who has been authorized by God. The miracles do this in the case of Jesus.

The miracles reveal God. God is seen in the miracles. Thus, the miracles of healing show that Jesus is the Lord and giver of life. The multiplication of the loaves shows that he is the sustainer of life. The healing of the blind man shows that he grants physical and spiritual sight. The list can be extended. Jesus refers to the evidential value of the miracles when he cries, "Do not believe me unless I do what my Father does. But if I do it, even though you do not believe me, believe the miracles, that you may know and understand that the Father is in me, and I in the Father" (10:37–38).

The Scriptures

The third supplemental witness that Jesus appealed to in support of his claims is the witness of the Old Testament Scriptures. This is the most important of the three. For of the three witnesses (the witness of John the Baptist, the signs, and the Scriptures), it is the evidence of the Scriptures upon which Jesus most fully dwells and in connection with which he most clearly links the witness of the Father. This witness is not referred to in passing, as is the witness of the signs. Nor is it overshadowed by others, as is the case with the witness of John the Baptist. Instead, Jesus concentrates upon this testimony, so much that the verses that deal with it (vv. 37–47) emerge as one of the most significant summaries of the importance of Scripture in the Gospel.

Jesus declares, "The Father who sent me has himself testified concerning me. You have never heard his voice nor seen his form, nor does his word dwell in you, for you do not believe the one he sent. You diligently study the Scriptures because you think that by them you possess eternal life. These are the Scriptures that testify about me, yet you refuse to come to me to have life. . . . But do not think I will accuse you before the Father. Your accuser is Moses, on whom your hopes are set. If you believed Moses, you would believe me, for he wrote about me. But since you do not believe what he wrote, how are you going to believe what I say?" (vv. 37–40, 45–47).

In this teaching Jesus claims that the Old Testament Scriptures are from God and are fulfilled in him, that the unbelieving Jews have perverted the Old Testament and misunderstood it (just as many do today), and that the Old Testament itself will accuse those who refuse to believe in it.

God's Signpost

We are going to come back to this subject in a subsequent study, but before we do we need to see one important point of Christ's teaching that bears directly upon the subject we are considering. What is the *primary* purpose of Scripture? Is it to record the history of God's dealings with men? It does record such history, but that is not its primary function. Is it to reveal certain truths to men? Does the word "truth" seem to make this the right answer? Although it does reveal truths, this is not its primary function either. The primary purpose of Scripture is to point men and women to Christ. It is true that it uses a variety of means to do this. History is one of them; the communication of truth, particularly about God's nature and about man's sin, is another. But the primary purpose is to point men to Christ.

Have the Scriptures done that for you? Have you given them a chance? I can tell you on the authority of the Word of God that there will be no real knowledge of the Lord Jesus Christ without them. And without him there will be no real knowledge of the Father.

The Scriptures, too, are a signpost. Suppose, as John Stott suggests in one of his books, that you and your family are determined to go on a picnic. You pick your spot and start driving toward it. At last you come to a sign that contains the name of the picnic grounds. What do you do now? Do you immediately stop the car and get out and have your picnic around the signpost? Of course not! You follow the sign to the grounds themselves and have your picnic there. In the same way, God gave the Scriptures so that you and I, sinners that we are, might come to Christ in whom we have a true knowledge of the Father.

A Demanding Revelation

The divine testimony to the person of Jesus Christ is centered upon three great supplementary witnesses: the witness of John the Baptist, the witness of the signs, and the witness of the Scriptures. The Baptist's witness is that of a prophet and thus of the *prophetic word*. The witness of the signs is that of the *acted word*. The final and most important witness is that of the Scriptures, which are the *written word*. All three witnesses involve the direct and supernatural activity of God and hence may be described as aspects of the Father's own testimony to the person and teaching of the Son.

But where does that leave us? Can we look at these witnesses to Jesus Christ and then simply disregard them, as though they had nothing to say to us personally? Or will we listen to them and heed them as that evidence of God's testimony in history that has permanent validity? Clearly, if the witnesses are what Jesus declares them to be, then they must be heeded and we must commit our lives to Jesus. What will you say to God in that day when you stand before him? Will you say, "I did not know about Jesus"? What nonsense! Will you say, "I did know about him, but I was not convinced by the evidence"? How shallow! Have you ever examined it? Is it not better to say, "I have examined the witnesses and have believed all that they have told me about him; therefore, I come to you not on my own merits but on the merits of Christ, my Savior"?

67

Why Miracles?

John 5:36

"I have testimony weightier than that of John. For the very work that the Father has given me to finish, and which I am doing, testifies that the Father has sent me."

In all my life I have never met anyone who has seen a ghost. But in the opening chapters of his book on *Miracles,* C. S. Lewis speaks of the one person whom he had met who had. "The interesting thing about the story," he writes, "is that that person disbelieved in the immortal soul before she saw the ghost and still disbelieves after seeing it. She says that what she saw must have been an illusion or a trick of the nerves."[1] According to Lewis—and I believe him—the person may be right. For since a miracle must always be presented to our senses in order for us to become aware of it—either to our sight, sound, hearing, or feeling—and since our senses are not infallible, anything that appears to be miraculous may well be only an illusion. In life seeing is clearly not believing. It is rather the other way around.

Here, of course, we come to our first difficulty in our study of the fifth chapter of John. For here Jesus appeals to miracles in defense of his extraordinary claims. He says, "I have a testimony weightier than that of John. For the very work that the Father has given me to finish, and which I am doing, testifies that the Father has sent me" (5:36). But is this appeal valid? We are right to ask: How do Christ's works bear witness to him? And besides, if the evidence of miracles *is* valid (as we have some reason to believe), what are we to say about Christ and his appeal to them?

The problem becomes even more acute and complex when we remember the story which Jesus told concerning the rich man and Lazarus. The rich man wanted God to send Lazarus back from the grave so that his brothers might repent. But Abraham, who spoke on this occasion, replied, "If they do not listen to Moses and the Prophets, they will not be convinced even if someone rises from the dead" (Luke 16:31). Apparently Jesus taught that even so great a miracle as a resurrection would not persuade the unrighteous. Moreover, if we want proof that this is so, we need only to turn to the story of that other Lazarus who was raised by Jesus but who thereby provoked not faith but hatred from the Jewish leaders. We are told that the leaders actually consulted how they might kill Lazarus because of the influence that his resurrection was having on the masses.

The question is clearly: What place does an appeal to miracles have in Christianity? Or, to put it another way, why and in what sense did Jesus himself appeal to them?

Christ's Signs

The best answer to these questions begins with the term "signs" or "signs and wonders." These words occur throughout the New Testament and mean "miracles." But the word "sign" does not always mean "miracle," and even in the cases where it refers to a miracle it always means more. Originally the word "sign" (*semeia* in Greek) meant "a distinguishing mark" or "token." Thus, in the Old Testament, circumcision is called a sign or token of the covenant that God made with Israel (Gen. 17:11). Paul repeats the same usage of the word in Romans 4:11. In the same way, the finding of the baby in the manger becomes a sign to the shepherds who were seeking the infant Jesus (Luke 2:12), and the "sign of Jonah" becomes a token of Christ's death and resurrection for the Jews (Luke 11:29–30). A sign is a symbol. It is a pointer to something signified. It is obvious that a miracle may become a sign by pointing to the unusual ability or character of the one performing it.

But what do the miracles point to in John? The answer is that they point to Christ's glory, which is only another way of saying that they reveal his divine worth or character. This is clear in the case of the changing of water into wine at Cana of Galilee, for John concludes that account by telling us that this was the beginning of miracles (the word is actually "signs") in which Jesus "revealed his glory" and on the basis of which "his disciples believed on him"

(2:11). In every instance the sign draws attention to Jesus himself and in particular to his divine nature revealed in his works. Jesus taught this by saying, "The . . . work which I am doing testifies that the Father has sent me."

Incidentally—and we need to see this aspect of Christ's teaching too—the works that Christians do also bear witness to Jesus. Pink, one of the great commentators on John, has written, "If our works are 'dead works,' wood, hay, and stubble which shall be burned up in the coming day, that proves we are carnal, walking after the flesh; and such a witness will dishonor and grieve Him whose name we bear. But if we abound in 'good works,' this will show that we are walking after the spirit, and men (our fellow-believers) seeing our good works will glorify our Father which is in heaven."[2]

The signs are also more than mere symbols. In some cases—above all in the miracles recorded by John—they actually contain Christ, are a part of him, just as his words are a part of himself. This means that they are actually part of the revelation.

Moreover, Christ's words and works belong together. This is made clear in two important texts. First, in John 15:22–24 Jesus speaks of his words and works together, showing that they are one in regard to their source and their effects. We can see the point best if the verses are printed as follows:

> If I had not come and *spoken* to them, they would not be guilty of sin.
>> Now, however, they have no excuse for their sin.
>> He who hates me hates my Father as well.
> If I had not *done* among them what no one else did,
>> They would not be guilty of sin.
>> But now they have seen these miracles, and yet they have hated both me and my Father.

The second text is John 14:10, in which "words" and "works" appear as interchangeable concepts: "The *words* I say to you are not just my own. Rather, it is the Father, living in me, who is doing his *work*."

The Major Signs

Christ's works are signs, not just his miracles, and so are his words. Everything he does is done to reveal God. In the nature of the case, however, some of the things that Jesus says and some of the things he does are more significant than others, with the result that John is compelled to choose from the many works at his disposal those that are most helpful for the church and that are most central to a true understanding of Christ's person. This, incidentally, is the true meaning of the concluding verses of chapter 20, which say, "Jesus did many other miraculous signs in the presence of his disciples, which are not recorded in this book. But these are written that you may believe that Jesus is the Christ, the Son of God, and that by believing you may have life in his name" (vv. 30–31).

What are the signs that John chooses? Among the many that reveal Christ's nature and character, John pays particular attention to the following:

1. *The transformation of the water into wine* (2:1–11). John tells us that this was the first of Christ's signs, and he uses it naturally to pass from the witness of John the Baptist, which occupies most of the first chapter of the Gospel, to the section of the Gospel that deals with the signs (chs. 2–11). The motive for this miracle cannot really be found in Christ's compassion for human suffering or in the conquest of evil, as is most often the case with the miracles recorded for us by Matthew, Mark, and Luke. The motive is solely that the "glory" of Christ might be revealed and that the disciples might believe as a result of that revelation.

What did this sign reveal? For one thing, it revealed Christ's unity with God the Father in creative power. This is an illustration of John 1:3 that says that "through him all things were made." For another, it shows Jesus to be the bringer of Christian joy. John's point is that Jesus alone makes life joyous and abundant.

2. *The healing of the nobleman's son* (4:46–54). We have already studied this sign, which John calls the second of Christ's miracles. It is a sign of healing, and thus shows the power of the Lord Jesus Christ to overcome sin and heal illness.

Even more significant than this is the fact that it also shows Jesus' ability to calm a troubled spirit and instill faith. We remember that the nobleman who came to Jesus did not have a strong faith originally. He was fearful, anxious, afraid that his son would die. Jesus led him to stronger faith, so much so that when the man left Jesus he actually went on calmly about his business and did not check on his son's condition until the next day.

3. *The healing of the disabled man* (5:1–18). John calls this the third sign, and it follows in his narrative closely upon the healing of the nobleman's son. What is the point of this miracle? Certainly it was not to provoke faith on the part of those who witnessed it. John tells us that it actually made the Jews angry, for they tried to persecute Jesus and kill him. It did not even provoke faith on the part of the man who was healed. For nothing is said about his faith at all, and his greatest loyalty seems to have been to the Jewish leaders rather than Christ even after his healing. Then what was the purpose? The point of the miracle is that *we* are like the disabled man spiritually. We have sinned, and spiritual inability to seek Christ has come from our sin. We cannot rise to meet him. We cannot even believe on him. Nevertheless, it is when we are disabled spiritually—blind, lame, and paralyzed—that Jesus comes to us to save us and to free us from sin's bondage. The miracle reveals God to be a God of great grace.

4. *The feeding of the five thousand* (6:1–14). This miracle is the first of three miracles whose significance is explained by Christ himself, in two cases by means of a long interlocking discourse. In this story, Jesus feeds five thousand people by means of a few small loaves and fish. The point is not just that Jesus

is able to multiple bread. The point is that he can satisfy the hunger of the soul. Jesus says, "I am the bread of life. He who comes to me will never go hungry, and he who believes in me will never be thirsty" (6:35).

Have you found that Jesus is able to satisfy your hunger, that He is able to quench your thirst? He can. I do not care what your need may be. You may have a thirst for companionship. Do you feel that no one understands you, that no one cares? Jesus cares. You may feel unloved. Do you have a hunger for love? Do you feel that no one loves you, that no one ever will, perhaps even that you are unlovely? Jesus loves you. He proved that by dying in your place. Do you have a thirst for direction and meaning in your life? Jesus has a plan for your life, designed before the foundation of this universe. The person who has found Jesus to be the perfect provider for these needs has already been convinced by the miracle.

5. *The walking upon the water* (6:16–21). John does not call attention to this miracle, and it is possible that it is included mostly because it was attached historically to the previous miracle of the multiplication of the loaves. It is in each of the other Gospels. The point of the miracle, if John intends it to make a point, is that Jesus obviously possesses power over the laws of nature.

6. *The healing of the man born blind* (9:1–41). This healing is actually a double miracle, involving the restoration of both physical and spiritual sight to one who had been born both physically and spiritually blind. The two parts of the miracle presuppose and reinforce each other. What is the point? Jesus tell us when he describes himself as the "light of the world." In the same story the faith of the man who had been born blind but who had come to both physical and spiritual sight is contrasted with the unbelief of the authorities who, although confronted with the true spiritual light, prefer to live in darkness.

7. *The raising of Lazarus from the dead* (11:1–46). In the last of the public signs Christ's progressive display of power over nature, sin, and sickness comes to a climax in the total victory of life over death. In this case the discourse is mingled with the narrative, but the key statement is outstanding: "I am the resurrection and the life" (v. 25). The miracle shows that Jesus is the source of eternal life, that it may be enjoyed here and now, and that the same power that assures it now will also, after the death of the body, raise the dead to a new and better existence beyond. It is significant that the Gospel specifically points to the raising of Lazarus as a sign (12:18), for this supreme manifestation of the glory of Jesus leads, not only to belief on the part of many from among the people but also to the most extreme and virulent hatred on the part of the authorities.

Taste and See

We come, then, to a summation of our answer to the question, What is the purpose of the miracles? The answer, on the negative side, is simply that the supernatural in itself does not prove the divine origin of the one performing it. Presumably even the devils can do miraculous things. The value of the miracles consists in their nature; that is, in what they reveal about God the Father and the Lord Jesus. This is the answer on its positive side. The miracles of Christ, as indeed all his works, both miraculous and nonmiraculous alike, show us his nature. They disclose his ability to fill the vacuum of the heart.

Let me state it in slightly different language. In John the signs are not occasioned *by* faith. They are occasions *for* faith. They are given to provoke faith and strengthen it.

Have they done that for you? If the miracles are true, then there has never been and doubtless will never be a person like this amazing Nazarene. Is this not provoking? Does it not demand that you investigate him personally to see whether the things written about him and claimed by him are valid? If you will not do this, then you demonstrate by your actions that the difficulties you have with belief are not rational. It is not as though God has not provided enough evidence for a thinking person to evaluate Christ's claims. Your difficulties are moral. The problem is sin. On the other hand, if you will investigate Christ's worth and character, you will find him to be what countless others have also found him to be—the Son of God and your Savior.

68

The Witness of the Scriptures

John 5:37–38

"And the Father who sent me has himself testified concerning me. You have never heard his voice nor seen his form, nor does his word dwell in you, for you do not believe the one he sent."

The fifth chapter of John's Gospel contains the evidences that the Lord Jesus Christ gives for his claims—the witness of John the Baptist, the witness of Christ's miracles, and the witness of the Scriptures. The first two have already been discussed. The third is discussed in the verses beginning with verse 37 and continuing to the end of the chapter.

To understand the importance of these verses, one needs to recognize that they come at the end of Christ's discourse and therefore are in a position of prominence. To give an illustration, they stand at the end of this discourse much the way a star witness might be introduced at the end of a trial to nail down the case for the prosecution. Suppose a man is on trial for murder and the evidence for his conviction is being presented by the district attorney. The first witness comes forward and demonstrates that the accused had an opportunity to commit the crime. He was present in the area of the crime at the time it was committed. The second witness shows that he had a motive for committing the crime. He would have profited by the victim's death.

The third witness proves that the accused had access to the murder weapon. Finally, the fourth witness was an eye witness of the murder itself and can identify the murderer.

This is an illustration, in part, of the way in which the Lord Jesus Christ built up the witnesses for his claims as they are recorded in this chapter. The witness of John was a real witness. It was the witness of a prophet. God spoke through John, and the leaders of Christ's day even acknowledged the importance of John's witness by appointing a delegation to visit John and question him. Still, in one sense, John's was but the witness of a man and only one man at that. It could be discounted. The witness of Christ's miracles follows. This is more important, for the miracles were evidence of God the Father working in Christ. The miracles revealed Christ's nature. Taken with the witness of the Baptist, they are quite important. Yet both fade into relative unimportance in light of the final witness, which is the witness of the Word of God.

So Jesus Christ begins to speak about the witness of the Bible to himself, stressing two points. The first is the divine origin of the Scriptures. The second is their primary purpose, which is to point to him. He is speaking of the first of these when he says, "And the Father who sent me has himself testified concerning me. You have never heard his voice nor seen his form, nor does his word dwell in you, for you do not believe the one he sent" (vv. 37–38).

Age of Decline

It is unfortunate that we need to stress the divine origin of the Scriptures as much as we do in our day. But it is necessary due to the fact that this truth is so widely contested, not only by scholars (from whom, of course, most of the doubts originate) but also by many regular church members. Doubt as to the divine origin of the Scriptures is so widespread in some quarters that many have even come to think that the situation is normal.

Actually nothing could be farther from the truth. The low view of the Bible that prevails in our day is a fairly recent development in light of the broad flow of church history. It goes back no more than two hundred years. A student of church history knows that up to the time of the Reformation (in some ways even for two hundred years beyond that) almost no one within the church doubted that the Scriptures of the Old and New Testaments are uniquely the Word of God. Even heretics accepted this principle. Thus, all who claimed to be Christians recognized that the Bible is a divine authority binding upon all men and that it contains objective truths that transcend human understanding.

Unfortunately, in the post-Reformation period the orthodox view of Scripture came under increasingly devastating attacks. Already weakened by centuries of appealing to the Fathers rather than to the Scripture in defense of a point of doctrine and in violent reaction to the Protestant Reformation, the Roman Catholic church in 1546 took the step of officially placing the tradition of the church alongside Scripture as an equally valid form and source of Christian doctrine. The full significance of this decision was no doubt overlooked at the time of the Council of Trent, but it was monumental. The act had tragic consequences for the Church of Rome as the continuing development of debilitating doctrines, such as Mariology and the veneration of the saints, indicates.

The Protestant church, as the result of its heritage and its sharp polemic against Catholicism, held on longer—for two hundred years. But then in the eighteenth century and particularly in the nineteenth century a critical appraisal of the Scriptures, backed by a naturalistic rationalism, succeeded in dislodging the Bible from the place it had previously held. For the church of the age of rationalism the Bible became man's word about God rather than God's word to man. And when people rejected the unique, divine character of the Bible, they rejected its authority also.

The Catholic church weakened the orthodox view of the Bible by exalting human traditions to the stature of Scripture. The Protestant Church weakened the orthodox view of Scripture by lowering the Bible to the level of traditions. The differences are great, but the results are similar. In both cases the unique character of the Scripture has been lost, its divine authority forfeited, and the function of the Bible as the reforming voice of God within the church forgotten for the majority of people.

Fortunately, neither position is tenable, and the confusion that haunts today's religious scene easily demonstrates this fact. The Protestant church is finding that without a valid basis for religious authority, theology withers and the church becomes increasingly powerless to preach the gospel. Thus, in an amazing milestone address to delegates to the Consultation on Church Union, meeting in Denver in the fall of 1971, Peter L. Berger of Rutgers University called for a return to "authority in the Christian community" and bemoaned its loss.[1] And in a most fascinating book published the following year, Dean M. Kelley, Director for Civil and Religious Liberty for the National Council of Churches, documented the inevitable decline of churches that lose a high degree of commitment and the corresponding growth of those who do not.[2]

The Roman community, on its part, is discovering that although two sources of authority are better than none, Scripture and tradition often conflict and the deep human preference for traditions rather than Scripture inevitably shifts the balance of authority away from the written Word of God. Many Catholics, including Monsignor George G. Higgins, a top executive of the U.S. Catholic Conference and author, are beginning to deplore preaching that omits the gospel and bypasses biblical authority. Says another executive, "The church is trying to pick up the ways of the world instead of preaching Christ crucified." In such a time there is a challenge for those who still adhere to the view of Scripture that the Lord Jesus Christ taught and who boldly exalt the Word as the final revelation of the Father and the final arbiter of human thought and conduct.

God's Word

We recognize, of course, even as we refer to the divine origin of the Scriptures, that in one sense all the biblical books have been written by men. That is, men did the actual writing. At the same time we also affirm that there is a great difference between the Bible and any other book that has ever been written by any man or woman. Men wrote, but God stood behind the writing. Men used their own vocabulary and literary style, but God nevertheless guided them in the choice of the words and guaranteed the outcome.

This point—which would have been heartily endorsed by the Lord Jesus Christ himself—is stated in a memorable way by Peter. Peter wrote, "No prophecy ever came by the impulse of man, but men moved by the Holy Spirit spoke from God" (2 Peter 1:21 RSV). In this verse the Greek word translated "moved" is the word used by Luke in the second chapter of Acts to compare the coming of the Holy Spirit at Pentecost to "the blowing of a *violent* wind" (Acts 2:2). Again, in the twenty-seventh chapter it is used to describe the force of the wind upon the ship that was carrying Paul to Rome. Luke notes that the ship was carried along by the wind. He says, "The ship was caught by the storm and could not head into the wind; so we gave way to it and were *driven* along" (v. 15). Again, "they . . . let the ship be *driven* along" (v. 17). Clearly, Luke wished to say that the ship was at the mercy of the storm. It did not cease to be a ship, but it did cease to have control over its course and destination.

In the same way, we are told through Peter that the writers of the Bible were borne along in their writing to produce the words that God intended to be recorded. They wrote as men, but as men moved by the Holy Spirit. The result was the revelation of God.

Someone might object at this point that if men had anything at all to do with the writing of the Bible, the results must at some point or other be filled with error. But this does not follow. An analogy can help. The analogy is one between the conception and birth of the Lord Jesus and the coming of our Bible. What happened when the Lord Jesus Christ was conceived in the womb of the virgin Mary? We read that the Holy Spirit overshadowed her so that the child that was born of her was called "the Son of God" (Luke 1:35). In this conception there was a touching of the divine and the human, and the result was also in its turn both human and divine. Christ was a real man. He was a particular man, a Jew, who had a certain measurable weight and a recognizable appearance. You could have taken a picture of him. Yet he was also God almighty and without sin.

In the same way, just as the Holy Spirit came upon the virgin Mary so that she conceived the human Son of God in her womb, so also did the Holy Spirit come upon the brain cells of Moses, David, the prophets, the evangelists, Paul, and the other biblical writers, so that they brought forth from their minds those books that constitute our Bible. All their writings bear the marks of human personality. They differ in style. At the same time, the ultimate source is divine, and the touch of the human did not stamp them with weakness or error any more than the womb of Mary imparted sin to the Savior.

Archaeological Evidence

We are going to go on from this point to see how this remarkable book with its divine authorship bears witness to Jesus Christ, how it can be misused, and why it will eventually condemn those who reject it. But before we do we need to answer the objections of someone who may have heard stories of how scholarship has supposedly disproved the reliability of the Bible and who are therefore inclined on those grounds to reject all that has been said about the divine origin of the Scriptures. Has scholarship demonstrated that the books of the Bible are fallible and therefore merely written by men after all? Is the Bible disproved?

There was a time not long ago when claims such as these were made by many influential spokesmen, and were made openly. In past years almost every biblical theologian and scholar spoke of so-called "certain results" or "assured findings" that were imagined to have laid the orthodox conception of the Bible to rest forever. Today, however, as anyone who had the opportunity to delve deeply into such questions knows, these phrases no longer occur with such frequency. In fact, they hardly occur at all. Why? Simply because, as the result of the continuing march of biblical and archaeological investigations, many of these so-called "assured results" have simply blown up in the faces of those who propounded them.

Here is an example. In 2 Kings 15:29 there is a reference to a king of Assyria named Tiglath-pileser. He is spoken of as having conquered the Israelites of the northern kingdom and as having taken many of them into captivity. A generation ago scholars were saying—their books are still in our libraries—that this king never existed and that the account of the fall of Israel to Assyria is something akin to mythology. Now however, archaeologists have excavated Tiglath-pileser's capital city and can give his whole history. They have even found his name pressed into bricks that read: "I Tiglath-pileser, king of the west lands, king of the earth, whose kingdom extends to the great sea. . . ." The English reader can find accounts of his battles with Israel in James B. Pritchard's *Ancient Near Eastern Texts Relating to the Old Testament.*

About the same time that some scholars were denying the existence of Tiglath-pileser, others were denying that Moses could have written the first five books of the Bible on the ground, which seemed irrefutable enough, that writing had not been invented in his day. Since that time, however, archaeologists have unearthed tablets and inscriptions that were written several hundreds of years before Moses and, ironically enough, in the very Sinai peninsula where Moses led the people of Israel for forty years.

In even more recent days, many scholars have denied that the historical books of the New Testament were written close enough to the events they purport to relate to be reliable. The synoptic Gospels in particular were dated late; and John, which seemed to have the greatest degree of Greek flavoring, was pushed back well into the second Christian century—and by some scholars into the third. In time, however, a piece of papyrus was uncovered in Egypt, on the basis of which it was necessary to date John no later than A.D. 125 and presumably much before that time. In other words, the results of scholarship in our day increasingly validate the biblical claims.

They do not prove infallibility—nothing can do that—but they do lead in the direction of reliability and reveal nothing that is not compatible with the highest view of the Scriptures.

Waiting on the Rock

The Christian need never fear to stand upon the Word of God, recognizing its full authority, as the Lord Jesus Christ did. At times there will be critical theories that run against it. The arguments may seem unanswerable, so much so that the one who tries to stand against them may well be dismissed as an obscurantist. The wise of this world will say, "You can believe that if you want to, but the results of scientific criticism teach us better." These things have happened before and will happen again. But the Christian who will stand upon Scripture will find even within his lifetime that, as the so-called "assured results" begin to crumble about the scholars, the view of the Bible held by the Lord Jesus Christ, the historical view of the church, will prevail.

Many years ago a former leader of the Church of England, Bishop Ryle of Liverpool, wrote wisely, "Give me the plenary, verbal theory of biblical inspiration with all its difficulties, rather than the doubt. I accept the difficulties and humbly wait for their solution. But while I wait, I am standing on the rock."

69

The Purpose of the Scriptures

John 5:39

"You diligently study the Scriptures because you think that by them you possess eternal life. These are the Scriptures that testify about me."

It is not unusual in our day for men and women to have a low view of the Bible. Many persons, including professors of theology and ministers, feel that the Bible is man's word about God rather than God's word about man and so devalue it. Therefore, it is necessary to speak as Christ did, stressing the divine origin of the Bible and pointing out its supernatural characteristics. At the same time, possessing a low view of Scripture is not the only error embraced by people today. Many misunderstand it. They do not know what it says or why it is written. As a result of this it is necessary also to speak of its purpose, which is, above all else, to reveal Christ Jesus.

What is the purpose of Scripture? According to Jesus Christ the purpose of the Scripture is to point to him and reveal him. Thus, in the verses we are studying, he said, "You search the scriptures, because you think that in them you have eternal life; and *it is they that bear witness to me*" (5:39 RSV).

Have you seen this truth? Martin Luther is one who saw it clearly. In a sermon on this text preached only months before his death he argued, "Here Christ would indicate the principal reason why the Scripture was given by God. Men are to study and search in it and to learn that He, *He*, Mary's Son, is the one who is able to give eternal life to all who come to Him and believe on Him. Therefore he who would correctly and profitably read Scripture should see to it that he finds Christ in it; then he finds life eternal without fail. On the other hand, if I do not so study and understand Moses and the prophets as to find

421

that Christ came from Heaven for the sake of my salvation, became man, suffered, died, was buried, rose, and ascended to Heaven so that through Him I enjoy reconciliation with God, forgiveness of all my sins, grace, righteousness, and life eternal, then my reading in Scripture is of no help whatsoever to my salvation. I may, of course, become a learned man by reading and studying Scripture and may preach what I have acquired; yet all this would do me no good whatsoever. For if I do not know and do not find the Christ, neither do I find salvation and life eternal. In fact, I actually find bitter death; for our good God has decreed that no other name is given among men whereby they may be saved except the name of Jesus (Acts 4:12)."[1]

One Author

If you will think about this purpose of Scripture for a moment, I am sure you will see that it is an additional reason why the Bible must be divine in origin. The Bible was written over a period of several thousand years by more than thirty human authors. If the product of these men was no more than a human product, it is inconceivable that they could have agreed even on an outlook on life, let alone on the grand overriding purposes of God in history as disclosed in their book. Yet this agreement is precisely what we find. The only explanation is that, although the human writers did write out of their own perspective and out of their own historical environments, nevertheless, the God who stands behind the Bible so inspired their writings that the resulting words were inerrant and consistent. What is more, the combined result was in an important sense *one book*.

It is no accident in this connection that in the verses we are studying, although Jesus does speak of Moses as having been responsible for part of the Bible (vv. 45–47), he nevertheless begins with the statement that the Scriptures in their entirety are God's witness to his messianic claims. This is the course of the argument in the fifth chapter. God bears witness to Jesus (vv. 30–32). He does so through the witness of John the Baptist (vv. 33–35). He does so through Christ's miracles (v. 36). Above all, however, he does so through the Bible (vv. 37–47).

We may sum up Christ's teaching in this chapter by saying that according to Jesus: 1) the Bible is given by God, 2) the purpose of the Bible is to point to himself, and 3) to use the Bible in any other way is ultimately to misunderstand it and pervert its intention.

One Subject

At this point someone might find himself thinking along these lines: "Granted that the purpose of the Bible (a Bible, I will admit, that is given by God) is to point to Jesus Christ. But how does it point to him? Is not the Bible mostly history? In the Old Testament, at least, does it not talk about anything but Jesus? How then can we say that it points to him? How can he be its subject?"

The answer to that question is that Jesus becomes the subject of the Old Testament in two ways: (1) by fitting in with its general themes and (2) by fulfilling the specific prophecies to be found there. He becomes the subject of the New Testament in a far more obvious way, for the New Testament tells his story and is almost exclusively about him.

Think, for instance, about the great themes of the Old Testament. One theme is the sin of man and man's need. The Bible begins with the story of the creation. But no sooner is this story told (in the first two chapters of Genesis) than we also are told of man's fall. Instead of being humbly and gratefully dependent upon his Creator, as he should have been, man was soon in a state of rebellion against God. He went his way instead of God's. So the consequences of sin, including death, passed upon the race.

In the rest of the Old Testament we see these consequences unfolding. Thus we have the murder of Abel, the corruption leading up to the flood, demonism, sexual perversions, eventually even great tragedy for the chosen nation of Israel in spite of great blessings. Israel is carried off in slavery. Although some eventually return to the land of blessing, they return to a much less glorious existence. The Old Testament story is best summarized in David's great psalm of repentance, which ought properly to be the psalm of the whole human race: "Have mercy on me, O God, according to your unfailing love; according to your great compassion blot out my transgressions. Wash away all my iniquity and cleanse me from my sin. For I know my transgressions, and my sin is always before me. . . . Surely I was sinful at birth, sinful from the time my mother conceived me" (Ps. 51:1–3, 5).

Here is one great biblical doctrine. But if we understand it rightly, even this doctrine is not an end in itself. It is true. The heart of man acknowledges it to be true. But the truth of our sin and need is expounded in the Bible not merely for the sake of expounding a truth but rather because at the same time it is able to point to Christ as the solution to the dilemma.

We get some idea of this aspect of the Bible's witness by thinking of it as a doctor's diagnosis. Here is a man who goes to the doctor complaining of nausea and abdominal pain. The doctor notes an area of tenderness in the groin, does a blood test, and diagnoses appendicitis. What is the purpose of the doctor's diagnosis? Is telling the truth the purpose? Well, yes, in a sense. That is one purpose, but it is not the ultimate purpose. The ultimate purpose is to get the man with the pain to the surgeon so that the threat of death may be averted. In the same way, the Bible diagnoses the spiritual condition of the race so that individual men, women, and children might turn to the Lord Jesus Christ, since he is the only one who can cure their condition and bring healing. This is one way in which Jesus becomes the theme of the Old Testament.

We might add that all who really believed during the Old Testament age saw this. Thus we have stories of Abraham, Isaac, Jacob, David, the prophets, Anna, Simeon, John the Baptist, and others, all of whom placed their trust in the coming Redeemer and waited for him.

This leads us to the second great Old Testament theme: the existence of a God who acts in love to redeem sinners. This God the Father did himself in partial ways throughout the Old Testament period. At the same time, even as he did it he pointed to the coming of his Son who would redeem his people perfectly and forever.

Take the dealings of God with Adam and Eve on the occasion of their having sinned in the garden. Sin had separated the man and woman from the Creator. They tried to hide. God, however, came to them in the cool of the evening, calling. It is true that God spoke in judgment, as he had to do. He revealed the consequences of their sin. Still, at the same time that he spoke in judgment, he killed animals. He clothed the man and woman with skins, covering their shame. Thus he began his teaching of the way of salvation through sacrifice. In the same story he spoke to Satan, revealing the coming of One who would one day defeat him forever. "He will crush your head, and you will strike his heel" (Gen 3:15).

Nine chapters later we find another, somewhat veiled, reference to the "seed" who shall crush Satan. This is God's first great promise to Abraham stressing that in him all men would be blessed (12:3). In chapter 22 it is restated like this, "And through your offspring all nations on earth will be blessed" (22:18). The blessing referred to here certainly is not a blessing to come to all people through Abraham personally. It is not a blessing to come through all Jews indiscriminately, for all Jews are not even theists. It is not even a blessing to come through believing Jews. The blessing foretold is that which was to come through *the* seed of Abraham, the promised seed, the Messiah. Thus, years later the apostle Paul, who knew this text, used it to show that (1) the seed was the Lord Jesus, (2) the promise to Abraham was one of blessing through him, and (3) the blessing was to come through Christ's great work of redemption (Gal. 3:13–16).

In the Book of Numbers there is an interesting prophecy spoken by the Lord through Balaam, that shifty, halfhearted prophet of Moses' day. Balak, a king who was hostile to Israel, had hired Balaam to curse the Jewish people. But every time Balaam opened his mouth to curse, blessings on the people came out instead. On one occasion he said, "A star will come out of Jacob; a scepter will rise out of Israel. . . . A ruler will come out of Jacob and destroy the survivors of the city" (Num. 24:17, 19). This was a prophecy of Christ's coming. In the same way the patriarch Jacob spoke of him while he was dying, saying, "The scepter will not depart from Judah, nor the ruler's staff from between his feet, until he comes to whom it belongs and the obedience of the nations if his" (Gen 49:10).

Moses also spoke of the One who would come. Speaking for God he declared, "The Lord your God will raise up for you a prophet like me from among your own brothers. You must listen to him" (Deut. 18:15). Again, with God speaking, "I will put my words in his mouth, and he will tell them everything I command him" (v. 18).

The Psalms contain great prophecies. The second psalm tells of Christ's eventual victory and rule over the nations of this earth. This psalm was a popular one with the early Christians who used it in reference to Christ, as is apparent from Acts 4. Psalm 16 foretells the resurrection (v. 10; cf. Acts 2:31). In the twenty-second, twenty-third, and twenty-fourth psalms are three portraits of the Lord Jesus: the suffering Savior, the compassionate shepherd, and the King. Other psalms speak of other aspects of his life and ministry. At last Psalm 110 returns to the theme of his rule, looking for the day when Jesus shall take his seat at the right hand of the Father when all his enemies shall be made his footstool (v. 1).

Dozens of prophecies concern details of Christ's life, death, and resurrection. They occur in the prophetic books—especially Isaiah, Daniel, Jeremiah, Ezekiel, Hosea, and Zechariah—but also elsewhere. Jesus deliberately submitted his life to the outline for it as revealed in such prophecies, and he fulfilled them in careful and specific detail. That he did do this is evidenced by his rebuke to Peter after Peter had tried to prevent his arrest in Gethsemane. Jesus said, "Put your sword back in its place. . . . Do you think I cannot call on my Father, and he will at once put at my disposal more than twelve legions of angels? But how then would the Scriptures be fulfilled that say it must happen in this way?" (Matt. 26:52–54).

Open Book, Open Mind

After his resurrection the Lord Jesus Christ appeared to two of his disciples, a man and his wife, who were on their way home from Jerusalem following the Passover during which he had been killed. The disciples were Cleopas and Mary. They were dejected. Mary at least had seen the crucifixion, and when Jesus had died her faith in him and her hope had died also. Neither of them had any understanding that Christ needed to die and rise. Thus, even when reports of the empty tomb reached them early on that first Easter morning neither of them was able to take in the news.

As they went on their way Jesus appeared to them, but he had changed himself so that they could not recognize him. He could have revealed himself to them at once. Instead he revealed the purpose of the Scriptures and so taught both this couple and ourselves a great lesson.

The Bible says that he "opened" the Scriptures to them. The opening itself takes place in the midst of the story, but the phrase does not occur until the end. In reporting their encounter with Jesus they said, "Were not our hearts burning within us while he talked with us on the road and opened the Scriptures to us?" (Luke 24:32). As we read on in the story, however, we soon find that this initial "opening," the opening of the Scriptures, is followed by another "opening." This is the opening of their eyes. We read that as a consequence of his teaching and as he sat with them and broke bread in their home, "Then their eyes were opened and they recognized him" (v. 31). Finally, at the end of the story we read that Jesus again appeared to them in the presence of the other disciples and "opened their minds so they could understand the Scriptures" (v. 45).

Here are three great openings—the opening of the Scriptures, the opening of the eyes, and the opening of the mind. All three need to be reproduced in the life of every growing Christian. To have the Scriptures opened in the right way is to open the eyes to Christ. This in turn opens eyes in a new way to the Scriptures.

Has much of the Word of God been a mystery to you? Have you failed to see its purpose? If this has been the case, try reading the Bible to find Christ. Find him as the seed of the woman and of Abraham. Discover him prefigured in the life of Joseph. Recognize him as the Passover Lamb. See him as the rock in the wilderness. Learn about him as the cloud who guides his people in the years of their wandering. Perceive him as the Righteous One of Deuteronomy. Carry through the pages of the Old Testament to Malachi where he is portrayed as the Sun of righteousness risen with healing in his wings. If this happens for you, the Bible will cease to be a book to be handled only and instead will become a tool to be looked through. It will become a telescope that will bring you close to Jesus.

70

The Misuse of the Scriptures

John 5:39–44

"You diligently study the Scriptures because you think that by them you possess eternal life. These are the Scriptures that testify about me, yet you refuse to come to me to have life.

"I do not accept praise from men, but I know you. I know that you do not have the love of God in your hearts. I have come in my Father's name, and you do not accept me; but if someone else comes in his own name, you will accept him. How can you believe if you accept praise from one another, yet make no effort to obtain the praise that comes from the only God?"

In the controversy the Lord Jesus Christ had with the Jewish leaders of his day concerning the Scriptures, there was at least one point of agreement and two points of disagreement. The point on which both Jesus and the Jewish rulers agreed was that the Scriptures had a divine origin. Many would disagree today, of course. But in Christ's day all recognized that the Scriptures of the Old Testament came from God. The points on which they disagreed were these: first, the purpose of the Scriptures and, second, the use of the Scriptures. All but the last of these points have already been considered. So in this study, we want to look at the ways in which the Bible can be misused.

427

Jesus spoke of this error when he said, "You diligently study the Scriptures because you think that by them you possess eternal life. These are the Scriptures that testify about me, yet you refuse to come to me to have life. I do not accept praise from men, but I know you. I know that you do not have the love of God in your hearts. . . . How can you believe if you accept praise from one another, yet make no effort to obtain the praise that comes from the only God?" (John 5:37–42, 44).

An End in Themselves

We must begin by asking the questions: How did the Jews misuse the Scriptures? Can we misuse them in the same way? The first answer, according to these words of Jesus, is obviously that the Jews misused Scripture by treating the words of Scripture as an end in themselves rather than allowing them to do their primary work, which is to point to Jesus. They searched the Scriptures, but they did not come to Christ. We err along the same lines whenever we allow Bible study to become academic and, as a result, do not allow ourselves to be drawn closer to God because of it.

No one could really fault the Jews of Christ's day for their meticulous study of the Scriptures. This was an acknowledged fact. The Jews did study the Scriptures. For this reason, I believe that verse 39 must be translated using the indicative mood ("You study the Scriptures") as many modern translations do, rather than using the imperative ("Study the Scriptures") as the Authorized Version does. The Jews prized the Scriptures. The difficulty did not lie there. The difficulty lay in the fact that in their high regard for the Bible they easily passed over its intention.

As a result, although they gained honor from men for their detailed knowledge of the Bible, they did not gain salvation.

We find an example of this just a few chapters farther on in John's Gospel. In chapter 9 John tells the story of the healing of a man who had been born blind. He was physically blind, of course. But the meat of the story lies in the fact that, like all men, he also was spiritually blind before Christ touched him. Afterward he came to spiritual sight. The man born blind began with the confession that, so far as he knew, he was healed only by a "man" named Jesus. He ended with the confession that Jesus is the "Lord," and worshiped him.

When the man was healed, he came into conflict with the Jewish rulers. They knew of Jesus, but they did not believe in him. In fact, they did not believe in him precisely because of their attitude to the Scriptures. For them the revelation recorded in the Old Testament was an end in itself. Nothing could be added. Nothing more, in fact, could be desired. They said, "We know that God spoke to Moses, but as for this fellow, we don't even know where he comes from" (9:29). The man who had been born blind did not try to compete with them in their acknowledged mastery of the Old Testament, but he pointed to the unquestioned fact of his healing. He concluded, "If this man were not from God, he could do nothing" (v. 33). In treating the Old Testament as an end in itself the Jews, therefore, actually perverted it and missed its true meaning. They failed to see that it is precisely of Jesus that the Old Testament testifies.

Let me bring this down to a very practical level—to our own day. Does anyone pervert the Bible by considering it an end in itself in our day? I believe that this happens frequently. Let me give some examples.

First, it happens in the world of biblical scholarship. Take the "historical Jesus" movement, which dates from 1768, the year in which the noted German scholar Hermann Samuel Reimarus died. Reimarus was not really a New Testament scholar, but at his death he left behind a manuscript that had far-reaching implications for those in the New Testament field. Reimarus argued that historians must distinguish between the "aim" of Jesus and the "aim" of his disciples. By this he meant that scholars should distinguish between the historical Jesus, who actually lived, and the Jesus of the New Testament, who was largely a product either of the faith or imagination of his followers. Faced with this choice, which he regarded as a choice between mutually exclusive alternatives, Reimarus chose the Jesus of history stripped of all supernatural elements. In his reconstruction Jesus then became one who went about preaching the kingdom of God but who died forsaken by God and disillusioned. Reimarus thought that Christianity was the product of the disciples who stole the corpse, proclaimed a bodily resurrection, and gathered followers.

It was obvious to many that Reimarus's views were extreme and his work polemical. Nevertheless, it turned out that his manuscript set the pattern for a whole century of historical-Jesus research. Scholars began to react against the supernatural element in the Gospels and cast about for a natural, alternative Jesus. Unfortunately, each scholar only succeeded in producing a Jesus in his own image. Rationalists saw him as the great teacher of morality. Socialists viewed him as a friend of the poor and a revolutionary. The most popular "lives of Jesus" volumes, those of David Friedrich Strauss, rejected most of the gospel as mythology, and Bruno Bauer ended his quest by denying that there ever was a historical Jesus. Bauer explained all the stories about Jesus as the products of the imagination of the primitive Christian community.

One can hardly fail to be impressed even today at the immense energy and talent that German scholars poured into this so-called "quest" for the historical Jesus, but the results were meager and the conclusions wrong. Scholarship had made the Gospels an end in themselves, so that the Bible became a book to be weighed and manipulated rather than believed and obeyed. What was the result? The result was that the Jesus produced was neither the historical Jesus nor the Christ of Scripture. Christ was the casualty. Here, then, was the error of Judaism, repeated on western soil and in recent history.

Let me give another example. Is it not true that the same thing happens in another way when a person buys a beautiful Bible to place in an important position in his or her home but fails to read it? Why do people do this? The answer is that in their minds the Bible is something special. They have a superstitious reverence for it. But their belief does not go beyond superstition. As a result, they never read it and, therefore, never come into contact with its author.

Third, the evangelical world may be in danger of doing almost the same thing with translations. I am for the use of any translations that actually help the user get into the Scriptures and obey them. I recommend the use of contemporary versions of the Bible along with more standard texts such as that of the Authorized, the Revised Standard, and the New American Standard versions. But alongside this legitimate use of translations there also is unfortunately an unhealthy preoccupation with the "best" and "latest" or most "contemporary" translation that I at least am convinced is harmful. Among those who get their minds fixed on the translations, it is the small variations between different texts that prove most interesting, rather than the teaching. Thus, obedience to Christ and a desire to know him better evaporates.

Personally I believe that there is absolutely no need for another English translation in our day. We have all varieties. Any taste can be satisfied. Perhaps much of our current interest in translations is traceable to the publishers who encourage our interest in them for commercial purposes. At any rate, I believe that the immense amounts of effort expended on producing such translations would be far better spent in getting the Bible into the languages of people who have not yet seen even one translation of the Scriptures.

Details Only

However, we must stop with these observations and go on. The first error that the Jews of Christ's day made, then, was the error of regarding Scripture as an end in itself. But this was not their only error. There was a second error also—that of becoming so preoccupied with the details of Scripture that they missed the truths contained there. For instance, the scribes, whose work it was to copy the Scriptures, subjected the pages of the Bible to the closest scrutiny. They gave attention to every syllable. They even counted up the words and letters so that they knew which of them came in the middle of the page and how many of each a given page should have. We can be thankful for this great care in one sense, for the accuracy of our present Old Testament texts is the result of it. Nevertheless, in the case of most scribes the reaction of the copier with the Word of God stopped with the copying. The words were accurate, but what is the value of accurate words without meanings? Or what is the value of letters if these are not inscribed on the fleshly tables of the heart?

We have a contemporary example of this error in those who have a high degree of biblical knowledge—those who can name the twelve apostles, all the cities Paul visited, the list of the Hebrew kings, and so on—but who have missed what the Scriptures have to teach about sin, justification, the Christian life, and obedience. Many others make this mistake in a preoccupation with prophecy.

Finally, the Jews also erred in considering the Scriptures rather than God as the source of life. This is easy to document. One Jewish writing, the Siphre on Deuteronomy 32:2, says, "As rain is life for the world, so also are the words of Torah life for the world." First Baruch 4:1–2 says, "This is the book of the commandments of God and the Law that endureth forever. All they that hold it fast are appointed to life; but such as leave it shall die." Hillel's words to the same effect are proverbial: "More flesh more worms; more wealth more care; more maidservants more lewdness; more menservants more thieving; more women more witchcraft; more Torah more life. . . . Whoso has gained a good name has gained it for himself; whoso has gained for himself words of Torah has gained for himself the life of the world to come" (*Pirke Aboth* 2:8). Quite clearly, this was believed literally. The important thing was the memorization of Scripture; this in itself won salvation. Against this view Jesus wished to point out that formal study of the Bible was *not* a guarantee of life to come, as the rabbis believed. Christ is the life, not the Scriptures considered in themselves. Only Christ can guarantee salvation.

What is needed then? The answer is that men and women need the new birth found in a new relationship to Jesus. The important story here is the conversation between Jesus and Nicodemus recorded earlier in the Gospel. Nicodemus was a Pharisee. He was a representative figure of the Jews. In this context a Jewish reader would expect a rabbinical debate, a discussion of the specific promises concerning a messiah, or something similar. Instead, the situation is no sooner introduced than Jesus moves the discussion to a higher and more spiritual plane. Jesus answers Nicodemus, "I tell you the truth, no one can see the kingdom of God unless he is born again" (3:3).

We may summarize this by saying that the Bible was given by God to point a man to the Savior and that he must come to the Savior if he is to find life. This is necessary, for unless the life of God takes possession of our hearts even the Word of God will be incomprehensible.

Those Who Find Jesus

Has the Word of God done that for you? Has it pointed you to the Savior? Let me give you one last story. One time in preparing a Christmas message I became impressed with the large number of men who missed Christmas even though there was no real need for them to have missed it. The innkeeper was one. He was too busy. Herod was another. But by far the most interesting of all those who missed the birth of Jesus were the religious leaders, the chief priests and the scribes, who missed it even though they had the Old Testament and knew where Christ should be born. You remember the story. The wise men had come to Jerusalem. Herod inquired of the scribes. The scribes said that the Christ was to be born in Bethlehem. It was on their word that the wise men started out to Bethlehem where they found him. These men had the

Scriptures. They knew them well enough to have the right answers. But they did not leave their own homes or the palace to investigate the Savior's arrival.

On the other hand, the Christmas story also tells of some who did find Christmas. They were not the kings of this world. They were not the religious leaders. They were not the thousands who were entirely engrossed in the countless minutia of materialistic lives. They were just poor folk who were looking to God and to whom God came.

Who were they? Some were shepherds. They were not important in the social structure of the ancient east. Yet they saw the angels. The wise men also found Christmas. They were not even Jews. Yet they saw the star. Finally, there were the poor but saintly folk like Simeon and Anna. These could well have been discounted either because of their means or social position or age. Some would dismiss them. Yet they saw and even held God's treasure. Why did these people find Jesus when the important of the world, as the world judges importance, so clearly missed him? There are two answers. First, they were honest enough to admit their need of a Savior. Second, they were humble enough to receive him personally when he came.

The Bible calls for this honest confession of sin and this humble commitment to the Lord Jesus Christ. You can read the Bible as the leaders of Israel did. You can misuse it out of pride. Or you can use it properly and come yourself to the Savior. Will you come in a spirit of humility?

71

The Accusation of the Scriptures

John 5:45–47

"But do not think I will accuse you before the Father. Your accuser is Moses, on whom your hopes are set. If you believed Moses, you would believe me, for he wrote about me. But since you do not believe what he wrote, how are you going to believe what I say?"

Do you remember the *Titanic,* that giant luxury liner built for passage of the North Atlantic sea lanes? The *Titanic* had been designed according to the latest of the scientific methods of its day and was supposed to be incapable of sinking. But she did sink. She hit an iceberg that ripped through nine of her watertight compartments. The resulting pressure was enough to burst through the rest of the ship. She went down, taking to the bottom many who were convinced that it could not happen. The *Titanic* disaster was a classic case of misplaced confidence.

We also discover a case of misplaced confidence in the three verses that close the important fifth chapter of John's Gospel. However, in this case the tragedy involves not merely the loss of life in this world. It also involves loss of life in the world to come. The Jewish leaders with whom Christ was speaking were not at all worried about salvation. They had the law of Moses, and they trusted their knowledge of it. It was evident from all that Jesus had to say, however, that a mere knowledge of the law was inadequate. The law was useful, but in itself it could not save; it was powerless. In fact, said Jesus, the law will actually condemn those who are trusting it. "But do not think I will accuse you before the Father. Your accuser is Moses on whom your hopes are set. If you believed Moses, you would believe me, for he wrote about me. But since you do not believe what he wrote, how are you going to believe what I say?" (John 5:45–47).

God's Standards

At this point the account that John gives of the conversation between Jesus and the Jews breaks off. But I suppose that if it were continued, the Jews would have been reported as asking the question we all want to ask when told that God's law condemns us. We ask it in different forms. Some ask, "If the law condemns us, then why did God give it?" Others say, "Why bother to keep the law, if this is the outcome?" Some ask, "What is the purpose of the law?" At the heart of these questions is the basic human objection that instead of pointing us to Jesus as the Savior God should take account of our nature and good works.

This is what the Pharisees had under the religious system that they had constructed. Jesus had said that these religious leaders desired the honor that comes from men (v. 44), and this was quite accurate. It was characteristic of them that they sought praise. They dressed so that everyone would recognize them. They prayed in a loud voice, publicly, so that everyone would observe what they were doing. They made sure that everyone knew what they were giving to the temple. In short, under this system people had taken their minds off God and were comparing themselves with others. They did quite well by this comparison, at least in their own eyes. So when Jesus came they obviously saw no need for a Savior.

Here, however, they missed the major point of the law, for the law was not given to help them do better than others but to show them that no matter how well they did they could not do well enough to satisfy God.

William Barclay says quite accurately, "The point is not: 'Am I as good as my neighbor?' The point is: 'Am I as good as God?' The point is not: 'Is my scholarship and is my piety greater than that of other people whom I could name?' The point is: 'What do I look like to God?' So long as we judge ourselves by human comparisons there is plenty of room for self-satisfaction, and self-satisfaction kills faith, for faith is born of the sense of need. But when we compare ourselves with Jesus Christ, and through Him, with God, we are humbled to the dust, and then faith is born, for there is nothing left to do but to trust to the mercy of God."[1]

It is only when we compare ourselves with God that we realize the need for a work of redemption accomplished by a Savior who comes from God to lift us up to himself.

Perfection

All this falls into an even clearer light when we go on to ask what God's standard is and find out, on the basis of the law, that this is perfection. I sometimes say in teaching on this subject, "Suppose that God were to come to you right now as you are and immediately take you as you are into heaven." If this should happen, heaven would not be heaven anymore. Heaven would be a little bit dirty. And it would be very dirty if God were to do this with us all. No, God's standard must be perfection. Nothing else can satisfy him. This is the message of the law. Thus, the law itself says, "Cursed is everyone who does not continue to do everything written in the Book of the Law" (Gal. 3:10; cf. Deut. 27:26).

This is the accusation of Moses, about which Christ was speaking. We hear it and tremble, for this is a terrible verdict. At the same time we need not tremble for long, for at the same time that God sets forth his standard he also sets forth the means by which that standard may be met. Instead of striving on our part, God tells us to rest on what he has done for us and to present it back to himself as he desires.

But before we go on to see what this means more precisely, we must deal more with this idea of perfection. Perfection is the standard, but what is perfection? One answer to that question comes from the law of the Old Testament. The Ten Commandments are the heart of the Old Testament law, and Deuteronomy 6:5 is the summation of the Ten Commandments. So we may deal with just this verse. It says, "Love the LORD your God with all your heart and with all your soul and with all your strength." This is the verse by which Jesus summed up the law in response to the question of the rich young ruler.

The point is that no one has ever done this. Moreover, it necessarily follows that if no one has been able to live up to it, and if this is the standard God gave, then there has never been anyone who has ever been saved by the law. One commentator has written, "I do not expect to meet anyone in Heaven who is there because of the Ten Commandments. Oh, I will meet men there who have measured themselves by the law and found that they had fallen short and therefore have learned they must run to the grace of God to be saved through the blood sacrifice He had provided, but no one will be there through the commandments themselves."[2]

Not a few men and women try to take comfort in the fact that although they are condemned by a verse like Deuteronomy 6:5, nevertheless there are some commandments that they seem capable of fulfilling. But this is misplaced confidence also. James 2:10 tells us, "For whoever keeps the whole law and yet stumbles at just one point is guilty of breaking all of it." This means that perfection is not to be measured by how well one can keep one particular commandment but by how well he keeps them all. By this measure a person is as imperfect by breaking one law as by breaking all ten. Suppose you had a boat that is fastened to a dock above a waterfall by a chain of ten links. How many do you have to break to set the boat adrift? The answer is: Just one. In the same way, men are adrift and condemned by the law no matter which one or how many of the commandments have been broken.

Another important expression of God's standard of perfection is found in the Sermon on the Mount. The entire sermon is an expression of it, of course. But again, we may take that one verse that is a summary. This is the Golden Rule. The Golden Rule says, "So in everything, do to others what you would have them do to you, for this sums up the Law and the Prophets" (Matt. 7:12). Who does this? The only honest answer is: No one. There are times when we try to please others. But we do not do it in all things or all the time any more than we love God with all our hearts, souls, and minds at all times. Again, no one will ever be in heaven as a result of the Golden Rule, except insofar as God has used it to reveal the person's own lack of perfection and turn him away from his own human goodness to the Savior.

An Internal Standard

There is another point that is obvious from these two great verses that summarize God's standards. Not only is God's standard perfection. Not only is this to be judged by the whole of God's laws, rather than just a part. This standard is also an internal standard, as well as an external one. Thus, it deals with thoughts, motivations, and desires, as well as with actions. Think for a moment of how Jesus looked at the Pharisees. When other people looked at the Pharisees they saw only what was visible from the outside, for that is all that human beings ever see. From that perspective the Pharisees were not too bad. At least they appeared better than others. Jesus, on the other hand, being God, was able to look at what was going on within, and he saw their motivations. They were striving for righteousness all right, at least as they conceived it, but they were doing it to outdo other people. It was not to please God. Moreover, in spite of their efforts to clean up the outside of their lives the Pharisees were as incapable as anyone else of cleaning up what was inside. On one occasion Jesus expressed this quite pointedly by saying, "Woe to you, teachers of the law and Pharisees, you hypocrites! You are like whitewashed tombs, which look beautiful on the outside but on the inside are full of dead men's bones and everything unclean" (Matt. 23:27).

These words are true of anyone. To a certain extent you and I can pull ourselves up by our bootstraps morally. A thief can reform himself and stop stealing. Having worked off a debt to society, he can even recapture a certain measure of respect and trust from his fellowmen. An alcoholic can overcome his weakness for drink. He can regain useful employment and again become a credit and asset to his family. We admire those who are able to do this. But the truth of the matter is that although we are able to do this outwardly so that people may admire us, as they did the Pharisees, we are nevertheless unable to do anything about the state of our hearts. Thus, we cannot make ourselves loving if we are not loving. We cannot make ourselves humble if we are not humble. Above all, we cannot make ourselves righteous (as God counts righteousness) if we are not.

The Scales of God

We sum it all up, then, and we find that the demand of the law is perfection. This is a perfection in all the law's requirements, and it is an internal perfection as well as an external one. Moreover, we see that all are condemned by this standard. Jesus was right. The law can do only two things, and the bringing of salvation is not one of them. The law can either condemn, or it can point to the Savior.

Has it done that for you? Perhaps I can help you to see this and make a commitment to Christ by an illustration that I first heard from Donald Grey Barnhouse. Sometime ago in a friend's house I came across an old balancing scale, the kind that was once used to measure out most dry goods and produce. It was a large one because my friend's family had been in the bakery business and had used this scale to measure flour and sugar for large recipes. In this type of scale a weight of fixed measure is placed on one side of the balance arm and the item to be weighed on the other. When there is enough flour or sugar or whatever it may be on the side opposite the weight, the arm balances.

Imagine now that you have before you that type of scale and that God has placed the pound measure of his perfection on the one arm. This is the perfection that the law portrays and that God must demand of you on the basis of his nature. Nothing less than perfection—in word, thought, and deed—can satisfy him. What can you furnish to meet his demands?

Here is a criminal, perhaps a thief or a murderer, who comes to present his goodness to God. He is not much by our standards, but even the most critical among us would not deny that he has some goodness. We acknowledge this when we say that there is honor even among thieves. The criminal comes; he places his goodness upon the scale. It is an ounce or two. But an ounce is not a pound, and the scales are unmoved. We set the criminal aside and write over him the words of God's judgment.

The average person now comes forward and places his good works on God's scale. He does much better than the criminal. The average person presents seven or eight ounces. This is three or four times better than the man who has gone before. Still it is not a pound. So the law accuses him also, and he too receives God's judgment.

Finally, the best men and women come forward. These are the acknowledged leaders of our society, just as the scribes and Pharisees were the acknowledged leaders of theirs. They may be social workers, ministers, professors, philanthropists. They are better than the average man. They present eleven or twelve ounces of attainment. Still their eleven or twelve ounces will not budge the scale of God's righteousness, and so they too join the rest of the race and are set aside. The Bible says, "For all have sinned and fall short of the glory of God" (Rom. 3:23).

Will a man live by law? Then the law will condemn him. But just here God comes in with his message of free salvation. Notice that he does not change his standard. The law is a good standard. It is the only possible standard. It is just that it cannot save people who have broken it. But God can! The efforts of men cannot move God's balance, but now God is going to move it for us. Jesus comes. He is the Son of God, our Savior. He is the embodiment of that total, internal, and external perfection of mind, soul, and body about which the law has been talking. He had the right to avoid us all. Yet he comes and is put to death for our sins. Since Jesus is the infinite God, his death is sufficient for any number of finite creatures. He was able to take the punishment of the law for an infinite weight of sin and cancel it for us in the hour of his death, so that now sin may be removed and righteousness be made available for all who trust him. God comes to us with the offer of salvation. He tells us that he wants us to be in heaven with him and that he has made the way. "I love you," God says. "I do not care on what level your life has been lived. I only want you to look to my Son who died for you. Do you see him dying there? He died for you. Do you see Christ rising from the tomb? This too is for you, for it is the evidence that I am forever satisfied with his sacrifice. If you will believe in him and commit yourself to him, I will take that death for your side of the scale. The standard is the same, but I will give my righteousness for your side of the balance." We take that righteousness, the righteousness given to us, and go (some boldly and others falteringly) to God's balance. We place Jesus' righteousness on our side of the scale, and immediately the balance is made. We are justified. We are accepted in the Beloved. God has nothing more against us forever.[3]

Have you done that? Remember, it is not enough to be like the Pharisees. It is not enough to possess the Bible. It is not enough to read the Bible. It is not even enough to study the Bible or memorize the Bible. You must obey the Bible. And it is the Bible that points you away from your own efforts to earn salvation, which you can never do, and instead directs you toward the Lord Jesus Christ, who is our Savior.

72

The Fourth Miracle

John 6:1-4

Some time after this, Jesus crossed to the far shore of the Sea of Galilee (that is, the Sea of Tiberias), and a great crowd of people followed him because they saw the miraculous signs he had performed on the sick. Then Jesus went up on a mountainside and sat down with his disciples. The Jewish Passover Feast was near.

There is only one miracle performed by the Lord Jesus Christ that is recorded by each of the four evangelists—Matthew, Mark, Luke, and John. It is the miracle in which he used only five small barley loaves and two fish to feed over five thousand people in Galilee just before the annual Jewish feast of Passover. It is important, moreover, not just because it is recorded in each of the Gospels but because of all that it signifies. Fortunately, the significance of the feeding of the multitude is spelled out far more clearly by John than by any of the other writers.

Each of the Gospel writers brings out of the story that which spoke to him personally. Matthew and Luke were most interested in the miracle itself, for they tell it without much embellishment. Mark stresses the loving compassion of Jesus; it was out of Jesus' compassion for the multitude, Mark tells us, that Christ fed them. In John the interest revolves around the historical significance of the event—it was a time of testing and a turning point in Christ's ministry—and around the fact that Jesus is himself the bread that satisfies men spiritually. Only in John do we learn that the miracle took place at the time of the Passover, that the loaves of the young lad were barley loaves (the poorest kind), the reason for gathering up the fragments that remained, and the effect of the miracle on the masses.

Incidentally, the difference in emphasis in the midst of an obvious agreement on all the details of the story by the four writers is evidence of the reliability of these men as historians. The agreements are such that the story could not have been made up by each man separately. The differences are such that they obviously were not collaborating. Thus, if they were not made up separately and if they were not made up in collaboration, the only remaining possibility is that they were not made up at all. They are true. In other words, we have in these accounts (Matt. 14:15–21; Mark 6:32–44; Luke 9:12–17; and John 6:1–15) the record of a true though supernatural event recorded accurately by four witnesses.

Anyone who wishes to dispute the factualness of the miracle must deal with such evidence.

A Needy People

The story is not recorded by the Gospel writers as evidence of their reliability, however, but rather to teach Christian truth. So it is to this that we must now turn. John tells us that sometime after the events recorded in the fifth chapter, Jesus, who was now in the north, crossed over to the eastern side of the Sea of Galilee where he was followed by a great multitude of people. It was the time of the Passover. Perhaps many of these people were on their way to Jerusalem to observe it, though we do not know this for sure. What we do know is that they were following Jesus because they had seen the miracles he did. Evening had come on as they had been listening to his teaching, and they were hungry.

Jesus anticipated the situation. He turned to Philip and asked a question that, together with the answer, is recorded by John to bring out the first important point in the story. Jesus asked, "Where shall we buy bread for these people to eat?" Philip answered to the effect that there was no place to buy it, that even if there were a place the disciples did not have enough money to pay for it, and furthermore that even if they had two hundred denarii (the normal wages of a laborer for six months), even this would not buy enough bread so that each one could have a little. In Philip's reply we have a confession of the failure of human resources in the situation. By extention, we also have an illustration of the failure of human resources in many circumstances of our own.

I do not doubt for a minute that this is one of John's main reasons for recording the story. It is obvious from a doctrinal point of view, of course. For John is soon going to show Jesus to be the One who can meet all needs, and there must always be a recognition of need before there can be a real turning to Jesus for help. But, more than this, the point is evident from John's passing reference to the Passover.

No alert Jewish mind would come to a word like this without thinking somewhat of the significance of the Passover. And it would be hard to miss the fact that the Passover marked the beginning of that period when Israel left the seeming security of Egypt and entered the wilderness where they were entirely dependent upon God. Things had been bad in Egypt, certainly. The people were slaves. They had been treated cruelly. Still, with grit and a little bit of humor a person could get by. In the desert it was different. In the desert there were vast extremes of temperature (from 140 to 160 degrees Fahrenheit in the daytime to below freezing at night). There were no towns and therefore no shops in which to buy food. Above all, there was no water, and without water a man cannot survive. This is the picture that John is setting before us in the opening verses of this chapter and that he is reinforcing specifically by reference to the desert wandering later. It is a picture of the failure of human resources—not only in a physical sense but also in the attempts of a person to please God.

On the physical level we do not need a great deal of reinforcement for this truth. We speak today of the eventual failure of natural resources such as fresh water, soil, natural gas, oil, and so on, due to the rate at which men and women of our century are consuming them. We speak of the failure of emotional resources, such as we find in nervous breakdowns, despair, uncontrolled temper, and such things. These failures are obvious. What is not so obvious is the failure of men and women to please God or to experience the life of God. This failure is invisible, yet it exists also.

You have failed to please God. You have failed to find the life of God by your own efforts. Do you not find that all you are able to do for yourself personally—whether it is in the area of success, wealth, fame, or sex—fails to bring happiness? I hope you have found this to be true, because it is true. Besides, it is only when you or I begin to acknowledge these things to be true that we begin to see and accept the solution.

The Sufficiency of Jesus Christ

The second point of this story, which is also the second reason why John tells it, is that Jesus Christ is all-sufficient. This is important particularly where human resources fail.

The matter of eating assumed a far greater importance in an ancient culture than it does for most of us who are living today. When we want something we merely go to the store for it, and it is rare when we cannot buy all we want. In ancient times it was different. Harvests were uncertain. There was not always enough to eat. As a result, to have enough food was considered a great blessing, and food itself became a symbol of prosperity. This is seen all through the Old Testament. For instance, at the beginning of Isaiah we read, "If you are willing and obedient, you will eat the best from the land" (1:19). Isaiah later said, "Come, all you who are thirsty, come to the waters; and you who have no money, come, buy and eat! Come, buy wine and milk without money and without cost. Why spend money on what is not bread, and your labor on what does not satisfy? Listen, listen to me, and eat what is good, and your soul will delight in the richest of fare" (55:1–2). David wrote, "The poor will eat and be satisfied; they who seek the LORD will praise him" (Ps. 22:26). We can see that this was also an important idea in Christ's time, for later on in this same chapter the Lord declared to his hearers, "I am the bread of life. He who comes to me will never go hungry, and he who believes in me will never be thirsty" (John 6:35).

Men and women find their real spiritual prosperity in God. We cannot find it on the human level. We cannot find the abundant life by indulging ourselves in all that life has to offer. We cannot find happiness by pursuing it. We cannot create satisfaction. These great blessings come from God. So we must feed on God as he is presented to us in the person of the Lord Jesus Christ.

Do you feed upon him? Do you come to him expecting to be fed?

There is a point here that becomes quite interesting in the actual working out of the story. In everyday business terms we would say that the supply outstripped the demand. We know it because, after the miracle had taken place and everyone eating had been filled, there were still twelve baskets of food left over. Food in abundance! It is always like that with God. In his valuable commentary Arthur W. Pink observes that when Abraham went up to intercede with God on behalf of the righteous in Sodom, God never ceased granting until Abraham had ceased asking. So also in the case of Elisha's oil. So long as there were empty vessels to be found in the land, the vessel of the widow who was helped by Elisha did not cease its supply. Pink writes, "This is what Jesus does to all His people. He comes to the poor bankrupt believer, and, placing in his hand a draft on the resources of heaven, says to him, 'Write on it what thou wilt.' Such is our precious Lord still. If we are straightened, it is not in Him, but in ourselves. If we are poor and weak, or tried and tempted, it is not that we cannot help ourselves—it is because we do not. . . . We have so little faith in things unseen and eternal. We draw so little on the resources of Christ. We come not to Him with our spiritual wants—our empty vessels— and draw from the ocean of His grace."[1]

There is a hymn that acknowledges this beautifully, though it is not widely known in America. It was written by Mary Shekleton.

> I am an empty vessel—not one thought
> Or look of love, I ever to Thee brought;
> Yet I may come, and come again to Thee
> With this, the empty sinner's only plea—
>   Thou lovest me.
> Oh, fill me, Jesus Savior, with Thy love!
> Lead, lead me to the living fount above;

> Thither may I, in simple faith, draw nigh,
> And never to another fountain fly,
> But unto Thee.

Have you asked God to do that, to supply what you need? Have you asked him really? God says that he is more than willing to fill the empty vessel of your life, in fact, that he is urging you to let him fill it. The Bible says, "And my God will supply all your needs according to his glorious riches in Christ Jesus" (Phil. 4:19).

How about you who are running away from God? You are unhappy, but you have never come to the point where you are willing to say, "Lord God, I have been running away from you and I have failed to recognize your claim on my life." You are unhappy. In some cases you are miserable. Why do you not stop running? Turn to Jesus and see if he is not able to satisfy you completely. You may be one who is tempted—perhaps in your home, perhaps out of your home. It may be a small thing; it may be a very great thing. Whatever it is, Jesus is sufficient for it. The Book of Hebrews says that Jesus was tempted as we are and is therefore able to help us in temptations (Heb. 4:15–16). Paul writes that God provides a way of escape in all temptations (1 Cor. 10:13). Perhaps your need is for comfort. You have lost a friend or relative, a wife, a husband. You are alone. Human resources have failed. Turn to the Lord Jesus Christ. He is the source of all comfort. He will provide it. Ask him. You are wise if you ask him for everything for which you stand in need.

Has God Forgotten?

This story contains a lesson for anyone who feels that God has forgotten him or her. Do you feel that way? If you do, notice that long before the disciples had expressed any interest in the welfare of the people, Jesus had initiated the matter of feeding them. He had spoken of it to Philip, knowing in advance what he was going to do. The disciples were interested—to a degree. They probably were hungry, too, so their concern would have been spurred on by self-interest. Still, whatever interest they may have had, the interest of the Lord Jesus Christ in the people was greater.

That is an encouragement for us, both if we fail to show concern for others—the multitudes about ourselves—or if we are one of the multitude and so feel forgotten. Let us take our attitude toward others first. We often fail to see human need. We miss the cry of loneliness, despair, or frustration expressed by some poor soul. Jesus hears it. Our hearts may be cold, but the heart of Jesus is warm with compassion.

Or suppose you are one of the lonely ones. Even when there are other people who *are* interested in you, that interest still is always imperfect and partial. There are people in your home, office, or church who care for you, particularly if they are Christian people. But they are beset by all the sin and failure that is common to men and women. Only One will not fail you. There is only

One whose interest does not waver. Jesus is eternal. He existed before the worlds began. He created you. He planned the circumstances of your life. He knows your situation. It is this One who desires to supply all your need according to his abundant resources.

Do you say that you cannot see it? There is no reason why you should. Just trust him. The patriarch Jacob, Abraham's grandson, was in his old age and was complaining about the harsh blows that life had dealt him. Years before, his son Joseph had been killed by wild animals, so he thought. Then famine had come, and he had sent ten of his remaining sons to Egypt to buy food. He had kept Benjamin, the youngest, at home. The sons came back, but without Simeon, who had been left as a hostage. When the famine continued it became necessary to send the sons back to Egypt for more food, but they refused to go, saying they could not return without Benjamin. The man in charge in Egypt had told them that if they did not return with Benjamin he would consider them liars about their family and would treat them as spies. Jacob was greatly distressed. He fought the inevitable. All things seemed against him. But it was at this moment that God was planning his greatest blessing for him. God knew the end from the beginning, and he cared about Jacob. He had actually sent Joseph to Egypt years in advance to prepare for this moment. Joseph was the man in charge. It was only when Jacob gave in to the situation that God brought to completion the blessing of a full reunion of all the brothers and their father in their new land.

Maybe you are going through a situation like that in your own life. Do not wring your hands and say, "God has forgotten." Trust him. He knows your need and where he is leading you.

73

Three and the Master

John 6:5–9

When Jesus looked up and saw a great crowd coming toward him, he said to Philip, "Where shall we buy bread for these people to eat?" He asked this only to test him, for he already had in mind what he was going to do.

Philip answered him, "Eight months' wages would not buy enough bread for each one to have a bite!"

Another of his disciples, Andrew, Simon Peter's brother, spoke up, "Here is a boy with five small barley loaves and two small fish, but how far will they go among so many?"

Not long ago I had an opportunity to attend a seminar on management skills conducted by the Servicemaster Industries Corporation. Many parts of the seminar were useful and instructive, but one part in particular impressed me as being of value in understanding this part of John's Gospel. There was an attempt to define management. The definition given was: "Management is getting the right things done through other people." This definition relates to Christ's miracle of feeding the five thousand people in Galilee because, among other things, the story gives us a splendid example of good management.

What did Jesus do on this occasion? He fed a great company of people, of course. But what precisely did he *do?* Or, we might ask, how did he do it?

He could have lifted up his hands and have demanded that manna come down from heaven. It would have come. He could have created a loaf of bread in each man's pocket. But Jesus did not do these things. Instead, he began to work through others—Philip, the lad, and Andrew. They helped. Thus, Jesus managed to get the job done through other people.

Philip

The first person the Lord turned to was Philip. Philip was from Bethsaida, and Bethsaida was in that area. It was natural that Jesus should turn to Philip, therefore, for Philip more than anyone else knew what food was available. The difficulty was that Philip got all caught up in his knowledge—perhaps he was proud that he knew that area of the country and could tell that there was no place to buy anything—and so forgot to turn the matter over to Jesus. In simple language, John tells us that Jesus asked Philip about food to test him and implies that Philip failed the test.

Philip had been confronted with a trying situation, much as we often are confronted. But his response was that which far too often is our own. A bill comes in the mail, and it is larger than the balance remaining in your checking account. What do you do? Do you wring your hands and say, "How in the world am I ever going to pay this bill?" Or do you take it to the Lord? You have a problem in your home, perhaps with your children or with your husband or wife. Do you say, "What is happening? How will I ever survive?" Or do you take it to the Lord? There is a problem at work. Do you say, "I don't know the answer; I'll just have to work weekends and work it out somehow"? Or do you take it to the Lord? You and I will have learned a great deal about walking with the Lord when we have learned to spread each difficulty before him as it comes along.

One hindrance to doing this is sometimes pride in our knowledge, the same hindrance that faced Philip. Philip was so flattered at being asked this question that he began to show off his knowledge and, in showing off his knowledge, actually revealed his ignorance. Knowledge can be a blessing, but it can also be a handicap to trusting the Lord. When placed in Christ's hands, it is valuable. When trusted in itself, it is not.

There was a second reason why Philip failed the test Jesus gave him. Philip not only had knowledge of the area where the miracle took place. He also had a head for figures, and this in turn led him to trust money. He began to calculate. He said to himself, "Let's see now, there are about a hundred people in that little group . . . there are about two hundred over there . . . two hundred . . . six hundred . . . Now if we gave everyone just a little bit, that would be so many times a few cents and. . . ." Then he gave Jesus the result of his calculations. He said, "Eight months' wages would not buy enough bread for each one to have a bite" (v. 7). Philip calculated, but he calculated without Christ.

I am convinced that if there is any one thing that most plagues Christian organizations in our day it is the thought that we can figure out the situation and then accomplish God's work primarily by means of money. I must not be misunderstood at this point, however. I said a moment ago that knowledge is a good thing if it is placed in Christ's hands. This is true also of money. Money can be well used. But to think that the needs of men and women can be met merely by collecting funds, even for an evangelical cause—it is this that is debilitating.

Moreover, it limits our vision. We think that when we are talking money and raising money we are thinking big, but actually, compared with God's plans for us, the opposite is generally the case. Think of Philip. He said, "Eight months' wages would not buy enough bread for each one to have a *bite*." Imagine even talking about "a little" in the presence of the Lord Jesus Christ! Yet we do that also. We have seen God work, as Philip had seen him work. But we come to him and say, "Oh, God, if you would just do so and so—it's just a little thing—if you would just do it, I believe I could get by." Actually, Christ's desire is to bless us *abundantly*.

Let us use our knowledge. Let us use our money. Let us use anything else God gives to us. But above all, let us look to God himself. Let us have that kind of vision for our own lives, our church, and our communities that stretches our minds and causes us to throw ourselves upon God. Let us say, "It is not just a little bit that we desire, our Father. We are not praying to have a little but to have much."

Someone might say, "But Philip had an excuse, didn't he? After all, he didn't know what Christ could do." I am not sure that this is a valid excuse. John has recorded several miracles that had taken place already. At the beginning of chapters 5 and 6 he has indicated a lapse of time in which, according to the other evangelists, other miracles had been performed also. Philip had been with Christ. He had seen these things. But when the question was put to him for this new situation his faith was inadequate. He said, "Yes, I know that you changed the water into wine at Cana. I know that you healed the son of the nobleman. I know that you made the paralyzed man walk. But I am not sure that you can do it for me." We say that. We see God working with others, but we do not allow that knowledge to carry over into our own lives.

There is nothing that God has done in the life of any other Christian at any period of history that he is not able to do in you if that is his plan for your life. You can know this. Moreover, you can know that if he has placed something in your life for a test, he has done it in order that you and others might see him bring blessing.

The Lad

The second person Jesus dealt with in this story was the lad. It is interesting to think about him for a moment. What do we know about him? For one thing, we know that he was poor. We know this because we are told by John that his lunch was composed largely of barley bread. Barley bread was the cheapest of all bread and was held in contempt. Thus, as William Barclay notes, bar-

ley bread was the kind of bread prescribed by the Mishnah as a meal offering for the sin of adultery because, says the Mishnah, adultery is the sin of a
beast and barley is the food of beasts. This kind of contempt is similar to that
which Samuel Johnson had for Scotland when, in his famous dictionary, he
defined oats as "a grain which in England is fed to horses and in Scotland is
fed to people." The lad had this bread and with it two small, pickled fish to help
make the dry, coarse bread go down.

Moreover, we know that the boy was insignificant. Someone has said,
"There is nothing in this world so insignificant as a boy." From a human
point of view this often is true. Here was a small boy, poor and insignificant.
Yet that boy did something that set him apart from all the other boys who may
have been in the crowd that day. That boy gave his lunch, poor as it was, to
the Lord Jesus. That lunch was as insignificant as it could be. It was as insignificant as the boy was. But the point of the story is that the insufficient from
the hands of the insignificant became sufficient and significant when placed
in the hands of Jesus.

It is true through the whole of biblical history. What is as insignificant as
dust? Nothing! You cannot even plant crops in it. Yet the dust became man
when molded by the hands of the Creator. The jawbone of an ass is insignificant. But God used a jawbone in the hands of Samson to kill one thousand
of the enemies of Israel. A shepherd's rod is insignificant, but it became powerful when God placed it in the hands of Moses. A sling is unimportant, but
God used it in the hands of David to kill Goliath. And what is as insignificant
as a poor girl, a virgin, in a distant town of the Roman empire? Yet God took
one such girl, a girl named Mary, and used her to bring forth the Redeemer.

Do not make the mistake of thinking that what you have is insignificant
and therefore useless. You may compare your gift with all the great talents
of this world—at least, those you think to be great—and imagine that your
gift is worthless. But if you do that you are forgetting to figure on God and
God's desires. What is it after all that makes a gift great in God's service? It
is not the magnitude of the gift. It is into whose hands it is given. If you will take
what you have, no matter how small or how great it may be, and place it in
the hands of the Master, you will find that it is more than sufficient for whatever task he sets before you.

What is your gift? Are you one who because of your age or your circumstances simply has time on your hands that many others, who are already engaged in work or projects, do not have? If so, that is a gift. Ask God to show
you how you can use your time in his service. Perhaps you have money? I
spoke earlier of the danger of trusting money rather than God, but that does
not mean for a moment that you cannot place your money in Christ's hands
to be used by him, if you have it. Recently a man who had joined our church,
and has since helped us in many ways, told me that one of the reasons why
he joined was that he realized our need for money and wished to help out
where he was able. He recognized that much of our work is with students who

contribute little toward our expenses. Perhaps God has given you abilities in administration, understanding the thoughts and problems of others, communicating the gospel.

If you think you may have any of these raw materials, you need to do two things. First, you need to ask God to clarify your gift so you will understand what it is exactly that he has given you. Second, you need to place it in his wonderful hands.

Andrew

We have considered already two important people in this story—Philip and the lad. There is a wonderful contrast between them, and much more could be said. But I do not want to end this study without looking at one more person. That person is Andrew, another of Christ's disciples.

I have learned over the years in which I have been preaching that some persons have a disposition for sermon outlines. They can figure them out almost as fast as the preacher. If you are one of these people, you probably have been wondering for some time why I did not mention Andrew sooner. The normal course of a study such as this would have been to speak of Philip and Andrew—they were disciples—and then the lad who had lunch. I have done it this way for a special reason. Philip was the first who was approached; he had the wrong answer. He was so caught up in his knowledge and in his ability with figures that he forgot Jesus. The lad was the one who responded, for he had something to give and was not too sophisticated or self-conscious to give it. But Andrew—Andrew was in Philip's position entirely so far as having anything to give was concerned. He had no food, just as Philip had no food. But Andrew went and got the lad.

Do you see what I am saying? I spoke in the beginning of how Jesus Christ was a good manager, according to the definition: "Management is getting the right things done through other people." By this definition Jesus was a first-rate manager in approaching Philip. But that is only what we might expect. The additional interesting and exciting point is that Andrew in imitation of Christ learned to be a good manager also. He said, "I do not have anything to offer, but I will go and see who does." It may be that you can be an Andrew. You yourself may not have the gift that is needed, but you can see what is needed and recruit someone who has it.

Moreover, I sometimes think as I read this story of the profound effect Andrew's approach must have had on the boy. Apart from what Andrew did that day in Galilee that boy was just like any other boy. He would have come and heard Jesus. But he would have been back on the far edge of the crowd somewhere, and the next day (after the people had gone) he would have been back home playing with his marbles. But Andrew got him. Andrew brought him into contact with the Lord Jesus and expanded his horizons. What is more, I am convinced that as the result of what Andrew did that boy went away remembering the day for as long as he lived. It will not surprise me in the slightest to find that boy in heaven someday, having later (as a result of this day's experience coupled with the preaching of Christ's death and resurrection) come to receive the Lord Jesus Christ as his Savior.

I thank God for those who did the work of Andrew for me. One of those was Donald Grey Barnhouse, the founder of the *Bible Study Hour* and a former pastor of the church I now serve. I was just a boy in the western part of Pennsylvania. So far as I knew, nothing of great importance ever happened in our town. But Barnhouse came there one year. Someone forgot to meet him at the airport, so he ended up in our house. He had known my parents from the years they had spent in Philadelphia. He stayed not only for that night but for each night of a ten-week series, and then for another ten-week series a couple of years later. During those weeks I had the privilege of sitting at the dining room table after school and listening to him as he talked about the state of the world and of what God was doing in various parts of it. He talked about the Bible, of what he was going to preach that evening, of what he was writing. All of this expanded my horizons, and I began to think of the day when I would preach, even though I did not know then that it would eventually be from the pulpit he was then occupying.

Where Is the Man?

Each of us has ways of measuring the importance of things in this world. Often we measure things by success. We look at this world and we consider those with power and wealth and extra intelligence to be important. God never measures things in this way. God tells us that the principal characters on the world stage generally are not those whom the world thinks prominent, but rather those who have surrendered whatever they have been given into his hands.

Will you do that? You may be looking only at your littleness, instead of looking at God's greatness. You may be complaining that your talents or opportunities are not great. You may be discouraged because your talents do not seem up to the tasks set before you. If any of these things are true, you need to remember that God used a little slave girl to bring the leper Naaman in touch with his healing power. He used a widow to provide the necessities of life for the prophet Elisha. Joseph was only a slave, but God used him to save both Egypt and Israel. We have already seen in this Gospel how God used the woman of Samaria, a prostitute, to save a whole town.

One day Dwight L. Moody overheard a man say, "The world has yet to see what God will do through one man who is fully surrendered to him." Moody answered—will you say it also?—"By the grace of God I am going to be that man."

74

Who's in Charge?

John 6:10–15

Jesus said, "Have the people sit down." There was plenty of grass in that place, and the men sat down, about five thousand of them. Jesus then took the loaves, gave thanks, and distributed to those who were seated as much as they wanted. He did the same with the fish.

When they had all had enough to eat, he said to his disciples, "Gather the pieces that are left over. Let nothing be wasted." So they gathered them and filled twelve baskets with the pieces of the five barley loaves left over by those who had eaten.

After the people saw the miraculous sign that Jesus did, they began to say, "Surely this is the Prophet who is to come into the world." Jesus, knowing that they intended to come and make him king by force, withdrew again to a mountain by himself.

T here is a very old proverb that says, "Nothing succeeds like success." The only difficulty is that the proverb does not say what success helps us succeed in doing.

In chapter 1 at the beginning of our study of the fifth chapter of John, I pointed out that there are two dangers that come to anyone who is seeking to please the Lord and walk in his way. They are: the danger of success and the danger of hostility. In John's Gospel the danger of hostility comes first, so we discussed that in connection with our study of Jesus's reaction to the hos-

451

tility of the Jewish leaders in chapter 5. When a person determines to live as Jesus has called him to live, that person can be certain that there will be some measure of hostility from the world, even at times from his Christian friends. This causes some followers of the Lord to become discouraged and to pull back from a full commitment. We have seen in our earlier studies that this did not happen to Jesus, and we saw why.

The second danger is the danger of success. This is no less frightening. Something can take place in the Christian's life that is so encouraging spiritually that the Christian becomes enamored with his success and comes to depend upon himself spiritually. He then goes off under his own wisdom, building a superstructure that is not of God's design. It is one rather of his own making. Those who gain reputations for themselves as Christian crusaders often provide us with examples of this, and the ends to which they go and the non-Christian means they employ to get there are disheartening. Fortunately, Jesus faced this danger also and was victorious.

Little Knowledge

In the sixth chapter of John we are told that after Jesus had used the five barley loaves and the two fish provided by the lad to feed five thousand people, the people who had witnessed the miracle determined to make him their king. In other words, they wanted to make him a political Messiah who would drive out the Romans.

This was wrong, of course, but the people for all their selfishness were not entirely unperceptive about what Jesus had done. For one thing, they were Jews and so possessed a religious heritage in which the idea of a Messiah was prominent. For another, they knew that in the law God had promised Moses that one day he would raise up a leader like himself. God had said, "I will raise up for them a prophet like you from among their brothers; I will put my words in his mouth, and he will tell them everything I command him" (Deut. 18:18). Knowledge of this promise explains the reaction of the people in saying, "Surely this is the Prophet who is to come into the world" (John 6:14). It also explains two other references in John in which the people wonder if some prominent figure might not be that "prophet" (1:21; 7:40).

Moreover, the people who had witnessed the miracle also knew of other verses that promised a certain measure of material prosperity to be provided by the Messiah during the days of his earthly rule. In fact, in Psalm 132:15 there is a promise that the Messiah would provide bread for the hungry. It says, "I will bless her with abundant provisions; her poor will I satisfy with food."

The people looked at these promises, filtering them through their own desires and prejudices, and then concluded, "Jesus is the Messiah. He is the One whom we should make king." The only difficulty was that they did not know the Scriptures as well as they should have known them and so made a big mistake. They knew that the Messiah was to be a great prophet. They knew that he was to be a great king. But they had failed to see that in between being a great prophet and a great king Jesus also had to be a great priest. In this role he was to offer up himself for the sins of the people. Jesus was a prophet, of course. He was speaking for God the Father. He would one day be king. We rightly sing:

> Jesus shall reign where'er the sun
> Does his successive journeys run;
> His kingdom stretch from shore to shore,
> Till moons shall wax and wane no more.

But before Jesus could be king he had to die. It was necessary for him to give his life "a ransom for many" (Mark 10:45).

Jesus knew these truths. He knew the Scriptures. Therefore, he did not allow the enthusiasm of the people based on the physical miracle to deter him from the proper path. We can apply this by saying that you and I must know Scripture well also if we are not to allow spiritual success to succeed in turning us away from God to our own plans and devices.

A Selfish Reaction

We need to say, too, that the reaction of the people to Christ's miracle was not altogether noble, even though it was partially scriptural. In fact, the more one thinks of the motives of the mob in wanting to make Jesus king, the less altruistic the reaction seems to be.

For one thing, the crowd was willing to support Jesus *only so long as he gave them what they wanted*. This means that their support was for selfish reasons. We see proof of this in their concern for more bread expressed later. We also see proof of it in the fact that within a short while another group of people just like this (perhaps even containing some of the same individuals, for these may have been on their way to the Passover) were crying out, "Crucify him! Crucify him!" There is such a thing as bought loyalty, and these people were expressing it. They were grateful for the meal. But their gratitude was that kind of gratitude referred to by Samuel Johnson, who defined it as "a lively sense of favours still to come."

When we begin to think along these lines the attitude of the mob repels us. But are we so very different? William Barclay writes at this point in his commentary, "When we want comfort in sorrow, when we want strength in difficulty, when we want peace in turmoil, when we want help when life has got us down, there is no one so wonderful as Jesus. Then we talk to Him and walk with Him and open our hearts to Him. But when He comes to us with some stern demand for sacrifice, with some challenge to effort, with the offer of some cross, then we will have nothing to do with Him. When we examine our hearts, it may be that we will find that we too love Jesus for what we can get out of Him, and when He comes to us with His great challenges and demands we too grow lukewarm, and even resentful and hostile to this disturbing and demanding Christ."[1]

This is one reason why the Bible speaks so plainly of the need to deny self and selfish desires as a Christian. Many verses speak along these lines, often using the ideas of death, crucifixion with Christ, and denial. For instance, Romans 6:4 says that we are to be "buried with him through baptism into death." Two verses farther on we read, "For we know that our old self was crucified with him so that the body of sin might be rendered powerless, that we should no longer be slaves to sin" (v. 6). The first part of Galatians 2:20 declares, "I have been crucified with Christ." In Galatians 6:14 Paul writes, "May I never boast except in the cross of our Lord Jesus Christ, through which the world has been crucified to me, and I to the world." Along with the message of death and denial there is also the message of resurrection and fulfillment. But, still, denial comes first. There must be a death to self before there can be an abundance of spiritual blessing.

What does it mean that we are to die to self? What does it mean that we are to be crucified with Jesus? Simply put, it means that we are to say no to anything that lies outside the will of God for our lives. This is true before conversion. We must say no to any plans we may have for earning God's favor and instead receive God's gift of eternal life in Christ. It also is true after our conversion, for the same principles that operated in our coming to Christ continue in the Christian life. We must say no to all our plans and personal desires (or at least be willing to say no) so that God's will rather than our own may be accomplished.

Here is an important question. I have said that we must say no or at least be willing to say no to anything that is contrary to the will of God in our lives. But how do we know when we have really said no? Our hearts and minds are subtle. It is easy to fool ourselves. How do we know when we have really said no to that which is contrary to the will of God in our lives? The answer is: When we have stopped complaining.

The Word of God has a good word for what we do when we really have not stopped complaining. It is the word "murmur." This is what the people of Israel did when they were in the wilderness and did not like what God was doing with them. It also is the word used by the ungrateful servants in Christ's parable about the householder. What is murmuring? Murmuring is expressing rebellion against something by mumbling under one's breath. It is called murmuring because that is what murmuring sounds like to anyone who is listening.

That is what we do with God. God tells us to do something, and the first thing we do is attempt to stare him down. We want to see if he really means it. After we find that he really does mean it, we murmur. And the reason we murmur is that we really do not want to do what he wants us to do. If you do that, then you are in the company of the great crowd who only supported Jesus when he gave them what they wanted. Grow up! Come to the point where you no longer murmur but say instead, "Yes, Lord, you know best." When you do that you will go away happy and fulfilled, because he does know best.

The Roman Yoke

There is also a second reason why the people were wrong in the particular kind of support they gave to Jesus: *they wanted to use him.* They wanted to use him instead of allowing him to use them and mold them into the kind of people he wanted them to be.

This is understandable, of course. The people had a great problem in their day. It was the occupation of their country by the Roman forces. Actually, this was not as bad as they probably imagined it was. For one thing, the Romans brought a measure of law and civilization. They built good roads and buildings. There really was such a thing as the Roman peace, and many of the conquered nations recognized this. However, the Jews did not. They were a fiercely independent people. Jews chaffed under this Roman yoke, and that which they most desired to have happen in their lifetime was to have the Roman yoke thrown off. Suddenly there was this unusual man Jesus. He had miraculous power. So they must have said something like this to themselves, "Wouldn't it be wonderful if we could get him on our side and get him to help us drive out the Romans?"

It is clear that the desire of this crowd was to make use of Jesus, far more than to be used by him. But again, are we really very different, many of us?

I think there are several ways in which we try to use the Lord Jesus Christ. One obvious example is the attempt to justify prejudice by appealing to the Scriptures. At times this has taken the totally unsupportable position that the African American race is descended from Ham, that Ham was placed under a curse by God, and that this therefore justifies any attempts to subject the African American to slavery. This is unbiblical, dishonest, and mean. Yet it has been done. It is a clear case of attempting to use Christ or use the Bible for wicked ends.

A second example is in the area of politics. Politicians love to quote the Bible. They quote it in support of any program they desire. Probably it is not even too cynical to suggest that as a rule they develop their programs first and get their supporting quotations second. There is no political program so ill-conceived that it cannot be justified by someone at some point by an appeal to Jesus Christ or biblical authority.

Finally, we use the Lord Jesus Christ to justify the American way of life. Do not misunderstand me here. I do not want to downplay America. We have been greatly blessed by God in this land. We probably have had a higher percentage of Christian people in America than in any other land at any period of history, with the possible exception of England under Cromwell or during the Wesleyan revivals. This has produced real advantages. Yet it also is true that today there is much that is not only non-Christian but even anti-Christian at all levels of our society and national life. The Lord Jesus Christ cannot be used to justify these things. He does not justify all that big business or labor does. He does not lend his support to Madison Avenue. You cannot quote Jesus in your pursuit of the second car, the second home, the lavish vacation, the indulgence of yourself in leisure time, and many other things that some consider their right. Some of these things may be God's gift to you. But if you are pursuing these things rather than pursuing God, spiritual growth, and advance in his plan for your life, if you are quoting the Bible as support of your inverted value system, then you are merely doing what the people who were fed by Jesus did. You are using him rather than allowing him to use you and mold you into the kind of person he would have you be.

Billions of Christs

What does Jesus want you to be? One answer to that question is from the eighth chapter of Romans in which God's purpose in calling an individual to himself is spelled out. It says, "For those God foreknew he also predestined to be conformed to the likeness of his Son, that he might be the firstborn among many brothers" (8:29). What is the purpose? It is that each one who has been called by God to faith in Jesus Christ might become like Christ so that—I say it reverently—eventually there might be many billions of Christs where there was only one before. The wonderful thing is that this can be done in us whatever our situation in life, whether we are rich or poor, educated or uneducated, black or white, male or female, or whatever it may be.

Moreover, it is only when we allow Jesus Christ to do that in us that we achieve any importance. If we take God and attempt to use him to justify what we want to do, all we succeed in doing is making Christianity petty. It becomes bounded by our own limited horizons. But if we allow God to use us, then no matter how insignificant we may seem as the world looks at things, we become important spiritually. For the Lord Jesus Christ himself is seen in the conduct of his followers.

75

The Fifth Miracle

John 6:16-21

When evening came, his disciples went down to the lake, where they got into a boat and set off across the lake for Capernaum. By now it was dark, and Jesus had not yet joined them. A strong wind was blowing and the waters grew rough. When they had rowed three or three and a half miles, they saw Jesus approaching the boat, walking on the water; and they were terrified. But he said to them, "It is I; don't be afraid." Then they were willing to take him into the boat, and immediately the boat reached the shore where they were heading.

If you have ever been to the Near East—to Turkey, Egypt, Lebanon, or Syria—you may have seen the oriental silversmiths working in the great bazaars. They work with coins that have been given to them by Western tourists, melting them down, and then forming them into small pieces of jewelry. Eventually they sell them back to any of the tourists who will buy them. This is done in a primitive way. Generally there is a small furnace over which sits a pot containing the molten silver. The coin is dropped in and melted. Every so often the silversmith goes over to the pot of silver, looks into it, scrapes off a bit of the dross that has collected, and then returns to his work. After a while he looks in, finds that the silver is ready, and begins to form it.

"Why do you constantly look into the silver?" we might ask.

The silversmith would answer, "I look into the silver until I find that the dross is all gone and the silver purified; I know when the dross is gone, because I can see myself reflected in the silver as in a fine mirror."

457

Here is the explanation of that wonderful passage in Malachi in which God tells us that he shall sit like a "refiner and purifier of silver," and of why Christians are so often called upon to go through the fires and testings of this life. God wants to make us like the Lord Jesus Christ. He does it by working to remove the dross of our lives, until his image is reflected in us for the world to see. The Bible tells us, "The Lord disciplines those he loves, and he punishes everyone he accepts as a son" (Heb. 12:6). This principle is illustrated in the story now before us.

The Storm

In the sixth chapter of John we are told that after the multitude who had been fed with the loaves and fish in Galilee had tried to make Jesus king, Jesus slipped away from them. He went up into a mountain alone to pray. We do not know how long he was gone. But the day wore on, and the disciples eventually went down to the Sea of Galilee and got into a boat in order to sail back to Capernaum. We must not think that they were rude in doing this, still less that they had forgotten Jesus, for Mark in his account of the incident tells us that Jesus had instructed them to go home (Mark 6:45). This is the first great fact of the story, for it means that Jesus himself had sent them across the lake by boat knowing full well what was to happen.

The night came on and with the night a great storm. This was a wind storm, as we can tell from the story, the kind that comes up quickly on the Sea of Galilee. Mark and Matthew tell us that the wind was against them. John adds that "a strong wind was blowing and the waters grew rough" (v. 18). This storm was dangerous. Besides this it made rowing difficult, for they rowed into the fourth watch of the night. That is, they began at dusk and rowed until approximately 3:00 A.M. or dawn.

I wonder what the disciples were thinking about as they rowed their boat through the storm for those six or seven dangerous hours. They were worried, no doubt. But did they ever think of Jesus and of his power to help them? Did they realize that even then they were in his care?

They should have recognized this, of course. In fact, it is even evident that Jesus sent them into the storm to teach them this lesson and to help their faith grow. For one thing, they had just witnessed Christ's care in the feeding of the multitudes. Here were at least five thousand people, many of whom Jesus and the disciples undoubtedly did not even know personally. Yet Jesus cared for them and fed them. Do you suppose that the disciples sensed that Jesus was able to care for them too? Did they trust him? Or did they do what we sometimes do—assume that this situation was different, that the power of Jesus was limited, or that he did not know of their predicament? The miracle of the multiplication of the loaves and fish should have taught them that Jesus did know, that his power was adequate, and that he did care.

For another thing, the disciples had already witnessed the power of the Lord Jesus Christ to calm troubled waters. This particular story from an earlier period in Christ's ministry is not told in John's Gospel, but Matthew, Mark, and Luke all record it (Matt. 8:23–27; Mark 4:35–41; Luke 8:22–25), indicating that it took place before the feeding of the multitude in Galilee. Sometime before the multiplying of the loaves, Jesus and his disciples had been in Galilee and had wished to cross from the more settled western shore of the Sea of Tiberias to the eastern shore inhabited by the Gadarenes. Jesus was exhausted from his preaching and fell asleep in the rear of the boat. A storm arose. The boat began to fill with water. The disciples feared that they would be drowned. They woke Jesus up crying, "Master, don't you care that we are about to perish?" Jesus arose and then quietly calmed the sea. He asked them, "Why are you so fearful? How is it that you have such small faith?"

Did the disciples remember this in the midst of the new storm as once again they found themselves rowing across the Sea of Galilee? Did they trust Christ to protect them? Or did they argue, as we do, that this time Jesus was not actually with them and could do nothing?

A thought that I find amusing has sometimes occurred to me as I have read this story. A few verses before this we are told that the disciples had collected twelve baskets of food left over from the feeding. What happened to these twelve baskets? I find it difficult to imagine that they threw the bread away after just having taken pains to gather the fragments up. The disciples could have taken the fragments with them. And in that case evidence of Jesus' supernatural ability and power would have been under their very noses as they rowed through the tempest.

I am not sure that there is a certain answer to be given to the question of whether the disciples had learned to trust Jesus or else were fearful, but as I read the story and contrast it with the earlier incident I sense that their faith had grown. In the earlier account we are told they were fearful. In this account, even though they were frightened when Jesus came walking on the water (they thought he was a ghost), we are not told that they were frightened by the storm. We are told only that they kept rowing.

Whatever the case, at length Jesus came toward them. This is the point at which Peter asked permission to walk toward him and did so for a time, although John omits this part of the experience. Jesus said, "It is I; don't be afraid." After this, John tells us, they were immediately at the land to which they went.

Growth of Faith

What did the disciples learn through this experience? It was a kind of testing—a trial by water if you will. It proved that, on the basis of their former experience, they had learned to trust Jesus a bit more. But what did they learn this time? What did they learn in this experience? I believe they learned at least three things, all of which are highlighted in the various accounts of the story.

First, they learned that, although they had not been aware of it, *Jesus was watching.* He knew what they were going through. Probably he told them this afterward, for Mark explains that when he was up on the mountain alone "he saw the disciples straining at the oars" (Mark 6:48). This is understandable when we remember that these events took place at the time of the Passover, when there was always a full moon, and that it was a windstorm, rather than a rainstorm with clouds, that churned the water.

Have the experiences through which you have gone taught you that Jesus is watching you and knows your circumstances? He does not make things too easy for any of us. He knows that muscles that are never used grow flabby. We must row in rough weather sometimes. There is work to be done. But do we know, even as we do the work, that Jesus' eye is upon us?

This is true in one sense for all men. It is one truth involved in the doctrine of the immanence of God. The immanence of God means quite simply that God is here. We can say that God is everywhere, and this is right too. But it is far more personal to say that God is where we are. He is here, wherever you or I may be. Take these examples. Adam sinned and in his panic of guilt tried to do the impossible: he tried to hide from God. At one time David must have had wild thoughts of trying to escape from God, for he wrote. "Where can I go from your Spirit? Where can I flee from your presence?" He then proceeded to celebrate the glory of the divine immanence. "If I go up to the heavens, you are there; if I make my bed in the depths, you are there. If I rise on the wings of the dawn, if I settle on the far side of the sea, even there your hand will guide me, your right hand will hold me fast" (Ps. 139:7–10). Solomon exclaimed, "But will God really dwell on earth? The heavens, even the highest heaven, cannot contain you. How much less this temple I have built!" (1 Kings 8:27). Paul assured the Athenians that God "is not far from each one of us. 'For in him we live and move and have our being'" (Acts 17:27–28).

If it is true that God is not far from anyone, that he sees what we do and knows all about us, how much more true it is that Jesus sees his own followers and knows what they are facing in all their circumstances! He has told us that not "a sparrow" falls to the ground without his knowledge and that the hairs of our head are "all numbered" (Matt. 10:29–31). He said, "And surely I will be with you always, to the very end of the age" (Matt. 28:20). Do you realize that he is with you? Do you sense that his eye is upon you as it was upon the disciples?

The second truth the disciples learned is that *Jesus helps*. Jesus watches us, it is true. But he does not watch with some kind of serene, unmoved detachment. He watches us in order to help. And he does help—at all times, of course, but particularly when life becomes too burdensome for us and when spiritual victory seems beyond our grasp.

At this point in his commentary William Barclay tells the story of a teacher in a little country school in England. She had told this story to the children; and she must have told it well, for the children obviously got the point. Some short time afterward there was a great snowstorm. The teacher had the job of getting the children home. Sometimes she practically had to drag them through the drifts. It was tiring. Finally, when they were nearly exhausted with the struggle, she overheard one of the youngest children say in his best British manner, half to himself, "We could be doing with that chap Jesus here now." Well, we could always be doing with Jesus and we never, no matter how difficult the circumstances, have to do without him.

Unfortunately, we often do without him, because we do not wait for his help or listen to his voice. In *Let Me Illustrate,* a collection of stories and illustrations from the writings of Donald Grey Barnhouse, there is a story of a man who owned an icehouse. One day he lost a fine watch in the sawdust. He offered a reward to anyone who would find it; and many went through the sawdust with rakes searching for the timepiece. No one could find the watch. Finally, when the searchers left the building for lunch, a small boy went into the icehouse. A few minutes later he came out with the watch. The men asked how he had found it, and he replied, "I just lay down in the sawdust and listened. Finally, I heard the watch ticking." Dr. Barnhouse then concludes, "Some of you have lost more than a watch. If you will be very still and listen quietly, the Lord will speak to you and show you just where you lost the power and victory which you so sorely miss."[1]

Finally, the disciples learned that *Jesus was also able to bring them home.* He not only helped; he got them to the place they were going. John indicates this aspect of the story by reporting, "Then they were willing to take him into the boat, and immediately the boat reached the shore where they were heading" (v. 21).

Jesus is able also to get you where you are going. Or, to put it more correctly, he is able to get you to the place to which he has called you or to which you are sent. This is true in life. If he has called you to be a missionary, he will see that you become one whatever the difficulties. If he has called you to a life of quiet witness in a drab undesirable spot, he will give you strength to make your witness there. He will help you in the shop, the home, the church, or wherever you may be.

Moreover, he also will see you safely through this life to your final home in heaven. I do not know whether John had this meaning in mind as he recorded this story. He could have, for he obviously saw levels of spiritual truth in each of the miracles he narrates. Still, whether or not John himself was thinking of this, what could be more descriptive of our age than that which John tells us was true of the evening in which the disciples crossed the lake—a stormy sea, a strong wind, a dark night? This we face. At times we cannot even see where we are headed. But we shall see Jesus one day, and he himself will guide us into port.

The psalmist says, "Commit your way to the LORD; trust in him and he will do this" (Ps. 37:5).

Becoming a Christian

But then, finally, I may be speaking to someone who has never trusted in Jesus Christ and who is saying, "Yes, it is all very well to speak to Christians like that. I suppose that they can know where they are going. But I do not know where I am going. I am not a Christian, and I do not know how to become one."

If you are saying that, let me explain the matter for you. In order to become a Christian there are two things you must believe and one thing you must do. First, you must believe on the authority of God's Word that you cannot help yourself spiritually. You can help yourself in this life. You can gain praise from others for your character or good works, but none of this will satisfy God. You are a sinner and are therefore as helpless as the disciples were in the midst of the storm.

Second, you must believe that Jesus is able to do what you cannot do. You cannot save yourself, but he can save you. You cannot satisfy God by means of your own character, but Jesus has already satisfied him and God is willing to place his character to your account. Jesus died for you to remove your sin. He rose so that you might know that God is satisfied with what Jesus has done on your behalf forever.

Finally, you must commit yourself to him. The Bible speaks of this in different ways, but in each case it is clear that it involves an act of our will. It says that we are to believe in Jesus, which means that we are to place ourselves in his hands. It says that we are to receive him, which means that we are to invite him into our lives. Will you do that? Will you admit your sin, believe that he is able to save you, and then commit your life into his keeping. When you do that you will learn that he came not merely to save you from the guilt of your sins but also to take charge of your life. Why not hand yourself over to him today? Say, "Lord Jesus Christ, I give myself to you—body, soul, and spirit. I want you to take charge of my life." It is a wise choice, for he is able to keep and bless all those who put their trust in him.

76

The Search

John 6:22–27

The next day the crowd that had stayed on the opposite shore of the lake realized that only one boat had been there, and that Jesus had not entered it with his disciples, but that they had gone away alone. Then some boats from Tiberias landed near the place where the people had eaten the bread after the Lord had given thanks. Once the crowd realized that neither Jesus nor his disciples were there, they got into the boats and went to Capernaum in search of Jesus.

When they found him on the other side of the lake, they asked him, "Rabbi, when did you get here?"

Jesus answered, "I tell you the truth, you are looking for me, not because you saw miraculous signs but because you ate the loaves and had your fill. Do not work for food that spoils, but for food that endures to eternal life, which the Son of Man will give you. On him God the Father has placed his seal of approval."

Among the most famous sayings of the early church fathers is this one by Saint Augustine: "Thou hast formed us for Thyself, and our hearts are restless till they find their rest in Thee." This universal restlessness of the soul is the cause of that apparent search for God that is to be found in most individuals and races. What the saying does not point out is that not every way of seeking him is correct.

The doctrine of prevenient grace means that before someone can seek after God, God must have first of all sought that person. Speaking of man in his natural state, the Bible says "There is no one righteous, not even one; there is no one who understands, no one who seeks God" (Rom. 3:10–11). It also says, "The man without the Spirit does not accept the things that come from the Spirit of God, for they are foolishness to him, and he cannot understand them, because they are spiritually discerned" (1 Cor. 2:14). This means that before someone can begin to think even one right thought about God or begin to desire him, God must first have done a work of enlightenment in that person's heart by means of the Holy Spirit. What also needs to be said, however, is that this prevenient and gracious work of the Holy Spirit should have its natural outcome in our thereafter following hard after God. We seek because we already have been found.

But how do we seek God? Do we do it in a way that will inevitably result in our finding him? Or do we seek selfishly and therefore wrongly? The following story will help us to answer that question for our own lives.

Seeking for Jesus

Jesus had crossed the Sea of Galilee by night in order to join the disciples in Capernaum. The people whom he had fed from the five loaves and two fish the day before saw in the morning light that Jesus was no longer in the area in which the miracle had been done. So they began to look for him. Eventually they made their way either around or across the lake and found him at Capernaum.

The reference to the boats in John's story is unclear. Generally commentators interpret the verses to mean that the crowd recalled that there had been but one boat the previous night—the other boats must have been driven in during the night by the storm—and that Jesus had not sailed away with the disciples. However, it also is possible that John means to say that there was only one boat available to Jesus and that he had not entered that. Or again, that only one boat was left on the shore and that Jesus was not in it, nor had he sailed in any of the others. Whatever the meaning of these references, the main point is obviously that the people could imagine no way by which Jesus had crossed the lake, for they could not have imagined that he had walked over it. So when they finally found him they came to him with the question, "Rabbi, how and when did you get here?"

Jesus' reply was to ignore the question and instead deal with the manner of their seeking. He did not praise them. Instead he replied, "I tell you the truth, you are looking for me, not because you saw miraculous signs but because you ate the loaves and had your fill. Do not work for food that spoils but for food that endures to eternal life, which the Son of Man will give you. On him the Father has placed his seal of approval" (vv. 26–27). Here was a sharp unveiling of the crowd's unworthy motives in seeking Jesus. But is it not true that these same motives operate in our own lives, even at times when we think we are most spiritual?

God or Man?

Let me outline what I mean in slightly more precise terms. First, although the crowd was obviously seeking Jesus in one sense, at the same time it is obvious that the minds of the individuals were on themselves. We see that clearly in the matter of the food, which Jesus mentions. We must remember that the crowd had been hungry when they were with Jesus the night before. He had fed them so that they had had all they wanted. The twelve baskets of leftovers are evidence of the fact that they had been fully satisfied. Still, the night had gone by and now part of the morning. It was time for a late breakfast or lunch; they were hungry again. Obviously their minds were primarily on their stomachs as they sought him.

Do you do that when you seek Jesus? Do you come with your mind filled, not so much with Jesus and his all-surpassing worth, but with your needs or with what you imagine your needs to be?

I am convinced that in our day in American Christianity there is a lamentable tendency to focus on human need rather than on God himself. I am equally convinced that this is the worst possible way to actually have the need met and to achieve a healthy Christianity. I know that someone will say, "But how can that be? Isn't it true that people do have needs?" The answer is: Yes, they do. "And isn't it true that Jesus is the answer to those needs?" The reply is: Yes, he is. "Shouldn't we therefore preach Jesus Christ as the answer to people's needs?" The only proper reply is: Yes, we should. "Well, then, what is wrong?" What is wrong is that it is tragically possible to so focus on our needs that we are actually focusing on ourselves rather than on Jesus, and so never get to the solutions to our problems that Jesus wants to bring. This occurs to different degrees in different people, of course. But I know of one case, a woman who has had a great deal of psychiatric counseling, in which there is no longer even a real desire to get better. She will talk endlessly about her problems. But she will almost come apart psychologically at any suggestion that God might have an answer that would bring her problems to an end.

Here is another example. I know of a small group Bible study in which the people involved think mainly of their problems. It is a kind of therapy group in which each one listens to the problems of the others so that the others will listen to him. There is almost a competition in problems. Who has the worst problem? Who should get the most sympathy? I do not want to be too harsh at this point, for I believe that it is always good (in a relative way) to get things out in the open. Nevertheless, the solutions are in Christ and not in our ability to articulate problems.

May I say it even more strongly? I am convinced that one of the major steps to achieving good spiritual mental health is getting your mind off yourself entirely and on the Lord instead. The author of an old English classic, *The Cloud of Unknowing*, was aware of this. He wrote in his volume, "Lift up thine heart unto God with a meek stirring of love; and mean Himself, and none of His goods. And thereto, look thee loath to think on aught but God Himself. So that nought work in thy wit, nor in thy will, but only God Himself. This is the work of the soul that most pleaseth God."[1]

Possessions

There was also a second thing that these people were doing in their search for Jesus and for which they were rebuked. It is related to the first. They had their minds on material things. The point of the miracle—which you will recall from our earlier study of miracles—was to point their minds to Jesus. He had fed them, but they were to see from the miracle that he was that spiritual bread who alone could satisfy the inner spiritual hunger of the soul. Instead they had their minds on material things alone and so missed the greater blessing.

Even before God created man he created a world full of varied and useful things for people to enjoy. These objects were part of God's plan. But it has fallen out since man's rebellion that those gifts that were for man's happiness today constitute what A. W. Tozer called "a potential source of ruin for the soul." So we find our minds filled with "things" and discover that we often come to God only when our possessions are threatened or when we want more.

It is not at all difficult to find examples of those who, although believers in God and followers of him, nevertheless allow the love of possessions to obscure their awareness of God and limit their growth. Achan is one of whom this was true. He was a soldier in the army of Israel that fought at Jericho. The spoil of that battle was to be dedicated to God, but Achan saw and took for himself a beautiful Babylonian garment, twenty pieces of silver, and a bar of gold. Because of his sin Israel lost her next battle at Ai, and Achan and his family were brought out into the open and judged. Solomon was a wise man in most respects, but he was not wise in regard to wealth and women, both of which ruined his spiritual life. Ananias and Sapphira lied to the Lord about money and were judged for it. Paul wrote of Demas, who "because he loved this world, has deserted me." Unfortunately, this is true to a large degree in our own century.

But is possessing things wrong for a Christian? No, it is not, even though there have been those who have taught this and in some cases teach it today. There is nothing wrong with the right of private property. There is nothing wrong with a Christian's possessing a home, a car, insurance policies, stocks and bonds, even more than one of these things. What is wrong, if there is a wrong in any individual case, is seeking these things to the exclusion of seeking after God, or seeking them more than God.

It is all a question of who or what is in control. I am assuming that you have some possessions. Well, do you control them? Or do they control you? What your attitude should be may be illustrated from a dramatic event in the life of Abraham.[2]

Abraham was a very old man when his son Isaac was born, and as the years went by he undoubtedly came to love Isaac with a great and possessing love. He loved him several times over—because he was the son of his old age, because he was the son of the promise. Perhaps the time came when this possession—

even, let us note, a God-given possession—came dangerously close to over-shadowing the place that God alone should have occupied in the aging pa-triarch's heart. At this point God stepped in with the command, "Take your son, your only son Isaac, whom you love, and go to the region of Moriah. Sacrifice him there as a burnt offering on one of the mountains I will tell you about" (Gen. 22:2).

The author of the Book of Genesis does not give us the details of the strug-gle that must have gone on in the heart of this sublime old man that night, but we can imagine what some of them were. How could he kill Isaac, whom he loved? It would be far better were he himself to die in Isaac's place. Besides this, Isaac was the promised son through whom Abraham was to become a great nation and the Messiah was to come. How could God fulfill the promises if Isaac were to die? At last Abraham came to a solution and made up his mind. He would do as God had directed. He would kill Isaac. He would lose him. But he would trust God to raise him up from the dead. This is what the author of Hebrews indicates when he writes that Abraham "offered Isaac as a sacrifice. . . . even though God had said to him, 'It is through Isaac that your offspring will be reckoned.' Abraham reasoned that God could raise the dead, and figuratively speaking, he did receive Isaac back from death" (Heb. 11:17–19).

God let Abraham go through with his plan up to the point where the knife was about to be plunged into the boy. But then he stopped Abraham—it was only a test, God said—and reiterated the promises. How glad Abraham was! He did not have to kill his son! He had him back! But God was glad too, for Abraham would no longer possess Isaac as he had previously. Now God would be all to Abraham.

One commentator writes on this story: "I have said that Abraham possessed nothing. Yet was not this poor man rich? Everything he had owned before was his still to enjoy: sheep, camels, herds, and goods of every sort. He had also his wife and his friends, and best of all he had his son Isaac safe by his side. He had everything, *but he possessed nothing.* There is the spiritual secret. There is the sweet theology of the heart which can be learned only in the school of renunciation." This writer adds, "The books on systematic theol-ogy overlook this, but the wise will understand."[3]

Do *you* understand? It is not our possessions that are wrong but our single-minded possession of our possessions. Do you seek for things? Or do you seek for God? How sad it would be if those things that are destined to per-ish should keep you from him who is eternal.

Halfhearted Seeking

Finally, there is a third error that characterized this seeking of the Galilean crowd. They came seeking, but they really did not seek wholeheartedly. What happened when Jesus refused to feed them physically the second time? I as-sume that most of them went home for lunch and are not heard from again in the narrative. Whatever the case, we know that after his speech in the synagogue "many of his disciples turned back and no longer followed him" (v. 66). Do you seek halfheartedly and then get discouraged when your prayer or Bible study is not all you had hoped it would be? Do you lose interest when you find that Jesus wants to lead you in a way that does not at first appeal to you? Or do you press on?

David explained some of his difficulties in Psalm 27. But he declared with determination, "My heart says of you, 'Seek his face!' Your face, LORD, will I seek" (27:8).

What, then, do we have to do to seek God properly and successfully? First, we must seek him where he alone can be found—*in Jesus Christ*. This is the point of Christ's reference to himself in the verse from the story which I cited earlier. Jesus said, "On him [meaning himself] God the Father has placed his seal of approval." What does that mean? In Jesus' day a seal on a document was the equivalent of a signature. It authenticated the document. It was that by which men knew that the document was the real thing and no forgery. It is in much the same sense that God has authenticated Jesus Christ by means of his life, character, teaching, miracles, and above all by the resurrection from the dead. This is the One in whom God is to be seen and found. Have you come to God in Jesus? He said, "I am the way and the truth and the life. No one comes to the Father except through me" (John 14:6).

Second, you must come *yourself*. No one else can come for you, not even a Bible teacher through whom you may even receive great blessing. Do you spend time praying—by yourself? Do you study the Bible? Do you spend time meditating on spiritual things? The Lord Jesus Christ is speaking to individuals when he declares, "Here I am! I stand at the door and knock. If anyone hears my voice and opens the door, I will go in and eat with him, and he with me" (Rev. 3:20).

Finally, you must come *wholeheartedly*. Jesus said, "Blessed are those who hunger and thirst for righteousness, for they will be filled" (Matt. 5:6). He was not speaking of the kind of hunger and thirst we know when he said this. The hunger and thirst we know hardly deserves to be called by that name. He was speaking of the hunger of people who seldom have enough to eat and of that thirst for water without which the thirsting man will die. He was saying that we are to hunger after him as a starving man hungers for bread and to thirst after him as a dying man thirsts after water. Do we do that? If we really would, it is hard to estimate how rich in the knowledge and fruitfulness of God we would be.

77

A Golden Sentence

John 6:28–29

Then they asked him, "What must we do to do the works God requires?"
Jesus answered, "The work of God is this: to believe in the one he has sent."

It is a great joy in the study of literature or history to discover a saying that seems to sum up a whole personality or a movement. Caesar supplied us with one of these sayings in his often quoted report on a military encounter in Gaul: *"Veni, vidi, vici"* (I came, I saw, I conquered). Winston Churchill did the same in England during the years of World War II. Who can forget his offer to the British people shortly after war had been declared against Germany? He said that he had not come to offer England an easy time or an easy victory but, rather, "Blood, toil, sweat and tears." Later, after Hitler had failed to break the English spirit through the bombing of London, Churchill joked about Hitler's promise to wring England's neck as if she were a chicken. "Some chicken," said Churchill. Then, after thunderous applause, "Some neck!"

Sentences like these are golden sentences, for they vividly capture a personality, a theme, or a spirited moment of world history. In another sense, however, even such striking statements seem less than totally gripping when placed alongside the truly golden sentences of the Word of God.

469

What are these sentences? You can think of many of them. John 3:16—"For God so loved the world that he gave his one and only Son, that whoever believes in him should not perish but have eternal life." Philippians 4:19—"And my God will meet all your needs according to his glorious riches in Christ Jesus" Psalm 23:1—"The LORD is my shepherd." I believe that our text, found in the sixth chapter of John, verse 29, is another. The crowd that had witnessed the miracle of the multiplication of the loaves and fish had crossed the Sea of Galilee to find Jesus in Capernaum and had asked him, "What must we do to do the works God requires?" It was a question that many people are asking. It was even a great question, though the answer was greater. Jesus replied in words that every human being on the earth should hear, read, and memorize: "The work of God is this: to believe in the one he has sent."

Faith or Works

In some ways it is almost unbelievable that the crowd should have asked this question in view of what Jesus had been telling them. He had said, "Do not work for food that spoils, but for food that endures to eternal life, which the Son of Man will *give* to you" (v. 27). Jesus had been speaking of a gift, but they had not grasped his meaning. Instead, they replied as the natural human mind, which is against God, always does; they replied that they wanted to do something to earn it.

It is always thus. Arthur W. Pink notes in his commentary: "It was thus with the woman at the well: until divine grace completed its work within her, she knew not the 'gift of God' (John 4:10). It was the same with the rich young ruler: 'Good Master, what shall I *do* to inherit eternal life?' (Luke 18:18). It was the same with the stricken Jews on the Day of Pentecost: 'Men and brethren, what shall we do?' (Acts 2:37). It was the same with the Philippian jailer: 'Sirs, what must I *do* to be saved?' (Acts 16:30). So it was with the prodigal son— 'Make me as one of thy *hired servants*' (one who *works* for what he receives) was his thought (Luke 15:19)."[1] None of those involved in these illustrations knew precisely what they must do or thought they must do, but they were certain that they had to do something.

The human mind is always flattered when it is conscious of doing something for God. What is more, for his doings man considers himself entitled to a reward. How pleased we should all be if we could only earn salvation! In that case we would have succeeded in bringing God into the humbling position of being in debt to us, and we would love it. But this is not the way of salvation.

What is the way? Jesus shows the way in our sentence: "The work of God is this: to believe in the one he has sent." It is not what we can do for God but rather what God has already done for us. All that is required of us is that we believe it. The Philippian jailer had asked Paul, "What must I do to be saved?" It was the question of the crowd that had sought Jesus. Paul answered just as Jesus had done before him: "Believe in the Lord Jesus Christ, and you will be saved" (Acts 16:31). Jesus is the One whom God has sent into the world to meet our deepest need. "The work of God" is to "believe" on him. What God requires of us is that we give up trying to please him by our own efforts and instead commit ourselves into the hands of our Savior.

Human Works

The burden of this study must obviously be upon what it means to commit oneself into the hands of the Savior. But before dealing with that it is necessary to deal just a bit further with the matter of human works, for it is these much more than the Savior that men would like to trust.

To begin with, someone might well ask the question, "But is it possible to enter heaven without good works?" The answer to the question is no. You cannot enter heaven without good character. But since we are talking about good works or character we must go on to the next question and ask, "But how good must that character be?" The answer is that your works must be without flaw. They must be perfect; you must be perfect. Clearly, nothing less than perfection could satisfy God. But do you have perfect character? Of course not! No one is perfect. Then, where can you get it? The answer is: Only from God. God offers you the perfect character of the Lord Jesus Christ. This will stand to your account just as the money of a rich man would stand to your account were it deposited in your account in your bank. Moreover, God will credit your sins to Jesus, who has died for them. God asks that you believe this, that you accept what Jesus has done.

What are you trusting rather than the Lord Jesus Christ? Is it rites and ceremonies? Some people think that their baptism will save them. But these are signs of what God has already done, not means of salvation. Baptize the devil, if you will, but his end will still be the lake of fire. Some people trust their humanitarian efforts. They give to the United Fund. They help the poor. But these things, while good in themselves, will not satisfy the righteous demands of a holy God in the day of his judgment. Then, what must you do? The answer is that you must do nothing—you can do nothing—except believe on the Lord Jesus.

I realize that no one will ever abandon his or her own attempts at righteousness until convinced that all human efforts are worthless. All must see that they fall short of God's perfect demands. On the other hand, when the worthlessness of human works in the area of satisfying God is revealed to a person by the Holy Spirit, then, I am convinced, he can lay hold on the Lord Jesus Christ in joy for his salvation.

"Put That on My Account"

I am now going to return to what it means to believe on the Lord Jesus. But I am going to do so by means of a story. It is a story from one of the short books of the Bible—Philemon.

Philemon was a rich man who lived in the city of Colosse. We know that he was rich because it was in his house that the Christians of Colosse were meeting. Besides, he had at least one slave (and probably more). Philemon had been converted through the ministry of Paul, though probably not at Colosse, since there are verses in Paul's letter to the Colossians that indicate that he had never been there. Since Paul had worked for a long time at Ephesus, and Colosse was nearby, it may be that Philemon had met Paul in Ephesus while he was on a business trip. Whatever the case, Philemon returned to Colosse as a Christian.

Time passed, and the day came when one of Philemon's slaves, a man named Onesimus, ran away. There is no evidence that Philemon pursued Onesimus. But this was still a serious matter. The law had been broken. And the law in the matter of a runaway slave (if accused by his master) proscribed death. Moreover, we know from Paul's letter that Onesimus had robbed Philemon before going. On these funds he probably made his way the great distance from Colosse to Rome.

We are told nothing about Onesimus's life in Rome, but few people would doubt that he had a good time, enjoying life to the full. He probably was something like the prodigal son who, we are told, "squandered his wealth on wild living." Onesimus probably did not have a thought for God. He had rejected that when he had turned his back on Philemon. But God had his eye on Onesimus and eventually brought him into contact with Paul, the very man through whom his master had been converted. How did he meet Paul? We do not know. Paul was in prison, so perhaps Onesimus had been arrested and met Paul in prison. God uses rough ways at times in dealing with those who run from him. But whatever the means, Onesimus met Paul and was converted.

After Onesimus's conversion we can be sure that Paul continued to instruct him in the faith. So I can imagine the day when, under the conviction of the Holy Spirit and in the light of the Word, Onesimus unburdened his conscience. "I need your advice, Paul," he might have said. Then the story came out—the theft, the flight, the loose living, the fear of capture, and now the seemingly impossible task of making right a great wrong. "I feel I ought to go back in accordance with the law and make right what I have done wrong. But I have no money to repay the loss. And returning might even mean my arrest and execution. What should I do?"

Paul replied—in what is surely one of the great examples of the love of Christ within the life of a redeemed sinner—that he would become surety for Onesimus. He would permit Philemon to charge any debt that Onesimus might have incurred to his own account. Moreover, he would write a letter to Philemon that would plead Onesimus's case.

What a picture we have as we imagine Onesimus hurrying back to Colosse with Paul's letter safely tucked into his belt. We can imagine Philemon standing at the gate of his beautiful Roman villa, looking down the road toward the heart of the city. Suddenly he looks up and exclaims, "Why, I believe I see that thief Onesimus coming! Oh, it couldn't be he! He wouldn't have the face to come back here after what he has done! But it does look like him. I'll wait and see." Probably Philemon is reasoning that, if it is Onesimus, it is because the money he stole is all gone and he is going to beg for pardon.

"Master! Master!" Onesimus cries.

"Well, it is Onesimus after all," says Philemon. "I'm surprised that you have the face to be seen around here again."

"Just read this," says Onesimus. He refuses to utter a word in his own behalf.

Philemon takes the letter, breaks the seal, opens the pages, and then slowly begins to read—*Paul, a prisoner of Jesus Christ.* "Why, this is from Paul!" says Philemon. "Have you seen him, Onesimus?" he asks eagerly of the returning slave.

"Yes, master, in Rome. It was in prison. He led me to Christ."

Philemon reads on—*and Timothy our brother, to Philemon, our dear friend and fellow worker. . . .* "How like Paul," he was thinking. *And to Apphia our sister.* "Come here, Apphia," Philemon must have called to his wife. "Here is a letter from Paul, from Rome. It seems that he is in prison."

Mrs. Philemon comes running and almost bumps into Onesimus. "Are you back?" she says in some surprise.

"Yes," says her husband, "but don't worry about that now. Onesimus has brought a letter from Paul, and first of all we must read it." *Therefore, although in Christ I could be bold and order you to do what you ought to do, yet I appeal to you on the basis of love. I then, as Paul—an old man and now also a prisoner of Christ Jesus—I appeal to you for my son Onesimus, who became my son while I was in chains.* "He means he was converted," Philemon must have thought. "But I wonder. He would not be the first slave to try to put it over on someone by using religion."

Formerly he was useless to you. "That's an understatement, if ever I heard one."

But now he has become useful both to you and to me. "Perhaps!"

I am sending him . . . back to you.

"Well," Philemon must have thought as he read through the letter, "Paul is certainly impressed with Onesimus, but I can hardly see how Onesimus could expect me to be. Not a word here about the robbery! Nothing about the wrongs that he did to me! Paul may believe that he is a Christian, but I will not believe it until the theft is out in the open and Onesimus admits his wrongdoing."

Philemon gets to the end of the letter, however, and there he finds this: *If he has done you any wrong or owes you anything, charge it to me. I, Paul, am writing this with my own hand. I will pay it back—not to mention that you owe me your very self.* I suppose that in that moment, Philemon's heart was conquered. He knew what Paul was saying. What is more, he knew that Onesimus had confessed his sin and had returned on Paul's recommendation and with confidence in Paul and in his relationship to Philemon. Paul was becoming surety for Onesimus. Although old and in prison, Paul was offering to pay. Onesimus had trusted him. Who can doubt that at this point Philemon freely forgave Onesimus and received him as he would have received Paul?[2]

A Pageant

The connection between this story, the failure of human works, and the need to believe on the Lord Jesus Christ for salvation is obvious. This is a pageant, if we may so understand it. Philemon is playing the part of God the Father. Paul is Jesus Christ. You and I are Onesimus. What have we done? We have wronged God. We have stolen from him that which is rightly his—honor, worship, glory, obedience—and we have run from him in order to sin our fill. There is no chance of our ever being able to make up that which we owe, and beyond that there is the whole matter of forgiveness and of the good will of the Father.

What shall we do? Shall we trust to good works, moral reformation, ceremonies? None of these things will do. Instead we come to Christ and find him interceding on our behalf. "Father," he says, "this runaway slave has wronged you. He owes what he can never repay. But he believes in me. He has been changed. Therefore, I ask that you charge all that he has done to my account."

Do you see that great picture of salvation? Will you come to God on the basis of that great offer of the Lord Jesus Christ? You can run farther, if you will. You can try to escape the consequences of your sin, if you wish—though you will not succeed. Or you can accept the work of the Lord Jesus Christ on your behalf and trust in him as your surety. If you look to yourself you may well tremble. But as you look to Jesus you will hear that still, quiet voice of the Holy Spirit that speaks comforting words on your behalf:

> Arise, my soul, arise! Shake off thy guilty fears;
> The bleeding sacrifice in my behalf appears:
> Before the throne my Surety stands—
> My name is written on his hands.

On this basis no charge shall ever be raised against you. And you will know that the true work of God is done when you believe on Jesus.

78

"I Am the Bread of Life"

John 6:30–35

So they asked him, "What miraculous sign then will you give that we may see it and believe you? What will you do? Our forefathers ate the manna in the desert; as it is written: 'He gave them bread from heaven to eat.'"

Jesus said to them, "I tell you the truth, it is not Moses who has given you the bread from heaven, but it is my Father who gives you the true bread from heaven. For the bread of God is he who comes down from heaven and gives life to the world."

"Sir," they said, "from now on give us this bread."

Then Jesus declared, "I am the bread of life. He who comes to me will never go hungry, and he who believes in me will never be thirsty."

In the early years of my ministry, when I was still doing graduate work, I had opportunity to study the Book of Amos in detail. I remember from those studies a passage that gripped me then and that still grips me whenever I remember it. Amos is speaking of a day when God's judgment will be such that there will be no one to preach true doctrine and when men and women will wander up and down and will not be able to find it. He casts the situation under the image of a famine and says, "'The days are coming,' declares the Sovereign LORD, 'when I will send a

475

famine through the land—not a famine of food or a thirst for water, but a famine of hearing the words of the LORD. Men will stagger from sea to sea and wander from north to east, searching for the word of the LORD, but they will not find it'" (Amos 8:11–12).

This is a horrible prophecy. But in some ways it is even more horrible to have the Lord Jesus Christ, the bread of life, available (as he is today) and yet have men refuse to come to him. Men have great hunger—a hunger for truth, righteousness, peace, joy, spiritual satisfaction, and other things. Jesus is the answer to this hunger. Yet the tragedy is that men will not come to him.

Jesus showed the wisdom of coming when he told the people who had followed him to Capernaum in Galilee, "I am the bread of life. He who comes to me will never go hungry, and he who believes in me will never be thirsty" (6:35).

Manipulation

Jesus had been talking to people who had been present on the other side of the Sea of Galilee when he had multiplied the loaves and fish. They were interested in having the miracle repeated. They had been taught by their rabbis that when the Messiah would come he would duplicate the miracle of the giving of manna that had been given originally by Moses. Jesus was claiming to be the Messiah. They could see that. Why, then, should they not expect him to duplicate Moses' miracle, particularly that aspect of the miracle that had to do with his repeating it six times a week for the entire forty years of desert wandering?

The Jewish writings said, "You shall not find the manna in this age, but you shall find it in the age that is coming" (Midrash Mekilta on Exod. 16:25). "For whom has the manna been prepared? For the righteous in the age that is coming" (Midrash Tanchuma, *Beshallach* 21:66). "What did the first redeemer do? He brought down the manna. The last redeemer will also bring down manna" (Midrash Rabba on Eccles. 1:9).

No doubt the people had heard such sayings as these and had them in their minds. But as I study the story of this conversation it seems to me more and more that they were far less desirous of that age of messianic blessing than they were of a successful outcome to their efforts to manipulate Jesus into doing what they wanted. Manipulation! That is the real clue to their questions. Jesus had spoken of the fact that he was God's gift to men and that God desired men to believe in him. They replied, in effect, that they would not believe unless they received a sign. We find it hard to imagine how they could overlook the sign they already had received. But they were actually saying something like this, "We admit, Jesus, that you did a wonderful thing yesterday. But before we believe in you as the Messiah we want to see a real sign. What you did was interesting, but we are Jews and we cannot forget that when Moses fed the people he did so for forty years. We will believe in you if you can do what Moses did and feed us now."

The Lord Jesus Christ does not stoop to answer this type of arrogant question on the part of sinful men. Thus, he simply overlooked the suggestion and instead directed his remarks to the real, spiritual issue. He said two things about Moses. First, Moses did not give manna. God gave it. It was God's miracle. Second, the manna that was given was not the true bread from the true heaven. It was only earthly bread from a visible sky. He then turned away from the person of Moses entirely and instead pointed to himself as that true bread which alone satisfies the real hunger of the human soul.

"I am the bread of life!" This solemn saying is the first of seven such sayings in John's Gospel: "I am the bread of life" (6:35); "I am the light of the world" (8:12; 9:5); "I am the gate" (10:7, 9); "I am the good shepherd" (10:11, 14); "I am the resurrection and the life" (11:25); "I am the way and the truth and the life" (14:6); "I am the true vine" (15:1, 5). So we take this first saying, spoken in this significant context, and we look at it for what it teaches about Christ and our condition.

The Message

It is obvious that when the Lord Jesus Christ spoke of himself as the bread, he was using an image about which everybody knew. So we turn to what people knew about bread for his meaning. What is important about bread? The first answer is that bread is *necessary for life*. When I was in the process of preparing this chapter I asked the following question at the dining room table one evening as a number of us were gathered around: "What makes bread important?" This was the answer I received: "Bread is necessary for life." What is more, as we talked about it we saw that in Christ's day bread was even more essential than in our own time, for it was the only staple in most persons' diets. Without bread, men died. If you see that, then you also see that Jesus was claiming to be the One whom men and women could not do without.

Are you trying to do without him? Are you going your way saying, "I'll take care of myself. I can get by. I live in an affluent age. I have a house, a car, plenty to eat, a good job, a wife, a family. I don't need Jesus"? What if everything in this entire life should go well for you, but you should lose your soul? Would that be a gain? Would you consider it a good bargain to do without Jesus forever?

You cannot do without him. You can manage after a fashion, for a time, but you cannot survive. In another of the "I am" sayings Jesus declared, "I am the way and the truth and the life. No one comes to the Father except through me" (14:6). He is the life. You will remain dead spiritually without him.

Second, bread is *suited for everyone*. Not everyone can eat everything. Some people can never eat sweets. Others cannot eat shellfish. Some cannot eat certain kinds of meat. The nursery rhyme says, "Jack Sprat could eat no fat; his wife could eat no lean." But bread is suited for everyone. In the same way, the Lord Jesus Christ is perfectly suited to the needs of all men. Sometimes people tell me, "Jesus may be all right for the kinds of people you talk to, but he is not for me." That is not at all uncommon. If a person is of more than average intelligence, he tends to think that Christ is only for the dull. If he is dull, he thinks that Christ is only for the intelligent. If he is sophisticated, he thinks that Jesus is only for the common people, and so on. But Jesus is for all. He is for you. He is the Savior of the world, and that includes the peasant as well as the king on his throne. Jesus Christ is great enough and glorious enough so that you will never exhaust him either in this life or in eternity. He has what you need. What is more, he knows you and he knows how to meet that need.

Our Daily Bread

Third, bread *should be eaten daily*. This brings us into a whole new area, the area of the Christian life. Everything before this has had to do with trusting Christ initially. But when a person trusts Christ as Savior this is hardly the end. Actually, it is the beginning, for it brings him into a living relationship with the Lord Jesus Christ in which he is to grow by feeding upon him day by day.

This point puts us in mind of that phrase in the Lord's Prayer that says, "Give us today our daily bread." There is a great emphasis upon the words "today" or "daily" in this prayer simply because by means of them the idea of a repeated fulfillment of a request occurs twice. The Lord's Prayer has only sixty-five words (seventy-two in Greek). So anything that is repeated twice is important.

But why is it important? For many years commentators on this prayer simply did not know the exact meaning of the Greek word that is translated "daily," for this is the only place where it occurs. They had a rough idea. The word is translated in our Bibles. Still, no one could be quite certain what precise shade of meaning to give to it. In fairly recent times, however, scholars have discovered a piece of Egyptian papyrus that seems to contain most of this word. It is part of an account book and contains the reading: "_ obol for epious—." The writing breaks off at this point. But the word epious seems to be the Greek word epiousios (daily) minus the last three letters. The reference seems to be to something like a daily ration.

Interestingly enough, this meaning now seems to be supported by a seemingly parallel inscription in Latin found at Pompeii. This, too, is a list of expenditures, and it contains the phrase "five assess for *diaria*" (a term based on the Latin word for "day"). Since both these phrases seem to be part of lists itemizing what we would call a day's supply of something for a person or group of persons, it seems right to take both words in the same sense and refer them to rations.

Put these two texts together—"Give us today our daily bread" and "I am the bread of life"—and think of the truths that emerge from them. One truth is that God cares for our bodies. The Lord's Prayer is certainly speaking of this. Unfortunately, there always have been some in the Christian church who have tried to minimize the importance of the body on the mistaken conviction that by doing so they were somehow becoming more spiritual. But that is not right. Christianity is the only religion in the world that takes the body with full seriousness. It teaches that God gave the body as well as the soul, and that a redemption of the body as well as a redemption of the soul is part of the divine plan. Therefore, it is right to pray for this world's needs, for food, homes, clothing, and other necessities. We have an illustration of the Lord's concern for physical needs in the fact that he fed the multitude.

On the other hand, there is also the truth that God is able and willing to provide for our spiritual needs, and this is far more important. We have spiritual needs as well as physical needs, though in our fallen state we may not be so conscious of them. Will we allow Jesus to satisfy those needs also? All we need to do is come to him, and come daily.

Tragically, many Christians allow the love of things to intrude between themselves and Jesus and, therefore, go on being spiritually hungry. In the Old Testament we are told that this happened repeatedly with the people of Israel. We are told that they desired things instead of God. Therefore, God gave them "things" but "sent a wasting disease upon them" (Ps. 106:15). We do the same thing today. One of our hymns describes us in the terms of God's description of the Jewish people in Old Testament times—"rich in things, but poor in soul." Is that your condition? Perhaps you have devoted most of your life to satisfying your hunger for objects, and yet you have never looked to God in order to be fed spiritually. You pray, "Give me my physical needs." But you have never made a habit of praying, "Give me that spiritual bread that comes down from heaven."

Most of our hungers are all right in themselves, of course, although we often get them out of proportion. They have been put within us by God. We have a valid desire for achievement, happiness, friendship, love, and success. But it is tragic that many Christians attempt to satisfy these hungers in the world's way while neglecting the truly satisfying task of spending time with God.

Fourth, bread also *produces growth*. We need to grow. The church of Jesus Christ is weak in our age, and it is weak simply because the individuals who compose it are not strong. Where are the great churches of a former age, churches filled with men and women who knew the great doctrines of the faith and were not afraid to trumpet them to a sleeping world? Where are the Augustines, the Luthers, the Calvins, and the Wesleys of our time? I do see some hopeful signs. The fact that some conservative churches are growing is hopeful. The Jesus movement is another hopeful sign. So are the great evangelistic crusades. But we do not have a strong church today. What we have is a weak, anemic Christianity, a lot of easy believism coupled with morality—and I include evangelical churches in that characterization. What is the reason for our sickly Christian postures? Undoubtedly, the reason is our deep failure to feed upon Jesus Christ who alone can make us grow.

The True Bread

Would you like to see such growth—in your church, in you personally? If so, you must feed on Jesus. This means, in the first place, that you must not look to other people as the source of your nourishment. That is what the people who had been talking to Jesus were doing. They were looking to the current teaching of their rabbis and to Moses. They were saying, "We are people of tradition. We look to what has been passed on to us by Moses through history." Do not look to the past. Do not look to men as the source of your teaching. I know that others can be the channels of good teaching. I am trying to be that myself for many people. But it would be terrible if a person should go away from hearing sound teaching and say, "But Dr. So and So said . . ." when you should go out declaring, "The Lord Jesus Christ has spoken thus." There is no power in the name of a human teacher. But there is power in that blessed name of Jesus, that name that is above all earthly names. Before him, every head shall bow and all knees bend.

In the second place, we must not look to earthly things for our satisfaction. The people of Christ's day were doing this. Are you looking only for your earthly needs to be granted? God will satisfy your earthly needs. He has promised to do it. But if that is the whole of your desire, even your major desire, then you are never going to see a great moving of the Holy Spirit of God in your life. We need to get our minds off ourselves and our needs, and we need to focus instead on the Lord Jesus Christ and his glory. And what great glory! What a great Lord!

Have you ever thought about all that grain must pass through before it becomes bread? It must first be planted and then grow. When it is ripe it must be cut down, winnowed, ground into flour. Finally, it must be subjected to the fiery heat of the oven. Only by this process does it become able to sustain life. This is what happened to the Lord Jesus Christ in order that he might become your bread. He was born into this world. He was bruised. He was cut down by sinful men. He passed through the fires of God's holy wrath as he took your place in judgment. This is his glory. He suffered this for you. How, then, can you refuse to feed upon him? Come to him! Draw from his fullness, and grow strong.

79

Those Who Shall Come

John 6:36–37

"But as I told you, you have seen me and still you do not believe. All that the Father gives me will come to me, and whoever comes to me I will never drive away."

$\mathbf{I}$n considering Jesus as the bread of life, it was pointed out in the last study that today's churches have not fed adequately upon that bread. The result is a sick and anemic Christianity in our century. If the verses to which we come now are understood and are allowed to penetrate the heart, they will cause the Christian who feeds upon them to be sickly no longer; instead, that person will grow and become strong. These are difficult verses—this section of John's Gospel may be among the most difficult portions of the book to assimilate—yet they are verses that carry us deep into the mind and heart of God.

These verses are given to fix our minds upon the grace and sovereignty of God in all things. They therefore take confidence away from anything that might be found in man and, instead, anchor it in God alone who alone is able to support it. They teach of man's sin and inability, God's electing and irresistible grace, the free offer of the gospel, and God's keeping power on behalf of his saints.

481

Another way of saying the same thing is to say that these few verses carry us deep into the principles of the Reformed or Calvinistic faith, although of course they do not date alone from the Reformation. This is the doctrine of Jesus Christ, Paul, Wycliffe, Luther, Calvin, Zwingli, Bullinger, Bucer, and other outstanding leaders of the Reformation period. These doctrines are reflected in many of our creeds, which in turn have become the official standards of many Protestant denominations. The official documents of the various branches of the Presbyterian and Reformed churches in Europe and America are all explicitly Calvinistic. The Baptist and Congregational churches, although they have no fixed creeds, have in many cases been strongly Reformed if we may judge from the writings of their major preachers and theologians. The Church of England and her daughter church, the Episcopal Church of America, have a Reformed creed in the Thirty-nine Articles. Moreover, even in Methodism (which is generally opposed to this system of doctrine) there is a body of Whitefield Methodists in Wales that even today bear the name of "Calvinistic Methodists."

In more recent times Hodge, Dabney, Cunningham, Smith, Shedd, Warfield, Kuyper, Spurgeon, and Berkouwer have all held these doctrines and taught them with conviction. In many cases they were taught under the acrostic of the "Tulip," which stands for: "total depravity," "unconditional election," "limited atonement," "irresistible grace," and "the perseverance of the saints."

These doctrines lie embedded in this section of John 6. And since they are so important, we are going to look initially only at the first two verses (vv. 36 and 37) where we find three great teachings: (1) man's inability, (2) election, and (3) the free offer of God's grace. After this we will return to the verses a second and a third time for a deeper study of these teachings.

Man's Inability

The first principle is the principle of man's total spiritual inability. It is taught in verse 36, in which Jesus says of those who had followed him from the far side of the Sea of Galilee to Capernaum, "But as I told you, you have seen me and still you do not believe." This is more than a mere description of the situation, for several verses later Jesus adds in speaking to the same people: "No one can come to me unless the Father who sent me draws him" (v. 44). In other words, the people *did not* believe because they *could not* believe, and because of this, Jesus was not in the least surprised by their attitude. They had witnessed all the evidence for Christ's claims that a person could wish. They had seen him, heard him. But they could not believe.

We must be careful as we say this to point out that the inability of man in spiritual things is not a physical inability and, therefore, that a man is not excused by his failings. He is guilty for his inability to believe. Let me explain in this way. Suppose that a man could be saved by literally getting up and walking over to Jesus. That would be easy to do if the man were in good health. But suppose he were lame. In that case, walking over to Jesus would be impossible; and because the inability was physical no one would blame the lame man. The same thing would be true if man's inability was analogous to physical blindness. We could say, "Look to Jesus and be saved." But if a man were blind, he could not look and no one would hold him guilty for that inability.

When we say, then, that the natural man has no ability in himself to turn to Jesus we are not speaking of a physical failing. We are speaking of something deeper, something that delves deep into man's nature, and for which he *is* guilty. A partial illustration can be found in the nature of animals. In the animal kingdom there are animals that eat nothing but meat—carnivores. There are animals that will eat only grass or plants—herbivores. Take a lion, which is a carnivore, and place a beautiful dish of oats or a bale of hay before him. Will he eat the oats or the hay? No! Why not? Is it not physically possible for the lion to eat oats? The answer is yes; it is physically possible for the lion to eat oats. But it is not in his nature to do so. Consequently, he will not eat them. In the same way, it is physically possible for a lamb to eat meat. But a lamb will not eat meat. So it is possible to say, in the same sense in which we are using the word of human inability, that it cannot.

In speaking of the will we come even closer to the true nature of man's problem. For the full tragedy of man's situation apart from God's grace is that man will not admit his need and will not come to the Lord Jesus Christ to have that need met. Moreover, since the will more than any other part of man's makeup is the real man, this means that man is totally depraved in spiritual things. Or, as we might also say, he is depraved at the very core of his being.

Those well-known verses from Romans 3 must be seen in this light. They say: "There is no one righteous, not even one; there is no one who understands, no one who seeks God" (vv. 10–11). Here are verses that express man's total inability to find or please God—in the area of the moral life ("there is no one righteous"), in the intellectual realm ("there is no one who understands"), and in the sphere of the will ("there is no one who seeks God"). Moreover, it is this combination that makes the case of man so desperate. Someone who does not hold to Reformed doctrine might say, "But surely the Bible teaches that anyone who will may come?" Of course! But that is not the point. On that we are all agreed. Certainly, anyone who will may come. But who wills to come? The answer is: No one except those in whom the Holy Spirit has already performed the entirely irresistible work of the new birth so that, as the result of the miracle, the spiritually blind eyes of the natural man are opened to see God's truth and the totally depraved will of the sinner is turned about to enable him to embrace Jesus Christ as his Savior.

When you as a sinner begin to understand this, when you begin to understand something of your nature and the absolute necessity for God's electing grace, then and only then do you begin to see how desperate your situation actually is. If you are holding onto the belief that you have some ability in spiritual things, no matter how small, then there is no great need to worry. Life is long. You can make yourself believe in the Lord Jesus Christ later, even on your deathbed, if necessary. At least you can take your chances on that being possible. But if you realize that the Bible is completely accurate and serious when it says that you are dead in trespasses and sins, that you cannot come to Christ apart from a miracle, the working of which is entirely in the sovereign choice of God, then you find yourself close to despair. For how can you be saved if it is neither in your nature nor power to trust in God and in the work of the Lord Jesus? You cannot. You have no hope; no hope, that is, unless God intervenes, in spite of yourself and your desires, to save you by pure grace.

Election

That, of course, brings us to the next verse. For if verse 36 says, as it does, that left to himself man is totally unable to believe on Jesus Christ or come to God, it is also equally and gloriously true that God does not leave all men to themselves but rather acts, in spite of man's will, to save some. So verse 37 declares: "All that the Father gives me will come to me, and whoever comes to me I will never drive away." It is because of this truth (and this truth alone) that Christians are able to preach and testify to Christ's gospel.

We need to enter into this sentence by looking into each of its parts. First, it speaks of the original position of all things, saying that all are in God's hands. This must be so if God is able to give some of those who are in his hands to Jesus.

I know that as we read this in the understanding of the flesh we are inclined to believe it is wrong. We like to think that we are each in our own hands so that we can each go in any direction we choose. However, that is not true. Within a certain limited sphere of activity it is true that you and I make our own decisions. But in this verse God is telling us the far greater truth, that we are held in God's hands in relation to everything important, whether we are believers in the Lord Jesus Christ or not. What is to be our fate, then, if we are not among those given by God the Father to the Lord Jesus Christ as his inheritance and for whom he died? Jonathan Edwards knew the answer to that question, and he presented it so graphically to those who heard him that men and women trembled in the pews and called out in desperation to God for salvation. "Sinners in the Hands of an Angry God" was his message. Terrible was the plight of those who spurned the Son but who could never escape the justified wrath of the Father! "There is no other reason to be given, why you have not dropped into hell since you arose in the morning, but that God's hand has held you up," he argued. "You need to consider yourselves, and awake thoroughly out of sleep."[1]

That is true. All you have and are—your health, wealth, mind, aspirations, even your very life—you have and are because God holds you. You would like to think that you are your own master, the captain of your own fate, but you are not. What happens to you is solely in God's pleasure.

But then, second, this verse also speaks of a great transaction, according to which some of those who have been held in God's hand in his suspended wrath have been handed over to the Lord Jesus Christ in his mercy. That is the greatest contract of all time, and this is not the only place in the Bible where this truth is mentioned. For instance, in the seventeenth chapter of John, Jesus speaks of those whom the Father has given him. In verse 2 he says, "For you granted him authority over all people that he might give eternal life to *all those you have given him.*" In verse 6 it is mentioned twice: "I have revealed you to *those you gave me* out of the world. They were yours; *you gave them to me* and they have obeyed your word." Verse 9 says, "I am not praying for the world, but for *those you have given me.*" And in verse 24 Christ says, "Father, I want *those you have given me* be with me where I am, and to see my glory."

Who are these who have been given by God the Father to Jesus Christ? They are those about whom Paul writes in Ephesians: "For he chose us in him before the creation of the world" (Eph. 1:4). These are the elect. We are told elsewhere that they are to form a vast and innumerable company.

Third, our text teaches that this great transaction that took place in eternity past between the Father and the Son is to be followed up by many specific changes in time. This is seen in the text in the contrasts between the tenses of the major verbs. In verse 37 where the Son is waiting for those whom the Father has given, the change is from the present tense to the future—"all that the Father *gives*" and "*will come.*" In verse 39, where the matter is looked at from the perspective of the eternal will of God, the change is from the past tense to the present—"of all that he *has given* me." In other words, the choice of God in eternity past has this effect—that men and women come to Christ now in time, coming as sinners who need to be saved, coming with nothing in order that they might receive everything from Christ.

It is in order to have men and women come in this way that the gospel is preached. It is why I preach it today. Will you come? Will you believe in Jesus? Do not say, as some do, "But if I am not among those whom God has given to Jesus, I cannot come." That is true. But you do not know whether you are among that number or not. All you know is that the gospel is proclaimed to you and that the command is given: "Believe in the Lord Jesus, and you will be saved." Will you come? I know that there are difficulties in sorting this out intellectually. But the text need not be a problem for you. It can be a blessed comfort. For if God has given certain persons to his Son—if this is irrevocably determined—why should you not be among them?

Finally, some should also be encouraged by the fourth point, which tells us that there is no exception in what is described here. For *all* that the Father has given to Jesus *shall* come. That is an encouragement even to the preacher of the gospel. There are periods in history when the gospel message seems to fall almost entirely on stony soil and little fruit is forthcoming. At other times the soil is receptive and much happens. What if the preacher, teacher, or lay evangelist were to peg his sense of accomplishment to these results? Well, it might be all right in periods of great blessing. But in times of drought how discouraged he would be! If, on the other hand, he is to take this text at full force, realizing that God is serious when he proclaims that *all* whom he has chosen shall come, then he can preach with full confidence and can rejoice to be a part of God's great plan of salvation.

Take heart, Christian worker! I do not know why God has chosen to save some through the foolishness of preaching and witnessing, but he has. Moreover, he has promised that all whom he has chosen to save will come. Nothing can stop them—not your failures (though you must take heed as to how you live), not even the devil! You may seem to be sowing seed at random and at times with little results. But God will see to it that some of that seed falls onto ground that he has prepared, and that it prospers. "Therefore, my dear brothers, stand firm. Let nothing move you. Always give yourselves fully to the work of the Lord, because you know that your labor in the Lord is not in vain" (1 Cor. 15:58).

The Free Offer of God's Grace

Finally, although it would be quite natural to stop at this point, it would not be right to stop without saying once more that none of these teachings is given to limit in any way the free offer of God's grace through the gospel. This is the offer of the second half of verse 37. In this study we have looked at John 6:36 and the first half of John 6:37. We are going to be looking at the second half of verse 37 in detail later, but even here it is not right to omit it. This half says, "And whoever comes to me I will never drive away." What a great offer that is! What a great promise! It is universal. It has no restrictions. It tells us that anyone is welcome to come in any way at any time. You can be young or old, bold or timid. You may have heard the gospel for the first time today or have been acquainted with it for the better part of a long lifetime. None of this matters. The only thing that matters is whether or not you will come to the Lord Jesus Christ as your Savior.

Someone will say, "But what must I do?" The answer is: You must stop doing. You have done quite enough for one lifetime, for you have ruined yourself by your doing. Your question should not be, "What should *I do?*" but rather, "What has *he done?*" The answer to that question is simply that it has all been done. He died for you. The work is finished. You need only to let go of your own attempts to earn God's favor and fall instead into the gentle and waiting arms of the Savior.

80

The Certainty of Divine Grace

John 6:37

"All that the Father gives me will come to me, and whoever comes to me I will never drive away."

John 6:37 demands discussion of a point passed over briefly in the last study. It is found in the first half of the verse, the half that reads, "All that the Father gives me will come to me." This is one of the great statements in the Bible of the doctrine of "the efficacious calling" of the sinner by God, or "irresistible grace." It is the teaching that all those whom God has chosen inevitably come to faith in the Lord Jesus Christ. This means that God's grace will not be frustrated, that the plan of salvation will come to a perfect completion, and that Jesus Christ will not have died in vain. This teaching necessarily belongs with those looked at earlier, for it is part and parcel of that Reformed system of doctrine that holds to the biblical teaching on man's total spiritual depravity and the necessity of God's electing grace.

Moreover, a little thought will show anyone who is willing to face these questions fairly that it must be this way. If we should attempt to make salvation ultimately dependent upon some act of man, no matter how small that act is, then nothing can be certain where salvation is concerned, and a statement like this—"All that the Father gives me will come to me"—is impossible.

Alpha and Omega

Let me explain what I mean. If Jesus Christ died not knowing if men would believe in him or not, and without the guarantee by God that they would believe, then it is entirely possible that no one would have believed and that his death would have been for nothing. He would have died, but no one would have been saved. You cannot have it both ways. Thus, God either determines who will be saved and sees to it that they are saved, or there is at least the possibility that no one will believe in Jesus. And if there is the possibility that no one will believe, or even that some whom God has chosen and given to Jesus will not believe, then John 6:37 is untrue and ought not to appear in the Bible.

Some have tried to avoid this conclusion by introducing the factor of God's foreknowledge. They argue that God in his omniscience foresaw that some would believe and therefore sent Jesus Christ to die for them. But that does not help anyone out of the difficulty. In fact, it makes the difficulty worse. For, instead of making the salvation of an individual depend upon the depraved will of man, it actually makes even the death of Jesus Christ himself depend upon the will of man. For if God had foreseen that none would believe, then Jesus would not have come and died and the great drama of salvation would have been nipped in the bud—and all because of us! We would have been dictating to the Savior.

Instead of this reasoning, we must come back to the great biblical principle that God is not only the author of salvation in the sense of being the One out of whom the plan flows, but also the author in the sense that, like any good author, he finishes the story. Thus, God brings the plan of salvation to its perfect conclusion by irresistibly drawing men, women, and children to himself. He is the Alpha and the Omega, the beginning and the end, the author and the finisher of our faith. Moreover, this is precisely what John 6:37 is teaching.

Cords of Love

As I say this, however, I am aware that there has been some disagreement even among Reformed theologians, as to how God does this. There have been various theories. Everyone is agreed that if God is drawing men and women to himself irresistibly, he is nevertheless not coercing them. He is not forcing or manipulating men. The Bible says that he draws us with the cords of love. But how does he do this? That is the question.

One of the theories advanced to answer this question is that God so orders circumstances that by ordering them he leads the will to do what he desires. What are we to say to this theory? Certainly, we may say that on a human level this often is true. We see it, for instance, in the raising of our children. I did this with my two-year-old daughter. We were at church for a supper meeting at which the children were to eat together while the adults began their meeting. My daughter did not want to eat. In fact, she would not! I sat down at the children's table, telling her that I was tired—which I was. When she would not eat, I asked for a plate for myself and had it piled high with lots of red Jell-O. I took the first bite. It was all I ate, but as I ate it I remarked how good it was. I took another spoonful, but as I took it I passed it by her nose. Her mouth opened, and the Jell-O was gone. "You ate my Jell-O," I exclaimed. That was a good joke to her. She brightened up, and soon she was eating it all. In a few minutes she pointed to the meat. She wanted some of that. She drank some milk. Finally, she had not only finished dinner, she had even had seconds and thirds on the Jell-O. That is bending the will toward its own best interests through circumstances.

The difficulty with this theory is that it does not do justice to what the Bible has to say about the will as it is since the fall of man into sin. Before the fall this theory would have been operative. But since the fall, it is not. Here we must remind ourselves about the character of people's inability to choose God. Our inability is not physical; it lies deep in our nature. We will not believe. But this lies so deep in our nature that for all practical purposes the "will not" actually means "cannot." This is why the Bible speaks of man as being "dead in trespasses and sins." He is as unable to save himself as a dead man is unable to return himself to life. Therefore, no matter how propitious the circumstances may be, the answer is always the same. It is to reject Jesus.

Rebirth

What would it take for a dead man to respond physically to the voice of Jesus? The answer is that it would take something like a resurrection, a miracle. That was true in the case of Lazarus. Lazarus had been dead four days. Jesus called, and Lazarus came forth. Why? Because Jesus did a miracle in raising him to life. In the same way it requires something like that miracle if a man or woman who has been dead in sin is to believe on Jesus.

This is what the Bible teaches. Therefore, a second, better theory is that God calls people to himself irresistibly by means of a miracle. It can be described as a resurrection. More often it is described as rebirth. Have you never heard someone say that the birth of a baby is a miracle? Of course you have, and it is. It is this same miracle that God does spiritually in the life of anyone who comes to believe in Jesus. The order is this: (1) God chooses, (2) God regenerates, (3) the individual believes. Moreover, it is because God alone is active in the first two steps that the calling of God is 100 percent effective. Here are some verses that teach this.

First, James 1:18: "He chose to give us birth through the word of truth, that we might be a kind of firstfruits of all he created." This verse speaks of the moment at which the Christian life begins as the moment at which a child is conceived. It is telling us that this is done according to the will of the Father and not of the child. Who ever heard of a baby deciding on the time or place where it should be born? The idea is preposterous! Yet it is no more preposterous than the teaching that you and I become children of God by deciding that we would like to be born into God's family. If you are a believer in Jesus Christ, it is because the matter of your faith in Christ was decided first of all by your heavenly Father. He engendered you. Moreover, we are told that the means by which he did that was the Word of God, the Bible.

The second important verse to tell about our spiritual conception and birth is John 1:13. This verse tells us that those who are born again are born "not of natural descent [blood], nor of human decision or a husband's will, but born of God." This teaches that there are three ways by which a man or a woman does *not* become God's child. It is not by physical birth. This is the significance of the phrase "not of blood." We do not associate birth with blood today, except in the phrases "noble blood" or "blue blood," but blood was associated with birth in antiquity; this is the sense in which John is writing. No one becomes a child of God simply because his or her parents are children of God. No one inherits the relationship. Then, too, no one becomes a child of God through emotion. This is the heart of the phrase "nor of human decision." A person can be moved to tears in a revival service, for example, and still not be born again. Finally, it is not of his own will either; for, according to John, no one becomes a believer merely by sitting down and deciding entirely in himself that he or she will believe. We cannot do that. Well, then, how do we come to believe? The answer is that we come to believe simply because God first does a miracle in order to make us alive spiritually.

A person must believe. You must accept Jesus if you are to be saved. But the question is: Why do you accept him when another person does not? Or, why do you reject him when another comes to him? Is it anything in man? Of course not! If that were the case, there could be boasting in heaven. Salvation is not of man, salvation is of God who intervenes. Men believe because God has first regenerated them, rather than it being the other way around.

Birth from Above

A third important verse on this subject is John 3:3: "No one can see the kingdom of God unless he is born again." In one sense this verse merely repeats what I have been saying. It tells us that a person must experience spiritual birth if he or she is to see spiritual things (cf. 1 Cor. 2:14). But it is also true that it adds a bit more. For one thing, there is a choice of words in the expression "born again" that is a clue to the fuller meaning. There are two words for "again" in the Greek language. One word is *palin*, which refers only to the repetition of an act. This is not the word used. The other word is *anothēn*, which means both "from above" and "again." Clearly, by using this word, John expressed the idea that the new birth must come from God alone and not from man.

Moreover, even the idea of repetition ("again") is not mere repetition. For *anothēn* also means to have the act repeated by the same one who acted the first time. In other words, just as God made Adam alive once by breathing into him the divine breath so that he became a living soul, so it is necessary for God to breathe into a man the second time in order that he might be brought to life spiritually. It is hard to miss the fact that this is precisely what is involved in the quickening of a dead soul, for a few verses farther on Jesus speaks of the fact that the new birth takes place by means of God's breath or spirit. He says, "No one can enter the kingdom of God unless he is born of water and of the Spirit" (3:5). God's spirit is his breath. His breath must fill our spiritual dust if it is to be animated.[1]

The last verse is 1 Peter 1:23: "For you have been born again, not of perishable seed, but of imperishable, through the living and enduring word of God." There are many images for the Bible in the Word of God. The Bible calls itself a lamp to our feet, a light to our path. It is a hammer, a rock, a mirror, a sword. It is milk for the infant. It is a schoolmaster to bring us to Christ. These are all great and good images, but none is so bold or striking as the image for the Word of God that occurs in this verse from 1 Peter. Here it is sperm, the male life germ. Peter is saying that God uses his Word to engender spiritual life in an individual, just as the human father implants his life within a woman in the act of engendering a child.

What happens when a man or a woman is born again? First, God takes the ovum of saving faith and gives it to the individual; for we are told that even faith is the gift of God (Eph. 2:8). Next, he sends forth the seed of his Word so that the living Word pierces the egg of faith and engenders life. In this act a new spiritual life comes into being. And if anyone should inquire after the mother, the answer is that the church fulfills this function. For it is within the womb of the church that the Word is preached and in which the embryo can grow until it comes to the point at which the new life becomes visible and the cry of confession announces the reality of new birth.

It Matters

If you are a Christian, this is a great truth for you, for it is a truth that gives tremendous importance to what you become in Christ and to what you do. God has a plan. So if he has chosen you and called you to himself in the course of his day-by-day unfolding of that plan, then where you are and what you do where you are matters.

Here is an illustration. According to any system of theology that places the ultimate decision in salvation with human beings, salvation is something like getting on a train that takes you away from your environment. It comes from somewhere else, passes through your town, and goes on to glory. Grace is involved, of course. God did not have to send the train. But still, your efforts are involved. You have to get on, and it takes you away. What I have been teaching is different. According to this system, you are not even on the platform. You are at home. But God comes on the train; he gets off; he goes to your house; he does a miracle in your life. And then, he instructs you to live for him there, because that is important to him.

If you see that, you will realize that the most important thing in this entire universe is, not what is happening in the halls of our heads of state or in the laboratories of the world's most brilliant scientists, but what is happening in you now. This gives importance to whatever you do. It means, you matter.

Are you saying, "But I am far too insignificant; I am not important"? In the world's eyes, yes, that may be true. But it is not true for God. In Shakespeare's *King Lear* there is a dungeon scene in which a number of selfish nobles are about to put out the eyes of an old man named Glouster. It is a wicked deed, and they are doing it for their own selfish ends. On the stage with them is an exceedingly minor character in the play. He does not even have a name. In the list of *dramatis personae* he is just called a servant. No one has been paying any attention to him. Nevertheless, in this one scene he rushes across the stage to defend Glouster. At once one of the nobles turns about and simply cuts him down with his sword. Then they go on and blind the old man anyway. Who is important in this scene? The world answers, "the noble." But if this were real life and we were looking at the play from God's perspective, the right answer would be, "the servant." For he did the right thing at the right moment.

We do not see this great drama of life clearly. God is the only One who knows the end from the beginning. We do not know the importance of our role, but we do know that he has created us and called us so that at this particular moment in the drama, in the play called "Time," we might take the part he has given in a way that is honoring to Jesus Christ. Will you take that role? Will you live for him? This is the spiritual meat of the text that tells us that all whom the Father has given to Jesus shall come to him and that no one who comes will be cast out.

81

No One Driven Away

John 6:37

"All that the Father gives me will come to me, and whoever comes to me I will never drive away."

The record of John 6:37 is one of the great texts of the Word of God: "whoever comes to me I will never drive away." This verse swings the broad gates of heaven wide open and promises that Jesus will receive all who come to the Father by him. It means that the gospel is for you if you will hear it and come to Christ. It is for you personally.

Years ago in the Midwest there was an old German farmer by the name of Klein. He was an ungodly man. Although he lived across the street from an Evangelical Lutheran Church, he never went in; and, of course, he did not believe the gospel. To his way of thinking, the gospel was for other people, not for him. One day, however, the Bible school of the church began to teach the Bible school children the chorus of the hymn that goes:

> Grace! Tis a charming sound,
> Harmonious to the ear;
> Heav'n with the echo shall resound,
> And all the earth shall hear.
> Saved by grace alone!
> This is all my plea:
> Jesus died for all mankind,
> And Jesus died for me.

From his listening post across the street Mr. Klein heard the children sing. He heard most of the words clearly. But when they came to the line "Jesus died for all mankind," he thought they were singing "Jesus died for old man Klein, and Jesus died for me." The thought that Jesus died for him personally finally sank into his heart. Klein crossed the street to the church, attended services, and eventually committed his life to the Lord Jesus Christ.

That is the message of John 6:37. Put your name in that song and say, "Jesus died for Mary Jones, John Smith, Paul Brown, Betty Harris, or whatever your name might be." Jesus died for you if you will come to him.

Belief and Trust

Before we go on to see just how wide this text is—how wide heaven's gates are flung open by it—we need to explain, first of all, what is meant by the word "come." Jesus said, "Whoever comes to me I will never drive away." What does it mean to come to him? One answer to that question is that Jesus is clearly talking about faith. To come to Jesus means to have faith in him. This channel of salvation is always spoken of in the Bible. "For it is by grace you have been saved through faith," Paul wrote to the Ephesians (Eph. 2:8). "Without faith it is impossible to please God," said the author of Hebrews (11:6). Faith in Jesus is commitment to Jesus based upon a belief that he is who he said he is and that he will do what he has promised to do for everyone who trusts him.

The great Baptist preacher Charles Haddon Spurgeon once wrote about faith: "Faith is not a blind thing; for faith begins with knowledge. It is not a speculative thing; for faith believes facts of which it is sure. It is not an unpractical, dreamy thing; for faith trusts, and stakes its destiny upon the truth of revelation. . . . Faith is believing that Christ is what He is said to be, and that He will do what He has promised to do, and then to expect this of Him."[1] Since Jesus said that he was dying for the sin of mankind and that he would save any who would commit themselves to him, saving faith is therefore just believing this and putting your life into the hands of the Savior.

Look at the same thing another way. What is faith? Faith is a simple thing. It is the eye that looks to Jesus, just as the eyes of the Israelites looked to the bronze serpent in the wilderness and were healed. Faith is the hand that grasps, just as Jacob grasped hold of the angel of the Lord, who wrestled with him by the brook Jabbok, and would not let go until he had been blessed. Faith is the mouth that feeds upon Christ, feasting on the bread of life and quenching its thirst with living water. Again, faith is clinging to Christ when it seems that this is all one can do. Faith is building on Christ so that a worthwhile structure begins to grow on that foundation. Faith is stepping out by faith in Christ when there seems to be nothing to step on, just as Peter stepped out onto the waters of the Sea of Galilee at Christ's bidding. Faith is trusting Christ and proving his promises.

Sometime ago a man introduced himself to me with the remark that he was a "C and E" Christian. I did not know what he was going to say, but I sensed what was coming.

"What do you mean?" I asked.

"Christmas and Easter," he answered. "I am the kind of Christian who goes to church on Christmas and Easter." I could easily have insulted him, but I held back and instead reminded myself of another Christian, an old saint from England, who called herself a "T and P" Christian. She wrote these letters in her Bible opposite promises that she personally had found to be true. The letters stood for "tried and proven."

Which are you? Are you a "C and E" Christian? In most cases that is no Christian at all. Or are you a "T and P" Christian, one who has tried God's promises by faith and has proved them personally?

I feel at this point that someone may say, "But I do not think that I can do even one of these things. I want to look up to Christ, but I cannot look. I want to grasp hold, but I cannot seem to do it. I want to feed on him, but I seem to lack the will even for that. I cannot seem to cling, build, step out, or prove his promises." But can you not simply let go then and fall into the waiting arms of Jesus? Suppose there is a fire and you are trapped on the third-story ledge of a building. The building is burning down around you and will soon fall. You are clinging to the ledge for dear life. Below are the firemen with their net. Well, can you not let go and fall into the net that will save you? That is all God asks. Merely release your hold on all that keeps you from him—whether this is your desire to run your own life, your own fine opinion of yourself, your low opinion of yourself, your good works, whatever it is—and fall into the net of salvation, into the waiting arms of the Savior. Jesus said, "Whoever comes to me I will never drive away."

Who May Come?

Let me make it even more personal. Who, according to this text, may come to Jesus? The answer is: anyone. How may they come? The answer is: in any way. When may they come? The answer is: at any time. How can it be more universal? The first half of verse 37 is written in the abstract—"*All* that the Father gives me will come to me." This is the part of Christ's sentence that deals with election. It is plural, designating a great number. It is abstract, for we do not know who those who are called by God are. The second half of the verse, however, our half, is both singular in number and personal—"him." It is Jesus' way of saying "You," whoever you may be, and however and whenever you may come.

Even if you are a great sinner, you may come. The Bible tells us that Jesus did not come to call the righteous "but sinners to repentance." What is your sin? Murder? Adultery? Theft? It does not matter. If you will come to Jesus, you will be received. "Whoever comes to me I will never drive away." Children of Christian parents, you who have been running away from the God of your father and mother, you may come! "Whoever comes to me I will never drive away." Backslider! "Whoever comes to me I will never drive away." You who are indifferent! "Whoever comes to me I will never drive away."

Some time ago I met a man who was indifferent toward Jesus Christ. He told me that he came to Tenth Presbyterian Church occasionally, adding that this

was "whenever my friends think I need a dose of religion." That kind of expo-
sure to religion will innoculate you against true faith and will lead you (with
a false sense of well-being) to a Christless eternity. Religion saves no one.
Christ saves. So Christ is for you if you are indifferent. Come to him. Jesus
said, "Whoever comes to me I will never drive away."

How May I Come?

Then, too, I want you to see that there is no restriction on how a person
may come, just as there is no restriction on who may come. How may you
come? The answer is: in any way.

Some come running. I have seen that many times. The gospel is preached;
these persons respond like Zacchaeus, who climbed a tree to get a saving view
of Christ, or like Peter, who jumped vigorously into the sea and swam toward
him. For these persons, the gospel is like a key in a lock, or a quarter in a soft-
drink machine. The results are immediate. Moreover, they seem to come in
the fullness of faith into a full knowledge of the gospel. Often, Catholics who
have not believed in Christ personally come in this way, for they often have
a true sense of God's sovereignty, righteousness, wisdom, and other attributes to begin with, and the gospel makes all of it fall into place.

Others come limping to Christ with poor, halting steps. They want to believe; they think they believe, a bit, in part; then they are not too sure, on the
other hand, that they do want to come. It makes no difference. These may
come too, for the words of Jesus do not specify how we may come any more
than they specify who may come. Coming is for anyone.

Perhaps you are one who has been holding back, resisting faith, just as Paul,
Augustine, C. S. Lewis, and many others have resisted. It makes no difference
here either, so long as you eventually commit your life into the hands of Jesus
Christ. Let me give you a personal illustration of this point. Some time ago, at
the University of Pennsylvania, workers for Campus Crusade for Christ began
speaking to a young black student who was apparently a Christian but who did
not seem terribly interested in Christian things. His chief interest was in making the freshman basketball team, and he had been working toward this goal
all through the fall of his freshman year. Actually he was resisting the gospel,
but the Crusade staff did not know this then. They invited him to a fall conference at which I was speaking. He did not want to go. He had no money, he
said. They gave him a scholarship. He then said he did not have a way to get
there. The staff offered him a ride. When he arrived at the conference he had
eaten no dinner, so he decided to go out for hamburgers instead of going to
the first meeting. His dinner did not take up the entire time of the meeting,
however, so he came in when it was just about halfway through. I did not see
this student enter but, apparently, just as he came through the door (wondering whether he would make the freshman basketball team—the final try-
outs were to be held on Monday) I said, "God loves you, whoever you are; he
offers you a plan for your life." This word struck him as directly from God. He

sat down and listened. He committed his life to the Lord, and he became the most effective witness of Christ's saving grace to the black community on the campus.

It does not matter how you come. You may come boldly, limpingly, reluctantly. The important thing is that you do come. Will you do that? Will you commit your life to Jesus?

When May I Come?

Finally, the words of Jesus are broad also as to when you may come. You may come at any time. You may come as a child. I am glad that children hear and respond to the gospel. Some say that you cannot preach to children, but that is untrue. Children can understand an enormous amount if someone will just take time to teach them. And they can follow Jesus. Are you a child? If you are, and if you can understand what I am saying, you should know three things: (1) you are old enough to sin, (2) you are old enough to die, and (3) you are old enough to come to Jesus. It is wonderful to come as a child. If you come as a child, you have a whole lifetime ahead of you in which Jesus can mold you into the kind of person he would have you be and can train you for the kind of work he has for you to do. I am glad that Jesus called me when I was young, for most of the decisions of my life, even at a young age, were made in view of that call and in view of the fact that I felt led to a preaching ministry. Children, will you not believe in Jesus and follow him?

You may be one who is saying, "But I have missed all that. I could have come as a child, but I did not come. Now I am old, and it is hard to change. It is too late for me." No, it is not too late! I will admit that there are increasing difficulties associated with advanced age. There are habits of mind. A young mind generally is more open. But God is equal to these difficulties, and men and women in old age come also. Why not you? If a number of those who have lived long lives before believing in Christ will come to Christ, why should you not be among them? You may not be able to do very much for Jesus because of your age, but he can do everything for you. Yours can be a great testimony. Though you will have only a short time on earth to serve him, you will have an eternity through which you can praise him.

Spurgeon once wrote, "Oh, my dear hearers, come to Jesus! Come in the morning when the dew is on your branch, for he will not cast you out. Come in the heat of noon, when the drought of care parches you, and he will not cast you out. Come when the shadows have grown long, and the darkness of the night is gathering about you, for he will not cast you out. The door is not shut; for the gate of mercy closes not so long as the gate of life is open."[2]

Will You Come?

Will you come to Jesus? The time is now; the place is wherever you find yourself at this moment.

A number of years ago I was in Egypt and stood on the banks of the mighty Nile River. Egypt owes her life to the Nile, so much so that the Egyptians have a proverb about it: "Egypt, the gift of the Nile." The Nile brings water, which makes the country one great oasis in the midst of the desert; the yearly inundations have long provided fertilization for the rich, dark soil. Nothing is greater or more valued in Egyptian life than the Nile. Yet for all its importance, the Nile is free and abundant to anyone who finds himself by its banks. Any dog, any cow, any person can drink of the river of Egypt and drink all he desires. So, too, with the grace of God. The river of God's grace is freely flowing. All may drink of it. Will you drink? You need only stoop down and scoop it up.

82

The Keeping Power of God

John 6:38–39

"For I have come down from heaven not to do my will but to do the will of him who sent me. And this is the will of him who sent me, that I shall lose none of all that he has given me, but raise them up at the last day."

Study of the sixth chapter of John has brought us to another great theme of the gospel, another plank in the system of doctrine known as the evangelical or Reformed faith. It is the keeping power of God. This aspect of theology has sometimes been referred to as the perseverance of the saints. But it is much better to speak of it as the keeping power of God, since it is God who perseveres with us far more than we with him. Simply put, this doctrine means that God never begins a work that he does not intend to finish and that, therefore, no one whom he has called to faith in Jesus Christ as Savior will ever be lost.

It is important that we understand this great truth, for, one way or another, our knowledge of it (or lack of knowledge of it) will affect our lives. If we do understand it, we will have a plank upon which we can stand, a foundation that is sure and upon which we can build.

499

Never, Never Drive Away

The doctrine of the keeping power of God is actually present in the verse that we studied in the last lesson, though we skipped over it then in order to stress the universality of the offer of the gospel to sinful men. The verse we were studying was John 6:37, which says, "All that the Father gives me will come to me, and whoever comes to me I will never drive away." The last phrase of that verse—"whoever comes to me I will never drive away"—certainly opens the gates of heaven to any man, woman, or child who will come. The gospel is for you, whoever you may be. At the same time, it also is true that the verse speaks of God's power to keep the one who does come, and to keep him eternally. We see this particularly in the original text, for the Greek contains a double negative that, in effect, denies that the one who comes to Christ will ever be driven away—either now or later. We can capture something of the effect by translating the verse—"whoever comes to me I will never, never drive away."

This theme is now developed more fully in the verses that follow. Here Jesus says, "For I have come down from heaven not to do my will but to do the will of him who sent me. And this is the will of him who sent me, that I shall lose none of all that he has given me, but raise them up at the last day" (vv. 38–39).

That . . . I should lose nothing! Not only is Jesus promising to reject no one who comes to him, he also is stating his determination to lose none of those who do come. Martin Luther saw this clearly and wrote, "Here Christ says: 'This is the will of Him who sent Me, that I should lose nothing.' He will not only refrain from expelling and rejecting anyone, but He is also resolved to keep them with Him and prevent anyone else from taking them from Him."[1]

For All Believers

Who are the ones about whom the verse is speaking? Who are those who will never be lost? The answer is that the verse applies to all who will come to the Lord Jesus. The "all" of verse 39 is the same as the "all" of verse 37. So, whoever you are and however you may have come, if you have come to Jesus as your Lord and Savior, this truth is for you. You may be aware of it, or you may not. You may believe it, or you may not. You may resist it, or you may not. It does not matter. If you have truly believed in the Lord Jesus Christ, then this verse is Jesus' own statement of the truth that you will never be lost. He will keep you. You can know that you will be in heaven one day as certainly as you can know that the Lord Jesus Christ himself will be there.

Let me make that explicit. In the last study it was pointed out that some people come to Jesus boldly. They hear the gospel, and immediately everything falls into place. They believe it, and they are as certain of their salvation in that moment as they will be forty years hence. Others come slowly and with many misgivings. They are constitutionally cautious and unstable. They are like butterflies in the garden that flit from flower to flower without settling down on any of them. In business they go from job to job. In Christian circles they go from church to church. They never are quite sure of their salvation. If you ask whether they have believed in Jesus as their Savior, they reply that they have but are not sure whether they have believed enough. Are people like that kept by God? Yes! They are as much in his perfect care as the one who comes boldly and completely at the beginning.

The same thing is true wherever a person may be along the normal span of human life. Take a child, for instance. Can that child who has responded to Jesus really believe these things? Does he know what he is doing? The answer is yes. "But so much lies ahead of him. He has so much growing and changing to do. Might it not be the case that his mind will be filled with other ideas later on and he will fall away from Christ?" Not at all. For Jesus Christ is keeping him. If you are a child, look forward to a lifetime of service for Jesus Christ. You will grow, and as you grow you will find that Jesus is even more wonderful than you think him now. You will find that he is indeed able to keep you and that you will not be lost.

Someone else is at the other end of the spectrum. You are in old age. You face sickness, increasingly restricted movement, eventually death. "Will I be able to keep myself strong in faith?" you are asking. The answer is that God is able to keep you. He will persevere with you. He will be as real to you in old age as he has ever been. In death he will be even closer. Moreover, even if you should be unaware of the fact that he is with you and will keep you and are fearful, that will not change the fact. For Jesus himself has said that he will lose nothing of all that has been given to him by the Father.

Are you saying, "But suppose I should get to the point where I would deny him?" May I be bold enough to answer that Jesus will keep you even then. Do you need an example? Take Peter. Peter lived with Jesus for three years, but at the time of the arrest and crucifixion Peter denied the Lord with oaths and cursings. Did Jesus forsake Peter? No! Peter was far from the Lord in that moment, it is true. But the Lord was not far from Peter. So we read that Jesus turned and looked on Peter and then later appeared to him personally and recommissioned him to service. This doctrine of the keeping power of God is for all. It is for you—whoever you may be, however you have come, whatever you may or may not have done.

God Is Faithful

Second, not only is the keeping power of God for all who have come to Jesus, it is also absolutely certain. It is certain because both the will and the power to keep those who have come to Christ from falling are God's. It would not be a certainty if the will and power were man's.

Our text speaks of God's will. We are going to look at God's will in more detail in our next study. God's power is spoken of in a dynamic and lucid way in 2 Timothy 1:12. In this verse Paul, who knew these truths, writes of God's power to keep his spiritual deposits. He says, "Yet I am not ashamed, because I know whom I have believed, and am convinced that he is able to guard what I have entrusted to him for that day." The verse is powerful in English, but it has a special power in the French translation. The French translation of one phrase says, *Il a la puissance de garder mon dépôt*. The metaphor is that of banking; and the translation literally means, "God has power to keep that which I have deposited with him." In other words, the verse is telling us that when we believe in Jesus Christ for our salvation we are actually trusting that God will be able to keep our spiritual deposits, and it is asserting that he will indeed keep them.

Capital Deposits

Have you trusted in God through faith in Jesus Christ? If so, think of the capital investments you have placed on deposit with him. First, your faith for salvation. Can God keep that? Of course he can! We turn to the Bible and discover Christ saying, "My sheep listen to my voice; I know them, and they follow me. I give them eternal life, and they shall never perish; no one can snatch them out of my hand" (John 10:27–28). Again we read, "Who shall separate us from the love of Christ? Shall trouble or hardship or persecution or famine or nakedness or danger or sword? . . . No, in all these things we are more than conquerors through him who loved us. For I am convinced that neither death nor life, neither angels nor demons, neither the present nor the future, nor any powers, neither height nor depth, nor anything else in all creation, will be able to separate us from the love of God that is in Christ Jesus our Lord" (Rom. 8:35, 37–39).

The love of the Lord Jesus Christ. What a theme! How wonderful to know that nothing can separate us from such love! There are things that would try. Paul lists three possible causes of separation from God's love in Romans 8, but then he dismisses them all.

First, there is sin. An honest Christian knows that although he is justified by God he is still a sinner and sins daily in thought, word, and deed. Such persons worry when they look at the sin that clings all too closely to their garments. "Well, what of sin?" asks Paul. "Christ has died for sin (past tense), and thus, in God's sight our sin is gone forever." Suppose someone should accuse us? "God is the judge," Paul answers. The Christian has been acquitted before the bench of the highest court of all, and no one is authorized to reopen his case.

Second, Paul speaks of physical suffering. And not only external suffering—tribulation, famine, nakedness, peril, and sword—but internal suffering too, that anguish of the soul that often is known by those who undergo persecution for the sake of their Lord and for the gospel. We read, "Yet for your sake we face death all day long; we are considered as sheep to be slaughtered" (Rom. 8:36, quoted from Ps. 44:22). It is in such suffering that we can be aware of the sustaining love of God.

All the words referring to this suffering are interesting, but the word "tribulation" in the King James Version has a particularly vivid mental picture associated with it. In the Greek language the word that is translated "tribulation" originally meant "pressure." It is the word *thlepsis*. This originally meant any kind of pressure—the pressure of a hand upon a table, the pressure of the wind against a sail, and so on—but in time it came to mean pressure that was oppressive or burdensome. At this stage the verb meant "to afflict" or "to harass," and the noun came to denote "affliction," "distress," or "oppression." In the Latin language, from which we got our English word "tribulation," the word referred to an instrument for threshing grain. This was done by beating the wheat from the chaff. Thus, when the word was applied to the calamities of this life it referred to their destructive characteristics.

We know such tribulation also. Sometimes it is the physical oppression of those harassed for their faith. At other times the pressure is mental, resulting from ridicule or from the tensions of our fast-paced society. Whatever it is, however, we are to know that it cannot separate us from Christ's love. God is able to keep our spiritual deposits for salvation in the life to come.

The third potential cause of separation from Christ's love is the existence of supernatural powers. But Paul says that even these cannot effect a separation. This was not an idle thought for Paul. He knew the extent of spiritual wickedness in this world and had wrestled against it himself. Moreover, he knew that this was the ultimate dimension of the struggle inherent in the Christian life. To the Ephesians he wrote, "For our struggle is not against flesh and blood, but against the rulers, against the authorities, against the powers of this dark world and against the spiritual forces of evil in the heavenly realms" (Eph. 6:12). But spiritual forces cannot be victorious over us.

The Bible says that Christ "having disarmed the powers and authorities, . . . made a public spectacle of them, triumphing over them by the cross" (Col. 2:15). Can we be separated from God's love through things present or things to come? Not by these things either. For God has chosen us in Christ from before the beginning of the world, and we shall be with him in glory long after time has ceased to have meaning.

God's Workmanship

Our faith for salvation is only one thing that we have deposited with God, however. If you are a Christian, you have also deposited your faith that he is able to accomplish his purposes in you in this life. Can God keep that? Of course he can! We turn to Ephesians 2:10 and read, "For we are God's workmanship, created in Christ Jesus to do good works, which God prepared in advance for us to do." In other words, when we come to Jesus we step out of one kind of life into another kind of life and are committing ourselves into the hands of One who is determined to form us, direct us, push us, and (if it is necessary) even kick us in order that he might mold us into the image of the Lord Jesus Christ.

We may take one more example. If you are a Christian, you have also committed unto God your faith that he is able to see you through temptation. Can

God keep that? Yes, that too. For we read, "No temptation has seized you except what is common to man. And God is faithful; he will not let you be tempted beyond what you can bear. But when you are tempted, he will also provide a way out so that you can stand up under it" (1 Cor. 10:13). Certainly God is able to keep our capital deposits.

And think what marvelous dividends he pays on the investment! It is not only that we are secure both for this life and the future but that we partake so richly of God's present blessings. There is a partaking of his love. There is joy. There is the peace that passes understanding. There are a thousand other blessings besides.

We are to be encouraged by the reality of these things in our lives. I once read the story of a little boy who went into a bank with just one penny to open an account. He went up to the teller and said, "Please, sir, I would like to deposit a penny in your bank." With a serious expression the teller took the penny and wrote out a bank book in the boy's name. Then he handed it to the boy and the boy went off. A little while later the boy came back and stood there looking up at the teller. "Yes. What is it, young fellow?" the teller asked. "Please, sir, I would just like to see if my penny is still in your bank." The teller held up a penny where the boy could see it. The boy smiled and went away satisfied.

It is our privilege to do that with God. He is not made weary with our childish questions. So, if the time comes (as it does to many Christians) when we begin to doubt the reality of spiritual things and our security, God has arranged it so we can come to him and say, "Please, Lord, I would just like to see whether the spiritual deposits that I have placed with you are still in the bank." If we ask him, God will provide the assurance. That is why Paul can write in the letter to the Philippians, mentioning just one of our dividends: "Do not be anxious about anything, but in everything, by prayer and petition, with thanksgiving, present your requests to God. And the peace of God, which transcends all understanding, will guard your hearts and your minds in Christ Jesus" (Phil. 4:6–7).

Where does it stand with you? Do you have faith in a God who is able to do all that he has promised—able to save, able to keep you from falling? Or are you uncertain, unstable? There is much that will make you unstable if you look first to the world instead of to God. Learn instead to look to God first, to that great God who is able to guard your spiritual deposits.

83

God's Will Confirmed by Jesus

John 6:40

"For my Father's will is that everyone who looks to the Son and believes in him shall have eternal life, and I will raise him up at the last day."

There is nothing certain in this world but death and taxes!" So goes a very cynical saying. This may be true in part for the unsaved person, but it is obviously not true for the Christian. For one thing, Jesus Christ may return for his own at any moment, in which case death will be avoided. For another, the Christian looks at that saying with the realization that whatever the case may be for others, in his case at least there are things that are far more certain.

We come to a number of these certainties in this particular portion of John's Gospel. They are certainties, Jesus tells us, because they are founded upon the combined wills of God the Father and God the Son. We can gain some feeling for the full strength of this combination of wills by recalling one of the promises that Jesus gave to his followers. He said, "Again, I tell you that if two of you on earth agree about anything you ask for, it will be done for you by my Father in heaven" (Matt. 18:19). If it is true that this shall be done upon earth in regard to our wills (when blessed and guided by the Holy Spirit), how much more true is it that this will be done when the wills of God the Father, God the Son, and God the Holy Spirit are combined.

This, then, is the sense of John 6:40 in which Jesus says, "For my Father's will is that everyone who looks to the Son and believes in him shall have eternal

505

life, and *I will* raise him up at the last day." As we try to enter into this text let us look first at the sovereign will of God; second, at the fact that this will is confirmed by Jesus; third, at the areas in which the wills of God the Father and God the Son combine; and fourth, at the truth that God is determined to carry out his will for us now. Our conclusion will be that this good and perfect will of God should be confirmed by everyone who calls himself a Christian.

God's Will

We begin with the sovereign will of God. What are we to say about that will? To begin with, it is beyond and above anything that we can know on this earth; indeed, it is the origin of all things and that according to which all things are ordered. God's will is absolute. It is unlimited. It is determined only by itself. God needs to consult no one in formulating and effecting his plans. God's will is independent. God's will is fixed, for it does not need to adapt to changing circumstances. It controls the circumstances, for it is omnipotent. "I the Lord," says God, "do not change" (Mal. 3:6). James writes that he is "the Father of the heavenly lights, who does not change like shifting shadows" (James 1:17). God's will is also irresistible, for he has foretold the end from the beginning and has promised to keep in his care all who come to him.

How would you change God's will? Would you change it for the better? You could not possibly change it for the better, for God's will is holy, just, good, and perfect. You cannot improve on perfection. Would you change it for the worse? Of course not, for we would not want God to be less than perfect even if that were possible.

"This is the will of him who sent me," says Jesus. We read that line, and we are terrified until we go on to read that the will of God is our salvation. Spurgeon wrote, "O God, I tremble at thy will, until I read those lines; I know not what thy will may be, and since I know it must be accomplished I cower down at thy feet in terror until I read that mercy is the Father's will, that love is the Father's will, that salvation is the Father's will, and then my heart flies into thy bosom with ecstasy and joy, to think that thine omnipotent, unchangeable will should be such good will; so full of benevolence, so full of love."[1]

God's Will Confirmed

Second, this section of John tells us that the good and benevolent will of God is confirmed by Jesus. Jesus says, in effect, "Yes, I agree; that is my will also; I pledge myself to see that this perfect and loving will is effected."

Let me illustrate this truth by the way in which a constable of the state might pledge himself as surety for a star witness scheduled to appear in a trial. The witness has been chosen by the court through subpoena. He is in danger, because friends of the man on trial might attempt to have the witness killed to escape the impact of his unfavorable testimony. The judge calls the constable. He says, "I want this witness to appear in court next Friday, and I want nothing to happen to him. I am committing him into your care. See that he appears at 10:30 A.M." The constable receives the witness and becomes surety for him, saying, in effect, "Your will is my will; I pledge myself to see that he appears next Friday at the hour appointed." That is what Jesus does for us, the only difference being that while a witness may be harmed in spite of the constable's care, with Jesus as surety none who are committed to him need ever fear being lost.

Jesus confirmed the will of God in the first instance by going to the cross. He said, "Here I am, I have come—it is written about me in the scroll. To do your will, O my God, is my desire; your law is within my heart" (Ps. 40:7, 8; cf. Heb. 10:7). He further confirms that will by drawing back to himself all who wander, by sanctifying them, and by bringing them irresistibly to that moment when they are presented to the Father without any sin, spot, or wrinkle.

A Sure Salvation

In this section of John, three areas of God's will concerning us are mentioned. First, verse 37 tells us that the will of God is seen in our *election*. "All that the Father gives me will come to me, and whoever comes to me I will never drive away." Quite clearly, the plain sense of this passage is that God has chosen a great company of persons, all of whom he has given to Christ and all of whom will come to him. The verse further tells us that Jesus confirms this aspect of God's will by promising never to drive away anyone who so comes.

I do not understand why this doctrine is so vigorously resisted by so many, unless it is due to the fact that this is simply unlike man's normal way of thinking and runs against his desires. People have imagined that the responsibility of human beings for their sin is lessened if one speaks of election. But this is not true. It is true that some have preached election in a way that implies that people are not responsible, but this comes from following the dictates of reason rather than the plain teaching of the Word of God. God elects, but we are also responsible. Thus, I can stand in the pulpit and preach anything that an Arminian can preach about man's sin and the necessity for him to surrender his will to the Lord Jesus Christ. If you have not believed on the Lord Jesus Christ as your Savior, your failure to do so is your own responsibility; you are already, therefore, justly under condemnation. If you would be saved, you must come to Christ. *You* must do it. You must yield yourself to him. At that same time, I can come to a text like this and declare with equal force that if you do come it is because God chose you in Christ before the foundation of the world and quickened you irresistibly by grace so that your eyes were opened to see who Christ is and your will was moved to embrace him.

Someone has illustrated this by describing the door of salvation as containing two signs. On the outside—"Whosoever will may come." On the inside—"Chosen in Christ before the foundation of the world." You say, "But am I among the elect?" I do not know. Believe in Christ; I will tell you the answer after you either receive or reject him. If you do believe, it is because the will of God the Father was confirmed by the will of God the Son in your election.

Second, verse 39 tells us that the will of the Father is confirmed by the will of the Son in the matter of our *preservation*. "And this is the will of him who sent me, that I shall lose none of all that he has given me, but raise them up at the last day." This verse tells us that God's will is that no one who believes in Jesus Christ should ever be lost. It tells us that Jesus confirmed this will of his Father by promising to raise up all who do believe at the last day.

I find it interesting that the promise is literally that Christ will lose "nothing" or "no thing." This certainly means "none," but the fact that the pronoun is neuter suggests more than this. The meaning is that not even one part of those who have believed in Jesus will be left behind. It is not a soul salvation about which Jesus Christ is talking; it is a whole salvation. We are to be saved spirit, soul, and body. This text reminds us of God's promise to Moses at the time of the Jewish exodus from Egypt. When God delivered the people, he did not deliver some and leave the rest behind. He did not deliver the people and leave their property behind. The promise was, "There shall not a hoof be left behind." So also for us the promise is that nothing that concerns any one of us will be lost.

Finally, the will of God is confirmed by Jesus in the matter of our entering into a *new quality of life now*. Verses 39–40 say, "And this is the will of him who sent me, that everyone who looks to the Son and believes in him may have eternal life, and I will raise him up at the last day." Eternal life is a present possession. Hence, this verse adds to the preceding thought of the keeping power of God the equally important thought that God is determined to accomplish his will in us now. We must not think that God begins a work in us at the moment of our initial faith in Christ, completes it at the moment of our death, but is completely indifferent to what happens to us in the meantime. That is absurd and unbiblical. On the contrary, the fact that God has placed his own, eternal and everlasting life within us is evidence that his will extends to the way we live, think, act, and grow now.

God Is Determined

Other verses also teach this. Philippians 1:6 is one: "Being confident of this, that he who began a good work in you will carry it on to completion until the day of Christ Jesus." This verse states that God is determined to carry out his plan in a Christian through this life until the moment in which the Christian dies or Jesus returns to take him home. Romans 8:28 and 29 also speak of God's present purpose in the life of a Christian: "And we know that in all things God works for the good of those who love him, who have been called according to his purpose. For those God foreknew he also predestined to be conformed to the likeness of his Son, that he might be the firstborn among many brothers."

This is a remarkable statement if we really understand it. To put the matter bluntly, it means that God's great purpose (of which our election, calling, and preservation are only a part) is to make each person who believes in Jesus Christ like Jesus. It means that God is so delighted with his Son that he has created and called millions of sinful men to himself in order that he might reproduce Jesus Christ in them and so populate the universe with millions of Christs where there was only one before. This does not mean that we will become divine. God is still God. We are his children, parts of his creation. But it does mean that we will be like him, like Jesus. This is the point in the whole matter of our present transformation.

I do not think this means that we will become increasingly aware of how good we are becoming. The opposite will be true. We will become increasingly aware of how sinful we are—like Paul, who early in his career called himself "the least of the apostles" (that is, he humbly called himself "number 13") but who toward the close of his life saw himself to be the "chief of sinners" (1 Cor. 15:9; 1 Tim. 1:15; cf. Eph. 3:8). We will not be conscious of increasing holiness. But we will be becoming more like Jesus even in becoming more aware of our sin. And we will be giving Christ more and more control over us so that his life will be seen in us increasingly. To put it in other words, it also means that what the Bible calls the fruits of the Spirit will be seen—"love, joy, peace, patience, kindness, goodness, faithfulness, gentleness, and self-control" (Gal. 5:22–23). This, too, is an aspect of God's will confirmed by Jesus.

There is a somber side to this subject, however. It comes from the fact that there will inevitably be times when the sovereign and irresistible will of God comes into conflict with our wills and we will attempt to resist the inevitable. When this happens, God will begin to deal with us, and his dealings will become sharper and sharper until we return to the path in which he has determined we shall go.

In the world of science today everyone is talking about the theory of continental drift that seems to be increasingly confirmed by various types of core samplings of the earth and by accurate measurement of positions upon the earth's surface. According to this theory, the world's surface (both above and below water) is divided into large segments called plates. These plates are slowly and ponderously moving. Thus, to give an example, North and South America are part of one plate, and this is moving away from the plate on which Europe rests at a rate of about one inch per year. On the western coast of the United States, this same plate is being passed by the enormous plate that underlies the Pacific Ocean. In this case the rate of drift is quicker, scientists estimating that adjustment along the edge is between four and eight inches annually. No one understands the forces that cause the great land masses to move. But they do move, and the movement is both fixed and irresistible.

The force of my illustration lies in the fact that earthquakes generally occur along the lines where these plates meet, but—and this is important—not at every point along the line. The San Andreas fault is an example. At places there have been violent earthquakes such as the San Francisco earthquake of 1906, or (farther south) the earthquake that devasted Managua, Nicaragua, in December of 1972. At other places along the same line there have never been earthquakes, and there will apparently never be any. What is the difference? The difference is simply that in the places where there are great earthquakes the edges of the two land masses lock in place and resist the movement. Pressure builds up; eventually the adjustment comes suddenly. In 1857, the Pacific side of the San Andreas fault jumped forward as much as 30 feet in the area of Fort Tejon near Los Angeles. On the other hand, in places where there are no earthquakes the land masses do not lock, and the adjustment is gradual. Geologists refer to the movement along these areas as creep.

May I apply that to the will of God for your life? God's will is as irresistible for you as the movements of the great, continental plates. We may not understand God's will, but it moves anyway and at its self-determined rate. What will you do? Will you resist it? If you do, the forces will build up and God will make the adjustment violently in your life. Or will you yield to it gradually? You will as by God's grace your eyes are opened daily to see his way and walk in it.

84

Murmurs of Disbelief

John 6:41–47

At this the Jews began to grumble about him because he said, "I am the bread that came down from heaven." They said, "Is this not Jesus, the son of Joseph, whose father and mother we know? How can he now say, 'I came down from heaven'?"

"Stop grumbling among yourselves," Jesus answered. "No one can come to me unless the Father who sent me draws him, and I will raise him up at the last day. It is written in the Prophets: 'They will all be taught by God.' Everyone who listens to the Father and learns from him comes to me. No one has seen the Father except the one who is from God; only he has seen the Father. I tell you the truth, he who believes has everlasting life."

It is one of the surest facts of Christianity that when the doctrines of man's total spiritual depravity and the necessity for God's electing grace in salvation are preached there will be resentment by many who hear them. That was true in Christ's day, and it is true in our own. Moreover, we do not have to go far to find either contemporary or historical examples.

The Jewish Leaders

In Christ's day this is precisely what happened. So we are not surprised to find that Jesus' teaching about the necessity for God's grace in salvation,

which we have in John 6:35–40, is immediately followed by an outbreak of
protest and resentment by certain of the leaders of Israel. The author of the
Gospel reports the moment by writing, "At this the Jews began to grumble
about him because he said, 'I am the bread that came down from heaven.'
They said, 'Is not this Jesus, the son of Joseph, whose father and mother we
know? How can he say, "I came down from heaven?"'" (vv. 41–42).

In these verses we have a change of persons from the verses that have gone
before, and probably a change of place. Up to this point Jesus has been speaking in the open to the crowds that had followed him from the other side of
the Sea of Galilee to Capernaum. Now he is speaking to the leaders who had
heard his teaching, and probably speaking in the synagogue of Capernaum,
as is suggested by verse 59. In this discussion Jesus restates his teaching and
supports it by evidence both from the Old Testament and from experience.

The first thing we are told, however, is that the Jewish leaders "grumbled
about him." The King James Version uses the word "murmur." What does that
mean? To understand what that means and to understand how close it comes
to what we do in our relationship to the gospel, we must realize that the word
"murmur" is one of those unique words in the English language that exist
solely because they sound like the thing they describe.[1] "Hiss" is such a word.
"Tinkle" is another; "buzz" is a third. Such words are often used in poetry
because of their unique character. One of the earliest examples of this device (known technically as onomatopoeia) is in Aristophenes' play *The Frogs,*
in which one of the lines given to those who represent the frogs sounds like
frogs croaking. Aristophenes wrote:

> Brekekekex co-ax, co-ax!

A better known example in the English language is Edgar Allan Poe's poem
"The Bells." To some degree the whole poem is built on this device, but these
lines will be an example:

> Hear the tolling of the bells,
>   Iron bells!
> What a world of solemn thought their monody compells!
>   In the silence of the night
> How we shiver with affright
> At the melancholy menace of their tone!

In this stanza the words chosen by Poe suggest the matter being described.
In exactly the same way then, murmur suggests by its sound what people do
when they disagree with someone and protest what he is saying. Murmuring
is the confused sound that runs through a crowd when people are angry and
in opposition to some teaching. This is what the leaders of Christ's day were
doing in regard to Christ's teachings. Others do it in our day. In fact, it is a
sin that few, if any, are preserved from.

Christ's Answer

It is interesting, too, that the objections of the Jewish leaders took the form of a criticism of Christ's person rather than a direct criticism of his teachings. They did not say, let us notice, "There are three reasons why we cannot agree with you and why we consider your views to be wrong." Christ's teaching was too consistent and too self-authenticating for that. Instead, they attacked him personally, saying, in effect, "Don't listen to him. He is a nobody from the sticks of Galilee, the son of a carpenter named Joseph. Listen to us." In this they revealed their consummate snobbishness, demonstrated their pride, and revealed their ignorance. The irony is that they did not recognize at all that there had been a virgin birth and that Christ's true Father was God.

What did Jesus answer? It is important to notice that Jesus did not answer by defending himself on the personal level, as we might like to do. He could have done it, of course. But instead of this he returned to his teaching and restated it, giving two proofs. This was a challenge to his hearers to investigate his teaching for themselves. Finally, after having restated his teaching and given his proofs, Jesus stated the doctrine again for the final time. The verses that contain this read as follows: "No one can come to me unless the Father who sent me draws him, and I will raise him up at the last day. It is written in the Prophets, 'They will all be taught by God.' Everyone who listens to the Father and learns from him comes to me. No one has seen the Father except the one who is from God; only he has seen the Father. I tell you the truth, he who believes in me has everlasting life" (vv. 44–47).

We need to take these statements one at a time. First, Jesus repeats what he had said earlier, but here he does so in even sharper language. Before, he had said, "You have seen me and still you do not believe. All that the Father gives me will come to me" (vv. 36–37). This implies that no one can come, apart from a special act of God on his behalf, but it does not say this negatively. Now Christ does. "No one can come to me unless the Father who sent me draws him."

This verse is so straightforward in its language that it has always been a battleground between those who are willing to accept the doctrine of election here taught by Christ and those who resist it on rational or humanistic grounds. It was discussed by Augustine and Pelagius, by Calvin and Arminius, by Luther and Erasmus.

The latter case is particularly interesting. Erasmus had been led to attack Martin Luther's teaching on the total spiritual depravity of man in a volume centering on the nature of the human will and on whether it can function in turning a man or a woman to God. Erasmus said it could. Moreover, he answered the obvious objection based on the argument of Christ in this verse— the objection that no one can come to Christ except the Father draw him— by saying that God draws people in the same way that an owner of a donkey might get it to move by holding a handful of carrots before its nose. The man draws, but obviously the will of the donkey is involved. According to this theory, God originates salvation but man nevertheless cooperates in it.

This may make good sense to the natural human way of thinking. But it is not what Scripture teaches, and Luther said so quite openly. What better drawing could there be, Luther argued, than the drawing of the Lord Jesus Christ himself? He was present among the people. He taught them personally. Still they did not come. In fact, they killed him. Luther concluded, "The ungodly does not 'come' even when he hears the word, unless the Father draws and teaches him inwardly; which he does by shedding abroad his Spirit. When that happens, there follows a 'drawing' other than that which is outward; Christ is then displayed by the enlightening of the Spirit, and by it man is rapt to Christ with the sweetest rapture, he being passive while God speaks, teaches and draws, rather than seeking or running himself."[2]

This was a good answer, of course. But we can go even further than this on the basis of Christ's statement. Luther's key word in answering Erasmus was "passive." He said that man was passive spiritually, inert, as inert as a dead man might be, if we may use that image. In John 6:44, however, there is in addition to this truth the thought that man also actually resists the work of God within. That is, he is not only passive; he also is perverse and obstinate.

We see this truth in the word that is chosen to speak of the Father's work in "drawing" a man or a woman to Christ. This word always implies resistance to the power that draws. William Barclay gives a number of examples of this in his devotional studies on John's Gospel. He shows that it is the word for drawing a heavily laden net to the shore, a net filled with a great number of fish (John 21:6, 11). It is the word that is used of Paul and Silas being dragged before the civil authorities in Philippi (Acts 16:19). It is used for drawing a sword from the belt or from its scabbard (John 18:10). Always there is the idea of resistance. So here also there is the idea that men and women resist God.

Curiously, however, Barclay adds that "God can and does draw men, but man's resistance can defeat the pull of God." The curious thing about this statement, though, is that not one of his examples shows the resistance to be successful. The fish do get to shore. Paul and Silas are dragged before the magistrates. The sword is withdrawn. Indeed, we can go even further than this. As Leon Morris notes in his commentary, "There is not one example in the New Testament of the use of this verb where the resistance is successful. Always the drawing power is triumphant, as here."[3] People resist. In this their depravity is seen. But the power of God always overcomes the resistance in those whom he has determined before the foundation of the world to give to Jesus.

Is this discouraging? Not at all. Actually, the fact that God does draw men and women to Christ in spite of themselves is our hope.

Evidence

At this point the Lord Jesus Christ gives two points of evidence to support his teaching. He did not need to give evidence, of course. His word was sufficient. Nevertheless, in speaking to these religious leaders he does support his statement—first, by a reference to the Old Testament, and then, second, by an appeal to experience.

His reference to the Old Testament actually is a partial quotation of Isaiah 54:13. Jesus says, "It is written in the Prophets, 'They will all be taught by God'" (John 6:45). As it stands in John's Gospel, we might read this verse with the thought that the "all" in the quotation applies to all men, thereby thinking that somehow God illuminates all, and men either come to Christ or refuse to come to Christ on their own volition. The full text, as Isaiah wrote it, shows that this is not the case. Actually, Isaiah wrote, "And all *your children* will be taught by the LORD." We see at once that the verse applies to God's children only, not to all men, and that it implies that one must first be a child of God through the new birth before one can really understand about Christ and come to him.

Jesus then goes on to show that this truth is also confirmed by experience: "Everyone who listens to and learns from the Father comes to me." Why is it that you and I can present the gospel to some people and never seem to get anywhere, even when the circumstances seem entirely favorable? And why is it that others with maximum problems and limited understanding believe? The only answer is that God has taught the one person and has not taught the other. Moreover, all whom God has taught do come to Jesus.

Life before Faith

Finally, after having stated his teaching and having given two points of evidence to support it, Jesus repeats his teaching about the necessity of God's grace in election a final time. He says, "I tell you the truth, he who believes has everlasting life" (v. 47).

I know there are many who have interpreted this verse in direct opposition to all that I have been saying. They have supposed that we are first to believe, after which, as a result of our having believed, we are given eternal life. But this would mean taking the verse in a way that would contradict all Christ's previous teaching. Actually, it is a summation of it all.

Perhaps this illustration, often used by Donald Grey Barnhouse, will help. We must imagine a battlefield over which troops are advancing in order to take a ridge that is just before them. Suddenly heavy fire opens up, and immediately the soldiers fall to the ground and hold their prone position until the enemy fire is silenced. Imagine further that all the soldiers are either dead, or alive and unwounded. When the firing stops the command comes once again to advance. Naturally, some of the soldiers do get up and move forward while others, the ones who are dead, do not. Why is it that the ones who do get up and advance get up? It is because they are alive and hear the voice of their commander. Does their getting up give them life? Of course not! It is rather the other way around. In the same way, he that "believes" on Christ does so because he already has "everlasting life." The hearing and believing are the marks of the existence of the new life of God implanted within the individual.

If you are not yet a Christian, this doctrine applies to you in the sense that the grace of God in election is your hope. There is no hope in yourself, either in your spiritual attainments or in your ability. In yourself you cannot even choose Christ. How wonderful, then, that God is able to do what you cannot do. He can draw you. Be cheered by that and prove that he is already at work in your life by coming to him.

On the other hand, if you are a Christian already, I challenge you to allow these great doctrines to have their proper and transforming place in your heart. I am convinced that to accept the principles of Christ's teaching in this chapter of John's Gospel would necessarily involve both a mental and spiritual revolution for many thousands of Christians at the present time. It would certainly involve a radically different approach to preaching and the practice of evangelism, as well as to most other parts of church life and theology. The great question is this: Will the Almighty God of the Christian Scriptures be our God? Or will our God be something less, something tailored to our own greatly limited horizons? Let us have the God of the Lord Jesus Christ, of Augustine, Luther, Calvin, and countless others, as our God. Let us stand with them in giving all might, majesty, dominion, power, and all glory in the matter of our salvation from beginning to end to that God only.

85

The Two Mannas

John 6:48–51

"I am the bread of life. Your forefathers ate the manna in the desert, yet they died. But here is the bread that comes down from heaven, which a man may eat and not die. I am the living bread that came down from heaven. If anyone eats of this bread, he will live forever. This bread is my flesh, which I will give for the life of the world."

Several years ago I heard a story about a Scotsman who was coming to America. He had purchased passage on one of the great ocean liners. He did not have much money, so he decided to save on food by stocking up on crackers, cheese, and fruit before his departure. The ship sailed, and he began to eat his Spartan meals. This went fairly well for the first four or five days. But as the ship drew closer to New York the crackers became increasingly stale, the cheese became moldy, and the fruit spoiled. Finally there was nothing left that was fit to eat. The Scotsman decided that he would go to the dining room and have one last, good meal before the liner docked in Manhattan and he went ashore. Imagine his surprise to discover that nothing in the dining room cost anything and that all that he could ever have eaten had already been included in the price of his ticket before he left the British Isles!

Unfortunately, this is the way in which thousands of men and women act toward the true bread of life that is offered to us without price in the person of the Lord Jesus Christ. He is there for all. But the sad fact is that many

517

would rather feed upon the dry crackers of human philosophy or the spoiled fruit of good works than come to him.

Jesus said, "I am the bread of life. Your forefathers ate manna in the desert, yet they died. But here is the bread that comes down from heaven, which a man may eat and not die. I am the living bread that came down from heaven. If anyone eats of this bread, he will live forever. This bread is my flesh, which I will give for the life of the world" (John 6:48–51). We will enter into the full meaning of these verses when we recognize that in them Jesus Christ voices a great claim, makes a requirement, and offers a wonderful promise.

Christ's Claim

The claim that the Lord Jesus makes in these verses is, quite simply, to be the "bread of life." It is the second time in this chapter that he has described himself by this image, and the image itself constitutes the first of the great "I am" sayings that are a characteristic of this Gospel. Here Jesus is portrayed as the bread of life. Later he will say: "I am the light of the world" (8:12; 9:5), "I am the gate" (10:7, 9), "I am the good shepherd" (10:11, 14), "I am the resurrection and the life" (11:25), "I am the way and the truth and the life" (14:6), "I am the true vine" (15:1, 5). By these images he shows that he is all that men and women need and that he is the sole way to come to God the Father.

Another way of setting the context for this saying is to notice that it is the third great Old Testament image that has been appropriated as a description of who Jesus Christ is and what he does. In chapter 1 Jesus has used the figure of Jacob's ladder upon which the angels of God were ascending and descending from heaven. This suggests that Jesus is the One through whom God the Father is revealed to men. In chapter 3 he is the brazen serpent that Moses lifted up in the wilderness. Here the crucifixion is portrayed, that work by which men and women are healed from the serpent bite of sin. Now he is the bread of life, the new manna, by which the new people of God are fed during the years of their desert wandering. There are two mannas, of course. There is the manna upon which the Jewish people fed in the wilderness under the direction of Moses. This manna sustained physical life for a time; but even this physical life did not go on forever, and eventually all who had eaten this literal manna died. There is also the manna that Jesus gives. This bread imparts and sustains that kind of life that will go on forever.

What does it mean when Jesus claims to be the bread of life? It means that he is able to satisfy the deepest needs and longings of the human soul. He is able to satisfy your needs, your longings, whatever they may be.

This does not mean that Jesus is going to satisfy every want or desire you may have or think you have. It means that he will satisfy that which you most deeply need. You say, "But aren't those two the same thing?" No, I do not think so. Let me give an example. Take a child who is beginning to grow up with a highly sharpened sense of what he "needs," as most children do. He thinks he needs candy—about every hour or so throughout the day. He thinks he needs to stay up to watch the late, late show on television. He thinks he needs to be able to set his own schedule—get up when he wants to, go in and out with his friends when he wants to, come to dinner when he wants to. He thinks he needs leisure time, particularly when he is asked to straighten up his room or help his mother with the dishes. All these items are "needs" from the child's point of view. But if the parent indulges the child in these, all he will produce is an unruly and obnoxious brat. What is more, when he grows up the child will attempt to inflict his unrestrained desires on everyone else and may well end up in jail.

What is it that the child needs? It is not what the child *thinks* he needs. Actually, the child needs discipline. He needs a standard of right and wrong conduct and someone to insist on that standard. He needs to be loved, to have goals, guidance, and encouragement.

In the same way, our real needs often differ from our imagined needs, and it is our real needs for which Jesus Christ is the answer. We find salvation in him. In him we have eternal life. We also are loved, receive goals and guidance, and are encouraged in life. "I am the bread of life," said Jesus. The implication is that we should feed upon him and grow.

In this chapter Jesus gives what would be called in theology a "progressive revelation" of himself as the bread. It is as though he held the mystery of himself as the bread in his hand and then slowly opened his hand one finger at a time so that those who were listening to him would see the truth gradually. First, he spoke of a bread from heaven that the Father gives to men (v. 32). This was the opening of the first finger. After the curiosity of the crowd had been aroused Jesus opened another finger by pointing out that he was the bread about which he was speaking (vv. 35, 48). Finally, in the verses that we are considering, he opens his hand the whole way and shows that the bread is his body that will be given up in death for men and women. He says, "And the bread that I will give is my flesh, which I will give for the life of the world" (v. 51).

I am glad that Jesus went on to speak of the cross, because Christ without the cross is of no use to us. We can look to his example, to the way he led his life. We can admire it. But the life alone does not help. We can admire the life, but we cannot live it. Besides, we are condemned by that life, for it is the standard of what God would require of us as his creatures. A Christ without the cross is of no use to us. He condemns us. Fortunately, there is more. For Jesus went on to speak of the cross and eventually to die upon it and rise again. Now there is hope. He died for our sin. The chastisement of our peace is upon him, and with his stripes we are healed. In his resurrection life we now have life. In his righteousness, through his death, we are now reckoned righteous in the sight of a holy and loving God.

To understand these things is to understand not only why Christ is truly the bread that came down from heaven but also why he is necessary for spiritual life.

The Requirement

These verses not only contain Christ's claim, which is a great claim; they also make a requirement. The requirement is that we feed upon him. This means to believe on Jesus, commit your life to him, take him into yourself so that he becomes a part of you and you of him. It is precisely the same act that is spoken of in verse 37, where we are encouraged to "come" to Christ, knowing that those who come to him will never be cast out. Have you come? I do not mean, do you know about Christ? Many people know about Christ but have never come to him. The devil knows about him but hates him. I mean, have you committed your life to him so that now your life, properly speaking, belongs to Jesus? If not, you need to say, "Lord Jesus Christ, I want you to know that I accept all the things said in Scripture about my sin and my need of you. I know that I am not holy. I recognize that I cannot please you by my own efforts. At the same time, I recognize that you died for me on the cross two thousand years ago, and I want that death to stand for my death. I want to be yours. Receive me now as one of your followers, as your child."

Men and women have used many different words as they have prayed along these lines. Many who read this have come in different ways and have said different words as they have come. Still, at its heart the experience is the same. It is the experience of letting go of anything that you might present, in order that your hands might be empty to receive that righteousness that Jesus Christ gives. There is no substitute for that. If you have not done that, you are not a Christian, no matter how much you may know about the Christian faith. On the other hand, if you have done that, then you are already a Christian and know that God has placed his eternal life within you and will keep you until the last day.

What I have been saying is born out in a forceful way by this imagery of eating. Think what eating involves. First, it is *necessary*. Other things are necessary too, but not to the same degree. A person might argue that exercise is necessary. Yes, it is good for you. But if you do not eat, before long you are not going to be able to do your exercises. Someone else might argue that the life of the mind is necessary. I agree. But if you fail to eat, pretty soon you will not even be able to sit up and read or think clearly. You must eat to live. So, spiritually, you must eat of the Lord Jesus Christ if you are to come to life spiritually and grow strong.

How do you feed upon Christ? It is through studying the Bible. That is one reason why I place such a strong emphasis upon a systematic study of the Word of God on the *Bible Study Hour.* It is why in my church I comment upon the Scripture readings at each of the services, as well as preach the sermon. It is why I encourage area Bible studies in which people can meet informally to learn and grow together as they eat and digest the Word. These are tools by which you and I can feed upon Jesus. There is no substitute for them.

If we use the Word, God will bring us into contact with Jesus. He will use it to bring to our minds what we most need to know; he will reveal sin in us and correct it; and he will most certainly lead us in the way that we should go.

Then, too, eating is always *a response to a need that is felt.* In physical terms the need is for nourishment and the feeling of the need for nourishment is hunger. It is the same spiritually. When does a person come to the Lord Jesus Christ as Savior or for daily feeding after he has believed on him initially? It is when he has recognized his need. If you consider yourself all-sufficient spiritually—sufficient for this life and for the next—then it is not likely that you will come to the Lord Jesus Christ. However, if you have tried the allurements of this world and have found them to be empty, as many have, then there will be within you that sense of inner need and hunger that will drive you toward Jesus. If you have been reading the Bible, God will show you that need for holiness that will turn you to him.

At one point in my ministry I was talking with a number of young people who had seen other young people turn to sexual indulgences as a means of satisfying the hunger they felt in their hearts. It had a hold upon them, as sin always does. They enjoyed it. They did not see how they could possibly stay away from this style of life. It was everything to them. But the interesting thing is that they were not happy. They were miserable. There is an old saying, "If you're so smart, why ain't you rich?" We could also say, "If sex is the way, why aren't you happy?" These young people needed to recognize that any way that is not God's way—that is divorced from Jesus Christ—is empty. They needed to see that Jesus is the bread that satisfies.

How I wish I could make that clear! Jesus is the only One who satisfies. You will never have to go far to find those who say the opposite. Madison Avenue exists for no other reason than to say the opposite. It says it all the time. Buy a car; you'll be happy. Take this vacation; you'll be happy. Use a detergent; you'll be happy. But it is not so. Do not permit yourself to be sold a bill of goods spiritually. Real joy comes from knowing the great God of the universe in Jesus Christ and from glorifying him forever.

Third, eating involves *appropriation.* Knowledge is not enough. It is possible to sit down at a banquet and identify all the dishes and even be able to address them by their French names—all the way from the *potage de légumes* to the *crêpes suzette.* But if you do not or will not eat of them, they do you no good whatsoever. In the same way, it is possible to understand Christian doctrine so well that you can tell where everyone else is wrong—where Barth is wrong, where Brunner is wrong, where Boice is wrong—but you are still lost unless you appropriate Jesus Christ personally.

That, of course, leads to the last significant point about eating. It must be *personal. You* must eat. No one else can do it for you. It also is true in regard to your relationship to the Lord Jesus. You cannot get along by saying, "Well, my husband believes . . . my wife believes . . . my children or my parents believe." The question is: Do *you* believe? Are *you* feeding on Jesus? I hope that you will never cheat your wife or husband or children or parents by asking them to do something that you refuse to do personally, but rather will give them the best of yourself by allowing God to make you into the kind of person he has always planned for you to be.

Life or Death

The last point is involved in all that has been said previously. It has to do with believing or not believing in Jesus. What are the issues? They are "life" and "death." It is not just a matter of a little bit of happiness versus more happiness or partial satisfaction versus greater satisfaction. It is life versus death. To know Jesus is to live—now and eternally. To refuse him is suicide.

There is no greater issue to be faced by anyone in the course of a normal human existence. Will you have life? God is the source of life; he gives it abundantly. Or will you choose that eternal death that comes from making yourself, rather than your Creator and Redeemer, the center of your spiritual horizons?

Do not do what the prodigal son did. He thought that he was going to find life when he left his father to enjoy himself in the city. We would say in today's jargon that he was determined to "live it up." So he took his inheritance and squandered it on riotous living. Did he find life? No, he found a life that to a Jew was a symbol of death. He was feeding unclean animals. When did life begin for the prodigal? Only when he saw his need, left his willful past behind him, and returned to his father. I covet that for you if you are one who has never really surrendered your will to Jesus and returned to him. Will you not come to him? Jesus is wonderful. He really is. He wants the best for you. Why do you not walk in that way willingly?

86

Food Indeed and Drink Indeed

John 6:52–59

Then the Jews began to argue sharply among themselves, "How can this man give us his flesh to eat?"

Jesus said to them, "I tell you the truth, unless you eat the flesh of the Son of Man and drink his blood, you have no life in you. Whoever eats my flesh and drinks my blood has eternal life, and I will raise him up at the last day. For my flesh is real food and my blood is real drink. Whoever eats my flesh and drinks my blood remains in me, and I in him. Just as the living Father sent me and I live because of the Father, so the one who feeds on me will live because of me. This is the bread that came down from heaven. Your forefathers ate manna and died, but he who feeds on this bread will live forever." He said this while teaching in the synagogue in Capernaum.

Years ago, before the United Presbyterian Church in the U.S.A. revised its Book of Order and with it the vows that were taken by ministers at their ordination, there was a phrase concerning "the peace, purity, and unity of the Church," which all who became ministers agreed to encourage. They promised to "study" these points, which meant to advance them. The difficulty lay in the fact that it was not always possible to promote the peace and purity of the church concurrently. Peace could be maintained without purity. Purity could be achieved without peace and unity. But to do both at the same time was difficult. The reason was that truth always will have enemies and that pure doctrine always will be opposed. Actually, I would go so far as to affirm as a rule of Christian experience that strong teaching of strong doctrine will inevitably produce discord in some quarter.

This is not experience limited to our own time either. It goes back to the time of the Lord Jesus Christ. An example is found in the verses that immediately follow Jesus' claim to be able to give his flesh for the life of the world.

Jesus had said, "I am the living bread that came down from heaven. If anyone eats of this bread, he will live forever. This bread is my flesh, which I will give for the life of the world" (v. 51). This bothered those who were listening to him, with the result (so we read) that they "began to argue sharply among themselves, 'How can this man give us his flesh to eat?'" (v. 52). This time, however, Jesus repeated his claim in even stronger terms. He said, "I tell you the truth, unless you eat the flesh of the Son of Man and drink his blood, you have no life in you. Whoever eats my flesh and drinks my blood has eternal life, and I will raise him up at the last day. For my flesh is real food and my blood is real drink. Whoever eats my flesh and drinks my blood remains in me, and I in him. Just as the living Father sent me and I live because of the Father, so the one who feeds on me will live because of me. This is the bread that came down from heaven. Your forefathers ate manna and died, but he who feeds on this bread will live forever" (vv. 55–58).

It is interesting as an insight into the problems of our own times, that in answering those who were in conflict over his teaching Jesus did not try to tone down the teaching to make it more palatable. If anything, he did the opposite. It would seem, then—to make a conclusion—that, according to Jesus, truth concerning doctrine leading to a genuine peace, rather than peace at the expense of doctrine, was to prevail.

Not the Lord's Supper

But what do these words mean? What does it mean to eat Christ's flesh and drink his blood? If we are to understand them, we must begin first by realizing that they do not refer—as many, including Raymond E. Brown in his comprehensive commentary for the Anchor Bible series, have believed them to refer—to the Lord's Supper or the communion service.

Many have looked at the sixth chapter of John in this way, of course, particularly those whose theology gives a high and mystical value to the sacraments. Generally speaking, there have been three major views of the Lord's Supper. The first is highly literal. It is the view of the Roman Catholic and Orthodox communions, as well as of some high church Anglicans and Episcopalians. According to these churchmen, the bread and the wine of the communion service are literally transformed into the flesh and blood of Jesus Christ by an ordained priest and thus become, at least to some, a reenactment of Christ's sacrifice. Clearly, to those who take such a position, the words of Christ in John 6 must refer to the mass, or Eucharist. They literally describe what is happening. The worshiper literally feeds on the Lord.

The second view of the Lord's Supper is that it is a mere memorial or testimonial. This understanding focuses on the words "Do this in remembrance of me" and on Paul's statement "For whenever you eat this bread and drink this cup, you proclaim the Lord's death until he comes" (1 Cor. 11:26). Certainly, there is truth in this view, but it is weak in that it does not indicate how Jesus can be present in any special way to those taking part in the service.

The third view, which was the view of John Calvin and of the Reformed church bodies, is that Jesus is actually present in the communion service but that he is present spiritually, not in any physical way. Calvin called this understanding the doctrine of the "real presence." We often say, in speaking of God, that God is everywhere present. It does not mean that he is physically present in physical objects, for that would be pantheism. It means that he is present spiritually. We also say that God is present in a special way with those who are his children; that is, he dwells within them. So he is present in Christians in some ways more than he is in the world. Moreover, even as Christians we often say that God is with us more at some times than at others, by which we mean (I assume) that we are more aware of his presence or that the lines of communication are more open. It is in this same progression but in an added sense that we speak of the real presence of Jesus Christ in the Lord's Supper. This presence is spiritual. It is, therefore, received spiritually, which is to say, by faith.

These, then, are the three great understandings of the meaning of the Lord's Supper which have prevailed in the church and according to which, particularly in the first instance, the sayings of Jesus in John 6 have been interpreted.

It is my view, however, that the Lord's Supper is not in consideration in these verses at all. Why? First, because at the time of the speaking of these words the Lord's Supper was not yet instituted. Second, because Jesus was addressing unbelievers in John 6, while the Lord's Supper is for Christians only. Third, because the eating and drinking spoken of in John is unto salvation, while the eating and drinking that is part of the Lord's Supper is for those who are already saved, and speaks of fellowship, growth, and communion. Fourth, because the Lord's Supper does not produce those results that are here attributed to the eating and drinking of Christ. This last is the greatest reason, for it is perfectly obvious that many thousands of persons partake each week of the Lord's Supper and yet do not possess that eternal life that Jesus says results from a true feeding upon him.

Feeding on Christ

If it is true, then, that the eating and drinking that Jesus speaks of in John 6 does not refer to the Lord's Supper, to what does it refer? Or, to put it in other language, what does it mean to feed upon Jesus? The answer to this question is that eating Christ's flesh and drinking his blood refer to that which Jesus has been speaking of all along. He has said that men and women must "believe" in him (vv. 29, 35, 47). They must "come" to him (v. 35). They must "look at" him (v. 40). They must "listen" and "learn from" him (v. 45). All these terms—believe, come, listen, learn—refer to what we would most naturally call faith. The last terms—"eating and drinking"—stress that the commitment that is involved in faith is as real, irrevocable, and productive of results as any literal eating or drinking.

Have you committed yourself to Jesus Christ so that he has become as real to you as that? Is he as real to you spiritually as something you can taste or handle? Is he as much a part of you as that which you eat? Do not think me blasphemous when I say that he must be as real and as useful to you as a hamburger and french fries. I say this because, although he is obviously far more real and useful than these, the unfortunate thing is that for many people he is much less.

If Jesus has not become as real to you as eating and drinking, let me suggest that you do something similar to that which a bride does in promising herself to her husband. Before the ceremony the bride can do anything she likes. In fact, if she wants to, she can even cancel the whole wedding, for she can decide even at 1:58 that she has made a mistake and cannot go through with a 2:00 ceremony. However, when the ceremony begins she comes to the place where she speaks her vows and, on the basis of those vows and those of her husband, is pronounced a wife, his wife. She is now no longer her own. At the same time, her groom pronounces his vows to her, and he becomes hers no less than she becomes his.

Apply this now to him who is the faithful lover and bridegroom of the church, and to you and me who are his bride. It is he who has courted us and wooed us. We did not choose him. It is he who has pronounced the vows first of all. His vows were pronounced in eternity long before the foundation of the world. He said, "I, Jesus, take you, John Smith (Mary Jones, or whatever your name may be), to be my wedded wife. And I do promise and covenant, before God and these witnesses, to be your loving and faithful husband, in plenty and in want, in joy and in sorrow, in sickness and in health, for time and for eternity." We looked up into his loving face and eyes, believed his promise, and repeated his vow.

In the case of the church something great happened between the speaking of this promise by Christ and our repetition of it. Between his vow and our vow, Jesus went to the cross where he paid an infinite price for our sin, purchasing us so that we could be free of sin, guilt, and shame as we come to him. We see his sacrifice. With that in mind we repeat, "I, sinner, take you, Jesus, to be my wedded husband. And I do promise and covenant, before God and these witnesses, to be your loving and faithful wife, in plenty and in want, in joy and in sorrow, in sickness and in health, for this life and for eternity."

That is what faith is. That is what it means to eat Christ's flesh and drink his blood. It is to commit yourself to him. It is to accept his promise and pledge on your behalf and to repeat his promise, vowing to be his for eternity. If you have done that, you have done the most important thing there is to be done in this life, regardless of what you may already have accomplished or may yet accomplish. If you have not, you should know that today is the day of salvation. Today is the day of your union with Christ, if you will have it so.

Results of Feeding

There is one more point that we must see in studying these verses. It is that there are certain results that come from feeding upon Jesus. The verses suggest three of them.

First, we receive the certainty of our salvation. This result is seen primarily in verse 54, where we are told of the gift of eternal life and of Christ's promise to raise us up at the last day. What is eternal life? Some who have disagreed with the doctrine of eternal security, the doctrine that no one who has come to Christ will ever be lost, have stressed that the eternal life that we receive in salvation is a special quality of life, rather than life of infinite duration. But while I would not deny for a moment that eternal life is a life of special quality, I am convinced that we must also go on to say that it is indeed eternal. Eternal life is the life of God. It is without end because he is without end. This truth is certainly affirmed in this passage, for Jesus immediately follows his mention of the gift of eternal life with the promise that he will raise up those who have been given eternal life at the last day (so also in verses 39, 40, and 44). What a great promise! How good to know that nothing will ever separate us from the One who loves us and who has taught us to love!

Second, we enter into a life-transforming union with Christ as a result of coming to him. This thought is expressed in verse 56, where the idea of union with Christ is mentioned for the first time in John's Gospel. It will become very prominent later, particularly in the last discourses. Here Jesus says, "Whoever eats my flesh and drinks my blood remains in me, and I in him."

What does it mean that we are joined to Christ and he to us? The fact that we are joined to Christ means that we have a change in our life and status. Let us go back to the wedding illustration. Before the wedding the bride has one status; afterward she has another. For one thing, there is the change in her name. Henceforth, she will bear her husband's name. There is a change in her legal status. Before, she could buy or sell property as she chose. Now there must be joint signatures. There is a psychological change; she senses a subtle difference between being single and being married. There is a social change that will penetrate even to the matter of who her friends will be, whom she will entertain, how her time will be spent, and other matters. When do these changes take place? The answer is that they take place instantly and simultaneously in the moment when she is joined to her husband. So it is spiritually. At the moment when we are joined to Christ through faith and by the new birth, we receive a new name—we are now Mrs. Christian instead of Miss Sinner—and a new way of life with new relationships and obligations is opened before us.

On the other side, the fact that Christ is joined to us means primarily that we receive his life and are to go on receiving it in increasing abundance throughout eternity. We are to be filled, as Paul says, with "all the fullness of God" (Eph. 3:19). Right now we are a bit like a quart bottle that has been filled with seawater. It is real seawater, but not much is in the bottle. But suppose you were able to enlarge the bottle so that it would contain a gallon. In that case, you could then put in three more quarts of seawater. The larger the bottle became, the more water it could hold—until, if it were big enough, it could conceivably be filled with all the fullness of the sea itself. In the same way, God promises to enlarge our spiritual capacities until the full life of the infinite Christ is reproduced in us.

Finally, the words of Jesus suggest that we receive strength for the living of this life as we feed upon him. He says, "So the one who feeds on me will live because of me" (v. 57). This verse is not talking about eternal life primarily; it is talking about our present daily life to be lived in Christ's power. Galatians 2:20 is another statement of that principle. "I have been crucified with Christ and I no longer live, but Christ lives in me. The life I live in the body, I live by faith in the Son of God, who loved me and gave himself for me."

Do you live by that life of the Lord Jesus Christ? That life is there in all its strength and purity. It is there to feed upon. By that life and that life alone we can grow.

87

Discipleship Tested by Doctrine

John 6:60–65

On hearing it, many of his disciples said, "This is a hard teaching. Who can accept it?"

Aware that his disciples were grumbling about this, Jesus said to them, "Does this offend you? What if you see the Son of Man ascend to where he was before! The Spirit gives life; the flesh counts for nothing. The words I have spoken to you are spirit and they are life. Yet there are some of you who do not believe." For Jesus had known from the beginning which of them did not believe and who would betray him. He went on to say, "This is why I told you that no one can come to me unless the Father has enabled him."

After the Lord Jesus Christ had left Judea, where he had encountered hostility, and had gone into Galilee, it seemed that for a time people were attracted to his teaching and were flocking around him. He had performed miracles in Galilee—turning the water into wine at Cana, healing the nobleman's son, multiplying the loaves and fish by the side of the Sea of Tiberias. This had attracted so much attention that for a time as many as five thousand people followed Jesus to hear his teachings. In a short while, however, the real nature of his claims became apparent. When this happened, many of his followers went back and no longer walked with him. We see the beginning of this toward the end of the sixth chapter of John's Gospel.

How did the ministry go in Galilee? Exactly as it had gone in Judea. The Lord Jesus Christ had been popular. Many had followed him. Then, as he began to teach, his doctrine became the measure of his followers' discipleship, and most dropped away. John, therefore, concludes the chapter by showing what happened, not among Christ's professed enemies but among his apparent adherents—the general company of his followers (v. 60) and the Twelve (v. 67).

Hard Sayings

If we are to profit from this section of the Gospel, we must be very clear in our understanding of why those who had appeared to be disciples dropped away. John says, "On hearing it, many of his disciples said, 'This is a hard teaching. Who can accept it?'" And he adds, "Aware that his disciples were grumbling about this, Jesus said to them, 'Does this offend you?'" (vv. 60–61). The reason lies in the fact that Christ's teachings were "hard" to accept. The Greek word is *sklēros,* and it clearly does not mean "hard to understand." It means "hard to tolerate." So long as Christ's followers could not understand him, they stayed around and asked questions. It was when they did understand him that they went elsewhere. They left because what they heard was so contrary to their own views that they would not accept it.

This applies to our own day and to ourselves. Often, when professing Christians criticize a true servant of God, one who is really giving out God's truth, and complain that his teachings are "hard," the real cause is not the difficulty of the doctrine but rather the unwillingness of the people involved to accept what they hear. Perhaps it conflicts with their own views. Perhaps it is different from the traditions of their fathers. Many of these persons also copy the men of Christ's day in another way, for they grumble among themselves as they drop away rather than coming directly to Jesus Christ to state their difficulties.

What were these teachings the crowd found difficult? They are the same ones that men and women find difficult to accept today.

First, there is the doctrine of Christ's incarnation with all that this implies for his person. Jesus said that he was the true bread that came down from heaven (vv. 33, 38, 51). This implied that he had existed before his physical birth and that he had a special relationship with God. He was God's Son, possessing the divine nature. He had come as God in order to take human nature upon himself. The crowd obviously understood what Jesus was saying, for we are told in the other Gospels that when he said such things they were immediately ready to interpret what he had said as blasphemy. God come in the flesh? This they could not accept. There are many who will not accept it today.

Secondly, Jesus was teaching that he needed to go to the cross. This truth lies in verse 51, which says, "And the bread that I will give is my flesh, which I will give for the life of the world." How hard this is to accept and truly understand! Those who heard Christ might have argued that they could understand how a person should pay for his own sin, even die for it if the crime were great enough. They could understand how salvation might be earned. But to think that Jesus Christ had to earn salvation for them and that they would therefore have to receive it as a free gift from him or not receive it at all—this they found objectionable. This is the primary difficulty that most of our contemporaries have in accepting Christianity.

Finally, Jesus had taught that the reason why most of those listening did not believe on him was that in themselves they could not believe and that they could come to believe eventually only if God had previously determined to give them to him. These are the rudiments of that system of doctrine known as the Reformed faith—man's spiritual inability to please God and the necessity of God's electing grace in salvation. Jesus had said, "No one can come to me unless the Father who sent me draws him" (v. 44). He had said, "All that the Father gives me will come to me" (v. 37). Nothing is more calculated to arouse the ire and rebellion of the human heart than this teaching. But it is true. Christ did not hesitate to proclaim it.

Each of these teachings ran counter to the normal way of thinking of those living in Christ's time, and they run counter to the normal way of thinking today. The question is: Are we willing to change our opinions to conform to the teachings of Christ? Or will we persevere in error? Obviously, we need to have our discipleship corrected by Christ's doctrine, and to learn not to evaluate spiritual matters by the measure of our own understanding.

Christ's Answer

Jesus answered by asking, "Doth this offend you? What if you see the Son of Man ascend to where he was before!" (vv. 61–62). I do not think the meaning of this verse is self-evident, at least it has not been self-evident to commentators, for they take different positions in referrring to it. Some think of it as a reference to the cross. Some view it as a prediction of Christ's ascension. Let me tell you what I think it means.

Years ago I heard a story told by Donald Grey Barnhouse, which will make this particular interpretation remain in your mind forever. Barnhouse had been visiting foreign mission fields, and while he had been doing this his family had been living in Berlin, Germany. There was a world-famous zoo in Berlin in those years to which Mrs. Barnhouse and the children went often. So when Barnhouse returned from his travels, and after the reunion, this was the first place the children wanted him to see.

In particular, they wanted him to see Rupert. Rupert was a magnificent sea lion weighing several tons, and he was kept in an immense pool that he had to himself. Everyone in Berlin loved Rupert. And they especially loved to be at the edge of the pool when he was fed each day by his keeper. Rupert would mount a platform and then catch the fish that his keeper threw to him. There were many fish, for Rupert had a great appetite. And with each fish Rupert would have to stretch out farther and farther to catch it. Finally, as the keeper reached the bottom of the bucket, the fish would be thrown so far out over the water that Rupert would have to leap from his perch, catch the fish in the air, and then come crashing down into the pool spraying water everywhere. It was this sight that the children wanted their father to see.

The family did see this together. And, in addition to seeing it, Barnhouse also filmed it on a small movie camera that he had purchased. Later, when they had left Berlin, the film was shown; and all this action unfolded on the screen. When he got to the end of the reel, however, Barnhouse stopped the projector before the film had entirely run through and threw the wheels into reverse. Now everything that the children had seen began to run backward. First there would be an enormous amount of water, which sprang up from all over the pool and began to disappear into a hole that had appeared in the middle. Then out of this hole came Rupert, all three or four thousand pounds of him, and he gracefully floated back through the air to land on the platform. Moreover, as he did it he spit out a fish that went flying back through the air and landed in the keeper's bucket. This show became far more popular than the right way of seeing the pictures. So, every time that the pictures were to be shown the children would cry, "Please, Daddy, make Rupert spit fish!"

You can see at once why this story has remained in my mind, and you will be able to see, I believe, how this graphically illustrates what Jesus meant when he asked, "What if you see the Son of Man ascend to where he was before!" It was not his future ascension that he was looking forward to, but rather his descension that he was remembering. He was saying, "Are you offended at my teachings? Do you find them hard? Well, then, what if I were to retract them and retract the whole plan of redemption? What if I were to put the whole film into reverse and go back through the early days of my ministry, back through my childhood, be unborn, and then reascend to my Father? What would you do then?"

What would we do? What could we do? Our case would be hopeless, desperate. But, thank God, Jesus did not do that. He went instead to the cross, giving his life as a ransom for our sins; he ascended, and he is sitting today at the right hand of the Father, watching as the Father through the efficacious working of the Holy Spirit brings men and women to him. I look at those truths and see my salvation written plainly in them. Jesus did die. He died for me. Therefore, my salvation is eternally secure unless Jesus should reverse the whole plan of salvation even now, which he obviously will not do.

Not Flesh, but Spirit

But then Jesus went on to say something else. His first answer had been to ask, "What if I were to reverse the whole plan of redemption?" The conclusion is that it is far better to have Christ's ministry, even though it has doctrines that are difficult to accept, rather than have no ministry at all. But then he went on to add: "The Spirit gives life; the flesh counts for nothing. The words I have spoken to you are spirit and they are life" (v. 63). This sentence adds the truth that it is only through the ministry of the Holy Spirit that we can understand his doctrine.

It is not difficult to understand what that means. We see it, first of all, in the earthly ministry of the Lord Jesus. People have said, "Wouldn't it have been wonderful to have known the Lord Jesus Christ in the flesh? Wouldn't it have been glorious to have walked with him, to have heard his voice, to have traveled about with him as he moved from place to place during his three-year ministry?" I suppose that for some it would be wonderful. But the interesting thing is that many in Christ's day did just that but nevertheless did not believe and eventually "turned back and no longer followed him." Knowing the Lord after the flesh did not necessarily profit those who were with him. Thus, Jesus was saying that it was his thoughts, words, and acts that were to bless them—not his outward appearance—and that even these had to be conveyed to the heart by the Holy Spirit if blessing should come.

On one occasion a woman said to Jesus, "Blessed is the mother who gave you birth and nursed you." But Jesus said, "Blessed rather are those who hear the word of God and obey it" (Luke 11:27–28).

Then, too, this principle is true of our life as Christians today. It is not the external trappings of religion that bless the soul, but rather the Word of God as it is carried to our understanding by the supernatural intervention of God's Holy Spirit in our lives. This is true of any outward form of religion. Baptism is a good thing; it is commanded by God. But baptism does not save an individual. In fact, it has even become a curse in some denominations where it has been practiced upon unbelievers, for it has given the impression that all is well with their souls when actually they are children of wrath and under condemnation.

Take communion as a second example. Communion can be a blessed event. But it is also true that it is observed regularly by thousands who have never truly committed their lives to Jesus Christ, and so it is totally ineffective. The works of the flesh profit nothing if the Spirit does not give life.

Bible reading is another example. So is prayer. So is church membership. These aspects of Christianity are of great value if the Holy Spirit is blessing them to us and if we are seeking his blessing. But they can also be used in an unbelieving, formal way and so achieve nothing. We grow in the doctrine of Jesus only when we allow the Spirit of Jesus to interpret his words and apply them to our hearts.

Words of Life

So, what will you do with Christ's words? Will you heed them, allowing the Holy Spirit to bless you through them? Or will you turn away from them, as many of Christ's followers did? It is true that no one can come to Jesus unless the Father draws him, but this does not eliminate human responsibility to heed Christ's words. Notice the balance of truth in Christ's statement. He said, "The Spirit gives life." That is the divine side. In this work God operates by himself, and no man participates. But Jesus also went on to say, "The words I have spoken *to you* are spirit and they are life." *To you* speaks of human responsibility. The teachings of Jesus are directed to you. Do you believe them?

If you are not a Christian, your obligation is to read God's Word and to see yourself and your need reflected in it. Moreover, it is to follow that true Word wherever it leads you and to come (for it leads in this direction) to the Savior.

On the other hand, many who read these words will be Christians. What is your obligation? Your obligation is to take these words to those who are lost and who will certainly perish without them. This is your prime responsibility. I know that we have other obligations also. We are obliged to feed the sick, comfort the sorrowing, care for the destitute, provide for widows and orphans. You will not neglect these good works. But even as you do them you will remember that the truly great and lasting changes in this world, those that determine history and human destiny, are those that take place in the realm of the spirit through the preaching of God's Word. You must give yourself first and foremost to that work.

You are to feed on Christ's words, digest Christ's words, live Christ's words, exude Christ's words. Many pressing concerns will attempt to dissuade you. People will try to discourage your commitment. Do not be discouraged. Proclaim Christ's teachings to those who will receive them and to those who will not. Proclaim them to the rich and to the poor, the educated and the uneducated, the high and the low, the privileged and the disadvantaged. As you do, God will use them to draw men and women to the Savior.

88

Nowhere to Go but Forward

John 6:66–68

From this time many of his disciples turned back and no longer followed him.

"You do not want to leave too, do you?" Jesus asked the Twelve.

Simon Peter answered him, "Lord, to whom shall we go? You have the words of eternal life."

I do not know if you ever attempt to visualize the scenes of Christ's life when you are reading about them in the Gospels, but I do occasionally. I have found myself doing this as I have read about the early enthusiasm and later defection of the crowds who came to hear Jesus in Galilee.

I see it in cinematic terms, contrasting the apparent success of the morning about which these verses are written with the pitiful sight that occurred later as Christ's former followers left him. I can see them coming in the early hours of the dawn as the sun rises over Galilee. They had been with Jesus in the wilderness the night before. Now they gather in the town of Capernaum until at last, with the streets bursting with crowds and the synagogue fully occupied, they press their questions upon him. Unfortunately, the answers of the Lord are not those they desire to hear. So, as the day wears on, these ap-

535

parent followers defect. At last the day ends as it had begun. Jesus is alone with his own close followers, the disciples. If I were filming the scene, I would contrast the morning with the evening, showing the small group who remain standing quietly, looking out over the lake as the last enthusiasts of the morning depart in the darkness to their homes.

This is a poignant scene, but now it becomes even more poignant. For, instead of congratulating himself on the fact that the Twelve had remained behind with him or allowing them to congratulate themselves, Jesus quietly turns about and asks this question: "Will you also leave?" It is a simple question, but it is one that must have cut deeply into their hearts and minds and that cuts into our hearts also. Will we go away? Will we be as some who have heard the Word of God, have even professed to believe it, but who have turned their backs upon Christ and Christianity? Or will we stay?

God grant that we may all be able to answer with Peter: "Lord, to whom shall we go? You have the words of eternal life" (v. 68). It was a profound question and a profound answer. Both the question and the answer are profoundly relevant to all who hear them and who should be able to echo Peter's answer today.

A Relevant Question

Look for a moment at why this question is so relevant for those who are living today. It is relevant, first of all, because some of whom it is asked are not true Christians and will surely go away.

Some will *betray* Christ. Do you doubt that? If so, look at the men to whom Jesus himself was speaking. Here were twelve men whom he had picked out to be with him and help him. He certainly had good judgment, much better judgment than any minister or officer who votes on admitting a person to membership in a particular congregation today. Yet one of these men was Judas. He was a man who had never believed in Christ in a saving way—for Jesus termed him a devil—yet he was with the other disciples and was unknown by them in his true character. Eventually he betrayed the Savior.

Is it too much to say that there are Judases within the visible church today? I think not. There are some who profess to be Christians, who even hold office in Christian churches, but who have never been born again and who may one day openly turn their backs on all they have stood for previously. These are those who go out from us because they are not of us. Are we among their number? Could we be? Instead of a glib answer, we should let that question go around among us as it went around the table in the upper room: "Lord, is it I?" We should search our hearts to see if we have really committed ourselves to the Savior.

Second, the question is relevant because, in addition to the fact that some will certainly betray Christ, each of us could *deny* him. Here was Peter. Peter was born again. Moreover, Peter is the very one who utters the correct answer to Christ's question in this story—"Lord, to whom shall we go? You have the words of eternal life." Later on he would say, "Even if I have to die with you, I will never disown you" (Matt. 26:35). Yet the time came when Peter was shaken and did deny Jesus. Jesus was arrested, and Peter stood by. A little girl asked him, "Weren't you with Jesus of Galilee?" Peter said, "No." Another declared, "This fellow was also with Jesus." Peter denied it. Later, another one said, "Surely you are one of them, for your speech gives you away." Peter denied for the third time that he knew Jesus, this time with cursings. I suppose that in the context of the Jewish culture of the day Peter would have sworn by some veiled reference to Jehovah. "In the name of God Almighty, I do not know Jesus Christ." What a comedown for Peter! But what about ourselves? If this could happen to Peter, it could happen to us. Will we also go away? Will we deny Jesus?

I would like to encourage you to be strong, to stay, to give a forthright and lasting testimony to the grace of God in Jesus Christ. It is not terribly difficult to gain an audience for the gospel message, particularly in this country in this day when, like the men of Athens, Americans seem to live only to hear or tell of some new thing. But to keep those who come for years and to build them up into a strong community where the gospel is openly confessed and the standards of Christianity are upheld—this is difficult, for men vacillate. Spurgeon wrote, "There is a constant winnowing going on in all churches, and this drives away the light and chaffy ones. There is a fan at work upon this floor. . . . Be not as the chaff. . . . Better far that we die than that we deny the Lord."[1]

A Searching Answer

We have looked at the question; we need now to look at Peter's answer. Peter said, "Lord, to whom shall we go? You have the words of eternal life." This has reference to the thought of going back, and Peter is expressing his view that having once come to Jesus such a thing is unthinkable. Is it unthinkable to you? Or would you consider turning back?

You say, "I am so discouraged right now, I think I might." Well, then, let me ask this: What would you go back to? Is there anything in your past that can compare with Jesus?

Would you go back to your *former way of life?* You know what your way of life was before you came to faith in the Lord Jesus Christ. It may have been characterized by a great emptiness or lack of meaning and purpose. God filled you and gave your life meaning. Would you go back to your emptiness? Your former life may have been filled with the excesses of sin. It may have been drunkenness, drugs, sexual licenses, or other things. You were ruining yourself by your sins. Will you turn back to those? The past may have been characterized by worldliness, in the sense of assuming the world's values. You may have been on a great ego trip from which you have been delivered by the Lord Jesus Christ. Would you go back to that? Was that so satisfying?

If nothing else should do it, your own self-interest should demand that your pathway be forward. When Christian was face-to-face with the devil in Bunyan's account of his travels to the celestial city in *Pilgrim's Progress,* he thought how dearly he would love to go back and escape the conflict. However, when he thought of his armor, he remembered that he had none for his back. He had a shield, a breastplate, a helmet, a sword, but nothing for his back. So he realized that if he should turn around, it would be the work of only a moment for the devil to slay him with his spear. He therefore resolved that however bad it might be to go forward, it would, nevertheless, be worse to go backward. So he fought on and gained victory. Think of that fact when you are discouraged or tempted. Retreat is impossible! Press on!

Let me remind you of a second inadequate alternative. Would you go back to the *secular ideologies* of our age? There is the ideology of progress. This word characterized the aspirations of the nineteenth century with all its advances in commerce, science, medicine, communications, and transportation. Some thought that we were headed toward a golden age in which all would live in peace and all forms of sickness and ignorance would be wiped out. But that has not happened. Sin is still with us. Science has not conquered it.

Some have been caught up in the ideology of world peace. This often was spoken of at the time of World War I, the war that was supposed to make the world safe for democracy. But World War I was followed by World War II, World War II by the Korean War, the Korean War by Vietnam. Foolish was the man or woman who thought that the American withdrawal from Vietnam would be the end of all wars!

Did your past hold the secular ideology of maximum human freedom? This philosophy billboards all forms of control or any type of restriction as an enemy and believes wholeheartedly that all will be well if only men and women are released to do their own thing. We have seen this philosophy at work in education and in other areas. But it is like saying that a garden will produce the most beauty if it is left to itself. Does it? I suppose there are some who might consider weeds beautiful and desirable—just as they consider crippling nationwide strikes, abortion on demand, open homosexuality, and anarchy beautiful and desirable—but for most sane men and women these are still weeds. They do not compare with the beauty that results from careful control and cultivation. Was freedom apart from Christ so wonderful? Was it real? Would you go back? Or did you first find real freedom in serving the Lord Jesus?

Perhaps your past held the ideology of agnosticism. This is the view that denies the possibility of finding answers to the deep questions of life—Who am I? Who is God? What am I here for? and so on. Questions are good, but what is the value of asking questions if you fail to find answers? What Christian would want to return to that?

There is a third area of the past to which you might be tempted to return. I have spoken of your former way of life, as well as the secular ideologies of our time. There are also *false religions and false religious leaders*. If your past contained these experiences, would you go back to them? How about the cults? How about the eastern religions? Were they the answer?

Finally, would you go back to that *dead moralism* that characterized the lives of so many of us before we became Christians? Before we came to Jesus Christ we were bent on a life of high moral attainment, but we found that the life we attained failed to satisfy anyone except ourselves—and it did not even satisfy ourselves most of the time. Did you have the sense that you were really pleasing God? I would be surprised if you did. Did your wife approve? Your husband? Your parents? Your children? If so, why did you have so much trouble with your personal relationships? Besides, when you came to Jesus, did not this involve the confession that your own efforts were empty and that you needed a righteousness that you could not find in yourself? Of course it did! So your experience is similar to that of the apostle Paul who pursued high ethical ideals but who, after he had found Christ, recognized that his past achievements were worthless (Phil. 3:8). Would you go back to the scrap heap of your morality?

"Lord, to whom shall we go? You have the words of eternal life."

I do not know where you could go to escape Jesus, even if you wanted to go back to those empty things that characterized your past. I doubt if you could even escape the suspicions of others that you have been with Jesus. Remember Peter. Peter denied the Lord with oaths and cursings. But he had just spent three years with Jesus, and as a result there was something in his speech that betrayed him. If you have been with Jesus, you will never be the same again either. No matter how you swear, someone will smoke you out and declare, "Surely you are one of them; you have been with him." David asked, "Where can I go from your Spirit? Where can I flee from your presence? If I go up to the heavens, you are there; if I make my bed in the depths, you are there. If I rise on the wings of the dawn, if I settle on the far side of the sea, even there your hand will guide me, your right hand will hold me fast" (Ps. 139:7–10).

Bound to the Master

The conclusion of this is that if you have believed on the Lord Jesus Christ as your Savior—if you are truly united to him through the miracle of the new birth—then there is no way for you to go but forward. A threefold cord binds you to him. Peter speaks of it.

First, there is nowhere else to go. Peter acknowledged this in the tone of his question. You have acknowledged it as I have reviewed the alternatives in this study. Who will have you after you have been with Jesus? Jesus was not wanted. He was killed. His followers down through the centuries have been killed. Who will take you in when the door has already been shut against your Master?

Second, you have learned that there is satisfaction in the words of the Lord Jesus Christ and that true satisfaction can be found in him only. Peter said, "You have the words of eternal life." It was said by the Greeks that that man would always be unsatisfied with human food who had once tasted the nectar of the gods. That is a description of your case if you are a Christian. Jesus said, "Drink of me, and I will satisfy your thirst; feed on me, and I will satisfy your hunger." You have done that. You have had heavenly food. Now anything else will seem flat by comparison.

Finally, as Peter says, "We believe and know that you are the Holy One of God." Thus, to go back now would be not only a crisis of faith; it would be intellectual suicide and dishonesty. It cannot be done. We know too much to prove faithless.

I wish I could tell you what the future holds for you, but I cannot. It may be that the future is bright. I often think this, for the trends of our day (in my opinion) are opening wide, wide doors for Christianity. It is a day of opportunity. The next generation may be the generation of the widest possible opportunity for the proclamation of the gospel and for witnessing and growth in history. If our day is the day of opportunity, we shall advance. We shall go forward. I am also aware, however, that days of opportunity often are followed by days of harsh persecution and that the chaff may be greatly winnowed out in our lifetime. The time may come when you and I may be persecuted. What shall we do then? How can we do less than those great martyrs of the faith who have gone boldly before us?

In the year 1555, in Oxford, England, Hugh Latimer, that great English bishop of the Reformation period, was led to the stake to be executed. Ridley was with him. These men had come to prominence as spokesmen for the Reformation in England under Henry VIII and had carried the true gospel of salvation by grace into every hamlet in the nation. But a change had come. Bloody Mary was now upon the throne, and godly men everywhere were being executed. Like one who had run a good race and who had kept the faith, Latimer went to the fires calmly. At the last he called out, "Be of good comfort, Master Ridley, and play the man; we shall this day light such a candle by God's grace in England as (I trust) shall never be put out."

If the time should come when you or I should find ourselves in that position, I trust that we too shall be strong. We cannot turn back. There is no place to go but forward.

89

A Disturbing Revelation

John 6:69–71

"We believe and know that you are the Holy One of God."

Then Jesus replied, "Have I not chosen you, the Twelve? Yet one of you is a devil!" (He meant Judas, the son of Simon Iscariot, who, though one of the Twelve, was later to betray him.)

I do not know why the apostle Peter appeals to me as much as he does, but I suppose it is because I am so much like him. I could say it is because Peter is so much like us Americans. On the negative side, he is impetuous. He speaks without thinking. Because he speaks without thinking he almost always is wrong. He also is overly confident. So one of the first things Jesus needed to teach him was that he was actually ignorant, weak, and cowardly. On the other hand, Peter is loyal, good-natured, and extremely anxious to learn and do the right thing. So when he is close to Christ and guided by the Holy Spirit he occasionally has great insight into divine truth and speaks truly.

This was the case in each of his great confessions of faith in the Lord Jesus Christ. One of those confessions is well known. It is recorded in the sixteenth chapter of Matthew in which Peter declares, "You are the Christ, the Son of the living God" (Matt. 16:16).

A lesser known but equally great confession occurs in the verses that close the sixth chapter of John. On this occasion Jesus had asked the disciples if they, like the Galilean crowd, would go away from him. Peter had answered on behalf of the others, "Lord, to whom shall we go? You have the words of eternal life." He then concluded, "And we have believed, and have come to know, that you are the Holy One of God" (6:69 RSV). In this confession Peter employed a phrase that is very uncommon in both the Old Testament and the New Testament—"the Holy One of God." It is so uncommon, in fact, that some of the scribes who were copying the New Testament during the early days of its transmission felt compelled to alter it and at the same time make this confession conform verbally to the confession of Matthew 16. The result was the version we have in most of our Bibles. But this was not what Peter said in Capernaum. Peter said, "You are the Holy One of God." The importance of the phrase lies in the fact that as he said it the others would naturally have thought of that other very popular phrase used of God himself—"the Holy One of Israel." In other words, there is no other possible place that Peter knew to assign to Jesus. He was the "Lord"—Jehovah. Peter was placing him with God and not with man.

Faith and Understanding

Peter's confession of faith is also interesting because of two words Peter used to indicate how he came to know this truth about Jesus. They are "believing" and "know." The most important thing about them is their order: first belief, then certainty. It is the divine order for true understanding in spiritual things.

Let us admit at the outset that this runs counter to our natural instincts and to our natural way of doing things. From a human point of view, who ever heard of believing in something in order to be sure of it? We want to make sure of something before we believe in it. We want to test out a person before we trust him. God reverses the order. Take these examples. David declared, "I am confident of this: I will see the goodness of the LORD in the land of the living" (Ps. 27:13). Jesus said to Martha, "Did I not tell you that if you believed, you would see the glory of God?" (John 11:40). In Hebrews we are told, "By faith we understand" (Heb. 11:3). There is a reason for this, of course. Quite simply it is because divine truth is beyond us. God's ways are not our ways. So we will begin to know and understand God's ways only as we begin to know and (in part) understand God. And we can begin to know God only through trusting him. Assurance, insight, knowledge—these are the fruit of believing. Certainty that Jesus is the Son of God comes, therefore, not by listening to the arguments of professors or by reading the latest of theological books or articles, but rather by believing what God has said about his Son in the Scriptures.

I admit that if this were a matter between men only, then to believe without seeing would be foolhardy. However, in dealing with God it is logical. God has never made a promise that he has not fulfilled in its proper time. His word is his bond. Moreover, if we do not believe him, then we actually are casting doubt upon his character.

Did you know that God has strong words to say about those who will not believe his testimony concerning Jesus Christ? We read this statement from him: "We accept man's testimony, but God's testimony is greater because it is the testimony of God, which he has given about his Son. Anyone who believes in the Son of God has this testimony in his heart. Anyone who does not believe God has made him out to be a liar, because he has not believed the testimony God has given about his Son" (1 John 5:9–10). This is a great and sweeping statement, but it is important because it affords an insight into the heart of God. God tells us that he wants to be believed. Moreover, he tells us that he wants us to believe him because of who he is.

These verses compare our belief in people with our belief in God, and they point out that we do believe other people. We believe in men, or in what men say, every day of our lives. If we did not, we could never ride a bus, go to work, attend a concert, sign a contract. These activities all involve acts of faith. They all involve the word of another person, sometimes even when we have not seen him or her. "Well," says God, "if you can believe other people, you can believe me; if you do not, you are dishonoring me." There are many men and women so refined and polite that they would never think of calling anyone a liar; yet they make a liar out of God every day by their unbelief. God says that they should believe him exactly as they believe other human beings.

The secret to arriving at a point of certainty in spiritual things is that we must believe what God tells us. Then, believing, we will find knowledge following. It is striking, is it not, that this is illustrated by the chapter we are studying. For the certainty Peter spoke of did not come primarily from viewing Christ's miracles—the turning of water into wine, the healing of the impotent man at Bethesda, the multiplying of the loaves and fish, or the walking on the water. It came rather from hearing and believing the "words of eternal life" that Jesus, the Holy One of God, had spoken.

One Is a Devil

At this point the sixth chapter of John reaches some sort of a climax as the result of Peter's confession. It is true that most of Christ's followers have left him. Still the Twelve have remained, and Peter has even spoken on their behalf to voice a great confession. If we were writing the Gospel, we would end the chapter at this point and go on to some new theme in chapter 7. Interestingly enough, however, John does not do this. For John is a realist, and he is portraying, not merely the growth of faith in Jesus, but also the emergence of hate for him and its intensification. Therefore, in this chapter Peter's confession of faith in Jesus is followed by a disturbing revelation.

There is some irony in the situation. Peter had spoken on behalf of the Twelve, saying, "We believe and know. . . ." But Jesus, who knew the hearts of men as his disciple did not, replied, "We? Did you say 'we,' Peter? You may not believe it now, but I tell you that one of you, one even of this small number, is a devil and will one day betray me." Actually, he did not say "betray" at this point, though he did so later. It is the evangelist himself who adds this note for clarification.

Here is a warning for us. We cannot see into the hearts of men either, though we would like to. We think at times that we have insight into men's character. Sometimes God gives insight. But still we usually see only the externals and so make many errors. "Man looks at the outward appearance, but the LORD looks at the heart" (1 Sam. 16:7). Then let us allow God to do it, and let us exercise great caution and humility in our evaluation of other men and women.

Why Judas?

Verses 70 and 71 tell us that Jesus saw into the hearts of men and knew that Judas was not a believer and would one day betray him. But if this is so (as it is), why did he choose Judas? Why not another?

The first and easiest answer to that question is that Jesus chose Judas because the Scriptures foretold it. John 17:12 tells us that, for it says, "While I was with them, I protected them and kept them safe by that name you gave me. None has been lost except the one doomed to destruction so that Scripture would be fulfilled." The reference is to Psalm 41:9 and similar passages. Jesus chose Judas to fulfill these passages. But to say this is only to push the question back one stage farther, for now we must ask, "But why did God cause such Scriptures to be written? Why did God ordain Judas to be among the twelve disciples?" Here we are helped by a number of well-thought-out comments by Arthur W. Pink, one of the most thoughtful commentators on John's Gospel.

First, as Pink notes, the choice of Judas by Jesus *furnished an opportunity for Christ to display his perfections.* When Jesus had come to earth he had professed, "Here I am . . . to do your will, O God" (Heb. 10:7). This will was written "in the volume of the book," and it included the choice of Judas as one who would betray him. This was a trial for Jesus, beyond any doubt. Judas was associated with Jesus for the three years of his ministry. They moved in the closest possible contact. Yet Judas was the devil's tool. Even when Jesus retired alone with the Twelve to escape the worst of his critics, Judas was there with him. Still He did not hesitate to do what the Father demanded. It is in his full subjection to the Father's will, written in the book, that his perfection as the incarnate Son may be evaluated.

If you are being tried, remember the perpetual trial faced by Jesus and learn that God has sent these trials into your life just as surely as he ordained the presence of Judas among the Twelve. Why? If there are no other reasons, there is at least this one—that God may display the perfections of Jesus within you as you endeavor to live for him.

Second, the choice of Judas *provided an impartial witness to the moral excellency of Christ.* Pink observes, "His Father, His forerunner, His saved apostles, bore testimony to His perfections; but lest it should be thought that these were *ex parte* witnesses, God saw to it that an *enemy* should also bear witness. Here was a man that was 'a devil'—a man who was in the closest possible touch with the life of Christ, both in public and in private; a man who would have seized eagerly on the slightest flaw, if it had been possible to find one; but it was not: 'I have betrayed . . . *innocent* blood' (Matt. 27:4), was the unsought testimony of an impartial witness."[1]

Third, the choice of Judas *gave occasion to uncover the awfulness of sin.* Imagine spending three years in the presence of the Lord Jesus Christ. Imagine all that Judas saw in that time—demonstrations of the love of God for a sick and sinful humanity; revelations of wisdom; a total lack of all the sinful aspects of human character, no pride, anger, lust, impatience, loss of self-control; total selflessness. Now imagine betraying such a One. That is how terrible sin is. The fullness of redemption brings to light the wonder of divine love. But it also was ordained that the fullness of redemption would expose something of the full horror of that sin for which the atonement was being made. Moreover, they are connected. For we will only begin to comprehend the height and depth of this divine love when we begin to see something of the nature of the sin for which Christ's blood was poured out.

Fourth, the presence of Judas *supplies the sinner with a solemn warning.* A person may experience the closest possible contact with Jesus and still not come to him for salvation. He may hear Christ's teachings, witness great miracles, observe the changed lives of others who have yielded to Christ and have believed on him, and yet not be born again. Judas was with Jesus, and he did not believe. Perhaps you are like him. You may have been raised in a godly home. You may have heard great preaching. You may have seen others believe, perhaps even in your own family. But you have not believed personally. Their faith will not save you. *You* must believe. Do not allow proximity to cheat you out of faith in the Savior.

Fifth, the presence of Judas *shows us that we may expect to find hypocrites among the followers of Jesus.* Judas was certainly a hypocrite. Think what it meant for any one of the Twelve to follow Jesus. It meant leaving home, going without any sure and certain shelter, being tired from hard journeys, preaching the gospel that Jesus instructed his disciples to preach. Judas did all these things and did them so well that, so far as we know, not one of the disciples ever suspected him of being what he was. Yet underneath it all he was no friend of the Lord Jesus Christ, and he eventually betrayed him.

There is no way of saying this nicely, but it must be said. There are Judases among the apparent followers of the Lord in our day. They are in our pews, even in our pulpits, and they are sometimes undetected. They betray the Lord and the gospel by both their words and actions. Jesus warned us to watch out for such. He called them wolves in sheep's clothing.

Sixth, the presence of Judas among the Twelve *affords us one more illustration of how radically different are God's thoughts and ways from ours.* Pink writes:

"That God should appoint a 'devil' to be one of the closest companions of the Savior; that he should have selected 'the son of perdition' to be one of the favored twelve, seemed incredible. Yet so it was."[2] Therefore, since we have seen that God did have good reasons for this selection (in spite of our thoughts to the contrary), let us learn to trust God in matters for which we can see no reason. Let us humble ourselves before him. Moreover, since we can see that God's thoughts are not our thoughts, let us learn that our thoughts must change.

Peter or Judas?

Here are two men brought together in the space of just three verses—Peter and Judas. One made a great confession. About the other we have a disturbing revelation. Which one most characterizes you? Both were with Jesus. Both gave evidences of a genuine interest in religion. But with one it was real; he was there because of Jesus. The other was there only for himself, or for what he could derive from the relationship. May I make it even more personal? What are you into Christianity for? Is it for Jesus? Or is it for yourself? I cannot promise that if you come to God out of a genuine love for the Lord Jesus Christ you will find the road easy. The company is usually good, but the road is rocky. It leads to a cross. Nevertheless, I can promise that Jesus is even more than you might hope for or realize, and beyond the cross there is glory.

90

What Time Is It?

John 7:1-10

After this, Jesus went around in Galilee, purposely staying away from Judea because the Jews there were waiting to take his life. But when the Jewish Feast of Tabernacles was near, Jesus' brothers said to him, "You ought to leave here and go to Judea, so that your disciples may see the miracles you do. No one who wants to become a public figure acts in secret. Since you are doing these things, show yourself to the world." For even his own brothers did not believe in him.

Therefore Jesus told them, "The right time for me has not yet come; for you any time is right. The world cannot hate you, but it hates me because I testify that what it does is evil. You go to the Feast. I am not yet going up to this Feast, because for me the right time has not yet come." Having said this, he stayed in Galilee.

However, after his brothers had left for the Feast, he went also, not publicly, but in secret.

Few things in this life are as important as time, but time often is wasted and thereby becomes unimportant. Moreover, it often is spent on that which later proves to have no meaning. When life is empty, time drags. Macbeth knew this and cried, "Tomorrow and tomorrow and tomorrow creeps in this petty pace from day to day." When life is full, time flies. Ovid declared, "The stream of time glides smoothly on and is past before we know." Seeing life and fortune fall before it, he also termed time "the devourer of all things." Shakespeare spoke of "the tooth of time." William James declared, "The great use of a life is to spend it for something that outlasts it."

547

But how do we know what will outlast it? Since we are bounded by time, how can we see beyond its horizons? One answer to how we can make our time count, not only for this life but for eternity also, is to be found in a saying of the Lord Jesus Christ to his brothers just before he went up to Jerusalem for the final time to begin the last phase of his work on earth.

Just before this, Jesus had concluded his work in Galilee. He had been there some time, and he had met with initial success. Nevertheless, as the true nature of his teaching became known and his claims became understood, the crowds that had once followed him willingly gradually drifted away. Eventually, he was alone with his disciples and, to judge from this narrative, in contact with his family. He seemed unwilling to leave Galilee, for he lingered there for approximately six months. This is the period between the time of the Passover, by which the events of John 6 are to be dated, and the time of the Feast of Tabernacles, which is the time note of chapter 7. The opening verse of chapter 7 explains the reason for Christ's delay in returning to Jerusalem—he was "purposely staying away from Judaea, because the Jews there were waiting to take his life."

At this point Jesus' brothers approached him. The Feast of Tabernacles was approaching, and it was their recommendation that Jesus go up to the feast with them and do miracles there. Perhaps they thought this would revive Jesus' sagging popularity. They were not altogether altruistic in their suggestions. John tells us that even his brothers did not really believe in him.

Jesus' reply was emphatic. It was not for them to tell him where and when to go. There was a great gulf between them and, besides, his steps were ordered. His exact words were, "The right time for me has not yet come; for you any time is right. The world cannot hate you, but it hates me because I testify that what it does is evil. You go up to this Feast. I am not yet going up to this Feast, because for me the right time has not yet come" (7:6–8). John goes on to tell us that Jesus remained for a time in Galilee but eventually made his way to Jerusalem secretly.

God's Time and Our Time

If we are to understand what Jesus meant by declaring that his time was not the same time as the time of his brothers (and if we are to gain insight from that for the time that is given to us), we must begin with the recognition that God's time is different from our time. In fact, it is questionable whether we can use the word "time" in reference to God's time at all. Time is a word for creation, and God is not in time. God is outside time. He stands in eternity. Consequently, we should not make the mistake of applying time concepts to him.

There is no good illustration of how God relates to what we call time, because every illustration, every word that we can draw upon, has time limitations. Nevertheless, some people have been helped by the following. We must imagine a river winding across a countryside. It begins in a mountainous interior, passes down through evergreen forests, across coastal plains, and into the sea. Moreover, we may imagine a man in a rowboat making his way down this river. He is in the mountains on Monday, among the trees on Tuesday, in the midst of the plains on Wednesday, and at the river's mouth on Thursday. For him, the mountains, forests, plains, and sea are in a time sequence. He sees only one of these geographical features at a time. On the other hand, we can imagine a pilot flying five miles above the earth's surface, and we can see that for him all the geographical features are present at the same time. He can see all the way from the mountains to the seas in one glance. God sees like the pilot because he is not confined by time. We can make the same point also by imagining time to be something like a motion picture. We view it in sequence. God views it as though it were millions of individual frames, all seen at once. From his perspective God sees Adam and Eve, Abraham and Isaac, Christ on the cross, you and me, simultaneously.

This is not just an interesting play of the imagination, of course, for it has bearing on what we understand of God and his relationship to our days. We see it primarily in the area of what you and I call "decision." For us, a life in time is filled with decisions. We make decisions constantly, and we do so in an effort to cope with variableness, ignorance, previous indecision, and other things. Our decisions are attempts to deal with problems not previously considered. God's decisions are not like this because of the nature of his relationship to time. There is no variableness or indecision with God. Consequently, his decisions are rather in the nature of eternal decrees, unchanging and unchangeable. The Westminster Shorter Catechism speaks of these decrees saying, "The decrees of God are his eternal purpose, according to the counsel of his will, whereby, for his own glory, he hath foreordained whatsoever comes to pass."

I believe that this could be a great step forward in your spiritual life if you can see it. God does not make decisions because he suddenly is confronted with a problem that he has not foreseen. He determines both the problems and their solutions in advance. He is never surprised, never caught off balance. Thus, there is never a problem that baffles him or a work that he does not intend to finish. Because of this we can rest in him and trust him for the ordering of our days.

The Time of Jesus Christ

The importance of these truths becomes particularly clear in relationship to the time of Jesus Christ, for here was God, the inhabitant of eternity, now living in time. What do we learn about the time of Jesus Christ? We learn that the time (or times) of Jesus Christ was fixed by the eternal decrees of God.

As we read the New Testament we are amazed at the number of verses that indicate that Jesus was born, lived, and died according to the fixed plan of God. For instance, Galatians 4:4–5 tells us, "But when the time had fully come, God sent his Son, born of a woman, born under law, to redeem those under law, that we might receive the full rights of sons." In Revelation 13:8 Christ's death particularly is placed in this context as John speaks of "the Lamb that was slain from the creation of the world." Paul links the same event to the prophecies of Scripture in 1 Corinthians 15:3, saying that "Christ died for our sins according to the Scriptures."

On the day of Pentecost, in the first truly Christian sermon, Peter linked both the element of prophecy and the fixing of time by the Father to Christ's crucifixion. "Men of Israel," he said, "listen to this: Jesus of Nazareth was a man accredited by God to you by miracles, wonders and signs, which God did among you through him, as you yourselves know. This man was handed over to you by God's set purpose and foreknowledge; and you, with the help of wicked men, put him to death by nailing him to the cross" (Acts 2:22–23). Later, in his first epistle, Peter repeats the same truths in writing to Christians: "For you know that it was not with perishable things such as silver or gold that you were redeemed from the empty way of life handed down to you from your forefathers, but with the precious blood of Christ, a lamb without blemish or defect. He was chosen before the creation of the world, but was revealed in these last times for your sake" (1 Peter 1:18–20).

Naturally, there are many more verses that could be cited. But we can draw all the important conclusions even from these. (1) The death of the Lord Jesus Christ was the most important event of his life, and it was eternally planned and determined by God. (2) Not only his death, but also the details of his death and other minutia of his birth and life were similarly determined. (3) When Jesus came to this earth, he was conscious that the events of his life were marked out for him by God. And (4) since these things are true, it follows that everything planned by God for Jesus Christ and revealed to us in the Scriptures has been accomplished.

One very important conclusion flows from this. If the events of Christ's life were ordered by God, as we have seen, then it follows that the most important thing that can be said about the death of the Lord Jesus Christ is that God the Father caused it. God the Father put Jesus to death. In the history of the church there have been times when men and women have emphasized the role that the Jewish leaders had in Christ's crucifixion. This has led in a very unjustifiable way to much anti-Semitism. It is true, of course, that the religious leaders did have a part in Christ's death, but this is relatively unimportant. Others, to counter this line of thought, have emphasized that it was actually the Gentiles, in the person of Pilate, who sentenced Christ to death. But again, while this is true, it is nevertheless relatively unimportant. The important thing is that God the Father put Jesus Christ to death and that he did so in order that there might be an atonement for our sins.

Imagine a trial in which a judge is obliged to impose a heavy fine upon his own son for some act of juvenile destruction. He imposes the fine, then steps down from the bench, taking his place next to his son, and pays the fine for him. This is an illustration both of the incarnation and of Christ's death.

The incarnation is God stepping down from the bench. The cross is God in love paying the fine that he in justice has imposed upon us. Can you understand this illustration? If you can, then you can see that the cross is God taking your place because he loved you and wants you to love him.

A Fixed Time Schedule

There is one more point that must be brought into focus here in order that we might understand John 7:6 and apply these truths to our own situation. The point is this: Not only were the events of the life of Jesus Christ predetermined by God, as we have seen, but even the time at which they occurred was determined. This is the only truth that gives meaning to our text. For on one day Jesus refused to go to Jerusalem, but then just three or four days later he reversed himself and did go.

The Bible does not provide us with detailed time references for every event of Christ's life. But in Daniel there is a reference to the time of his death that is so exact that we are justified in applying the same principle, the principle of time-determination, to all the events of his birth and ministry. The revelation to Daniel concerning the coming of Christ was focused in a period of seventy weeks. A week, in this phrase, as is evident from the context, concerns a period of seven years; that is, a week of years. We might say a "heptad" if we had that word in our language. There were to be seven weeks of years, by which time the city of Jerusalem was to be rebuilt, following its destruction by the Babylonians. Then there was to be a period of sixty-two weeks of years, by which time the Messiah would have come and died. The prophecy says, "Know and understand this: From the issuing of the decree to restore and rebuild Jerusalem until the Anointed One, the ruler, comes, there will be seven 'sevens,' and sixty-two 'sevens.' It will be rebuilt with streets and a trench, but in times of trouble. After the sixty-two 'sevens,' the Anointed One will be cut off and will have nothing" (Dan. 9:25–26). Here is a full prophecy of the substitutionary death of Jesus Christ for sin, and it is dated in history from the year of the issuing of the decree to rebuild Jerusalem.

When was this decree? It has been dated from several sources as having been issued in 445 B.C. Consequently, the latest possible date for the death of the Messiah, according to this prophecy, was to be 483 years later (that is, sixty-nine weeks of years, or sixty-nine times seven). The year arrived at by this reckoning is A.D. 38. Jesus must have died by then. Moreover, if the more accurate reckoning of the great British scholar Sir Robert Anderson in his book *The Coming Prince* is accurate, the dating may be even closer that this. Anderson's calculations place the end of the 483-year period on April 6, A.D. 32.[1] Clearly, then, even the precise years and days of the events of Christ's life were determined.

Moreover, this tells us a great deal about the nature of the Scriptures. In the seventeenth century an English astronomer by the name of Edmund Halley announced, on the basis of Newton's newly discovered laws of gravity, that the brilliant comet that had been seen in Europe in the year 1682 would return in 1759. Halley died in 1742, seventeen years before the time he had predicted for the comet's return. But in 1759 the comet did return, right on schedule, and the laws by which he had calculated its orbit were vindicated.

In the same way, the Scriptures of the Old Testament foretold the time of Christ's coming, even though those who had originally been the vehicles of their writing and who had received them died. The years dragged on. Throughout the ages all who had faith in God looked to the heavens and awaited the fulfillment of these prophecies. Finally a star was seen in the sky, and the wise men who followed it arrived at Bethlehem where the young child was found. The birth gave way to the life, the life to the crucifixion, the crucifixion to the resurrection and ascension. All that had been planned and determined by God concerning Jesus Christ was accomplished. The Scriptures were vindicated. Thus we were also given a firm basis for our confidence in God and our hope in Christ's return.

The conclusion to this is simple. It is that our time can either be like the world's time, like the time of Jesus' brothers, or it can be like the time of Jesus. If it is like the world's time, our time has no meaning—at any rate, no more than we ourselves are able to give to it. On the other hand, if it is like the time of Jesus, it can be filled with meaning.[2] Your time can become part of that great and eternal drama of salvation that is God's plan for the ages. If you are not a Christian, I encourage you to come to Christ for salvation and begin to allow him to plan your time. If you do, he will give your life meaning and fill all your times with opportunity.

Perhaps you are already a Christian and yet do not see how your time has been made meaningful. Do not be discouraged just because you cannot see it. God sees it, and he both knows and has planned what is happening.

Years ago I saw a film I will never forget. It was produced by the Moody Institute of Science by using both high speed and time lapse photography. It was called *Time and Eternity,* and its premise was that many things in this world escape us because we are locked in a fixed time progression. Some things move too fast for us to see. The flight of an insect is an example. The film revealed this by filming at a very high speed and then slowing the film down for projection. Other things move too slowly—the growth of a flower or the moving of clouds. When these are filmed slowly and then speeded up for viewing, the dance of a growing flower or the churning, billowing excitement of the clouds is breathtaking. We can see each of these things physically, but we miss the beauty because we are locked in our own time system. In the same way, we often miss the beauty of what God himself is doing in our lives, not because we cannot see the individual features of his work but because his work is either too slow for our comprehension or too fast. Trust him, and rejoice in the fact that one day your perspective will be his own.

91

What Do You Think of Jesus?

John 7:11–13

Now at the Feast the Jews were watching for him and asking, "Where is that man?"

Among the crowds there was widespread whispering about him. Some said, "He is a good man."

Others replied, "No, he deceives the people." But no one would say anything publicly about him for fear of the Jews.

Once, in preparation for an interview period on the *Bible Study Hour*, the staff of the radio program went out onto the streets of Philadelphia to ask people this question: "Who is Jesus Christ?" Sometimes they asked, "Do you think Jesus Christ is God?" The answers they received were illuminating, for they revealed the confusion that exists in many person's minds about the identity of this remarkable man from Nazareth.

One young woman responded, "Jesus Christ was a man who thought he was God." Another young woman, a biology student, replied, "Jesus Christ is pure essence of energy. God to me is energy, electric energy because it's something that's not known." A man told us, "I think that's something you have to decide for yourself, but he had some beautiful ideas." Others replied, "He is one that we look up to as our leader"; "he is an individual who lived two thousand years ago, who was interested in the social betterment of all classes of people"; "he was well liked; he meant well; he was a good man." Most people asked were just confused. They answered, "I haven't any idea. . . . I don't know. . . ."

The confusion that exists in most people's minds about Jesus of Nazareth was not the only thing our interviewers detected, however. The interviews also showed the fact that, in spite of their confusion, most of those who were asked about Jesus could not quite escape him. No one said, "I couldn't care less." Quite a few actually seemed embarrassed by the question.

Who is Jesus Christ? This is a question that men and women have been asking ever since Christ's time and that needs to be asked and answered again and again in each generation. Jesus had delayed in going up to the Feast of Tabernacles in Jerusalem, and while he delayed the people were asking questions about him. "Where is he?" asked the priests. "Who is he?" asked others. John then says, "Among the crowds there was widespread whispering about him. Some said, 'He is a good man.' Others said, 'No, he deceives the people'" (John 7:12).

The One Impossibility

Who is Jesus Christ? I want to help you answer that question (in case you have never faced it squarely). But I want to begin by talking about the one truly impossible answer. The one truly impossible answer is the answer that was given first by the people of Jerusalem. They said, "He is a good man." Many give this answer today, but it is the one thing that Jesus most certainly cannot be.

Why is that? It is because of the peculiar nature of his teachings. One of their most obvious features is what John Stott calls their "egocentric character." Jesus' teaching is all wrapped up in himself. For instance, Jesus often spoke of the Fatherhood of God, but whenever he did that he seemed always to go on to speak of the special relationship that he had to the Father, possessed by no other. He even had a special word for God, *abba,* which revealed his special relationship. It meant "daddy." No contemporary Jewish figure ever used this word for God; it would have been thought irreverent or even blasphemous. Yet Jesus used it. Moreover, he went on to teach that because of what he would accomplish on the cross, and *only* because of that, others could come to enjoy this relationship also.

The egocentric character of Christ's teaching is seen also in the great "I am" sayings that are so prominent in John's Gospel. "I am the bread of life," Christ said. "I am the light of the world." "I am the gate." The last of these— "I am the way and the truth and the life"—is categorical in its teaching that faith in Christ is the sole way by which a sinful man or woman can find a right relationship to God and enter heaven.

A careful study of Christ's teaching will reveal that Jesus considered the Scriptures of the Old Testament to have been written mainly about him. Moses "wrote about me," he maintained (John 5:46). "Abraham rejoiced at the thought of seeing my day; he saw it and was glad" (John 8:56). Using the books of the Old Testament as his text Jesus explained to his disciples those things that were written "concerning himself" (Luke 24:27). One great example of this outlook occurred early in his public ministry in the synagogue at Nazareth. Jesus had been asked to read from the prophets, as any male Jew might be asked to do on any Sabbath, and he had chosen to read from Isaiah 61:1–2. "The Spirit of the Sovereign LORD is on me, because the LORD has anointed me to preach good news to the poor. He has sent me to bind up the brokenhearted, to proclaim freedom for the captives and release for the prisoners, to proclaim the year of the LORD's favor." At this point, however, he closed up the scroll and applied the prophecy, saying, "Today this scripture is fulfilled in your hearing" (Luke 4:21). This was a remarkable declaration, for it was nothing less than the claim that Isaiah had written of him and that he was fulfilling this prophecy.

With such an estimate of himself it is not surprising that Jesus called men and women to follow him. In fact, he commanded them to follow him, and then later dispatched them on a world-encompassing evangelistic ministry.

The impossibility of regarding Jesus merely as a good man is seen also in his claim to be able to forgive sins, not merely sins against himself but also against others. No mere man can forgive sins, no matter how good he is. In fact, as C. S. Lewis notes, "Unless the speaker is God, this is really so preposterous as to be comic." We do not have much difficulty in imagining how a person can forgive an offense against himself. If a person should hit you, you have a right to forgive him. "Don't mention it," you might say, particularly if he said he was sorry. If he steals from you, you can also forgive him. But suppose the person should go around hitting other people, thousands of them, and stealing from them. In that case, you have no right to forgive him; and you should not regard highly anyone who thought he had this right. Yet this is precisely what Jesus did.

On one occasion, a paralyzed man was lowered into his presence from a hole cut in the roof of the house where he was teaching. Jesus said, "Son, your sins are forgiven" (Mark 2:5). On another occasion Jesus forgave a woman who was known to be a sinner in some open way. She had entered the house where Jesus was eating, wept so that her tears fell on his feet, and then wiped his feet with her hair. Jesus told her, "Your sins are forgiven" (Luke 7:48). On each occasion the onlookers objected, saying, "Who is this that forgives sins? Who can forgive sins but God only?" None of the observers was prepared to admit Christ's claim at this point, but at least they saw the issue clearly. How could he forgive sins? The claim was preposterous if he was not really God.

Finally, the impossibility of considering Jesus to be merely a good man is seen in the fact that on several occasions he openly claimed to be God. In the climate of the Judaism of his day this could not be done often or openly, for it was blasphemy and a capital offense. Nevertheless, there were times when Jesus allowed the issue to become clear.

For example, in the eighth chapter of John there is the record of a conversation between Jesus and the Jewish rulers over the relationship of Jews to Abraham. They thought they were saved because of their physical descent from Abraham. Jesus denied it. They became angry and attacked him personally. "Are you greater than our father Abraham?" they asked. Jesus answered, "Before Abraham was born, I am" (John 8:58). This so offended those who heard him that they began to pick up stones to throw at him and kill him. They did this because they recognized the claim to divinity that Christ's words implied. At the least these words were a claim to preexistence; that is, Jesus claimed to have existed in the beginning with God before Abraham was created. In addition, however, they were also a claim to be God himself. For Christ's "I am" was the very name for God—Jehovah—which means, "I am who I am" (Exod. 3:14). It was because of this claim that those who heard Jesus took up stones to kill him.

A second example of the same claim occurs when Jesus appeared to Thomas shortly after the Resurrection. Thomas had said that he would not believe in Jesus' resurrection unless he could put his finger in the nail prints of Jesus' hands and his hand into Jesus' side. But when Jesus appeared, Thomas did not insist on these tests. Instead, he fell at Jesus' feet, declaring, "My Lord and my God." What did Jesus do? Did he reply, as Paul and Barnabas did later in a similar situation, "Men, why are you doing this? We too are only men, human like you" (Acts 14:15)? Not at all! He accepted the designation of this doubting apostle, adding, "Because you have seen me, you have believed; blessed are those who have not seen, and yet have believed" (John 20:29).

What are we to do with these claims? We cannot escape them. As John Stott observes, "The claims are there. They do not in themselves constitute evidence of deity. The claims may have been false. But some explanation of them must be found. We cannot any longer regard Jesus as simply a great teacher, if He was so grievously mistaken in one of the chief subjects of His teaching, namely Himself."[1] In the same way C. S. Lewis has written, "You must make your choice. Either this man was, and is, the Son of God: or else a madman or something worse. You can shut Him up for a fool, you can spit at Him and kill Him as a demon; or you can fall at His feet and call Him Lord and God. But let us not come with any patronizing nonsense about His being a great human teacher. He has not left that open to us. He did not intend to."[2]

The Possibilities

I have said, then, that the one impossible explanation of the person of Jesus Christ is that he was a good man. But the quotation from C. S. Lewis has already begun to suggest the true possibilities. There are three of them.

First, if the unusual and egocentric claims of Jesus of Nazareth eliminate the possibility that he was merely a good man or an exceptional teacher, they nevertheless do not eliminate the possibility that he may have been mad, or, if you will, that he was suffering from a severe case of megalomania. This is the view of those who in this chapter say, "You are demon-possessed" (v. 20). This has been the case with other men. Hitler suffered from megalomania. It is probable that Napoleon did too.

Perhaps Jesus was crazy or possessed. Before we jump too quickly at this explanation, however, we need to ask whether the total character of Jesus (as we know it) bears out this speculation. Did he act like one who was crazy? Did he speak like one suffering from megalomania? It is hard to read the Gospels and be satisfied with this explanation. Rather, it is hard to escape the conclusion that Jesus was actually the sanest man who ever lived. He spoke with quiet authority. He always seemed in control of the situation. He was never surprised or rattled. He just does not seem to fit our easy classifications.

There is another reason why Jesus cannot have been crazy. It is the reaction of others to him. Men and women did not merely tolerate Jesus; they either were for him or else violently against him. This is not the way we react to those who are crazy. We may be irritated by a madman's irrational behavior. We may ignore him. We may lock him up if his delusions are dangerous. But we do not kill him. Yet this is what men who did not want to follow him tried to do to Jesus.

The second possibility is that Jesus Christ was a deceiver—the view of some others (v. 12). That is, he was out to fool men deliberately. He wanted to be a big man; therefore he made messianic claims and deluded men and women into believing them. Before we settle on this answer, however, we need to be perfectly clear about all that is involved. In the first place, if Jesus really was a deceiver, he was certainly the *best* deceiver who ever lived. Jesus claimed to be God, but we must remember that this claim was not made in a Greek or Roman environment where the idea of many gods or even half-gods was acceptable. It was made at the heart of monotheistic Judaism. Nowhere else in the ancient world could one find a strict belief in one God, but this belief was present in Judea in Christ's century. Jews were ridiculed for it. At times they were persecuted. Nevertheless, they stuck to this doctrine and were even fanatical in its defense. It was in this hostile theological climate that Christ made his claims. What happened? The remarkable thing is that he got people to believe in him. Lots of people—men and women, peasants and sophisticates, priests, even eventually members of his own family. So if Jesus was a deceiver, he was at least a good one. He was the best.

On the other hand, if Jesus was a deceiver, he was also the *worst* deceiver—so much so that he could be termed a devil if he were not God. Think it through clearly. Jesus did not merely say, "I am God," and then let it go at that. He said, "I am God come to save fallen humanity; I am the means of salvation; trust me with your life and your future." Jesus taught that God is holy and that we are barred from him because we are not holy. Our sin is a great barrier between ourselves and God. We cannot come into God's presence. Moreover, he taught that he had come to do something about our problem. He would die for our sin; he would bear our punishment. All who would trust in him would be saved. This is good news. It is even great news—but only if it is true. If it is not true, then we are of all men the most miserable and Jesus Christ should be hated as a fiend from hell. If it is not true, Jesus has condemned millions. He has sent generations of gullible followers to a hopeless eternity.

But has he? Is he a deceiver? Is this the only explanation that we can give of one who was known as being "meek and lowly"; who took the place of a poor itinerant evangelist in order that he might help the destitute and teach those whom others despised; who said, "Come unto me, all you who are weary and are burdened, and I will give you rest"? Somehow the facts do not fit. We cannot face the facts of his life and teaching and still call this man a deceiver. What then? Well, if he was not a deceiver and he was not mad, there is only one possibility left. Jesus is who he said he is. He is God, and we should follow him.

The Inescapable Christ

Do you believe that? I hope you do. Or, at least, I hope you are on the way to believing it. Who is Jesus Christ? The one thing you must try not to do is escape the question.

Some try to escape the question by running away. If you have been doing that, let me challenge you to be entirely honest with yourself on this question. You will not want to believe in Christ without evidence, but consider the evidence. Read one of the Gospels. Read it carefully and critically. Ask yourself: Is Jesus mad? Is he a deceiver? Is he God? And before you read, ask God to help you understand what is written. You do not even have to believe in God for certain. Just pray, "God (if there is a God), I want you to know that I am an honest seeker after truth, and I want to understand who Jesus Christ is. I know that I cannot be impartial about so great an issue; therefore, I promise that if you show me that Jesus of Nazareth really is your Son and our Savior, I will obey and follow him." I assure you that if you will pray this prayer, God will lead you into his truth. Just a few verses farther on in John's Gospel the Lord himself declares this saying, "If anyone chooses to do God's will, he will find out whether my teaching is from God or whether I speak on my own" (v. 17).

Finally, you may be one who is already intellectually convinced of the truth of Jesus' claims, yet you have not yet committed yourself to him and thus come to know him personally. If you are in this position, you should know that your position is untenable. Do not delay. Honesty demands a response, and divine love draws you to Jesus. Say, "Jesus, I have tried to go my own way until this time. I have tried to avoid you. I was wrong, and I will do so no longer. From now on I accept your death on my behalf. I promise to be your follower."

92

Man's Doctrine, God's Doctrine

John 7:14–18

Not until halfway through the Feast did Jesus go up to the temple courts and begin to teach. The Jews were amazed and asked, "How did this man get such learning without having studied?"

Jesus answered, "My teaching is not my own. It comes from him who sent me. If anyone chooses to do God's will, he will find out whether my teaching comes from God or whether I speak on my own. He who speaks on his own does so to gain honor for himself, but he who works for the honor of the one who sent him is a man of truth; there is nothing false about him."

We come in this chapter to a second important question raised about the Lord Jesus Christ. The first question, which we looked at in the last study, concerned his person. It was expressed in the form: "Who is he?" In answering that question we saw that Jesus of Nazareth cannot be either a good man, a deceiver, or crazy. Hence, he must be God. The second question concerns his teaching: "Is it true? Can it be trusted?" This question was raised by Christ's contemporaries.

"Not until halfway through the Feast did Jesus go up to the temple courts and begin to teach. The Jews were amazed and asked, 'How did this man get such learning without having studied?' Jesus answered, 'My teaching is not my own. It comes from him who sent me. If anyone chooses to do God's will, he

559

will find out whether my teaching comes from God or whether I speak on my own. He who speaks on his own does so to gain honor for himself, but he who works for the honor of the one who sent him is a man of truth; there is nothing false about him" (7:14–18). We realize from these verses that so long as Jesus was hidden from the crowds, as he was for the first half of the feast, the questions of the people concerned him personally. However, when he suddenly appeared and began to teach, the questions shifted from who he was to what he was saying. These were marvelous teachings. The people had never heard anything like them. They were coming from one who had never received formal training in the rabbinical schools.

"Where did he get this teaching?" Hidden within their question was the deeper question as to whether or not anything so radical and new could be trusted. We see the importance of this question when we realize that many persons ask it today when they hear true Christian teaching for the first time.

Not of Human Origin

It is interesting to note how Christ replied, for his reply stressed the enormous gulf that exists between all human teaching and that which is divine in origin. If we had been in this situation, we might have been inclined to stress our own originality, which, in a sense, Jesus himself might have done. However, if he had done that—if he had said that he was self-taught or that he needed no teacher—he would have been discredited at once. For no one in Christ's age prized originality. The rabbis taught by quoting other rabbis, particularly those who had lived before them. The Jewish Talmud today is composed largely of such rabbinic quotations. So Jesus did not do that. Instead, when he was questioned about it he replied, not by denying the need for external authority but by citing the highest authority of all. "My teaching is not my own," he said. "It comes from him who sent me." The tradition out of which Jesus spoke was God's.

This being true, however, it follows that there is an enormous gulf between human traditions and the revelation of God: in other words, between man's doctrine and God's doctrine. These are not the same. They are not even variations of the same basic principles. They are opposed. Consequently, in all spiritual things we need revelation. And we need to be suspicious of any teaching that originates in man.

Many Differences

God says, in speaking to men, "My thoughts are not your thoughts, neither are your ways my ways" (Isa. 55:8). This is true, and it can be seen by comparing the teaching and views of the world with God's teaching on all the great spiritual issues.

Take the *doctrine of God* himself. What does the world think about God? Well, the world has differing views. Some of them have been cited by the English writer and Bible translator J. B. Phillips in the book *Your God Is Too Small.* There is God the Policeman, God the Parental Hangover, the Grand Old Man, God the Managing Director, and so on. If we turn to the books of philosophy, we find definitions that are more carefully constructed but no better. God is the Ideal. He is the Prime Mover. In more modern terms he is the author of the "big bang" that got the expanding universe expanding. Basic to all these ideas, however, is the thought that God is not particularly involved in life now or that, if he is, he is not particularly righteous or fair in the way he goes about it.

How different this is from the Christian view. According to the teaching of Jesus Christ, God is the holy and sovereign God of all eternity and all history. He planned the world from before its creation. He brought each thing into being according to a perfect plan. He sustains life now and guides history. He came in the person of his Son to redeem a fallen humanity. He constantly intervenes to save men and women as an expression of his grace. Moreover, he will one day conduct a righteous and final judgment.

We may also see the difference between the views of human beings and the truth of God in regard to the doctrine of *Scripture.* What is the Bible? Many will answer that the Bible is a record of man's seeking after God and of his views about God—if indeed they do not say something worse. But God tells us that the Bible is his word about man and to man in his lost condition. Is the Bible human in origin? If so, it is dispensable. Is it divine? If that is the case, it is the only sure foundation for us in a faltering universe.

Unfortunately, even Christians sometimes get off the track on Scripture. This is true of enthusiasts, for instance—those who feel that fervor is the important thing and that teachings do not matter. But they do matter. Those who think this way are a bit like a couple who bought a house shortly after World War II. Houses were not being built too well in those days, but this couple finally thought that they had found a good one. Besides, they noted, it had a fireplace. That was a rare thing in a new home then. The first night in the house was a chilly and windy night, so the husband decided to build a fire in the fireplace. He did, and they watched it burn. Suddenly the fire dropped through the floor into the basement, and when they examined the fireplace they discovered that it had no base. There was nothing for the fire to rest upon except the floor. There is similar waste and uselessness for anyone who attempts to kindle the fires of religious enthusiasm on any other base than the firm teachings and principles of the Word of God.

Man's doctrine and God's doctrine also differ where *man himself* is concerned. Man's doctrine rates man by man's standards, and by man's standard he is not too bad. At any rate, most people are not too bad, and almost everyone can take comfort from the fact that he is better than someone else in something. If we were to express morality in inches, we would all acknowledge that there are Wilt Chamberlains as well as midgets, and take courage from the fact that we are (at least in our own opinion) somewhat above the average.

But God does not look at man from man's perspective. He looks from his perspective, and from that point of view all persons fall woefully short of his requirements. To return to the illustration of physical height, it is as though God were looking down on us from the top of the Empire State Building in New York. Down on Thirty-eighth Street people might be four, five, or six feet tall and that might seem important. But from God's perspective they all seem like midgets. The Bible says, "For all have sinned and fall short of the glory of God" (Rom. 3:23).

If you doubt God's verdict upon you and question his evaluation of your character, you need to present your case before the bar of Scripture. Study the law. I am convinced that if you do you will accept yourself after the examination as being far more sinful than you previously imagined.

Sometime ago a San Francisco policeman stopped a car for having a noisy muffler. He found that it was not registered. When he called up the warrants bureau he found that there were fifty-nine parking violations registered against the car and that the total charges were $1,217. Finally, he also learned that the driver was the son of Joseph Alioto, the mayor of the city. When word of the unpaid tickets reached the mayor he exploded, but he also ordered a check on the rest of his family. Imagine his surprise when he learned that eight different Aliotos—including the mayor himself, his wife, and four of his sons—owed $422 on twenty-two separate violations. He paid them. In the same way the law exposes our sin and teaches us our true standing before God.

The differences between human opinions concerning the *Lord Jesus Christ* and the Father's teaching about him are another example. The present chapter of John's Gospel is full of such human opinions. We find some calling Jesus "a good man" (v. 12). This is the most impossible view of all. Some called Christ a "deceiver" (v. 12). Others were willing to call him a "prophet" (v. 40). Some said he was possessed by a demon, another way of saying that he was crazy (v. 20). Some felt that he was very courageous (v. 26) and that he was what we would call a "spellbinder" (v. 46). The truth of the matter is that Jesus is God.

We turn to the *death of Jesus Christ,* and we find the same variation. Some say that the cross was a tragedy; others, an example of brave suffering. The Bible teaches that the cross was the place of vicarious sacrifice, that Jesus died there for sinful men, and that from before the foundation of the world this great sacrifice was planned as the means by which God would save those whom he had previously determined to save.

You say, "But that is hard to understand and accept." You are right, and that is the whole point. These things are hard to understand and accept. But for that reason God has taken time to explain them. It is why, in the case of the sacrifice of Jesus Christ, God the Father began to teach about it back in Old Testament times. The Jewish people were no more prone to accept the idea of vicarious sacrifice than we are. But God used the animal sacrifices, which he established and regulated, to teach that one day the perfect Lamb, his Son, would come and die for the sin of the world.

Finally, we think of *judgment,* and we find that men scoff at it. "The only hell we shall ever know is the hell we make for ourselves on this earth," they argue. But the Bible says, "In the past God overlooked such ignorance, but now he commands all people everywhere to repent. For he has set a day when he will judge the world with justice by the man he has appointed. He has given proof of this to all men by raising him from the dead" (Acts 17:30–31). Can you dismiss this doctrine? Must you not rather receive it as the teaching of Christ and of the whole Word of God?

No Satisfaction

The tremendous difference that exists between man's doctrine and God's doctrine leads to a few conclusions.

First, it is only God's doctrine that satisfies. There is no comfort in the speculations of men, at least not in the moments of crisis. If we can be shaken, that which is the product of our minds or hands can be shaken also. The story is told of a Roman Catholic sculptor who lived in Europe years ago. He was dying, and so was visited by his priest. The priest talked to him and then, seeing how ill he was, prepared to give him final unction. "You are dying," he said. He held up a beautiful crucifix. "Look upon your God, who died for you."

The sculptor looked and then cried out, "Alas for me; I made it." There is no satisfaction in that which is the fruit of our own hands. Human theories will not satisfy in the hour of death. Only divine truth will stabilize.

Satisfaction

The second conclusion is that we can be sure of God's doctrine even though it is strange to us. How? Jesus told how in these verses, showing that the key is to be found in a willingness to obey God and follow in the direction that true doctrine leads, even before we know what it is. He said, "If anyone chooses to do God's will, he will find out whether my teaching is from God or whether I speak on my own" (v. 17). God does not give assurance in spiritual things merely to satisfy curiosity. He does not teach divine truth to those who will not live by it. However, if a man determines in advance that he will live by it—that he is serious with God—then God will disclose the truths of his Word to him. In particular, he will disclose the truth concerning the Lord Jesus Christ to those who determine that they will follow him.

Harry Ironside tells of a young man who did that. He was a cowboy out in Arizona, and he had gotten away from God. For years he had ridiculed and rejected the Bible. But at last, when he was under deep conviction of sin, someone said, "Why don't you just go to God yourself and ask him to make it clear to you?" He took these words to heart. One night by the side of his bed he knelt and prayed, "O God, if there is a God and if you can look down on a poor lost sinner like me and if you can hear my prayer, if Jesus Christ is your Son, reveal this to me; for if you do, I promise that I will serve you for the rest of my days." The cowboy then began to search the Bible. Afterward he said that, although he could not explain it, a change took place and within three days he knew beyond a doubt that the Lord Jesus Christ was indeed the Son of God and his Savior. This man became a faithful servant of the Lord for many years, until God finally took him home to heaven.

If you say, "But I can't believe the Bible," I will tell you why you cannot. You have not yet determined to go the way God's truth leads. However, once you determine to go God's way, you will know these things are true. What will it be for you—God's doctrine or the doctrines of human beings? Will it be truth or error? Make truth your guest. God's truth is the best of all guests. Entertain it, and it will bless you as Abraham was blessed by the visiting angels.

93

Judging by Right Judgment

John 7:19-24

"Has not Moses given you the law? Yet not one of you keeps the law. Why are you trying to kill me?"

"You are demon-possessed," the crowd answered. "Who is trying to kill you?"

Jesus said to them, "I did one miracle, and you are all astonished. Yet, because Moses gave you circumcision (though actually it did not come from Moses, but from the patriarchs), you circumcise a child on the Sabbath. Now if a child can be circumcised on the Sabbath so that the law of Moses may not be broken, why are you angry with me for healing the whole man on the Sabbath? Stop judging by mere appearances, and make a right judgment."

The fundamental spiritual error of the human heart is to think that a person can please God by his own natural efforts. But this error leads to others. It leads to errors in estimating the person and work of Christ, for example. If we are doing all right by our own efforts, or think we are, then we think that we are obviously not much different from Christ himself and certainly do not need a Savior. It also leads to errors concerning the law of God. We are encouraged to believe that the law was given to be followed as a way of salvation—which is nowhere taught in the Bible— rather than as a standard that is meant to condemn sinners and to drive the one who feels its condemnation to the Lord Jesus Christ.

This latter error—the error of thinking that the law was given to be kept as a way of salvation—lies behind the following story.

565

Christ in Judea

For a number of months, perhaps for the better part of a year, the Lord Jesus Christ had been carrying on a ministry in Galilee. Galilee was north of Judea, and, more than that, it was divided from it by the entirely different and independent land of Samaria. Therefore, what Jesus did in the north was of relatively little concern to the rulers of Judea. After the turning of public opinion in the north, however, and as the time of his prophesied crucifixion grew closer, Jesus returned to Jerusalem and thus at once plunged into the midst of the hostility of the authorities.

What Jesus had done in the north was not really much in the minds of these religious leaders. But there was not one of them who had forgotten that on his last visit to Jerusalem a year before, Jesus had violated their understanding of the sabbath by healing a paralyzed man. That was work, according to their understanding. The law said, "Remember the Sabbath day by keeping it holy. Six days you shall labor and do all your work, but the seventh day is a Sabbath to the LORD your God. On it you shall not do any work, neither you, nor your son or daughter, nor your manservant or maidservant, nor your animals, nor the alien within your gates" (Exod. 20:8–10). If Jesus could do such things on the sabbath, he was obviously dangerous. He was a sinner, and he was teaching others to sin. At the time of this miracle the leaders had, therefore, tried to kill him. Jesus had escaped. But he had now returned, and they remembered.

The common people as a whole did not recognize this malignant hatred on the part of their leaders. Jesus did, but they did not. Consequently, they did not understand why Jesus was speaking as he was in answering these leaders. Some of the ambiguities of the conversation vanish when we recognize this. Moreover, the purpose of the law becomes clear for us also. For Jesus told why God gave the law at the same time that he was teaching both what are the right and wrong attitudes men hold toward it.

This becomes personal for us, particularly toward the end of Christ's conversation with the people and leaders. For Jesus concluded, "Stop judging by mere appearances, and make a right judgment" (v. 24). To be sure that we do judge rightly, particularly where the law is concerned, we need to pay close attention to Christ's statements.

The Law Condemns

The first statement that the Lord Jesus Christ made was that anyone trusting in the law will be condemned by the law, for no one keeps it perfectly. I know that this is somewhat veiled in this specific conversation, due to the fact that Christ was speaking directly to those men who hated him. Yet this is the general teaching. Jesus said, "Has not Moses given you the law? Yet not one of you keeps the law. Why are you trying to kill me?" (v. 19). Would these men make the law their standard? Well, then, the law would condemn them.

They would use the law to attempt to prove that Jesus Christ was a sinner, but even while they were doing it the law would condemn them for their hatred and murderous designs.

The law always does that. It condemns. Someone said to me once that you should never point a finger at someone else and say, "He is responsible." For every time you point a finger at another you have three fingers pointing at yourself. Will you attempt to find another guilty before God's righteous standards? You yourself are condemned. Will you attempt to live by the law? The law will pronounce its judgment upon you.

We find a great illustration of this from an incident in the life of King David. David had sinned in committing adultery with Bathsheba and then in having her husband killed. So God sent the prophet Nathan to the king. Nathan told the king this story. "There were two men in a city," he said, "one rich and the other poor. The poor man had nothing except one ewe lamb, which he had raised as a member of his family. The children played with it, and it ate from his own table. It was almost like a daughter to him. The rich man, on the other hand, had many sheep. One day, when a traveler came to the rich man, the man who had much was not willing to take one of his own flock to prepare it for the traveler but rather took the poor man's lamb and served it to his visitor." David became terribly angry, too angry, in fact. He said, "As surely as the LORD lives, the man who did this deserves to die!" Nathan allowed David to finish his speech, and then told him that David was the man. What does the law do? The law condemns. It shows that we have violated it. Thus, there can never be hope of salvation by observing the law.

There is another reason for this also. The reason is seen in the nature of God's law, which is to demand perfection. The law says, "Cursed is everyone who does not continue to do everything written in the Book of the Law" (Gal. 3:10; cf. Deut. 27:26). If salvation could come by any law, it would come by God's law. God's law is perfect. But no one keeps it. Hence, its very perfection condemns us. Christ's first point was an important one. Anyone trusting in the law will be condemned by the law. If we are to be saved, salvation must come by a different road entirely.

Second, Jesus showed that trusting in the law makes one a hypocrite. For the legalist will condemn in another what he excuses in himself. Here were Jewish leaders condemning Christ for healing a man on the sabbath, but they were refusing to see that they themselves did things that basically were no different. Jesus revealed this in regard to their enactment of the rite of circumcision.

His argument went something like this. It was the law of the Old Testament that a male child should be circumcised on the eighth day after his birth (Lev. 12:3). Naturally, the eighth day would often fall on the sabbath. But it was the teaching of the rabbis, recorded in the Mishnah, that "everything necessary for circumcision" could be done on the sabbath day. "Well," said Jesus, "don't you see what you are doing? You say that you fully observe the law that was given to you through Moses, including the laws concerning the sabbath. The laws of the sabbath forbid work, and you have interpreted that to mean every kind of activity except that which is absolutely necessary to save life. Technically, this should exclude circumcision. Yet you permit it, and it is right that you do. Moreover, notice that circumcision is a form of mutilation. How hypocritical then for you to blame me for curing a man's body, making it whole, when you for the sake of religion actually mutilate it on the seventh day!"

This is an unusually intricate argument, suited to the particular type of hypocrisy prevalent in Christ's time, but the principle is no less true for ours. Legalism gives birth to hypocrisy. So for this reason also law cannot be the basis for a saving relationship to God Almighty. Besides, it makes men hard. Had the Jewish leaders understood the implications of the Mosaic provision for circumcision on the sabbath "they would have seen that deeds of mercy such as he had just done were not merely permissible but obligatory" for men, as Morris indicates.[1]

The Use of the Law

At this point, then, we have come to the end of Christ's specific teachings about the law in John 6. But we are still left with a question. If no one can be saved by the law and if trying to live by law actually tends to make one a hypocrite, why then did God give the law? Did God give the law to condemn? Does God take delight in the law's verdict upon sinful humanity? The answer is that the law was given to point men and women to Christ. The law was not given with the thought that anyone would ever keep it as a way of salvation. The law was a standard given in order to convince men of their true and hopeless condition so that they might turn from their own efforts at salvation and come to God for grace.

The law can be compared to a mirror. The function of a mirror is to show you your face and, if your face is dirty, to show you that it is dirty. The purpose of a mirror is not to wash your face. Imagine a person coming into the house after a hard day's work, looking in a mirror, and discovering that his face is dirty. Then imagine him taking the mirror off the wall and attempting to wash his face with it. How ridiculous! Yes, but it is no more ridiculous than the folly of a man who thinks that he can be made righteous by the law's righteous standards. The purpose of the mirror is to drive one to the soap and water. Similarly, the function of the law is to drive the one who discovers his sin by means of the law to Christ.

But how could he know about Christ? Particularly, how could a Jew living in Old Testament times know that there was to be a Savior? The answer is that at the same time God gave the law, he also gave the instructions concerning the sacrifices. At the same time that he gave Moses, he also gave Aaron, who was the high priest.

It is as though God in the same moment in which he declared, "Thou shalt not," also went on to say, "But I know you will, and so this is the way to get out of it."

Nearly all the sacrifices prescribed in the Old Testament point to Christ, of course. But the meaning of the sacrifice is made particularly clear in two sacrifices always performed in Israel on the Day of Atonement. The first sacrifice was that of a goat that was driven away into the wilderness to die there. This goat was brought to Aaron or to those high priests who followed him. The high priest placed his hands on the head of the goat, thereby identifying himself and the people with it. He then confessed the people's sins, symbolically transferring them to the goat, which was then driven out into the wilderness. The text says, "The goat will carry on itself all their sins" (Lev. 16:22).

The other sacrifice was the sacrifice made in the courtyard of the temple. After making a sacrifice for himself, Aaron was to take another goat, kill it, and then bring its blood into the Holy of Holies where it was to be placed upon the mercy seat of the ark of the covenant beneath the wings of the cherubim. All this was symbolic. The ark contained the stone tablets of the law of Moses, which were broken. The space between the outstretched wings of the cherubim represented the presence of God. Without the blood of the innocent substitute the picture is one of stern judgment and inevitable condemnation. God looks down upon the law that all men have broken. The broken law calls for death. But then, the blood of the goat is placed between God's presence and the law, and God's wrath is averted. Death has occurred. Sin has been punished. Now God looks in grace upon the sinner.

I do not know how much of the great plan of salvation concerning the birth, life, and death of Jesus Christ most of those living before his time understood. Some undoubtedly understood much; others, little. But I do know this: The sacrifices were given to show the way in which salvation was to come, so that when a person despaired of finding salvation by means of the law he might look for a Savior.

Jesus Christ is that Savior. He bore your sin upon himself, if you are one whom the Father has given to him. He carried away your sin, as the scapegoat carried away the sins of the nation. He intervened between the wrath of God and the law that you have broken, as the blood of the sacrifice intervened on the Day of Atonement. He died for you. He died that you might be made the righteousness of God in him (2 Cor. 5:21).

We sing it in many of our hymns.

> What can wash away my sin?
> Nothing but the blood of Jesus;
> What can make me whole again?
> Nothing but the blood of Jesus.
>
> O precious is the flow
> That makes me white as snow;
> No other fount I know,
> Nothing but the blood of Jesus.

Or again:

> Not the labors of my hands
> Can fulfill thy law's demands;
> Could my zeal no respite know,
> Could my tears forever flow,
> All for sin could not atone;
> Thou must save, and thou alone.
> Rock of ages, cleft for me,
> Let me hide myself in thee.

Cleansed from Sin

Many years ago, toward the end of the twelfth century, Scotland's great king Robert the Bruce was being chased by English soldiers. They were almost upon him, so when he realized that he was not making the speed he should he left the path and darted through the moorlands and thick forest, hoping to escape. Robert ran mile after mile. But then, just as he was telling himself that perhaps at last he had escaped the vengeance of King Edward, he heard a sound that made his blood run cold. It was the baying of his own bloodhounds. He knew that the English, fearing that they would lose him in the thicket, had let loose his own bloodhounds, putting them on his track. The animals that were supposed to protect their master faithfully were actually serving the English by running him down. Robert knew that it was all over for him unless he could succeed in putting something between himself and the hounds that might throw off his scent. Desperate now and exhausted, he stumbled on until suddenly he came to a clear mountain brook. At once he plunged in, allowed it to sweep him a mile or two downstream, and then came out on the other side of the forest, where he hid and listened as the hounds came up to the water and were able to go no farther. The scent was gone. The king had escaped from his enemies.

You can easily see the application. The law, which is supposed to do us good, actually serves to our hurt and betrays us. We are lost unless we plunge into that one stream that will wash out the scent of sin forever. Jesus is that stream. Will you come to him? Will you drink of him? Will you allow his blood to cleanse you?

94

Who Has Done More Than Jesus?

John 7:25–31

At that point some of the people of Jerusalem began to ask, "Isn't this the man they are trying to kill? Here he is, speaking publicly, and they are not saying a word to him. Have the authorities really concluded that he is the Christ? But we know where this man is from; when the Christ comes, no one will know where he is from."

Then Jesus, still teaching in the temple courts, cried out, "Yes, you know me, and you know where I am from. I am not here on my own, but he who sent me is true. You do not know him, but I know him because I am from him and he sent me."

At this they tried to seize him, but no one laid a hand on him, because his time had not yet come. Still, many in the crowd put their faith in him. They said, "When the Christ comes, will he do more miraculous signs than this man?"

It is a good thing to ask questions. But there is no point in asking questions unless what we ask leads to answers. Only a fool or a child asks questions just to ask questions. In the verses in John to which we now come there are three questions, each asked by a group of persons who had witnessed a part of the ministry of the Lord Jesus Christ. Each of these is important; in fact, one of them is terribly important. Yet not one is answered. We turn, therefore, to the questions, not for the questions themselves but for the answers and, in particular, so that we may arrive at the

571

all-important answer to that question that concerns our own personal estimate of the Lord Jesus Christ and our relationship to him.

Three Questions

The first question is found in verse 25. It is asked by a group of people who
were knowledgeable about affairs in Jerusalem. Most of the people did not
know of the hostility directed against Jesus by the religious leaders; but some
did know of it, and these were puzzled by the fact that Jesus apparently was
allowed to go on teaching. Their question was: "Isn't this the man they are
trying to kill?" John does not give the answer to this question, but the answer
is obvious. "Yes, it is!" Since Jesus is the sinless Son of God, this answer tells
us much about the corruption of the human heart.

The second question follows immediately upon the first one as the result
of a kind of reasoning by those who had asked it. "Have the authorities really
concluded that he is the Christ?" (v. 26). The answer was, "No, they have not"—
and that is because they did not wish to know. This answer exposes the truly
lost condition of men and women, for none are so blind as those who will
not see, or deaf, who will not hear.

Finally, there is a question by another group who, we are told, actually believed in Jesus. Their question deals with Christ's actions and is expressed
as follows: "When Christ [that is, the Messiah] comes, will he do more miraculous signs than this man?" (v. 31). The answer at this point, although John
once again does not give it explicitly, is: "No, he will not." Consequently, the
conclusion must be that Jesus is the Christ, and that we should believe on
him as the Savior.

Do you believe on him? Is he your Savior? If not, you must ask yourself this
question: When the Messiah comes, will he do more—could he do more—
than Jesus?

Christ and the Scriptures

Let me help you a bit with your answer, and let me do so by bringing to
mind some of the things that Jesus has done. First, *Jesus alone has fulfilled the
Scriptures.* This is his own teaching. He said, "Do not think that I have come to
abolish the Law or the Prophets; I have not come to abolish them but to fulfill
them" (Matt. 5:17).

It is also confirmed by observation. Toward the end of the brilliant ministry of John the Baptist, after he had been thrown into prison, John's spirits
sagged. The time came when he sent friends to Jesus to ask whether Jesus was
indeed the Messiah or whether he and his followers should look for another.
Jesus did not answer directly but instead sent back a quotation from Isaiah in
which he detailed the accomplishments of his ministry. He said, "Go back
and report to John what you hear and see: The blind receive sight, the lame
walk, those who have leprosy are cured, the deaf hear, the dead are raised,

and the good news is preached to the poor. Blessed is the man who does not fall away on account of me" (Matt. 11:4–6). Jesus' claim was based on an appeal to the Scriptures, and his point was that he alone was fulfilling them. In time, as we know, he fulfilled them completely, even to the point of the prophecies concerning the specific details of his death and resurrection.

When the Messiah comes, will he do more to fulfill the detailed prophecies of the Old Testament than Jesus has done?

Jesus Is God

Second, because of fulfilling the Scriptures and for other reasons, *Jesus has convinced millions that he is God manifest in human flesh* and that he alone has answers to the deep problems of life.

We must not think that believing in an incarnate God came easy to Christ's contemporaries while it is hard for us today. It may have been easy for Greeks or Romans, for much of their mythology contained similar ideas. But it was not easy for Jesus' Jewish contemporaries, and it was among orthodox Jews that the gospel first gained a foothold. Here were people who had been raised in a culture based upon centuries of ardent monotheism. They declared in their synagogues, "Hear, O Israel: The LORD our God, the LORD is one LORD" (Deut. 6:4). They abhorred the polytheism of the gentile cultures of the day. Yet, through talking with Jesus and through observing him as he went about the countryside teaching and doing good, these men came to believe that he was more than man, that he was God incarnate. Many of them later died as martyrs rather than renounce that belief. Peter declared, "You are the Christ, the Son of the living God" (Matt. 16:16). Thomas called him "My Lord and my God" (John 20:28). Paul wrote that he was "declared with power to be the Son of God by his resurrection from the dead" (Rom. 1:4).

It is the same today. Millions confess Jesus to be the One whom he claimed to be. Centuries separate us from the time in which Jesus Christ lived and carried on his ministry. The weight of secular opinion, steeped as it is in skepticism, is against the conclusion that Jesus is God. Yet Jesus has spoken to us and convinced those of us who have studied his life and been moved by it that he is God and that he has the answers to life. Who else has convinced millions of this truth, as Jesus has done?

When the Messiah comes, will he convince more people of his godhead than have already been convinced by Jesus?

A Social Revolution

Third, Jesus has launched *the only great and lasting social changes the world has ever seen.* That is a categorical statement, but it is justified. At the time of Christ's coming the world was a place of great cruelty and horror. Slavery was universally practiced and accepted. Gladiatorial contests brought literal death before the eyes of millions for amusement. Unwanted children were exposed upon the hillsides to die. Pride divided the free man from the slave, Jew from Gentile, man from woman, Roman from Greek. It was a barbarous age, as Fellini has so well depicted in his *Satyricon* and *Roma* and as the historians of the time have reported.

But Jesus changed that. He came, not with a social program alone, but with a new ethic founded upon a new life that was his life within all who should follow him. The change did not happen at once. In the early years, the preachers of the gospel were fortunate if they were given an opportunity just to preach the gospel. But, in time, the life of the risen Lord took hold of at least some people, and a number of others, even those who were not Christians, responded.

The greatest changes took place during the reigns of the emperors Constantine and Justinian. Cruel sports, such as those of the arena, were checked, for Christians opposed them. Laws came into being that protected the slave. He could no longer be branded as a sign of ownership, for instance. He could no longer be killed at the whim of his owner. Children were given legal rights that they had never before possessed. Hospitals and orphanages came into being. At times the progress was slow. There were setbacks. The Middle Ages were in some ways a return to barbarism. Those who went by the name of Christian often did non-Christian things. Still, at the time of the recovery of the gospel during the Reformation period, the social conscience of Christianity was found not to be lost. So we find Zwingli instituting social reforms at Zurich, and Calvin creating jobs for the thousands of refugees who thronged the streets of Geneva.

Zwingli transformed the preacher's monastery into a poorhouse where food was dispensed each day to those who wanted it. Begging was abolished. Apprentices were subsidized. Poor children were clothed. The register in which the rules were recorded regarding the care of beggars still exists; and the inscription at the top of the page begins, "Be merciful, says the Lord, as your Father in heaven is merciful."

Please do not misunderstand me. I do not mean to say by this rehearsal of history that non-Christians have never done a charitable deed, still less that Christians have always done them. In ancient times there were acts of charity practiced by some individuals. In our day much is done by non-Christians in proper imitation of Christian standards. But Jesus is the starting point nonetheless. He alone has inspired men, not only to do, but to persevere in the doing of that which we call social concerns and actions.

When the Messiah comes, will he bring about greater social changes than those occasioned by Jesus?

The Emancipator

Fourth, *Jesus has liberated the souls of millions.* When Jesus was on earth, at the beginning of his ministry on one occasion he entered the synagogue at Nazareth where he had been brought up and was asked to read the Old Testament lesson. He took the scroll of Isaiah and began to read from the sixty-first chapter. He read: "The Spirit of the Lord is on me, because he has anointed me to preach good news to the poor. He has sent me to proclaim freedom for the prisoners and recovery of sight for the blind, to release the oppressed, to proclaim the year of the Lord's favor" (Luke 4:18–19). He then declared, "Today this scripture is fulfilled in your hearing" (v. 21).

In this Old Testament quotation two phrases speak of emancipation: "to preach deliverance to the captives" and "to set at liberty them that are bruised." This was one of the most important parts of Christ's ministry. In Christ's day men and women were in physical bondage, but an even greater truth is that in his day, as in ours, many more were in spiritual bondage. They were bound by sin. Never more than one-half or two-thirds of the people on earth have ever been held in physical slavery at any one time. But all men at all times have been held captive by sin. Jesus has set millions free. Some were held down by drink, but Christ freed them. Others were enslaved by drugs, but Jesus broke those shackles. He has freed men of pride, arrogance, selfishness, and thousands of other debilitating things.

Has he done that for you? Or are you still caught in something from which you cannot free yourself? He can free you. Above all, he can liberate your soul. Charles Wesley wrote a magnificent verse of a great hymn about it. The stanza goes:

> Long my imprisoned spirit lay
>   Fast bound in sin and nature's night;
> Thine eye diffused a quick'ning ray,
>   I woke, the dungeon flamed with light;
> My chains fell off, my heart was free,
>   I rose, went forth, and followed Thee.

When the Messiah comes, will he provide us with a greater measure of true spiritual freedom than Jesus provides for those who come to him?

Healer of Broken Hearts

Finally, there is a phrase in these verses that points to *Jesus as the healer of broken hearts*. He said that God sent him "to heal the brokenhearted," and this he has done.

We do not often talk about broken hearts, for the subject is much too personal. Yet there are broken hearts, millions of them. They are all around us, and we often are touched in this way ourselves. There is no one who is exempt. I talk to men whose wives have been unfaithful to them. Sometimes they are in the ministry. I talk to women who have lost their husbands to other women, but who still love their husbands. Some have had their hearts broken by death or by the fact that their children have left home and have to all appearances rejected Christ and Christianity. Some have failed in life. Some are homeless. These are the heartbreaks of human existence; and if Jesus Christ does not have the answer, there is just no answer.

But there is an answer, of course, and he has it. Jesus said that God sent him to heal the brokenhearted. Will Jesus Christ fail? Abraham succeeded in the task that God gave him. Moses succeeded. So did David and all the rest. Is Jesus Christ only to fail? Not at all. He has done what the Father sent him to do in millions of cases, and he is still doing it today. Heartbreak may be all too real, but those who have known Christ's love and power have been able to go on with their lives, rejoicing in him. Horatius Bonar sang,

> I have no help but thine, nor do I need
> Another arm save thine to lean upon:
> It is enough, my Lord, enough indeed;
> My strength is in thy might, thy might alone.

Jesus heals broken hearts. When the Messiah comes, will he heal more hearts than Jesus?

Come to Jesus

At the time of the Civil War in America a young man still in his teens was court-martialed by the Union Army and sentenced to be shot. He had gone to the war before he had to, because his friend had gone, and in friendship he had been willing to stand guard one night while his friend was somewhere else. Unfortunately, he had been on duty himself the night before; so, having been awake for two nights, he could not resist drowsiness and fell asleep at his post. For this he was sentenced to death.

When news of what had happened reached the boy's parents in New England their hearts were broken. To think that their only and beloved son should be shot! The boy's sister, a little girl who had read the life of Lincoln and knew from her reading how much he loved his own children, said, "If Abraham Lincoln knew how my father and mother loved my brother, he would not let him be shot." She determined that she would see the President. Security was not so strict in those days as it is today. So when the little girl reached the White House and told her story to the sentinel on duty, he was touched by her imploring looks, and passed her in. Mr. Lincoln's private secretary did the same thing. She was ushered into Lincoln's office and found herself in the company of Lincoln and his generals. The little girl told her simple story, stressing the grief of her parents. Lincoln was touched. He then wrote out a dispatch canceling the sentence and paroling the boy so he could return home to his father and mother.

This is a story of how a mere man can be moved by compassion. But it makes the point that if a man can be so moved, how much more compassionate and ready to heal hearts is Jesus Christ, who is more than man. Bring your need to him. Accept the comfort he can give you. And learn, as countless others have learned, that there is no one who can do more than Jesus.

95

"Where I Am, You Cannot Come"

John 7:32–36

The Pharisees heard the crowd whispering such things about him. Then the chief priests and the Pharisees sent temple guards to arrest him.

Jesus said, "I am with you for only a short time, and then I go to the one who sent me. You will look for me, but you will not find me; and where I am, you cannot come."

The Jews said to one another, "Where does this man intend to go that we cannot find him? Will he go where our people live scattered among the Greeks, and teach the Greeks? What did he mean when he said, 'You will look for me, but you will not find me,' and 'Where I am, you cannot come'?"

It is impossible to read the first seven chapters of John's Gospel without becoming aware of the hostility that was building up against Jesus Christ on the part of the religious leaders and without beginning to anticipate the nature of the conflict that was to come. At the beginning of the Gospel we are warned that although Jesus came unto his own people, nevertheless "his own did not receive him" (1:11). Later we are told that the leaders of the nation repeatedly schemed to kill him. Up to this point, however, nothing overt has been done against Jesus. Now this changes, for an attempt is made to arrest him. John writes that when "the Pharisees heard the crowd whispering such things about him . . . the chief priests and the Pharisees sent temple guards to arrest him" (7:32).

It is a strange mixture of good and evil, of light and shadow that we find in this chapter. On the one hand, we learn of a favorable response toward Christ by some of the people; this response precipitated the Pharisees' action. On the other hand, we hear of an official attempt at suppression. Here we see the Pharisees and chief priests—the phrase generally denotes the official body of the Sanhedrin in John's Gospel—sitting in judgment on Jesus. In the following verses we see one of their own number, Nicodemus, defending him. Even the attempted arrest presents the same ambiguity. For although in this section we see the officers dispatched to arrest Jesus, in just a little while we find them returning with the task unfinished. "Why didn't you bring him in?" they are asked.

The officers reply, "No one ever spoke the way this man does."

What is the situation at this point? It is an awakening of belief by some, accompanied on the part of others by the most intense hatred. In this situation it is of great value to study the response of the Lord Jesus Christ to his adversaries, for his response can help us when we are confronted by similar situations.

The most important verses are 33 and 34. Jesus said, "I am with you for only a short time, and then I go to the one who sent me. You will look for me, but you will not find me; and where I am, you cannot come."

"I Am with You"

There are many lessons that can be drawn from this response, but the first, and certainly one of the most valuable, is that the servant of God cannot be held back from his work or be killed before he has completed that which God has given him to do. Thus Jesus replies, first of all, that regardless of what they may try to do he will be with them "only a short time."

It would not be a great while, of course. It was only to be six months—the period between the Feast of Tabernacles in the fall of the year, around which these remarks are dated, and the Passover at which Christ would be crucified in the spring. Still, so long as those six months had not passed, no one could take him. His hour, as the evangelist says in verse 30, had not come.

It is the same today. Luther, who faced similar problems in his time, wrote on these verses: "Who is Christ's protector? Who fends off his enemies? No one. . . . Nothing is said about many thousands of mounted soldiers or about thirty thousand foot soldiers who defended him. No, his entire armor is a little hour granted him until his crucifixion. That hour was not yet at hand, and since it was not, all the designs of his enemies against him were futile."[1] Luther then concludes by noting that it will be so always. Nothing can touch the Christian unless it coincides with God's explicit command and order.

This includes even the hatred and schemes of the devil. Let me illustrate this by one of the great stories of the Bible.

Back in the Old Testament, just before the Book of the Psalms, there is the story of Job, a man whom we would classify as a rich but otherwise insignificant gentleman farmer but who becomes great in spiritual things because of what God allowed to transpire in his life. God allowed a great struggle brought on by the assaults of Satan. Yet God only allowed it because he knew in advance that through the strength that he would give to him, his servant Job would triumph. The point of the story in which we are most interested is that Satan was unable to do anything to Job until God first permitted it and even then it was permitted only because God knew that Job would be the victor. In other words, the story is an illustration of 1 Corinthians 10:13: "No temptation has seized you except what is common to man. And God is faithful; he will not let you be tempted beyond what you can bear. But when you are tempted, he will also provide a way out so that you can stand up under it."

God's Hedge

The Bible tells us that Job lived in the land of Uz and that he was fairly prosperous, though not by the standards of a very wealthy landowner or rancher in our time. His inventory was 7,000 sheep, 3,000 camels, 500 yoke of oxen, and 500 donkeys. Besides this, there were all the necessary servants for such a household. Job also had seven sons and three daughters. The Bible tells us that Job was "blameless and upright; he feared God and shunned evil" (Job 1:1).

The day came, however, when the sons of God with Satan in their midst came to present themselves before the Lord. God initiated the conversation, directing his initial question to Satan: "Where have you come from?" Satan replied that he had been going to and fro in the earth and had been walking up and down in it.

Then came the important question: "Have you considered my servant Job? There is no one on earth like him; he is blameless and upright, a man who fears God and shuns evil" (1:8). The question is important because it indicates that the sufferings of Job began not only by God's permission, which Satan certainly needed to have, but also by God's direction. For it was God and not Satan who brought Job into the conversation.

Satan had undoubtedly heard of Job. Perhaps a lesser demon had brought Job to his attention, or perhaps Satan had even investigated Job himself. We do not know the details. All we know is that Satan did know of Job by the time God asked the question. For when God asked, "Have you considered my servant Job?" Satan immediately replied, "Does Job fear God for nothing? . . . Have you not put a hedge around him and his household and everything he has?" (1:9–10). He added, "But stretch out your hand and strike everything he has, and he will surely curse you to your face" (1:11).

The last part of this reply was untrue, of course, as the story shows. For Job did not curse God even when his substance was taken from him. Nevertheless, we must note that the first part was true and that it contained a great admission. Satan imputed the wrong motives to Job, to be sure. He implied that Job served God only because God protected him. But the true part—the interesting part—is that God had been protecting Job. Satan admits it. In other words, by admitting that God had placed a hedge about Job, Satan was also admitting that either he or one of his minions (or many of them) had been attacking Job but had been unsuccessful because of the protecting shield that God throws about all those who have put their trust in his grace.

Satan would pass over the hedge if he could. But he cannot. He would make the righteous fall if it were possible. But it is not. We see how God later shielded the people of Israel against the Egyptians, David against Saul, Peter against Herod, and the Lord Jesus Christ against all who would have sought to have hindered his ministry in any way contrary to the Father's will. In the same way we are protected.

The Assaults of Satan

Satan admitted that he could not touch Job, but he also made the accusation that Job remained faithful to God only because of that fact. So with great brevity God replies that in order to make the matter clear and to prove that Satan's accusation is untrue, he will lower the hedge. He will not remove it completely. But he will lower it so that Satan may touch all that Job has, excepting his person.

Now the full force of Satan's wrath falls against this aging saint. A servant arrives to tell him that marauders have carried off his oxen and donkeys and that they have killed the servants who were attending them. Another comes with news that lightning has killed both the sheep and those attending them. A third servant tells him that bandits have stolen the camels and that those servants have died. Finally, a messenger arrives to say that a whirlwind struck the house in which his children were eating and that they were killed in an instant. No doubt Satan steps back, waiting for his prophecy that Job would curse God to be fulfilled. But Job stands firm. He is filled with legitimate sorrow and great grief. But faith wards off the defeat that Satan is looking for. Instead of cursing, "Job got up and tore his robe and shaved his head. Then he fell to the ground in worship and said: 'Naked I came from my mother's womb, and naked I will depart. The LORD gave and the LORD has taken away; may the name of the LORD be praised'" (1:20–21). Job had triumphed, and God was vindicated.

Again the time came when the sons of God presented themselves before Jehovah, and the same questions were asked.

"Where have you come from?"

"From roaming through the earth and going back and forth in it." This time the reply seems a bit evasive, for the heavenly host knew Satan had actually been in Job's backyard.

God continued, "Have you considered my servant Job? There is no one on earth like him; he is blameless and upright, a man who fears God and shuns evil. And he *still* maintains his integrity. . . ."

Satan answered, "Skin for skin! . . . A man will give all he has for his own life. But stretch out your hand and strike his flesh and bones, and he will surely curse you to your face" (2:1–5). This was also untrue, of course, as were aspects of Satan's former challenge. But God permits the challenge, this time giving Satan permission to touch Job's body, but not to take his life. At once Satan leaves and inflicts Job with boils which, we read, covered him "from the soles of his feet to the top of his head." What happened? Once again Job stood firm in his faith. And he did not falter even though his wife turned against him and his friends began to give him worldly counsel.

God's Blessing

We get to the end of the story and find that God again blesses Job and doubles all that he had given to him previously. When his friends were speaking to him, trying to convince him that he must have been guilty of some sin because of what had happened, Job replied to them argument by argument. But when at the last God spoke, Job remained silent. Job listened. Then he gave a great statement of faith and prayed for those friends who had given him bad counsel. At this point the Lord rescinded Satan's permit to attack Job and restored to him the outward marks of his favor. We are told, "After Job had prayed for his friends, the LORD made him prosperous again and gave him twice as much as he had before" (Job 42:10).

Incidentally, although it is extraneous to the point I have been making, we should not pass over the ending without noticing that it contains a lesson for all believers concerning their children. The lesson is that the children of believers can never be lost to them. For even if the children should die, the children are still theirs and will be reunited to them one day.

We see this truth by comparing the opening list of Job's family and possessions with the list that closes the book after God is said to have doubled them. Before, Job had owned 7,000 sheep; now there are 14,000. Before, there were 3,000 camels; now there are 6,000. Before, 500 each of yokes of oxen and donkeys; now, 1,000. But then we come to the list of children and find the numbers identical. Before, there were seven sons and three daughters; now there are seven sons and three daughters. Is something wrong? Not at all. It is merely God's way of saying that the original sons and daughters—unlike the animals, which did not possess immortal souls—were not lost to Job and that in the end he actually possessed fourteen sons and six daughters, though half of them were with God in glory. Thus it is for every Christian parent who has lost a child.

If you have lost a child, as Job did, never say that you once had a child but do not have one now. Say that you have a child and that he or she is in heaven.[2]

Now Is the Time

This story has taken us far afield, but it has nevertheless illustrated the first great point of Christ's reply to his critics in Jerusalem. They were threatening to arrest him. He replies that nothing can touch him so long as he still has work to do. In other words, nothing can touch him (or ourselves) until it has first been filtered through the perfect and loving will of our heavenly Father. We are to take comfort in that and be strong in the work that has been entrusted to us.

There is one other lesson also. Jesus referred to himself by saying, "I am with you for only a short time." But then he went on to remind his hearers that although he would be with them for a short time, nevertheless, the day of God's grace for them would not last forever. "Then I go to the one who sent me. You will look for me, but you will not find me; and where I am, you cannot come." That was true in an obvious, historical way for Judaism. Christ was present among the Jews for three years. His three-year ministry was followed by a forty-year-ministry by those whom he had specifically chosen as apostles. But then Jerusalem fell to the Romans, and the Christians were scattered throughout the world to preach the gospel. In an ironic way they went to the persons mentioned in the question put by Christ's hearers: "Where does this man intend to go, that we cannot find him? Will he go to where our people live scattered among the Greeks, and teach the Greeks?" (v. 35). When the Christians did go to the dispersed Jews and to the Greeks the day of national opportunity ended at least for a time for Judaism.

It will end also for Gentiles when God in his own time brings this age to its close. It might end for you tonight. What is the state of your commitment? Have you sought Jesus and found him? Have you entered into that deep security that commitment to him brings? I hope you have or else that you will make that commitment now. He loves you. He died for you. He wants you to live for him. The Bible says: "Seek the LORD while he may be found, call on him while he is near" (Isa. 55:6). It says, "I tell you, now is the time of God's favor, now is the day of salvation" (2 Cor. 6:2).

96

An Invitation and a Promise

John 7:37–39

On the last and greatest day of the Feast, Jesus stood and said in a loud voice, "If any-one is thirsty, let him come to me and drink. Whoever believes in me, as the Scripture has said, streams of living water will flow from within him." By this he meant the Spirit, whom those who believed in him were later to receive. Up to that time the Spirit had not been given, since Jesus had not yet been glorified.

During the course of a year each of us receives many invitations. Some of them are gladly received: invitations to a wedding of good friends, to an intimate dinner, to a concert, to an evening of quiet conversation. Other invitations are not so welcome, and we find our-selves asking, "Do I have to go there?" or, "How can I get out of responding to that one?" In this chapter we come to the most important and happy invi-tation you and I can ever receive, and the great promise that goes with it. It is in the words of Jesus. "If anyone is thirsty, let him come to me and drink. Whoever believes in me, as the Scripture has said, streams of living water will flow from within him" (7:37–38).

The Setting

By now we are acquainted with the setting in which these words, the last spoken by Jesus in this chapter, were uttered. Jesus had gone to the Feast of Tabernacles at Jerusalem and had begun to preach. Most were astounded at his teaching and were asking themselves if this might indeed be the Messiah whom all were expecting. The rulers, on the other hand, only increased their hatred of him and schemed how they might have him arrested and removed. Within a short time this enmity would build to a climax and Christ would be crucified. Moreover, since many had come up to this feast from other places and would soon be going back while Jesus remained in Judea, many would be seeing Christ no more.

As a result of this situation we find a new intensity in Christ's teaching. We are told that it was now the last day of the eight-day feast; on the next day the crowds would be gone. We are told that the invitation was given as Christ "stood and said in a loud voice." Here is intensity of appeal and great simplicity. Here is the core of the gospel. Other occasions would remain for deeper teaching and for secondary matters. But this was not the time for that. This was the time to touch men's souls and to draw them to Christ for salvation. It was now or never for many. So the invitation is given. "Do you have a thirst?" Christ asks them. "Do you want salvation? Then come; come to me. Here and here alone is where you can find it."

What a day this would be if we, unlike that great crowd of a former day, should all come to Jesus and drink from him freely! And why should we fail to come to him? May the living Spirit of our God accomplish that as we examine both the extent of Christ's invitation and the nature of the promise in this study.

A Great Invitation

We must appreciate the extent of Christ's invitation. On the one hand, it is as broad as humanity, for Jesus says, "If anyone. . . ." As in his day, so also in ours—all are included in the invitation.

We get a sense of the breadth of this invitation when we think of the extent of that original Jerusalem congregation. Who was there at the feast? Jews were there—Jews from every part of Palestine and from every part of the empire. Jews were always going to Jerusalem for these feasts. Moreover, Gentiles were there also—some no doubt as proselytes, others simply as interested bystanders. We have a feeling for the mixed nature of this multitude when we remember that on the day of Pentecost, as the result of Peter's preaching, Parthians, Medes, Elamites, Libyans, Romans, Cretans, Arabians, and Greeks of Mesopotamia, Cappadocia, Pontus, Asia, Phrygia, and Pamphylia, heard him. A similar situation would have existed on this earlier occasion. Yet we do not find Jesus limiting his offer. "If *anyone* is thirsty, let him come!" All may come. Today the same sound flows forth from every true Christian pulpit and from all who bear a faithful witness to Christ in our land.

Have you heard it? Have you listened to that great invitation? I wonder if you have noticed that in this verse Jesus does not even detail the nature of the thirst. He might have been more specific. He once said, "Blessed are those who hunger and thirst for righteousness" (Matt. 5:6). He might have said, "Blessed are those who hunger and thirst after goodness or purity or holiness; for they shall be filled." He could have said, "If anyone is thirsty for me, let him come and drink." But he was not specific. There were no limitations. Is there a thirst? Then come! You are the one to whom the Lord Jesus Christ is speaking.

You may say, "But I am thirsting for pleasure, and the pleasure I am seeking is not Christian." Very well. But if you want real pleasure, pleasure that lasts and that truly satisfies, you will find it in Christ and not in the direction you are going. The Bible says, "At thy right hand there are pleasures for evermore" (Ps. 16:11 KJV).

Someone else may say, "I am not concerned for pleasure; I am concerned for wealth. Will I find wealth in Jesus?" In your sense, no. But in a better sense, yes. The Bible says that if we become God's children, then we are heirs, "heirs of God and co-heirs with Christ" (Rom. 8:17). It also says, "What good is it for a man to gain the whole world, yet forfeit hs soul?" (Mark 8:36). Oh, that there might be men and women who thirst today, for even thirst after the wrong thing is better than apathy. Oh, that men and women might come to him!

In these words, then, there is an invitation as wide as humanity.

On the other hand, there is also a sense in which, sadly, the great scope of this text is realistically narrowed down. It is true that the Lord Jesus addressed the invitation to "anyone," but we can hardly miss the fact that he did so in the midst of a conditional sentence. He said, "If anyone is thirsty. . . ." And that is as much as to admit that there may not be many.

I can imagine that at this point our Lord's eyes swept over the vast congregation listening to him. The expressions in the eyes that glanced back were like those of our day. Some showed callousness; some hatred—they were the ones intent on his destruction. Some showed indifference. Some eyes were blank and uncomprehending. All preachers experience this. I never stand to preach the gospel but I am made aware of the fact that there are many who do not understand the gospel and who, even if they do understand it, will not receive the Savior. To such we preach soul-satisfaction. We share Christ's invitation. But they, although they are in the midst of a spiritual desert of their own making, will not drink from this fountain. We warn them of their danger, and they dismiss it lightly. We speak of the law's condemnation, and they laugh at such old-fashioned notions. The mass of men never thirsts after salvation. Do you thirst?

You say, "I do not know whether I do or not." Well, find out. Turn your eye inward and ask, "Is there no thirst within me? Am I not dissatisfied about something? Is there not some area of my life in which I am unfulfilled?" If you are such a one, then God has placed that hunger and thirst within you.

Rejoice! And come to Jesus! He said, "If anyone is thirsty, let him come to me and drink. . . . streams of living water will flow from within him."

Come to Me

I have already anticipated my next point, as you will see, for it has to do with directions. What are they? They are directions that point you to Jesus. Do not say, "But what am I to believe? What doctrines must I accept?" That will come in time, but it is not the step for you to take now. If you are thirsty, come to Jesus. He said, "Come to me."

Above all, do not make the mistake of coming to the church as an institution or become preoccupied with its rites and ceremonies. Ceremonies are intended to point you to Christ. If you look to them in themselves, they will deceive you.

This was true in Christ's day and is well illustrated by the procedures that were taking place at this season. There were eight days to the great Feast of Tabernacles, and on each day certain public ceremonies were enacted. All were intended to remind the people of God's provision for them during the days of their desert wandering and to point them forward to the Messiah in whom they would all be fulfilled. On the eighth day, the day on which Jesus stood up and cried out this invitation, the ceremonies were particularly impressive. On that day the priests, accompanied by the worshipers, went outside the city to the pool of Siloam—the pool to which Jesus later sends the blind man. Here they filled golden pitchers with water. Then, returning to the city, they marched seven times around the altar and concluded by pouring the water from the pool upon it. Clearly, the ceremony reminded them of God's provision of water for the people during their forty years in the wilderness.

This was done on the last great day of the feast, as I have said; and it was against this background, perhaps at this very climactic moment, that the voice of Jesus rang out—"If anyone is thirsty, let him come to me." The ceremonies had value in reminding the people of God's past provision. We must not scorn them. But they also pointed to Jesus as the One who truly satisfied. Hence, he called upon the people to turn from the ceremonies and come to him.

Have you done what Christ's invitation requires? It is expressed in two parts, and the parts are synonomous. That is, they reinforce and interpret each other. First, you are to "come." That is not hard, especially when the One to whom you are to come is so lovely. And it need not be lengthy, for Jesus has already taken the greatest part of the journey in coming to you. "Come" means to believe, to have faith in him, to commit yourself to him. Will you do that? I wrote earlier that you will get to the fullness of the doctrines by and by. But you should notice even now that if you come to Jesus, you will be coming to the One who came to this earth to redeem you, who died on the cross for your sin, and who then rose again and was glorified by God, his Father. The author of the Gospel has this full picture of the victorious Christ in view, for the next verse alludes to it in the remark that "Jesus was not yet glorified."

Second, you are invited to "drink" from Christ, as you would from a fountain. All that has been said about coming applies to this word too, but drinking involves one further idea. It involves appropriation. That which you drink becomes a part of you. If it is wholesome, it helps you grow. Thus does Christ want to become part of your life and personality.

Will you come? Will you drink? There is no other prescription for the thirst of the human soul. There is no other drink but Jesus. Do not delay in coming. You have not come before, and that was wrong. But you may come *now.* That is the great invitation.

A Great Promise

Finally, one should see that there is also a great promise. Jesus said, "If anyone is thirsty, let him come to me and drink." Then he added, "Whoever believes in me, as the Scripture has said, streams of living water will flow from within him."

I wonder if you would have written the verse that way if you had been speaking or if you were (humanly speaking) the author of John's Gospel. I rather doubt it. Is it not true that if you or I had been writing, we would have tended to say, "And if anyone comes to me and drinks, he will be satisfied; his thirst will be quenched"? Of course we would. But that is not the nature of this promise. It is not the fact that we will be satisfied that Christ mentions. It is rather that we will become the means by which others, in addition to ourselves, will be satisfied. This means that to be Christ-centered is not to be self-centered. It is to be others-centered. It is to be made a blessing.

Now it goes without saying that we ourselves will be satisfied. In fact, we must be satisfied. Here Christ is telling us that we shall be overflowing vessels, but no vessel was ever overflowing until it had first been filled. Of course, we must be filled if this is to happen. But the point is that, if we drink of him, our minds of necessity will not be on our own satisfaction, but rather on the satisfaction of others.

It is at this point that much of our present-day Christianity is found wanting. To hear most Christians talk you would think that the sole purpose of Christ's coming was to save them and to satisfy them. That is one purpose, of course. But that is not the way in which I find the Christian life described in my Bible. That kind of Christianity—when not balanced by the truth we are considering—produces a shallow, experience-centered, introverted, and eventually selfish approach to life and to those around us. We are not called to that. Jesus did not die to give us warm feelings. The work of the Holy Spirit—for this promise is ultimately about the Holy Spirit—is to make you precisely as Christ was in this world. And that means getting outside yourself, getting interested in others, and becoming useful. Have you entered into this promise? Are others experiencing abundance of blessing through you?

If not, you need to ask God to make you, not only a satisfied believer who has drunk of Christ for himself and has found his own needs met, but also a

useful believer who overflows his family, neighborhood, and church with blessing. I assure you that you will never know the true extent of your own satisfaction until you become the channel for such a blessing for other people.

A Flood of Blessing

What would happen if we were each—each one who knows Jesus as his
Savior—to become such a blessing? I suppose that, if each one were to become such a river, we should have a veritable flood of God's blessing.

I long for such a flood, don't you? What a wonderful thing it would be!
Spurgeon spoke of it back in the nineteenth century, comparing it to the in-
coming tides on the Thames that lifted the great river barges. When the tide
was out nothing could move those barges as they lay in the mud of the river's
bottom. A team of men could not move them. Machinery could never get them
moved out to the sea. But then the tide would come, and soon they would be
floating. When the tide returned, even a child could move them by his hand.

Oh, for a floodtide of God's grace! I know of some boats that need floating. They do not work for God. They are not interested in the spiritual well-
being of others. They do not come out to prayer meetings. They do not witness. I cannot move them. They need to be set afloat. Pray with me that there
might be such a flood of God's grace through deeply satisfied hearts that we
all might be borne up together and that these along with many others might
become active. God grant it, for their sake and for the world.

97

Christ, a Divider of Men

John 7:40-44

On hearing his words, some of the people said, "Surely this man is the Prophet."

Others said, "He is the Christ."

Still others asked, "How can the Christ come from Galilee? Does not the Scripture say that the Christ will come from David's family and from Bethlehem, the town where David lived?" Thus the people were divided because of Jesus. Some wanted to seize him, but no one laid a hand on him.

I am sure that I do not have all the answers to why the Lord Jesus Christ produces divisions among men, as he does. But this is the case, and I am not at all sure that it is to be regretted.

For one thing, Jesus himself prophesied that this was to be the case. He said, "Do not suppose that I have come to bring peace to the earth. I did not come to bring peace, but a sword. For I have come to turn 'a man against his father, a daughter against her mother, a daughter-in-law against her mother-in-law— a man's enemies will be the members of his own household'" (Matt. 10:34–36). For another thing, divisions are natural where truth is concerned. They go with strong doctrine. The great Baptist preacher Charles Haddon Spurgeon once wrote of the reality of this in his day, saying, "I have heard of a whole

589

parish in which there were no religious bickerings because there was no religion; there were no religious strifes because nobody had anything worth striving for. And that," he added, "is not a state of things over which I can rejoice."[1]

Nor can anyone rejoice in such a situation. At the same time we must sorrow over the fact that any division between men and women over Jesus necessarily means that some will not believe in him or come to him for salvation. And we want many to come. This is the point of the verses to which we now come in our verse-by-verse study of John's Gospel, which tell us that at this point of Christ's ministry "the people were divided because of Jesus" (7:43).

A Division between Nonbelievers

In the first place, there was a division among nonbelievers because of him. Indeed, the verses talk primarily about this division.

There were those who thought him to be "the Prophet" (v. 40). This means that they were *willing to accept a portion of his claims* but not all of them. The prophet, of course, was the Messiah whose coming was foretold by Moses in Deuteronomy 18:15. But in popular usage in the time of Christ this phrase had come to denote that prophet who was expected to come as a forerunner of the Messiah (Mal. 4:5–6). In other words, the prophet was thought to be the one who would point to the answer to man's need but who, nevertheless, was not himself the answer. In calling Jesus by this title, the people were acknowledging that he was a good man who spoke wisely. They were even recognizing a certain grandeur about him that might indicate that he was sent by God. But they were not admitting the full import of his claims—that he was God and that men and women could find spiritual satisfaction only by coming to him.

There are many today who act in this way. We speak of Jesus Christ and his teaching, and those who act this way merely sort out what is said so that all that might possibly exert a personal claim upon them is excluded. They will come to Jesus for inspiring thoughts. Perhaps they will even go to church on a Sunday morning for the "good" it will do them—or send their children. But they will not follow Jesus. They will not acknowledge him to be their Lord.

Second, there were people among the crowd who went further. These were *willing to acknowledge that he actually was all that he claimed to be.* They said, "He is the Christ" (v. 41). However, although they admitted Christ's claims, they did not do that one additional thing that is absolutely necessary. They did not follow out the proper consequence of their belief by coming to him.

Is it too much to suggest that there are people in any congregation and in any Christian group who can be described in this manner? It is probably most always the case. That may be the case for you. You have heard the Christian gospel over a long period of time, and you understand what it is that we are talking about. You do not deny the truthfulness of the Scriptures. You affirm it. You do not doubt that Jesus Christ is the unique Son of God. You believe it. You do not question the factualness of the crucifixion nor the meaning of Christ's death for your life. You understand this. You know that he died for you. In fact, if you were to go elsewhere and hear a different gospel, you would know at once that it is different and would say, "But that is not what Dr. Boice has been teaching." All this is true, and yet you have never accepted Jesus Christ as your personal Savior. You have never determined to follow him. What a sad state! How tragic to have an orthodox head wedded to a rebellious heart! Why not make today the day in which you go the whole way and receive Jesus Christ as your Savior?

Third, there were people who *rejected Jesus entirely* and who did so apparently on a quibble. Their friends had said, "He is the Christ." But they replied, "How can the Christ come from Galilee? Does not the Scripture say that the Christ will come from David's family and from the town of Bethlehem, the town where David lived?" (vv. 41–42). In other words, they thought that Jesus failed to satisfy one of the prophecies of the Old Testament about the Messiah. So they dismissed him. They had no further use for him or for his teaching.

How this reveals the true nature of their hearts! And with what irony John records their reaction! For instance, we cannot help noticing how this particular reaction revealed a great deal of pride in those who provided it. These people were largely from Jerusalem or from the outlying areas of Judea. Galilee was to the far north, "in the sticks" to their way of thinking. So when they said, "How can the Christ come from Galilee?" they really were implying that Jesus was just not sophisticated enough to be their leader. We see this reaction today in those who consider Christians to be uneducated persons and who think of Christianity as being beneath their social level.

Moreover, the reaction of this part of the crowd also reveals a strange hypocrisy. For they were dismissing Jesus on a quibble while at the same time refusing to investigate his claims, particularly whether or not he might actually have fulfilled this particular condition. The condition was twofold: that the Messiah be of David's line (he was to sit on the throne of David) and that he be born in Bethlehem (Micah 5:2). Jesus had fulfilled both parts. He had descended from David in a way that exhausted the Davidic line, combining in himself both the royal line through Joseph and the legal line through Mary.[2] And he had been born in Bethlehem, though many did not know it due to the fact that he had grown up in Nazareth. Jesus fulfilled all the Old Testament requirements. Yet the people who objected to him did not bother to investigate these requirements.

Are you one who has been rejecting Jesus Christ on a quibble? Do you refuse to come because you cannot understand where Cain got his wife? Or how God can punish sinners? Or why we are to believe in a virgin birth or a resurrection? There are answers to these questions; you will come to know them in time. But they must not be used as excuses for a failure to come to grips with Christ personally. Investigate him. Study his life and claims. But do so honestly. Honesty demands a determination to follow him if his claims are verified.

What a change there would be if men and women would really investigate Christ's claims! Years ago a friend of Harry Ironside was forced to leave his mission work in India because of ill health. Some time after his return from the field he received a letter from an elder in his church in India saying how much they missed him and assuring him that in his absence they were doing a great deal more praying and reading the Bible. In fact, the letter said, they were having a real "re-Bible." Well, the elders were right. For where the Bible is prayerfully studied spiritual insight and a genuine "revival" will follow.

Finally, some of those who heard Jesus at the feast *wanted to harm him.* John says "Some of them wanted to seize him, but no one laid a hand on him" (v. 44). How are we to understand this group? There is no way to understand it. There is no way to understand men who would crucify the Lord of glory.

What shall we who know the Lord do? We must pray for those who cannot see the truth concerning him. God must open their eyes. We must help those who have seen in part but who have not yet made a commitment. We are to be witnesses, and we must love them. Indeed, we must love even those who are enemies. For by such love and through it God may call some.

Nonbelievers and Believers

There was clearly a division among nonbelievers then concerning Christ. But note: there is a far greater and categorical division between nonbelievers and believers.

It is impossible to overestimate this difference. On the one hand, we have the one who is not yet a Christian. He is described as "dead in . . . transgressions and sins." He walks according to "the ways of this world and of the ruler of the kingdom of the air." He fulfills "the cravings of our sinful nature." He is a child "of wrath." On the other hand, we have the believer who through the grace of God is "alive" in Christ, seated "in the heavenly realms in Christ Jesus," and "created in Christ Jesus unto good works" (Eph. 2:1–10). The difference lies in the relation of each individual to the Savior.

We can see the differences in the practical outworking of their lives. The believer trusts Christ. Indeed, Christ is all in all to him, the only one who can be trusted totally. The nonbeliever trusts either in himself or in other people.

The believer loves Christ. Indeed, how could he help but love him! Jesus is the One who gave up the glory of heaven, laying it aside, in order to become man and die for him. Love sent the Savior to die in his place. Now he loves him. "We love because he first loved us." The nonbeliever does not love the Savior.

The believer also serves Christ. He is called to service. Recognizing his past, that before Christ's coming he was in bondage to sin, and knowing something of the deliverance that Jesus has bought for him through his death, the Christian now recognizes himself to be no longer his own but the Lord's. He recognizes the truth of Paul's challenge: "You were bought at a price. Therefore honor God with your body" (1 Cor. 6:20). The unbeliever does not have this orientation to life's service.

Finally, the Christian is striving to be like Jesus. He may not be much like him. At times he may be much unlike him. Still this is his goal, and he can say with Paul, "Brothers, I do not consider myself yet to have taken hold of it. But one thing I do: Forgetting what is behind and straining toward what is ahead, I press on toward the goal to win the prize for which God has called me heavenward in Christ Jesus" (Phil. 3:13–14). The goals of the unbeliever are a product of this world's culture or of his own desires.

Where do you find yourself in that contrast? Do you trust, love, serve, and strive to be like Jesus? Or are you living for yourself and serving yourself? If it is the second of those pictures, I trust that something of the power, love, and character of Jesus himself may reach you, so that you will come to him and do so without delay. The danger in delaying is that the end may come—you may die or Jesus may return—and the divisions of this life will be established for eternity.

Unity for Believers

Finally, although it is true that Jesus is the cause of these divisions, it is true also that he is the cause of the most profound and happy unity among believers. Jesus divides? Yes. But for those who know him he is also that which draws us together.

He is the only one who can draw us together. We who are Christians do not come from only one walk of life, as though we could be drawn together by a culture that we hold in common or by our backgrounds. We do not come from one race, as though we could be united ethnically. We are not even all of one nation or sex or intellectual attainment or status. All the causes for the divisions of the world at large exist within the Christian church. But there is this difference. Within the church and for Christians these divisions simply cease to matter. We are one. As Paul says, "There is neither Jew nor Greek, slave nor free, male nor female, for you are all one in Christ Jesus" (Gal. 3:28).

Let me share an early example of such unity with you. About the year A.D. 56, the apostle Paul was in Corinth where he had been dictating a letter to the Christians in Rome. While doing this he had been living in the home of a rich man named Gaius, who had presumably only recently been converted to Christ. He had been dictating through a slave who ranked number three among the slaves of that household. The slave's official name was Tertius, which means "three." Probably Paul had been composing this letter over a period of time, and as he had been dictating it various people had dropped by. Now, on this particular day, as he came to the end of the letter, some of these people came by again to hear him close it. They sensed its importance. Paul's fellow workers were there—Timothy, Lucius, Jason, Sosipater. Gaius was there, as well as his friend Erastus, an elected official in the city. Archeologists have since found Erastus's name, together with his office, inscribed in marble. And there are the slaves: Tertius (number three) and Quartus (number four).

Now observe what happens as Paul brings his letter to a close. Paul has already addressed the Romans, many of them by name. He has wished them well and added a benediction. Now he looks about him and begins to send greetings from those who are present in the room.

> Timothy, my fellow worker, sends his greetings to you,
>   as do Lucius, Jason and Sosipater,
>   my relatives. . . .

Paul pauses, but as he does so Tertius, the scribe, keeps writing, as slaves sometimes did in antiquity.

> I, Tertius, who wrote down this letter,
>   greet you in the Lord. . . .

Then, as Paul picks up his dictation, Tertius continues on Paul's behalf.

> Gaius, whose hospitality I and the whole church here enjoy,
>   sends you his greetings.
> Erastus, who is the city's director,
>   sends . . . greetings. . . .

Here, Quartus, the least important person in the room but one who feels his brotherhood with the Christians in Rome, as do the others, and who is afraid of being left out, raises his hand to catch Paul's attention. Paul quickly adds, "And our brother Quartus." Now all have been included, from the most important elected official of Corinth to the least important slave in Gaius's household, and all have expressed their sense of belonging to the Roman Christians who live hundreds of miles away and whom most of them have never seen and would not see until they were united in heaven.

Here is a great example of the reality of unity in Christ and of Christian brotherhood. Christ is a divider of men. But he also is the source of a most blessed and transforming unity for Christians.

98

None like Jesus

John 7:45–52

Finally the temple guards went back to the chief priests and Pharisees, who asked them, "Why didn't you bring him in?"

"No one ever spoke the way this man does," the guards declared.

"You mean he has deceived you also?" the Pharisees retorted. "Has any of the rulers or of the Pharisees believed in him? No! But this mob that knows nothing of the law—there is a curse on them."

Nicodemus, who had gone to Jesus earlier and who was one of their own number, asked, "Does our law condemn anyone without first hearing him to find out what he is doing?"

They replied, "Are you from Galilee, too? Look into it, and you will find that a prophet does not come out of Galilee."

Earlier in these sermons on the Gospel of John, verses were studied that spoke of the uniqueness of Jesus Christ, of the fact that by any measurement there is no one quite like him. The verses were in John 1 (vv. 15–18), and we saw as we considered them that Jesus is unique in his origin, in being the sole source of blessing for men and women, as being full of grace and truth, and as the only one in whom you or I may see God. In this study we come to verses that speak of his uniqueness in yet another sense—the uniqueness of his words. These verses contain the reaction of the temple guards to his teaching. No doubt they had heard plenty of prisoners. But although they had been sent to take him, they returned empty-handed, saying, "No one ever spoke the way this man does" (v. 46).

These words, which obviously are of great importance, will be the jumping-off place for the present study.

The Story

We are helped a bit in our appreciation of these words by realizing that the guards had been some time in their unproductive attempt to seize Jesus. The attempt itself, mentioned for the first time in verse 32, had been initiated by the Pharisees and priests because they had found Jesus to be a threat to their teaching. They had observed him for some time, and they had realized (correctly) that he was opposed to any thoughts of salvation by legalism, the system of religion on which they prided themselves, and that he was therefore a threat to them. Besides, he was a blasphemer because, as they could see, he was making himself equal to God.

At the same time, it also was true that Jesus was relatively popular. And since they could not run the risk of looking like men who were opposed to a true man of God, a prophet, they did the only thing they could. They sent their own temple guards—not Roman soldiers—with orders to observe Jesus and then to arrest him whenever the occasion was suitable. "Arrest him," they said, "but do it quietly." Six months later, at the Passover, they were following the same course of action when they actually succeeded in having Jesus arrested by night in the Garden of Gethsemane. We do not know how long it was between the giving of the order on this earlier occasion and the report of the guards to their superiors recorded here. But we do know that it must have been some time. For at least a day had gone by, according to verse 37, and it may well have been longer. At all events, the picture we have is that of the guards lingering on the outskirts of the crowds for some time as Christ taught the people.

It is dangerous to linger around the Lord Jesus for whatever reason. It is dangerous to be exposed to his teaching. As time went by, these guards became impressed with what he was saying, and being impressed they found themselves unable to proceed with their mission.

Sent from God

What precisely had these men heard Jesus teaching? One thing they had heard Jesus saying was that He had been sent from God. We read, "Yes, you know me, and you know where I am from. I am not here on my own, but he who sent me is true. You do not know him, but I know him because I am from him and he sent me" (vv. 28–29).

There are times in our study of the Word of God when it is necessary for us to give particular attention to the smallest of words. We have such a case here. To do it helps us to see something very important about Jesus. Notice that Jesus said he was sent *from* God. He did not say that he was sent *by* God, though that would have been true and also important. He said that he was sent *from* God. This implies a previous existence with God; that is, a life with God before his incarnation. This in turn points to his full divinity. There are many men who have been sent by God. All the Old Testament prophets fall into this category. John the Baptist is an example. So, in another sense, are all of God's people today, for we all are sent by God as witnesses to this world. Many have been sent *by* God. Only one, the Lord Jesus Christ, has been sent *from* him.

Moreover, this and this alone meets our deepest need and longings. We hear much talk today about the "image" of God. The question involved in such talk is this—"How are we to picture God or visualize him?" We know, of course, that the Old Testament firmly forbids any attempt to make an image of God, for that tends to idolatry. Instead, the Old Testament suggests that we think of God in terms of his names—Jehovah, Adonai, El Shaddai, El Elyon—which reveal his nature. But at the same time when we recognize the value of this, we also recognize that names are not quite enough for those who wish to know God in a deeper and more personal way. "Can we never see God?" we ask. "Can we not know him?" It is just at this point that Christ's statements about himself and his origin come into the picture, for it is in Christ that we see the Father. "No one has ever seen God," as John says earlier. Nevertheless, "God the One and Only, who is at the Father's side, has made him known" (1:18). The fact that Jesus is from God and is God dispels whatever previous mystery there may have been and meets our longing.

When we see this about Christ's teaching we see that Jesus was saying something so extraordinary that it should properly make an impression upon us, just as it did upon the guards who had been sent to arrest him.

His Life Controlled by God

Second, having been sent from God, Jesus also knew and taught that the details of his life had been arranged and were controlled by God. That is, nothing ever entered into his life that was not sent into it by the Father, and he was doing nothing that deviated in any respect from the plan for his life that had been previously outlined in the Old Testament. In one sense, many of his words imply this. In this chapter, however, it is taught most explicitly in Christ's words to his brothers just before they went up to the feast. They wanted him to go up and try to recapture some of his declining popularity. He answered, "The right time for me has not yet come; for you any time is right" (v. 6).

What was the basis upon which Jesus could make such a statement? His brothers could go wherever they wished, and at any time, because their time was in their own hands. Their time had only the meaning they themselves were able to give it. Jesus, however, could not go to the feast at the time their question was asked, because his time was in the hands of the Father and received the significance that he alone gave it.

Words from God

Third, Jesus not only taught that he had been sent from God and that all the details of his life had been ordered from God. He also taught that his words were from God, so that anyone who heard him heard God. We read about it like this: "Jesus answered, 'My teaching is not my own. It comes from him who sent me. If anyone chooses to do God's will, he will find out whether my teaching is from God or whether I speak on my own'" (vv. 16–17).

This gives us the true answer as to why his words made such an impact upon his hearers and why they continue to influence and motivate people today. If Jesus' words were merely human words, they might be of historical or even inspirational value. But they would have no ultimate influence or lasting authority. However, since Jesus' words are words from God, they are unlike other words and indeed possess full authority. They are true, for one thing. God is truth itself, and words that are from him will always be true. We can count upon them. Moreover, the words are powerful, for they convey something of that creative energy seen in the creation of the world by means of God speaking.

Once a leper came to Jesus with the claim of faith: "If you will, you can make me clean." Jesus replied, "I will; be you clean," and the foul disease left him. Once Jesus was in the house of a man named Jairus, whose daughter had just died. Jesus said, "My child, get up," and at once she returned to life. At the tomb of his friend Lazarus Jesus called out in a loud voice, "Lazarus, come out," and Lazarus (who had been dead four days) came out from the tomb. What power! What love! It is a privilege to say that this power can be applied to you also as you respond to Christ's words, for he has promised forgiveness of sins and new life to all who ask him to be their Savior.

Hunger and Thirst

Fourth, Jesus declared that he was himself the answer to human need. He said, "If anyone is thirsty, let him come to me and drink. Whoever believes in me, as the Scripture has said, streams of living water will flow from within him" (vv. 37–38). The same idea is present in Christ's earlier claim to be the bread of life.

What hunger and thirst there are in the hearts of men. There are times, of course, when the hunger and thirst are not evident. In times of prosperity people seem to have everything, and we find ourselves asking, "What more could they want?" Sometimes we ask, "What more could I want?" Still, the thirst is there and it betrays its presence through a general uneasiness, anxiety, and depression, sometimes even through suicide or other irrational behavior. At other times in history—perhaps we are moving into such a period even now—the hunger is obvious, and we find people searching everywhere for something with which to satisfy themselves and not being able to find it.

Christ satisfies! If nothing but those two words could sink into those who follow this study, I would be satisfied. Christ satisfies! He does this by removing sin, which is always at the heart of man's problems, and then on that basis restoring the relationships between the individual and God and between the individual and others, which sin has broken.

A Blessing to Others

Finally, Jesus also claimed to be able to make all who come to him a blessing to other people. In fact, this claim is involved in the verses I have just quoted. For he said that the one who would drink from him would find within himself a river of water that would be overflowing (v. 38).

I know of no other way in which the great problems of our world will be affected. What is the source of our problems, whatever they may be—hunger, disease, exploitation, bigotry, war? Where do they come from? It is not the environment, though that is a factor in some cases. It is not the inherent evil of the authorities, for the authorities are merely people like ourselves in positions of power. The cause is mankind itself and, in particular, the sin of mankind. Until that is dealt with there will be no strong or lasting solutions. Therefore, we must begin with our sin, yours and mine, and then, having our own sin dealt with and being filled with the joy that comes from knowing God, we will have something to offer others. When we are a blessing, then and only then will we be able to deal with those external problems that affect everybody.

The Words of Men

The words of Jesus *are* wonderful. They speak to us where we are. But how different they are from the words of men or from human teaching. This contrast is made for us in this story, for after we are told of the report of the temple guards—"No one ever spoke the way this man does"—we also are told some of the things the Pharisees and the chief priests said in responding to it. One of the responses to the guards was filled with pride. They said, "You mean he has deceived you also? Have any of the rulers or of the Pharisees believed in him?" (vv. 47–48). They obviously thought they were better than other people. Another of their replies was filled with contempt for the common people. They said, "But this mob that knows nothing of the law—there is a curse on them" (v. 49). Actually, the people knew the law pretty well, but the Pharisees despised them because they had not had opportunity to be educated in the rabbinic schools, as they were. Moreover, it was also true that their replies were filled with ignorance even of the true situation. For no sooner had they denied that any of the rulers had believed on Jesus than Nicodemus, one of their very number, spoke up for him. And no sooner had they expressed scorn for those who were ignorant of the law than they were chided by Nicodemus for their own disregard of it—"Does our law condemn anyone without first hearing him to find out what he is doing?" (v. 51). Besides, in their answer to him, they showed ignorance even of the prophetic Scriptures, for they denied that any prophet could come from Galilee, when, in fact, Jonah—and perhaps others—had come from there.

There is pride, contempt, and ignorance in the best speeches of even the best of men. But many do not see this. In fact, no one does see it until he has first listened to and been enthralled by the Lord Jesus. Have you heard him? Have you recognized that there is indeed none like Jesus? Hear him; he speaks to you. He says, "Come to me, all you who are weary and burdened, and I will give you rest." He says, "Come to me and drink." Let your heart respond with joy: "No one ever spoke the way this man does. I am coming, Lord Jesus!"

99

The Woman Taken in Adultery

John 7:53–8:11

Then each went to his own home.

But Jesus went to the Mount of Olives. At dawn he appeared again in the temple courts, where all the people gathered around him, and he sat down to teach them. The teachers of the law and the Pharisees brought in a woman caught in adultery. They made her stand before the group and said to Jesus, "Teacher, this woman was caught in the act of adultery. In the Law Moses commanded us to stone such women. Now what do you say?" They were using this question as a trap, in order to have a basis for accusing him.

But Jesus bent down and started to write on the ground with his finger. When they kept on questioning him, he straightened up and said to them, "If any one of you is without sin, let him be the first to throw a stone at her." Again he stooped down and wrote on the ground.

At this, those who heard began to go away one at a time, the older ones first, until only Jesus was left, with the woman still standing there. Jesus straightened up and asked her, "Woman, where are they? Has no one condemned you?"

"No one, sir," she said.

"Then neither do I condemn you," Jesus declared. "Go now and leave your life of sin."

When the rulers of the Jewish nation failed in their attempt to have Jesus arrested by the temple guards, they immediately devised a plot to trap him. This plot is the most despicable action by these men recorded in the Gospels. At the same time, it became an occasion by which Jesus not only revealed the depth of his justice, wisdom, and compassion but also provided a message of hope and great peace for those

601

who come to him. The story is that of the woman taken in adultery. The problem of the story is how justice and mercy can be harmonized while, at the same time, neither encouraging sin nor condemning the sinner. In this respect it is a central, even a pivotal, point in John's Gospel.

Textual Problems

Before beginning our study of this story, I must be frank to admit that it involves us in a serious textual problem. The difficulty, simply put, is that the majority of the earliest manuscripts of John do not contain these verses and, moreover, that some of the best manuscripts are of this number. The best evidence for the story is its presence in Codex Bezae, of the fifth or sixth century, now in the University Library at Cambridge, England. But it is not in the older Codices Sinaiticus or Vaticanus, nor in the Washington or Koridethi manuscripts. In fact, of the older manuscripts, eight omit it entirely, though two manuscripts leave a blank space where it would have come. And not until the medieval manuscripts does it seem to have been included with any regularity. Some early manuscripts attach it at other places, such as at the end of the Gospel or after Luke 21:38.

Does that mean that we should just throw out these verses? Should we place them in the same category as the apocryphal gospels? Interestingly enough, very few scholars (even many of the liberal ones) seem willing to do this, and the fact that a good case can be made out for the other side, should make one cautious in how he deals with it. I am willing to deal with the story as genuine—though perhaps not a part of the original Gospel as John wrote it—for the following reasons:

1. While it is true that most early manuscripts omit this story, it also is true that the story itself is old, regardless of who wrote it or whether or not it was originally in John's Gospel. We find it in *The Apostolic Constitutions* (third century A.D.). And Eusebius, the church historian, tells us that Papias (who died not long after A.D. 100) knew a story "of a woman who was accused of many sins before the Lord." Later, Jerome unquestioningly included it in the Latin Vulgate.

2. A good case can be made for its inclusion at this particular place in John's Gospel. For one thing, without it the change of thought between the fifty-second verse of chapter seven and the twelfth verse of chapter eight is abrupt and unnatural. We do not know where Jesus is in John 8:12, nor to whom he is speaking. For another thing, the introduction of a story at this point seems to fit the pattern that John has been using in these opening chapters. In each case, from chapter 5 onward, a story is used to set the theme of the teaching that follows. Thus, the miracle of healing the disabled man, which begins chapter 5, becomes the text of the sermon that follows. The feeding of the multitude in chapter 6 leads into the discourse on Christ as the bread of life. The discussion between Jesus and his brothers about going up to the feast in chapter 7 is an introduction to Christ's words at the feast. So, likewise, is the story of his

dealing with the adulterous woman an introduction to that speech on the combination of righteousness and freedom in Christ that the rest of the chapter declares that Christ brings.

3. Third, there is an excellent reason why the story may have been omitted in the early manuscripts. In a contest with paganism, it is easy to see how the story might have been used by enemies of the gospel to suggest that Christ condoned fornication. Indeed, this is the reason for its omission given by both Augustine and Ambrose in the late fourth and early fifth centuries.

4. The fourth and last reason for dealing with the section is the feeling, which many have had, that this story is indeed true to Christ's nature, in accord at every point with his perfect holiness, wisdom, and deep compassion.

As we turn to the story we must see three things primarily: first, the horror of sin; second, the mastery by God of all circumstances; and third, the word of the Savior to the sinner.

Sin's Horror

First, the story reveals sin's horror. And, of course, I do not mean the sin of the woman. I mean the sin of the rulers. Adultery is sin, certainly. The woman was guilty of adultery. But compared to the sin of the men who were using her in an attempt to trap Jesus, her sin was minimal—a mote in her eye compared to the beams that were in their eyes (Matt. 7:1–5).

To understand precisely what these men were doing we must understand that not only was their approach to Jesus a trap; they actually had already been active in trapping the woman. In fact, it could hardly be otherwise, on the basis of their testimony and in light of the very exacting requirements of Jewish law in this and other capital cases. Under Jewish law, as it was practiced by the rabbis in the time of Christ and later, it was necessary to have multiple witnesses to the act of intercourse before the charge of adultery could be substantiated, and even this was to be under the most exacting of circumstances. Thus, as one scholar points out, "There is absolutely no question of [the witnesses] having seen the couple in a 'compromising situation,' for example, coming from a room in which they were alone, or even lying together on the same bed. The actual physical movements of the couple must have been capable of no other explanation, and the witnesses must have seen exactly the same acts at exactly the same time, in the presence of each other, so that their dispositions would be identical in every respect."[1]

Under these conditions the obtaining of evidence in adultery would be almost impossible were the situation itself not a setup. We are justified in supposing that the liaison had been arranged, perhaps by the very man who committed adultery with the woman. Was he a member of the Sanhedrin? Whatever the case, the arrangement must have involved the posting of witnesses in the room or at the keyhole.

We see the horror of the sin of these men in another way too. For the fact that only the woman was brought to Jesus reveals their dishonesty. If adultery could be proved only by the testimony of witnesses who had seen the couple in the very act of adultery and if this is what the rulers were claiming, as they were, where then was the man in the story? Why was he not brought with the woman? At the least, the rulers allowed the man to escape. At the worst, the man had been in on the plotting and had been granted immunity beforehand. How horrible! Yes, but it is only the old case of the double standard that exists still today. Men should take their stand with the women in such cases, confessing their share of the guilt, which is usually greater anyway. But they do not. The poor woman had to bear the shame alone.

God of Circumstances

The horror of sin is not the only subject these verses introduce, however. They also reveal the mastery by God of all circumstances.

We will appreciate this aspect of the story better if we realize that this was a serious problem with which the Lord was confronted. This was not like the problems with which he had been challenged before. On an earlier occasion the Sadducees, who did not believe in the afterlife, had come to him with a trick question about the resurrection. They imagined the case of a woman who had married seven brothers in turn, each one having died and having left her with no children. "In the resurrection, therefore, when they rise, whose wife will she be?" they asked. It was a stupid, almost infantile question. So Jesus answered that they had erred, knowing neither the Scriptures nor the power of God. On another occasion some of the rulers tried to trap him with a question regarding taxes. But again this involved only the conflict between public sentiment and the law of Rome, and Jesus dealt with it easily.

It was not this way with this problem of the adulterous woman. In this case three important matters were at stake: (1) the life of the woman, (2) the teaching of Jesus about the compassionate nature of his kingdom, and (3) the divinely given law of Moses. The way the matter was posed—so it seemed to the rulers—there was little doubt that Jesus would have to relinquish one of these items.

Everyone knew that the ministry of the Lord Jesus Christ had been marked by compassion. He had moved about among publicans and sinners. He had befriended the outcasts. He had said, "Come to me, all you who are weary and burdened" (Matt. 11:28). But if he was consistent with this teaching and if, on the basis of his compassion for the woman, he actually waived the law of Moses, then the rulers could rightly denounce him as a dangerous and false prophet. What prophet could speak against the law? Jesus had already been suspected of this because of his attitude toward the sabbath regulations. If he rejected Moses' judgment, they had him. On the other hand, if Jesus upheld the law— if he said, "Kill the woman"—then they were also sure that they had him. For they reasoned, "If he says that, then we will ridicule him to the end of his days. We'll say, 'Sure, he says, "Come to me, all you who are weary and burdened," but he neglects to tell you that when you do come he's going to stone you.'"

With devilish insight these men had hit upon *the* problem of *all* problems in respect to the relationship of a sinner to God. How can God show love to the sinner without being unjust? Or, as Paul states the problem: How can God be both just and the justifier of the ungodly (Rom. 3:26)? From a human point of view the problem is unsolvable. In this the rulers were right. "Even if Jesus wants to show love, he cannot," they argued. But they were not aware that they were not dealing with a mere man when they dealt with Jesus. They were dealing with God, and with God all things are possible.

At first Jesus appeared to ignore them. Instead of replying he simply bent down and began to write on the ground.

I do not know why he wrote on the ground, and, what is more, I do not believe that anyone else does either. I have read numerous commentaries on these verses, and I have been surprised to find that nearly every one of them gives a different answer. Some have suggested that Jesus wrote on the ground to gain time. Others argue that he did so to force the accusers to repeat their charges, thinking that perhaps the shame of the situation might become evident even to them as they said it. Lawyers sometimes follow this procedure in courts of law. One person has suggested that Jesus was himself overcome with shame and horror in much the same way as he shuddered at the tomb of Lazarus or wept over the city of Jerusalem. Some suggest that this was a symbolic action, intended to remind the accusers of Jeremiah 17:13—"O Lord, the hope of Israel, all who forsake you will be put to shame. Those who turn away from you will be written in the dust." Perhaps, since Jesus knew their hearts, he was writing out their sins. Perhaps he wrote the words he later spoke. Whatever the case, the fact of Christ's writing had no effect on the rulers, who rudely continued to press for an answer. One of the sad effects of sin is that it hardens the sinner.

After a while Jesus stood up and replied, "If any one of you is without sin, let him be the first to throw a stone at her" (v. 7). How simple and, at the same time, how disarming! So we read that "those who heard began to go away one at a time, the older ones first, until only Jesus was left, with the woman still standing there" (v. 9). Obviously, there was something in the gaze of the Lord Jesus Christ, or in the tone of his voice, or simply in the power of his presence that got through to these men, unrepentant as they were, and left them powerless. Think of the efforts they had gone through! Think of the plotting! Yet they were destroyed in a moment when they were confronted by the God who masters circumstances.

Words to the Sinner

At last, Jesus turned to the woman and for the first time addressed her directly. "Woman, where are they? Has no one condemned you?"

She answered, "No one, sir."

"Neither do I condemn you," said Jesus. "Go now and leave your life of sin" (vv. 10–11).

On what basis did Jesus make the statement, "Neither do I condemn you"? Some have suggested that at this point Jesus took advantage of the requirements of the law itself according to which it was necessary to have two or three witnesses in any judicial hearing. Jesus was one accuser perhaps, because he knew all things. But the others were gone, and so the requirements of the law could not be met. This may be right in part. Certainly it freed Jesus from having to condemn the woman. Yet to handle the matter like this is to miss the real meat of the story. For when we ask, "Why did the Lord Jesus Christ not pronounce judgment?" the only substantial and ultimately satisfying answer we get is that he did not pronounce judgment against the woman for precisely the same reason that he does not pronounce judgment against those who come to him in faith. It was because of the cross upon which he was about to bear the full penalty of God's wrath against every sin ever committed by those whom the Father had given to him. He did not give forgiveness easily. He did so only because he was about to make forgiveness possible by the act of suffering in place of the sinner. This is the gospel. This is the only solution to the problem of how God can remain just and also excuse the sinner. To us, salvation is free. But it is free only because the Son of God paid the price for us.

Finally, Jesus told the woman to stop sinning. This always follows upon divine forgiveness, for we cannot be saved by God and then continue to do as we please. We must stop sinning. At the same time, we can be glad that the order is as Jesus gave it. For if he had said, "Go, sin no more; and I will not condemn you," what hope would there be? We all sin, so there would be no forgiveness. Instead he says, "I forgive you on the basis of my death. Now, because you are forgiven, stop sinning."

I hope this has been your experience. I hope you have heard and understood these words of Jesus.

You must place yourself at some place in this story. Are you like the crowd, who stood watching? These witnessed forgiveness, but they did not enter into it. Are you like the rulers? These were sinners, like the woman, but they went away from Jesus without even hearing the words of forgiveness. Or, finally, are you like the woman, who not only heard but also received the gospel message? Of all who were there that day by far the best one to be is the woman. The crowd was indifferent, as crowds always are. The rulers went out from Christ into darkness and six months later were killing the sinless Son of God. But the woman—well, the woman was forgiven through Christ, who died for her sin and for yours, whoever you may be.

100

Never a "Thing"

John 7:53–8:11

Then each went to his own home.

But Jesus went to the Mount of Olives. At dawn he appeared again in the temple courts, where all the people gathered around him, and he sat down to teach them. The teachers of the law and the Pharisees brought in a woman caught in adultery. They made her stand before the group and said to Jesus, "Teacher, this woman was caught in the act of adultery. In the Law Moses commanded us to stone such women. Now what do you say?" They were using this question as a trap, in order to have a basis for accusing him.

But Jesus bent down and started to write on the ground with his finger. When they kept on questioning him, he straightened up and said to them, "If any one of you is without sin, let him be the first to throw a stone at her." Again he stooped down and wrote on the ground.

At this, those who heard began to go away one at a time, the older ones first, until only Jesus was left, with the woman still standing there. Jesus straightened up and asked her, "Woman, where are they? Has no one condemned you?"

"No one, sir," she said.

"Then neither do I condemn you," Jesus declared. "Go now and leave your life of sin."

There are two worlds, the impersonal world and the world of persons; not so much a world of things and a world of men, as a personal and an impersonal view of both men and things. Between these two worlds there is an invisible frontier which is within ourselves, and it is very difficult to cross."[1]

607

These words by the noted Swiss physician and author, Paul Tournier, speak to a great problem of our time, the problem of treating persons as things and vice versa. And they suggest, quite rightly, that the source of the problem, as with nearly all problems confronting us, is in ourselves. People are not things, of course. They were not created as things by God. God himself does not regard them as things. Yet we often treat other people as things—whenever we try to use them for some end of our own, fail to listen to them, or refuse to see them as those for whom Christ died. Have you never heard said, "I'll be all right if I can just get Mary to do so and so"? Or perhaps, "Why worry about Joe? He doesn't matter"? Or, "Let's just ignore him"?

If you have ever said these things or something like them, then you are guilty, as we all are, of that which Tournier is describing; and the attitude of the Lord Jesus Christ toward people, which we find so brilliantly illuminated in the story of the woman taken in adultery, is for you and should prove helpful.

The Attitude of the Rulers

The first point we need to notice is the attitude of the religious leaders toward the woman, for it was the opposite of Jesus' attitude. In brief, the rulers tried to use the woman. We see this in the fact that the situation itself was a setup. Under rabbinic law it was next to impossible to secure a death penalty in a case of adultery. There had to be witnesses—two or three of them—and these had to observe, not merely a compromising situation but the very act of adultery. Moreover, in their testimony they had also to agree in every particular. An illustration of the failure to do this is found in the apocryphal story of Susanna in which the innocent Susanna is acquitted when the witnesses, who had conspired to perjure themselves against her, fail to agree in naming the tree of a garden under which the act supposedly was committed.

Under such circumstances it is almost self-evident that the rulers must have arranged the liaison, having stationed the witnesses in the room or at the keyhole. It was a situation quite similar to the use of private investigators and photographers in order to prove adultery today.

Moreover, the horror of this insensitive use of the woman is heightened by the probability that the woman was young. This is impossible to prove, of course, but it is suggested rather forcibly by the significance of the particular penalty called for by the woman's accusers. These men were calling for death by stoning, and the importance of this is that stoning was the penalty specified in the case of adultery by a betrothed bride, who usually would be young.

The general text prescribing death in the case of adultery is Leviticus 20:10, which says, "If a man commits adultery with another man's wife—with the wife of his neighbor—both the adulterer and the adulteress must be put to death." Here the penalty is death, but the means of inflicting death are not specified. In Jewish practice at the time of Jesus the penalty was death by strangulation. On the other hand, in Deuteronomy 22:23–24 the penalty is death by stoning; but in this case the punishment applies only to a case involving an engaged girl who has proved unfaithful to the engagement by having relations with another man. Since engagements almost invariably involved young people, perhaps as young as thirteen or fourteen years old, we are justified in thinking that this was probably the case of the woman brought before Jesus. So we have a young girl, caught in what may have been her first offense, perhaps seduced and betrayed, if indeed this is what was required to secure her conviction. All this makes the situation more horrible.

Furthermore, we need to notice that, as the rulers used this woman, they were even found quoting Scripture, for they referred to the law and its punishments. It is sad and ironic, but so it was; and so it is for many who use the Word of God as they use people—for their own ends and apart from the grace and mercy of God that the Word communicates.

It is too bad that the rulers did not give even more attention to the Old Testament, rather than less. For if they had understood the full teaching of the Scriptures, they would have understood that in the sight of God each person is an individual, created by him for a specific purpose, and that the Word of God is not supposed to be used as merely one more tool to manipulate people.

In *A Doctor's Casebook in the Light of the Bible*, Paul Tournier, whom I quoted earlier, speaks of what he calls the extraordinary "personalism" of the Bible. "What distinguishes the God of the Bible from the divinities of every other religion is that He is a personal God, who speaks personally to man," he argues. God called Abraham by name, taking him out of his own country into a new land. "He makes a person of him through his personal obedience to a personal command. The personal God makes man into a person." Tournier shows how God called to Moses, saying, "I know thee by name" (Exod. 33:17). He said to Cyrus, "I [am] the Lord, who call thee by thy name" (Isa. 45:3). "One is struck, on reading the Bible, by the importance in it of proper names," Tournier observes. "Whole chapters are devoted to long genealogies. When I was young I used to think that they could well have been dropped from the biblical canon. But I have since realized that these series of proper names bear witness to the fact that, in the biblical perspective, man is neither a thing nor an abstraction, neither a species nor an idea, that he is not a fraction of the mass, as the Marxists see him, but that he is a person."[2]

Tournier is clearly right. And he is right when he calls upon Christians to share the biblical attitude. "If I forget my patients' names," he adds, "if I say to myself, Ah! There's that gall-bladder type or that consumptive that I saw the other day,' I am interesting myself more in their gall-bladders or their lungs than in themselves as persons."[3]

The religious rulers were obviously guilty of precisely this and worse. And we are also guilty, though on different levels. To them the woman was just a case. She had no feelings, no future, no need for saving. It was only in the presence of the Lord Jesus Christ that she found mercy and regained her identity.

The Attitude of Jesus

This brings us to the attitude of the Lord Jesus Christ toward the woman, and we find ourselves asking: What characterized his attitude? There are a number of answers.

First, the attitude of the Lord Jesus Christ was characterized by *understanding*. This is the point at which everything else begins, for Jesus clearly knew what was going on both in the attitude and actions of the men and in the life of the woman. He was not fooled by circumstances nor by appearances. He was not deceived by the religious talk of the leaders, nor by the unrighteous actions of the victim. The expectations of the crowd did not move him. In short, he saw both the good and the evil and moved accordingly.

We need to grow in such understanding if we are to become like Jesus. Apart from this understanding there are two errors into which we fall in dealing with men and women. The first is naïveté. This is the error of believing that people are better than they are; it comes about by overlooking sin and evil. A person who is guilty of this error may be excessively optimistic. He may be loving and think well of all people and, as a result, be taken for a ride in many of his personal relationships. He will be used by the less scrupulous or more realistic. If such a person becomes disillusioned, however, he then runs the risk of falling into the other error, which is cynicism. This results in suspecting low motives in the best of actions and, in extreme cases, in refusing to enter into meaningful relationships with others at all.

In avoiding these errors—both naïveté and cynicism—Jesus becomes our pattern. For he was able to look the worst of life in the face without being astonished or embittered and at the same time retain the purity out of which he was enabled to move in love toward the sinner. Earlier John tells us that Jesus "knew all men. He did not need man's testimony about man, for he knew what was in a man" (2:24–25).

Naturally, we will never be able to understand other people completely, for our knowledge is limited by sin and by our human perspectives. Still, it is true that we can know people much better than we do and can be a help to them because of our understanding. Where does such understanding come from? It comes from the Word of God, for it is only in the Word that we can gain accurate insight into human nature and human problems. The Scriptures will show both the depravity of man, with all its complications in individual and corporate life, and the destiny of the redeemed as the result of God's perfect remedy for sin in Jesus Christ.

Second, the attitude of the Lord Jesus was characterized by *compassion*. This was linked to his understanding. Jesus knew the woman intuitively. He knew her sin and shame. He knew her potential. Because he knew her, he loved her. It was always thus with Jesus. He saw people as sheep without a shepherd, as sinners without a Savior; from that understanding came compassion.

It is impossible to explain such compassion. We may point to its link with understanding, but that does not explain its real origins. It does not explain it in ideal situations, let alone in this one, or in any situation that involves the love of the righteous God for a sinner.

Imagine for a moment that you are a parent and that you have one of your children sitting upon your lap. The child says, "Daddy [or Mommy], do you love me?"

You say, "Yes, I do," and you give the child a kiss.

Then the child says, "Why do you love me?" Well, what do you say to that question? There is just no answer. You cannot say, "I love you because you are good," for that is not true, and it may even be harmful. You would love the child even if he were bad, which he certainly will be sooner or later. And you would not want the child to think that your love depends upon his being good, for he would then doubt your love when he disappoints you. Then again, you cannot say, "I love you because you are beautiful." You would love the child even if he were not beautiful. You would love him even if he were retarded or deformed. Nor can you say, "I love you because you are mine," for you would love the child even if he were adopted. Why do you love him? Well, you love him in part because you understand him, but that does not explain your love. Love is unexplainable. The best you can say is that love is divine and that you love him because God himself has loved us.

Apply this to Christ's love for the woman. What can explain it? It is beyond reason, for every argument from reason would suggest that Christ should condemn her. She had broken the law. She had debased her own person. She even had violated that great illustration of Christ's love for the church and of the church's love for Christ: marriage. For marriage was given by God to illustrate that greatest of all relationships. And yet, Christ loved her. He wanted to spare her, to save her. There was no love in the attitude of her accusers.

Third, the attitude of the Lord Jesus Christ was characterized by *forgiveness*. This was his desire from the beginning—from the moment at which he stooped and wrote on the ground to the final moment in which he said to the woman, "Neither do I condemn you. Go now and leave your life of sin."

But it was not an easy forgiveness. It was not what Dietrich Bonhoeffer has aptly termed "cheap grace." It was costly, for it meant that Jesus would himself have to bear the justified wrath of God against the sinner. The Bible tells us that "the wages of sin is death" (Rom. 6:23), and it was precisely this that the Lord Jesus Christ bore for those whom he desired to forgive. Death means separation. In the physical sense death means the separation of the soul and the spirit from the body. In the spiritual sense it means the separation of the soul and the spirit from God. This, Jesus bore in our place. We probably will never understand in its fullness what this meant to the Savior, but we gain a sense of what it meant in that awful cry of dereliction wrung from his lips on the cross— "My God, my God, why have you forsaken me?" In that moment God the Father turned his back on God the Son so that Jesus knew the reality of spiritual death and separation. At the time of his talking to the woman this was before him, but it was on the basis of what was coming that forgiveness was given.

Today we look back on Christ's sacrifice, and the horror of what He bore for us compels us to come to him. Someone has said, "No other god has wounds." It is true. No other god ever was able to give himself in death for the sinner.

Fourth, the attitude of the Lord Jesus Christ was characterized by a *challenge*. He said, "Go now and leave your life of sin." This was not the same thing as merely allowing the woman to go her way, forgiven but free to do as she might choose. She was forgiven, but she was told to do better. It was, in short, the challenge of the sinless life. In the same way, Jesus confronts us. He understands us, loves us, forgives us; but he does this in order that we might not sin. Moreover, the element of challenge is also to characterize the Christian's relationships with other people.

Persons or Things?

The conclusion of this is that our attitude toward others should be that of the Lord Jesus Christ toward us and not that of the rulers who had accused the woman. They had used the woman. Jesus had saved her. What made the difference? We can say that the men were only sinful human beings while Christ was divine, of course. That is correct. But it is not very helpful. What is helpful is to notice that before this incident Jesus had spent the night upon the Mount of Olives, where we know from other sources he was accustomed to spend the time praying, while the leaders for their part had spent the night scheming with one another and (some of them) in peeping through keyholes.

Where does this compassionate attitude toward other persons come from in practical experience? It comes only from communing with our heavenly Father. We are personal with others only when we know ourselves to be persons. We know ourselves to be persons only when we see ourselves as persons before God.

101

"I Am the Light of the World"

John 8:12

When Jesus spoke again to the people, he said, "I am the light of the world. Whoever follows me will never walk in darkness, but will have the light of life."

It is not an accident that the claim of the Lord Jesus Christ to be the light of the world occurs immediately after the story of the woman taken in adultery, the story that introduces the eighth chapter of John's Gospel.

The story of the woman taken in adultery may not have been in the original text of John's Gospel, that is, in the first copy of the book as John wrote it. But whether it was there initially or not, few can doubt that the place where it finally was put was well chosen; for it follows well on the failure of an original plan by the rulers of Israel to arrest Jesus, and leads naturally into Christ's statement about being the light of the world. The story of the woman and her accusers is a greater revelation of the dark nature of sin than anything yet recorded in John's Gospel, and in it the purity and brightness of Jesus shine through abundantly.

It is appropriate to turn from the story itself to hear the Lord say, "I am the light of the world. Whoever follows me will never walk in darkness, but will have the light of life" (8:12).

Jesus already has been described as light in John's Gospel. In the opening chapter John wrote, "In him was life, and that life was the light of men" (v. 4). He spoke of the light six times in that context. In chapter 3 there is a similar reference. John said, "This is the verdict: Light has come into the world, but men loved darkness instead of light because their deeds were evil" (v. 19). This verse and those immediately following refer to light five times in reference to Jesus. In each of these cases the image is in John's words only, however. So we read these verses and, if we have not read further, we find ourselves asking, "But why does John refer to Jesus in this way? Where did he get this image? How did he develop this idea?" It is only when we get to our present text that we discover the answer. John refers to Jesus as the light because Jesus referred to himself as the light. Indeed, John obviously remembered this and so developed the images even further in this Gospel and in 1 John.

Jesus' claim to be the world's light is the second of the seven great "I am" sayings that are a unique feature of this book. The others are: "I am the bread of life" (6:35), "I am the gate" (10:7, 9), "I am the good shepherd" (10:11, 14), "I am the resurrection and the life" (11:25), "I am the way and the truth and the life" (14:6), and "I am the true vine" (15:1, 5).

The Cloud in the Desert

If we are to understand the full import of what Jesus was claiming when he claimed to be the light of the world, we must understand this verse in terms of that to which Jesus was undoubtedly referring. This is particularly important because it is not what we would most naturally think. We read this verse—"I am the light of the world"—and we think of the sun. Indeed, we are encouraged to do that by uses of this image elsewhere, as in Malachi where the coming Messiah is spoken of as the "sun of righteousness . . . with healing in its wings." This is not a bad thing to do. There is even much to be learned from it. But it is not the image Jesus is using in John 8:12.

To understand what Jesus had in mind as he spoke to the people we must remember that these words were spoken shortly after the Feast of Tabernacles in the courtyard of the temple area (v. 20) where the ceremonies that were a part of that feast were conducted.

We already have noted one of these ceremonies. On each morning of the eight-day feast the priests of Israel joined in a procession to the pool of Siloam from which they drew water in golden pitchers. Then, returning to the temple area, they poured this water upon the altar of sacrifice. As they did this the people, many of whom accompanied the priests, sang and chanted. One verse used was Isaiah 12:3: "With joy you will draw water from the wells of salvation." Another was Psalm 114:7–8: "Tremble, O earth, at the presence of the Lord, at the presence of the God of Jacob, who turned the rock into a pool, the hard rock into springs of water." The use of Psalm 114 shows that the ceremony was conceived primarily as a remembrance of God's provision of water for the people of Israel during the years of their wilderness wandering, though it also pointed forward to the spiritual water that men would draw from God in the day of God's future visitation. It was probably at the high point of this ceremony that Jesus broke into the festivities by crying, "If anyone is thirsty, let him come to me and drink. Whoever believes in me, as the Scripture has said, streams of living water will flow from within him" (John 7:37–38).

The second ceremony was similar. On the first night of the feast, and probably on succeeding nights also, after the sun had set, two great lamps were lighted in the courts of the temple. These were said to have cast their light over every quarter of the city. The lamps were meant to recall the pillar of cloud and fire that had accompanied the people in their wanderings in the desert. This was the cloud that had appeared on the day when the people left Egypt and had stood between the Israelites and the pursuing armies of the Egyptians the night before the crossing of the Red Sea. It kept the Jewish people from being attacked. Later it guided the people through the wilderness. It also spread out over them to give shade by day and light and warmth by night. I believe that it was in clear reference to the ceremony of lighting the lamps and naturally, therefore, also to the miraculous cloud itself that Jesus referred when he claimed to be this world's light.

This conclusion is supported by the fact that if it is so, then we have a striking succession of three great wilderness images in chapters 6, 7, and 8 of John's Gospel. In 6, Jesus is the new manna sent down from heaven. In 7, he is the water miraculously provided from the rock. In 8, he is the cloud. We therefore turn to the cloud itself and to its functions in order to determine the full meaning of this second of the "I am" sayings in John's Gospel.

God's Presence

Why was the cloud important? The most obvious way in which the cloud was important was that it symbolized God's presence with the people. This would be obvious from the fact that the cloud gave off light. For in an age that did not know an abundance of artificial light, light would always suggest God's presence. Besides, the cloud was so huge and so striking that this in itself would suggest a theophany.

We see this in the texts that refer to this unique phenomenon. For instance, the first reference to the cloud in the Old Testament clearly identifies the presence of the Lord with it. "By day the LORD went ahead of them in a pillar of cloud to guide them on their way and by night in a pillar of fire to give them light, so that they could travel by day or night" (Exod. 13:21–22). Other passages tell us that God spoke from the cloud and that he sometimes broke forth from it in judgment upon the sins of the people. In one striking passage the cloud is even addressed as God, for God is said to have raised himself up when the cloud rose and to have descended when the cloud descended. "Whenever the ark set out, Moses said, 'Rise up, O LORD! May your enemies be scattered; may your foes flee before you.' Whenever it came to rest, he said,

'Return, O LORD, to the countless thousands of Israel'" (Num. 10:35–36). At no time in their wandering were the people of Israel able to forget that the presence of God went with them and overshadowed them in all they did.

Apply this now to the claim of the Lord Jesus Christ. Long years before, the cloud of God's glory had departed from Israel. It once had filled the Holy of Holies of the temple before which Christ was standing. Now the innermost shrine was empty, and even the lamps that commemorated the departed cloud had gone out. In this context and against this background Jesus cried, "I am the light of the world. I am the cloud. I am God with you." Here was God once again with his people.

Have you found God in Jesus? Is Jesus, God with you? There is no other place in which you may find him. Come to him if you have never done so, and learn to say with John and the believers of all ages: "The Word became flesh and made his dwelling among us. We have seen his glory, the glory of the One and Only, who came from the Father, full of grace and truth" (John 1:14).

Protection

Second, the cloud was important in that it was the primary means by which God protected the people. Without it the people would have perished many years before they entered Canaan, either from their human enemies like Pharoah and his armies or from the natural dangers of the desert.

We must remember at this point that when the people of Israel left Egypt there were probably about two million of them. The Bible says that there were 600,000 men, but, of course, wives and children need to be added to that number. This vast company of people was being led out into a desert region that, as anyone who has ever been there can tell you, is one of the most inhospitable regions on earth. In the daytime the temperature can easily reach 140 or 150 degrees, and at night it can fall below freezing. To survive in such a region the vast host of Israel needed water and a shelter from the sun. The rock, which Moses was instructed to smite with his rod, provided water. Shelter was provided by the cloud, which spread out over the camp of the people to give them protection. Without this special and miraculous provision the people would have died.

We sing about God's protection of the people in one of our hymns, a hymn that many who sing it probably do not understand.

> Round each habitation hov'ring,
> See the cloud and fire appear
> For a glory and a cov'ring,
> Showing that the Lord is near!
> Thus, deriving from their banner
> Light by night and shade by day,
> Safe they feed upon the manna
> Which he gives them when they pray.

In the same way the Lord Jesus Christ is a protector for all who come to him and follow him.

The Moving of the Cloud

Third, the cloud was important because it was the primary means by which God guided the people while they were in the desert. There were few, if any, landmarks in the desert, and the people would not have recognized landmarks even if they had seen them. Besides, the heat of the desert produces mirages, distorts distances, and makes most terrains indistinguishable. How were the people to find their way? How were they to avoid wandering into hostile territory or around in circles? The answer God gave was the cloud. When the cloud moved they were to move; indeed, they had to move, for if they had remained where they were they would soon have died from the heat of the desert by day or from the cold at night. When the cloud remained in one place, they remained.

One long passage in Numbers makes this particularly clear. "Whenever the cloud lifted from above the Tent, the Israelites set out; wherever the cloud settled, the Israelites encamped. At the LORD's command the Israelites set out, and at his command they encamped. As long as the cloud stayed over the tabernacle, they remained in camp. When the cloud remained over the tabernacle a long time, the Israelites obeyed the LORD's order and did not set out. Sometimes the cloud was over the tabernacle only a few days; at the LORD's command they would encamp, and then at his command they would set out. Sometimes the cloud stayed only from evening till morning, and when it lifted in the morning, they set out. Whether by day or by night, whenever the cloud lifted, they set out. Whether the cloud stayed over the tabernacle for two days or a month or a year, the Israelites would remain in camp and not set out; but when it lifted, they would set out. At the LORD's command they encamped, and at the LORD's command they set out. They obeyed the LORD's order, in accordance with his command through Moses" (Num. 9:17–23).

We can easily see how this applies to Christ's statement. For when he claimed to be the light of the world in clear reference to the cloud of Israel's wandering, he was claiming not only that he was God with his people, or that he was the one who would protect them, but also that he is the one who gives guidance. Thus, when Jesus moves before us we are to move. When he abides in one place we, too, are to remain there.

Moreover, we are to avoid two errors. The first error is to be overly hasty in following him; that is, to follow so closely upon the moving of the cloud that we mistake its moving and find ourselves going in another direction. If we tend to make this mistake, we must remember that there was to be a clear space between the guiding ark over which the cloud rose and the people—about "two thousand cubits" (three-fifths of a mile)—that there be no mistakes about the road. Alexander Maclaren, who writes on this theme, observes, "It is neither reverent nor wise to be treading on the heels of our Guide in our eager confidence that we know where He wants us to go."[1]

On the other hand, we are not to be slow either. For, as Maclaren states, we are not to "let the warmth by the camp-fire, or the pleasantness of the shady place where [our] tent is pitched, keep [us] there when the cloud lifts."[2] The only place of true blessing is under the shadow of God's presence.

Will You Follow?

To summarize: When the Lord Jesus Christ claimed to be the light of the world he was claiming to be these three things for his people—God with them, the source of protection, and the One who guides. These are great claims. But we must not overlook the fact that they are only for those who follow him. He said, "Whoever *follows* me will never walk in darkness, but will have the light of life." To follow Christ is almost synonymous with believing in Christ; for in another, parallel passage Jesus uses the same image in declaring, "I have come into the world as a light, so that no one who believes in me should stay in darkness" (John 12:46). Faith in Christ is following Christ, or at least leads to following Christ. And following Christ is possible only for those who have faith in him.

Do you have faith in Christ? Are you following him? You should; for if you are, you have Christ's promise that you will no longer be walking in darkness but will possess the light of life. The last phrase is another way of saying that you will possess Christ himself, who thereafter will become all things to you. The Bible says that he is made unto us "righteousness, holiness, and redemption," and that it is a joy to follow him (1 Cor. 1:30).

102

The Witnesses Agree

John 8:13–18

The Pharisees challenged him, "Here you are, appearing as your own witness; your testimony is not valid."

Jesus answered, "Even if I testify on my own behalf, my testimony is valid, for I know where I came from and where I am going. But you have no idea where I come from or where I am going. You judge by human standards; I pass judgment on no one. But if I do judge, my decisions are right, because I am not alone. I stand with the Father, who sent me. In your own Law it is written that the testimony of two men is valid. I am one who testifies for myself; my other witness is the Father, who sent me."

If you were an unscrupulous person and were about to be accused of a crime in court by a certain witness, what would you do to eliminate the impact of his testimony? Most of us would do nothing, of course, especially if we were innocent. But if you were guilty and were also unscrupulous, I suppose you would have three courses of action open to you. First, you could eliminate the witness; you could have him killed, perhaps, or else threaten him so that he would keep quiet. This has happened many times in actual criminal trials, as we know. Second, you could seek to discredit the witness. That is, if you could show that he does not possess good character, perhaps that he has lied in court before, you could get people to discount what he has to say on this occasion. Third, you could seek to have his testimony thrown out of court on a technicality.

619

Here are three lines of attack for anyone who is unscrupulous, and I mention them now because they are precisely the lines of attack followed by those who tried to discredit Jesus Christ in that testimony he bore to men of God's nature and of man's need for salvation.

The first line of attack was to eliminate him. We saw an attempt at that in the closing verses of John 7, for these verses record an attempt by the leaders of Israel in Christ's time to have him arrested. They failed on that occasion, but they succeeded later, with the result that Jesus was brought to trial and executed. Second, they tried to discredit him by throwing such doubt upon his character that no one would listen to him regardless of what he had to say. This was the object of the abortive attempt to trap Jesus in the incident concerning the woman taken in adultery. The final attempt was to eliminate the force of his testimony as the result of a technicality. It is this to which we now come in our verse-by-verse study of John's Gospel.

Two or Three Witnesses

In the last verse we studied we found the Lord Jesus Christ making a stupendous claim. To be sure, he has made many stupendous claims thus far in the Gospel, but in this particular verse he states something that is very close to a claim to be God. He says, "I am the light of the world. Whoever follows me will never walk in darkness, but will have the light of life" (8:12). Since God was thought of in terms of light and life, and since this claim referred to the cloud of Israel's desert wandering that symbolized God's presence with the people, Christ's words must have seemed almost blasphemous to his listeners. By any standard it was at least a claim to his right to have men and women follow him. The leaders rejected both inferences.

But how were they to eliminate this testimony? They had already tried to have him arrested, and that had failed. He had proved too smart for them in the matter of the woman. Perhaps a technicality would do. At all events, they would try it.

In Jewish law there was a maxim to the effect that no one could ever be convicted on the testimony of a single witness. Always two or three witnesses were required. This principle was expressed in Numbers 35:30: "No one is to be put to death on the testimony of only one witness"; Deuteronomy 17:6: "On the testimony of two or three witnesses a man shall be put to death, but no one shall be put to death on the testimony of only one witness"; and Deuteronomy 19:15: "At the mouth of two witnesses, or at the mouth of three witnesses, shall the matter be established." This had been interpreted in the broadest possible way by the rabbinical authorities so that it came to be applied eventually to all testimony. Nothing was to be believed unless more than one person could attest to it. And, of course, no one could testify concerning himself. The rulers now applied this to Jesus, their point being that whether or not his claim was true, at least insofar as evidence was concerned it was invalid. It was the testimony of just one man concerning himself and should be discounted. John tells us, "The Pharisees challenged him, 'Here you are appearing as your own witness; your testimony is not valid'" (v. 13).

I must admit at this point that in some ways the subject we are covering is both technical and related to a past age. But in other ways it is simple and relevant to people today. There are many who would discount Christ's witness, not because it is untrue necessarily, but because according to their way of evaluating evidence, there is no way of telling whether it is true or not. They do not really disbelieve Christ, but so far as he is concerned they are agnostics. To such people particularly, and indeed to all of us, Christ's answer to the charge of the rulers is of great importance.

Superior Knowledge

In answering the charge that his testimony concerning himself was invalid on technical grounds, Jesus makes three points, the first being that in terms of the kind of matter to which he is testifying only a person with a superior source of knowledge can qualify and that he and only he possesses such knowledge. In his own words the reply was, "Even if I testify on my own behalf, my testimony is valid, for I know where I came from and where I am going. But you have no idea where I come from and where I am going" (v. 14). In other words, if this were only a matter of something within the framework of human experience and apprehension, then the rabbinic maxim would hold true and would be useful. But in terms of knowing God, only God can testify. In this case, God the Son is bearing witness both to himself and to God the Father, and the testimony should be accepted because of these unique circumstances.

Perhaps there is even an indirect reference to another Jewish legal principle in this answer. For it was another principle that the character and status of the witness were involved in accepting or not accepting his testimony. This principle expresses itself largely in a listing of those who for their personalities, professions, or questionable activities were discounted as witnesses. Among such persons were thieves, shepherds (because they seem to have permitted their sheep to graze on another person's property), violent persons, and all suspected of dishonesty in financial matters, among whom were tax collectors and customs officials.

Now, so goes Jesus' argument, if the rabbis reject the testimony of men whom they consider unreliable, and if they accept the testimony of an upright man when substantiated by that of another upright witness, why should they not then in Jesus' case accept the testimony of One who is more than a man? Jesus knows his origins and destiny, things that no other can know (v. 14). He judges according to truth and not, as do his opponents, according to the flesh (v. 15). He works in complete spiritual unity with God the Father (vv. 15–16).

This understanding of the passage is encouraged also by the fact that in the citation of the legal principle in John 8:17, Jesus is quoted as changing the original phrase "two witnesses" to "two men," thereby stressing the great gulf that exists between merely human and, therefore, limited testimony and his own.

Do you recognize this distinction? Have you seen that if Jesus is who he claims to be, then he is able also to bear testimony about God and to certain things about man that we could learn about in no other way? If he is not God, then we have no sure knowledge of God. If he is God, his statements and claims can be trusted.

Impartial Testimony

Second, Jesus defended his right to give testimony about God and man on the basis that his testimony is impartial. This is what he means in verses 15 and 16, where he says, "You judge by human standards; I pass judgment on no one. But if I do judge, my decisions are right." The "human standards" in this verse stand for all that is human in man as opposed to that which is of God; it involves the limitations of being human, including limitations in knowledge and in objectivity. Here were men who were testifying about men. They were partial in their estimate of men. They excused themselves and others. In opposition to this, Jesus declares that his judgment is not limited as theirs is, but rather is impartial.

Moreover, it also is sinless. For being of "human standards" in biblical language also implies being sinful; and this, too, Jesus is denying. He is the sinless One. So the distortions of sin do not enter to invalidate his testimony.

Sin always enters where human testimony and judgment are concerned. The story is told by lawyers of a not altogether honest judge from Virginia. He had been asked to decide a case concerning two railroads, and when the briefs came to him from the two lawyers representing the two railroads, they contained bribes. The first lawyer had sent a check for $10,000. The second lawyer had sent a check for $15,000. The judge looked at the two checks, thought a moment, then called his secretary. "Make out a check for five thousand dollars," he said, "and send it to the lawyer representing the second railroad. We're going to decide this case on its merits."

Men, even at the best, are sinful. So we should clearly accept the testimony of the sinless One over testimony rendered by any man or woman.

The Witness of the Father

Finally, the Lord Jesus Christ also pointed out, as he had done earlier in his ministry, that in the final analysis his testimony did not stand alone but actually was supported by the word of God the Father, thereby satisfying the rabbinical requirement that in the mouth of two or three witnesses every word should be established. We find him saying, "In your own Law it is written that the testimony of two men is valid. I am one who testifies for myself; my other witness is the Father who sent me" (vv. 17–18). The witness of God the Father consists of a witness through John the Baptist (5:33–34), the witness of Christ's signs (5:36), and the witness of the Old Testament Scriptures (5:39–47).

What, then, can we say of Christ's testimony? When we put it all together we have the testimony of Jesus himself, characterized by superior knowledge and impartiality, corroborated by the witness of the Father. Two great, two superior witnesses! And the witnesses agree!

Who can discredit such testimony? No one can discredit it; and no one has, though many have tried.

Three Applications

There are a few important applications to our own lives from these teachings. First, we must not trust our own judgment in spiritual matters. Our knowledge is limited. We are not impartial. We must not trust our own way of looking at things. This is the point of Proverbs 3:5–6, which says, "Trust in the LORD with all your heart and lean not on your own understanding; in all your ways acknowledge him, and he will make your paths straight."

Second, we should trust the word of the Lord Jesus Christ implicitly. We should not trust our own understanding, but we should trust him because of who he is. There may be much in the Christian faith that we do not understand. There will be aspects of Christian truth that we will not like and wish could be eliminated. But that is not an option for us. Whatever Jesus says must be believed without question, and our own reasonings on spiritual matters must be subordinated. The Bible speaks of our duty along these lines by pointing to the proper goal of "[demolishing] every pretension that sets itself up against the knowledge of God, and . . . [taking] captive every thought to make it obedient to Christ" (2 Cor. 10:5).

Third, if the word of Jesus Christ is true, then we should accept him as our Savior and follow him as our Lord. Have you done that? If not, let me challenge you to test his testimony and then to follow him if that testimony is valid.

The great Bible teacher and lecturer Reuben A. Torrey tells of a man who accepted this challenge. Torrey had been lecturing to a number of his students in Chicago and had been confronted at the end of the lecture by a man who claimed that his experience contradicted everything that Torrey had been saying. Torry had been telling how doubt in spiritual matters could be overcome, and this man felt that he had done everything Torrey had suggested and yet was unconvinced.

"Let us be very definite about this," Torrey replied. So, calling his secretary, he dictated, "I believe that there is an absolute difference between right and wrong, and I hereby take my stand upon the right to follow it wherever it carries me. I promise to make an honest search to find if Jesus Christ is the Son of God, and if I find that He is, I promise to accept him as my Savior and confess him publicly before the world." The secretary brought two copies. "Will you sign this?" Torrey asked.

"Certainly," said the visitor, as he signed one copy and returned the other to Torrey. "But there is nothing to it," he added. "My case is very peculiar."

"Now, another thing," said Torrey. "Do you know that there is not a God?"

"No, I do not know that there is not a God," was the answer. "I am an agnostic in the matter. I neither affirm nor deny."

"And in that case, you also do not know that God does not answer prayer," Torrey continued.

"That is correct."

"Well, then," said Torrey, "here is a clue for you in your search to discover if Jesus Christ is the Son of God. You must pray. Pray something like this, 'God, if there is a God, show me if Jesus Christ is Your Son or not; if You show me that He is Your Son, I promise to accept him as my Savior and confess him to be such before the world.' Will you do that?"

"Yes, I'll do that, too," the man answered. "But there is nothing to it. My case is very peculiar."

"There is also one final thing. In John 20:31, John says, 'These [things] are written that you may believe that Jesus is the Christ, the Son of God, and that by believing you may have life in his name.' Here John tells us that his Gospel was written to show men the proof that Jesus is the Christ and God's Son. Will you read the proof? And will you pray the prayer I have suggested each time before you begin to read it?" The man replied again that he would. But he added once more that there was nothing to it.

The two men parted, and each went about his own affairs. Two weeks later the two met again in Torrey's lecture hall. But this time the skeptic said, "You know, there was something to that. Ever since I have done what you suggested I feel as if I have been caught up and am being carried along by the Niagara River. The first thing you know I shall become a shouting Methodist."

Torrey became one for the occasion and cried, "Praise the Lord!"

Again several weeks went by, in which Torrey lectured in the East, but when he returned, the man was waiting for him. He had become a Christian. His testimony was, "I can't understand now how I ever listened to anything else."

If you are not yet a Christian, this can become your story if you will face the evidence. Will you face it? God does not want you to be in confusion but to be certain in your knowledge of Christian truth.

103

Three Questions

John 8:19–27

Then they asked him, "Where is your father?"

"You do not know me or my Father," Jesus replied. "If you knew me, you would know my Father also." He spoke these words while teaching in the temple area near the place where the offerings were put. Yet no one seized him, because his time had not yet come.

Once more Jesus said to them, "I am going away, and you will look for me, and you will die in your sin. Where I go, you cannot come."

This made the Jews ask, "Will he kill himself? Is that why he says, 'Where I go, you cannot come'?"

But he continued, "You are from below; I am from above. You are of this world; I am not of this world. I told you that you would die in your sins; if you do not believe that I am the one I claim to be, you will indeed die in your sins."

"Who are you?" they asked.

"Just what I have been claiming all along," Jesus replied. "I have much to say in judgment of you. But he who sent me is reliable, and what I have heard from him I tell the world."

They did not understand that he was telling them about his Father.

Once, when a member of Tenth Presbyterian Church and I were joking about the course of much theological discussion, we pointed out how such discussion often goes downhill in quality and ends up in personal invective. We were imagining how it might be between the pulpit of this church and an opponent, whom we shall call John Smith. Smith disagrees with the doctrines of the Reformed faith that he hears me

625

teaching; so he writes a book questioning them. It is called *Calvinism Surveyed*. The second step in the debate is my reply; it bears the title *Arminianism Refuted*. Now John Smith gets lengthy. He compiles a three-volume work entitled *The Teachings of James Montgomery Boice Exposed*. I reply with *The Heresy of John Smith*. The final work in the debate is by the man who started this controversy; it is a pamphlet called "Come out from among Them and Be Ye Separate."

We were only being humorous, of course. I don't even know a John Smith. But what we were saying unfortunately does illustrate the course of much theological discussion. What is more, it illustrates a point that I would like to make in connection with the eighth chapter of John's Gospel.

Scorn of the Pharisees

We need to understand, if we are to enter fully into the spirit of this chapter, that the relationship between Jesus Christ and the rulers of the people was deteriorating. At least that is the way we would describe it from a human point of view. These chapters (chapters 5 through 8) record the rejection of Jesus by the leaders, beginning with their opposition to him on the sabbath question in chapter 5 and ending with a complete break in chapter 8. In fact, the next chapters will begin a new theme: the relationship of Jesus to those whom the Father has given him and his provision for them. At this point, however, John is still tracing the deteriorating relationship between Jesus and the leaders and is showing us that it reached a new low.

It had sunk quite low already, of course. First, there was the attempt to arrest Jesus (7:32). This failed. Next there was the attempt to trap him in the matter of the woman taken in adultery (8:3–11). Jesus showed himself to be too smart for the rulers in this situation. Third, there was the attempt to have his testimony discounted on the basis of a legal technicality (8:13). He had an answer even for this. So, after Jesus had escaped arrest, overcome them in the test, and answered their objection to his testimony, the Pharisees and other leaders sank to the lowest level of all and began to make fun of him personally. They did this by asking insulting questions.

There were three questions. The first was, "Where is your father?" (v. 19). At the least this was a scornful rejection of Jesus' statement that there was a second witness to his claims. But it may also have been a reference to the peculiar nature of the facts surrounding his birth and to their belief—with insulting and demeaning overtones—that Joseph was not Christ's father. This slur may also be evident in the saying recorded later: "We are not illegitimate children" (v. 41).

The second question was, "Will he kill himself?" (v. 22). The force of this query is seen in the Jewish belief that those who killed themselves went to the lowest part of Hades. Jesus had just said, "Where I go, you cannot come." They had correctly understood that he was speaking of his death, but they reasoned that since they would surely be going to heaven he must be going to hell, and the lowest part at that.

The final question, "Who are you?" (v. 25), had the effect of calling him a nobody. It implied a rejection of all the things he had said about himself previously.

What was Jesus' response to such questions? What was his reaction to the scorn they expressed? It is interesting that Christ answered by the strongest series of statements about the fate of the unregenerate person that we have thus far in John's Gospel.

God Gave Them Up

The first thing the Lord Jesus Christ said when faced by the scornful questions of these men is that *such questions are not asked by those who know him* and that, therefore, those who ask them do not know either him or God the Father. This point was so important that Jesus repeated it in different terms after having said it the first time. He first said, "You do not know me or my Father . . . if you knew me, you would know my Father also" (v. 19). Then he added, "You are from below; I am from above. You are of this world; I am not of this world" (v. 23). In other words, these men (despite their position and learning) did not know God, and it was because of this that they asked such scornful questions.

This is quite interesting for us, because it runs counter to our natural way of looking at things. To our way of thinking, asking questions is good. We say, "How are we going to learn if we don't ask questions?" That is right, to a degree. Even in Bible study it is right, for we need to ask, "To whom is this written? Who is speaking? What does it say? How does it apply to me?" and so on, if our Bible study is to be helpful. At the same time, we need to recognize that in spiritual matters there is a type of question that is not at all helpful. This type of question is aimed not so much at finding out the truth but at resisting the truth. It really is an attempt to justify a refusal to believe what God has already made known to us.

This is what God is speaking about in the first chapter of Romans where we are told that God gave certain men over to a reprobate mind because "they did not think it worthwhile to retain the knowledge of God" (1:28). Certain things about God are known to all men. Romans 1:20 speaks of them. But because men and women do not like what they know and do not want to recognize the conclusions that flow from it, they refuse to retain this knowledge of God and therefore willfully reject him.

David tells us why in slightly different language. He writes in Psalm 77:3: "I remembered you, O God, and I groaned." God will always trouble those whose hearts and minds are not at peace with him through the death of Jesus Christ. Therefore, since men do not like to be troubled in their minds and pricked in their consciences, they do everything they can think of to banish God from their knowledge. One way is to ask questions, even the kind that are asked by many theologians and ministers: Who is God? What was Jesus really like? What is the meaning of the cross to men today? The sad thing is that this is unnecessary, for the knowledge of God exists to be seized by those who will have it since God is revealed in the person of Jesus Christ and in the Scriptures.

The first chapter of Romans reminds us of one more truth. The truth is in the form of a warning of what God does to those who will not retain the knowledge of him. We are told that God "gave them over." The Greek suggests the thought that since men have abandoned God, God has abandoned them. They gave God up, so God gave them up.

This is a terrible phrase: "God gave them over." It occurs three times in Romans 1. In the first instance we are told that because men refused to glorify God as God and were not thankful, God gave them over to uncleanness (v. 24). The reference is to sexual sins. Second, we are told that because men exchanged the truth of God for a lie and worshiped and served the creature more than the Creator, God gave them over to vile affections (v. 26). This refers to sexual perversions—homosexuality, lesbianism, and so on. Finally, after it is said that they did not like to retain God in their knowledge, we are told that God gave them over to something that is far worse than these sexual sins. God gave them over to a reprobate mind (v. 28). That is, he abandoned them to their own corrupt judgment. This is a terrible fate, as is proved by the horrible list of sins that follows this verse, which sins, God says, flow from man's reprobate judgment.

The Day of God's Grace

Second, Jesus taught that *the day of God's grace would not last forever.* He taught this in two ways: first, by reference to his own death and departure, after which they would seek for him and would not be able to find him and, second, by reference to the fact that they would die also (8:21). The day of God's grace either in historical or personal terms is not endless. Hence, the personal act of entering into a right relationship with God through faith in the Lord Jesus Christ should not be delayed. To delay is folly.

Why is it that people will exercise common sense in a thousand matters of daily need in this life but will not exercise common sense in the matter of eternity? People will provide for themselves financially, saving up for the day of retirement when they no longer will be able to continue working as before. They will provide for their health. Not only will they go to the doctor when ill; they will exercise preventive medicine by following a series of regular checkups, tests, and inoculations. They eat well. They take vacations and provide for periods of exercise. In all these matters, men and women will exercise the most commendable common sense. But they will not prepare to meet God in this, the day of his grace.

Years ago an evangelist preached a sermon on the text, "Prepare to Meet Thy God," and his first point was this: "The greatest reason why you should prepare to meet your God is that you must meet your God." That is true. Unless your case is settled out of court through your personal response to

Jesus Christ, you must appear before the judgment bar of God the Father and answer for your rejection of Christ. Will you respond to him? The Bible declares, "Now is the time of God's favor, now is the day of salvation" (2 Cor. 6:2).

No Excuse

Third, Jesus replied to the scorn of the Pharisees by the truth that if they would not believe on him as their Messiah and Savior, *they would die in their sins* (vv. 21, 24). There are two ways to die, according to the Bible. You may die "in the Lord"—Revelation 14:13 says, "Blessed are the dead who die in the Lord from now on"—or you may die "in your sins." To die in sin means to die with the burden of one's sin upon oneself and, as a result, to be forced to bear the penalty of sin, which is spiritual death. God says that "the wages of sin is death" (Rom. 6:23). Physical death is the separation of the soul and the spirit from the body. Spiritual death is the separation of the soul and the spirit from God. To die in sin is to die separated from God and to remain so forever.

Moreover, it does not at all matter whether or not you are aware of this. It is true nonetheless. You may try to forget about this, but the day of God's judgment will reveal the sin that many have tried to cover over with the world's values and activities.

What people have tried to do may be illustrated by a particular type of manuscript called a palimpsest. A palimpsest is a manuscript with two entirely different writings on it, one over the other. When the manuscript was first written it was written as any other manuscript is written, with line upon line of characters reproducing some ancient text. Later, however, when the earlier writing had faded somewhat and paper was scarce, someone took the old parchment or papyrus, turned it sideways, and wrote a new text over it. These palimpsests vary in quality. In some, both writings can be clearly seen. In others, the newer writing has almost entirely replaced the old. Scholars often recover this older and more valuable writing by using acids, ultraviolet light, and X-rays. So it is with the heart of man. In the early ages of the human race God wrote his standards of conduct upon the heart of man. But when man violated God's standards and when his conscience was troubled by that fact, man allowed the original writing to fade and eventually, turning the page sideways, wrote over God's writing with the darker ink of his own dark deeds. Some day, however, the acid of God's judgment will eat away the newer writing, and men will be exposed as sinners to be judged by that standard that God originally placed within the life and conscience of all.

Separation from God

Finally, Jesus said the most sobering thing of all. He said that if the men who refused to believe in him continued to refuse him and therefore died in their sins, *they would go to hell and not to heaven.* It is true, of course, that

Jesus does not mention hell by name in these verses, though he does elsewhere. But the existence of hell and the fact that hell is the destiny of those who refuse him is still stated. Jesus said, "You will die in your sin. Where I go, you cannot come." Where was he going? He was going to heaven. So if they could not come where he was going, they could not come to heaven and would remain without God and apart from God forever.

The frightening thing about this statement is that there is no escape from it. If it were only a matter of human judgment, then there would be a possibility of escape at least. For instance, a criminal might escape prosecution if his crime should go undiscovered or if no one should discover that he is the criminal. Apparently this happens often, for in many cases police are unable even to find a suspect though a crime has been committed. Or again, a criminal may escape from the sphere of the law's jurisdiction, as the financier who fled to South America in order to escape prosecution on charges of tax evasion. Finally, a criminal may escape on a technicality.

Here are three ways in which a criminal by human law may escape the law's judgment. But there is no escape from God's judgment. Do you think that a crime and the one who has committed it are unknown to God? Do you think that you can escape God's jurisdiction? Do you think that a technicality can get you off? These abuses of the law may pass on earth, for human judgment is imperfect. But they will not pass in heaven. There is no escape. No escape! You must meet God and answer for your sins.

Someone will say, "But that is frightening. Are you saying those things just to frighten me?" In a sense I am, for I would like you to be so frightened by the warning the Lord Jesus Christ gives that you will turn from your sin and cleave to him. The gospel tells us that Jesus died for your sin. He died both physically and spiritually—he was separated from God—so that you and everyone else might not have to die spiritually. He removed our sin, so that all who believe on him might have eternal life and be able to follow him to heaven.

You can assess your relationship to the Lord Jesus Christ by the way in which you would answer the questions that were posed by the Pharisees and with which we began. "Where is your father?" Can you say, "Your Father is God Almighty, and you are his Son"?

Will he kill himself? Can you say, "In one sense, yes, for he gave himself for us"?

Who are you? Can you say, "You are the Christ, the Son of the living God; you are my Savior"?

104

The Uplifted Christ

John 8:28–29

So Jesus said, "When you have lifted up the Son of Man, then you will know that I am the one I claim to be and that I do nothing on my own but speak just what the Father has taught me. The one who sent me is with me; he has not left me alone, for I always do what pleases him."

Our text tells us that the Lord Jesus Christ was to be "lifted up" and that, when he was lifted up, certain consequences would flow from it. These two words—"lifted up"—introduce us to some wonderful truths from John's Gospel.

We should notice from the beginning that John in three different places speaks of Jesus being lifted up and that these should rightly be taken together in order to gain the full force of his teaching. The first text is John 3:14–15: "Just as Moses lifted up the snake in the desert, so the Son of Man must be lifted up, that everyone who believes in him may have eternal life." The verses stress the necessity of Christ's crucifixion. The second text is the one to which we have now come in our study, John 8:28–29. Jesus says, "When you have lifted up the Son of Man, then you will know that I am the one I claim to be, and that I do nothing on my own but speak just what the Father has taught me. The one who sent me is with me, he has not left me alone, for I always do what pleases him." The last passage is the well-known cry of Jesus in John 12:32: "But I, when I am lifted up from the earth, will draw all men to myself."

These three passages, all of which stress the truth that Jesus was to be lifted up, carry us to the heart of the gospel and stress its consequences. We should therefore explore this theme by a careful study of each passage.

Jesus Must Die

The first text, then, is John 3:14–15. It is a good one with which to begin, for it makes clear precisely what is meant by this unusual phrase. Sometimes preachers have used the last of these three verses—"But I, when I am lifted up from the earth, will draw all men to myself"—as though the phrase referred to our need to lift Christ up in our preaching. We do need to lift Christ up in our preaching, of course. But while it is true that if we lift Christ up in preaching he will indeed draw men and women to himself, this is nevertheless not the primary sense of the metaphor. To be lifted up means to be lifted up on the cross in death. It is a reference to Christ crucified. Consequently, John 3:14 compares Christ's being lifted up to the lifting up of the serpent upon a pole in the wilderness when the wandering Israelites were afflicted by the poison of deadly serpents and were dying. John 12:33 says simply, "He said this to show the kind of death he was going to die."

Moreover, the first of these verses also stresses the divine necessity in Christ's death, for it says, "So the Son of Man *must* be lifted up." Why is this so? Why was it necessary for Christ to die?

One answer to that question is that it was necessary because Christ's death was part of God's eternal plan to save sinners. But that is too general to be of much help. A far better answer is that it was necessary because nothing else could accomplish God's purpose. In the first place, no other person existed who could pay the price of our sin so that we might be forgiven for our sin and go free. No man could do it. Men are sinners, and each one (except those who are Christ's) must pay the price of his or her own transgressions. Only Jesus, who is more than a man and without sin, could pay the price of sin and so save us. This he did, as we correctly sing:

> There was no other good enough
>   To pay the price of sin;
> He only could unlock the gate
>   Of heaven, and let us in.

It was necessary for Christ to die, for no one else was able to die that death that would save sinners.

Moreover, it was necessary for Christ to die also because nothing but a crucified Christ will draw men to God. Nothing but this will even draw men to hear preaching. Liberalism does not draw men. The cults do not draw men in great quantities. Men and women will not long attend a man-centered religion. But preach Christ crucified—preach him in the power of the Holy Spirit—and men and women will begin to come to him. They begin to leave their comfortable homes in the suburbs and come to city churches, where they would have come for no other reason. They begin to take weeks of their vacation time and attend seminars or attend Bible conferences. At times they will even mass in the millions as they did in Korea for the Billy Graham crusades in that country.

Preach any Christ but a crucified Christ, and you will not draw men for long. But preach the gospel of a Savior who atones for the sins of men and women by dying for them, and you will have hearers. Moreover, as Christ is lifted up, many of those who hear will believe.

Source of Knowledge

The second text is John 8:28. Here the emphasis is upon the fact that the leaders of the people would come to know certain things about Christ, the truth about Christ, only after they had killed him. Consequently, the verse points to the cross as the only basis for true knowledge in spiritual things. Jesus said, "When you have lifted up the Son of Man, then you will know that I am the one I claim to be and that I do nothing on my own, but speak just what the Father has taught me."

There are two senses in which this is true. First, it is true because it is only at the cross of Christ that the stubborn and rebellious will of man is conquered. Since a rebellious will is the major barrier to a reception of God's truth and since it is only at the cross that the barrier is removed, it is therefore only at the cross that the light of God's revelation is enabled to illuminate the soul. Jesus said, "If anyone chooses to do God's will, he will find out whether my teaching is from God or whether I speak on my own." It is at the cross that we are enabled to will it.

But then, too, it is in the glory of the cross and in those manifestations of God's power that surround it (particularly in the resurrection) that we have the fullest proof of Christ's divinity and teaching. So the evidence leads people to knowledge. This is indicated in the word that John uses when he says that Jesus was "lifted up." There are different words in Greek that are translated as "lifted up" in English. Most common are *airo* and various compounds based upon it—*egeiro, espairo,* and so on. John does not use these words in the verses we are studying. Instead, he uses the verb *hupsoo,* which means "to exalt" or "to elevate." The overtones of this word show that John is thinking of Christ's glorification even as he writes of his crucifixion, thereby indicating that the cross, as the first step in that glorification, becomes a proof of Christ's teachings.

Jesus said that after he had been lifted up—by the crucifixion and eventually to the Father by means of the resurrection and the ascension—the rulers of the people would no longer be in ignorance of who he is but would know that he is indeed Jehovah. These are sobering words. If they are true—and they must be true if Jesus said them—they mean that the rulers were later found to be rejecting Christianity in large measure not for a lack of knowledge about him but because of sin. They knew who he was, many of them at least, and yet they would not have him as their Savior.

Perhaps the situation is repeating itself today, for there has never been a period in history when there was more knowledge about Jesus Christ and yet in which so few seem willing to follow him. Lack of knowledge can hardly be pleaded as an excuse by those of our well-educated and informed generation.

The Great Attraction

The final verse of the three we are considering is most important, for it speaks of the drawing power of the uplifted Christ. It tells us that he is the great attraction. "But I, when I am lifted up from the earth, will draw all men to myself." Why is it that Jesus as the crucified Son of God draws men and women to him? There are two reasons. Let me share them with you from a great message on "The Uplifted Christ" by Reuben A. Torrey.

"First of all," Torrey writes, "Christ crucified draws all men unto Himself because Christ crucified meets the first, the deepest, the greatest and most fundamental need of man. What is man's first, greatest, deepest, most fundamental need? A Savior? A Savior from what? Underlying all else, a Savior from the guilt of sin. Every man of every race has sinned. As Paul in Romans 3:22–23 says, 'There is no difference: For all have sinned and come short of the glory of God.' There is no difference between Jew and Gentile at this point, nor is there a difference between English and German at this point. There is no difference between American and Japanese at this point, no difference between European and Asiatic, no difference between the American and the African. 'There is no difference: For *all* have sinned and come short of the glory of God.' Every man of every race is a sinner; 'there is no difference' at this point. Every man shall have to answer for his sin to the infinitely holy God who rules this universe. Therefore, all men need an atoning Savior, who can by His atoning death make propitiation for, and so cover up our sins. . . .

"In all the universe there is no other religion but Christianity that even offers an atoning Savior. Mohammedanism offers Mohammed, 'The Prophet,' a teacher, but not a savior; Buddhism offers Buddha, supposedly at least a wonderful teacher, 'The Light of Asia,' but not an atoning savior; Confucianism offers Confucius, a marvelous teacher far ahead of his time, but not an atoning savior. No religion but Christianity offers an atoning Savior, offers an atonement of any real character. This is the radical point of difference between Christianity and every other religion in the world; yet some foolish preachers are trying to eliminate from Christianity this, its very point of radical difference from all other religions.

"But such an emasculated Christianity will not reach the needs of men and will not draw men. It never has and it never will. The Bible and history are one at this point. Jesus Christ offers Himself lifted up on the cross to redeem us from the curse of the law, by becoming a curse in our behalf, 'Christ hath redeemed us from the curse of the law, being made a curse for us; for it is written, Cursed is everyone that hangeth on a tree' (Gal. 3:13). People know their need; they may try to forget it, they may try to deny it, they may try to drown their sense of it by drink and dissipation or by wild pleasure-seeking or wild money-getting, or by listening to fake preachers in supposedly orthodox pulpits. . . . But in spite of all our attempts to drown or stupefy or silence our sense of sin, our consciousness of guilt before a holy God, we all have it, and like Banquo's Ghost it will not quiet down. Nothing gives the guilty conscience abiding peace but the atoning blood of Jesus Christ. So, Christ *lifted up* draws all men unto Him, and even wicked ministers of Satan . . . sometimes come to their senses and flee to the real Christ, *Christ crucified*, as I hope they all may. . . . Happy the man or woman who yields to that drawing. Woe be to the man or woman who resists that drawing; final gloom, despondency and despair are their lot."

Drawn by Love

"In the second place," continues Torrey, "Christ lifted up on the cross, Christ crucified, draws all men unto Him, because lifted up there to die for us He reveals his wonderful love, and the wondrous love of the Father for us. '*Hereby* perceive we the love of God, because he laid down his life for us' (1 John 3:16), and 'God commendeth his love toward us, in that while we were yet sinners, Christ died for us' (Rom. 5:8). There is nothing that draws men like love. Love draws all men in every clime, but no other love draws like the love of God. John 3:16, 'For God so loved the world, that he gave his only begotten Son, that whosoever believeth in him should not perish, but have everlasting life,' has broken thousands of hard hearts."

Torrey then tells this story. "Many years ago in Chicago at a Christian workers' Convention, I preached in the First Methodist Church on Sunday night. When I gave out the invitation, among many who stood up was a beautifully dressed young woman, but she did not come to the altar with the others. The next night I saw her at the regular session of the conference, and calling to someone else to take the chair I went down to the back of the church so that I could speak to her when the meeting was dismissed. As soon as the benediction was pronounced, I hurried to the seat where she was standing before she had time to leave, and asked her to sit down while I spoke to her. I asked why she had not taken a decided stand when rising the night before. She gave a light, frivolous laugh and said, 'Oh, you don't know my life.' Then with apparently utter shamelessness, before I could speak, she began to pour out a story of awful sin. She told me how she had spent the past Easter, and then said with a laugh, 'Funny way to spend Easter, wasn't it?' I was appalled at the disgusting shamelessness of it all," said Torrey, "for she was a woman in good position. I simply took a little Bible that I had, and opening it at John 3:16, asked her to read it. The print was fine and she had to hold it close to her eyes to read. She began to read flippantly, 'For God so loved the world,' then she became suddenly still. She read on, 'that he gave his only begotten Son,' but now the tears welled up in her eyes, and dropped down on the beautiful gown she wore. The love of God was conquering, the love of God was drawing. The picture of Christ lifted up has won millions."[1]

Christ lifted up is not something that may easily be dismissed as irrelevant. It is of great importance, and that for three reasons. First, it is important because it was absolutely necessary, because it was within the eternal plan of God to save sinners. Second, it is important because it is the sure basis for all true knowledge in spiritual things. You must come to the cross if you would know God or know him more completely. Finally, it is important also because of the fact that the uplifted Christ draws sinful, ignorant, and rebellious men and women to him, conquering them by the unimaginable, unfathomable love that is so clearly displayed there.

May that love conquer your heart. If it has not yet done so, look now to Jesus. See him lifted up on the cross for you, dying in your place, wounded for your transgressions that by his stripes you might be healed. And come to him. The world has never before seen nor ever again will see such a Savior.

105

Believing on Jesus

John 8:30–32

Even as he spoke, many put their faith in him.
To the Jews who had believed him, Jesus said, "If you hold to my teaching, you are really my disciples. Then you will know the truth, and the truth will set you free."

Across America on any given Sunday thousands of sermons will be preached to those who are Christians to urge them to live like Christians, and many thousands more will be preached to those who are not Christians to urge them to believe in Jesus. I doubt if many are preached to those who already believe the doctrines of Christianity and who think they are Christians but who, nevertheless, have never come to the point of accepting the Lord Jesus Christ personally as their Savior. This study is for such people.

The interesting thing about the situation that I have just described is that most people who listen to Christian preaching are, I am convinced, in the last of these categories. That is, they are not genuinely born-again Christians, but neither are they hostile to Christianity. They believe the doctrines. It is just that they have never committed themselves to Jesus Christ and are not really his. They believe, but they are not disciples. They do not deny Christ, but neither do they follow him. A sense of the magnitude of this problem can be seen from the fact that in both Britain and the United States, well over 90 percent of the people surveyed in opinion polls claim that they believe in a personal

God. But very few, obviously, do anything about him. In many cases they do not even expose themselves to Christianity.

What should be said about this situation? Or, more particularly, what should be our attitude to such people? The correct answer comes from the lips of the Lord Jesus Christ when he said to those who in his day believed what he had to say but, nevertheless, had not committed themselves to him, "If you hold to my teaching, you are really my disciples. Then you will know the truth, and the truth will set you free" (8:31–32).

Two Kinds of Belief

To understand what the Lord Jesus Christ is saying in these verses and to apply them properly, we need first to understand that there is a great deal of difference between merely believing Jesus and believing *in* him or *on* him.

In most of our English versions this difference is not overly clear in this section of John's Gospel, and in some cases is completely obscured. But in Greek the distinction is plain. In verse 30 of this chapter, John writes of those who really did trust Jesus and who had personally committed themselves to him. John says, "Even as he spoke, many put their faith in him." In the next verse, however, the phrase is changed so that we find ourselves reading of those who merely "believed him." Unfortunately, the Authorized Version and the Revised Standard Version translate the phrases identically (either "believed on" or "believed in"). But the New English Bible, the New American Standard Bible, the New International Version, and others preserve the distinction. The New English Bible is explicit; it says, "As he said this, many put their faith in him. Turning to the Jews who had believed him, Jesus said. . . ." The New International Version says, "Many put their faith in him. To the Jews who had believed him, Jesus said . . ." In other words, the verses distinguish between those listeners who had believed on Jesus unto salvation and those who had merely believed certain things that he had said.

It is worth noting that this contrast—between those who merely believe doctrines and those who believe on Jesus personally—is also made elsewhere. Thus, to give one example, in the sixth chapter we find Jesus calling for saving faith by saying, "The work of God is this: to believe in the one he has sent" (v. 29). But then, immediately after, those who refuse to believe on that level declare, "What miraculous sign will you give then, that we may see and believe?" (v. 30).

Someone will say, "But is it really possible to believe certain things about Christ or to believe him and yet fail to believe on him?" Yes, of course it is. What is more, we have examples of precisely this failure. One example is Judas, one within the very limited and privileged circle of Christ's disciples. Judas obviously believed something about Jesus. He believed enough to be one of the early preachers. When Jesus sent his disciples out two-by-two, Judas undoubtedly went with them. Yet Judas was not a saved man. Simon Magus is another example. We are told that he believed after he had seen the miracles and signs that Peter and the other apostles performed. He was baptized and became a member of the church. But he was not a true believer either and later was rebuked for his unbelief by Peter. The greatest examples of all are the devils who, we are told, "believe and shudder." Each of these believes certain things about Jesus. But they do not believe unto salvation.

It is not saying too much to suggest that there are many such today. If you are one, I want to encourage you to go the whole way and believe *on* Jesus. It would be a pity to believe so much, to believe the doctrines, and yet fall short of salvation.

Back in the nineteenth century there was a famous acrobat, known all over the world. His real name was Jean Francois Gravalet, but he was known by his stage name—Blondin. Born in France in 1824, Blondin became well known in France while still a child. As he grew older his skill plus his flair for the spectacular soon brought him the acclaim of many in Europe and then in America. His most spectacular feats, those that also drew most attention, were his crossings of Niagara Falls on a tightrope 1,100 feet long and 160 feet above the water. Once he pushed a wheelbarrow across. On another occasion he stopped halfway and cooked an omelet.

Once, in an unusual demonstration of skill, Blondin carried a man across Niagara Falls on his back and then turned around and carried him back. After he had put his rider down, the acrobat turned to the large crowd that had been watching and asked a man who was near at hand, "Do you believe that I could do that with you?"

"Of course," the man said. "I've just seen you do it."

"Well, hop on," said Blondin, "and I'll carry you across."

The man answered, "Not on your life!"

That is the difference between believing something on the intellectual level only and believing in the sense of belief that the Bible calls for when it asks us to believe on Christ. To believe in the biblical sense is to commit yourself to Christ, to trust him to carry you over the churning cataracts and wild whirlpools of life. The other belief is only intellectual assent. God wants the first kind of belief. And yet—this is the point that we need to fix clearly in our minds—Jesus' words were directed not to those who had believed properly, but rather to those who had believed only on the inadequate, intellectual level. It was to these, the weak in faith, that he said, "If you hold to my teaching, you are really my disciples. Then you will know the truth, and the truth will set you free."

An Eye for Faith

This fact leads us naturally to the second point, which is the most important. The point is simply that Jesus takes notice of even this inadequate faith and seeks to encourage it. Intellectual belief is not saving faith, but saving faith may come from such beginnings. Therefore, Jesus spoke to those who only believed his teachings and tried to lead them farther.

Spurgeon once wrote on this subject: "It is written, 'When the Son of man cometh, shall he find faith on the earth?' Certainly He can find it if anyone can. He has a very quick eye for faith. He deals with little faith as we used to do with a spark in the tinder, in the days of our boyhood. When we had struck a spark, and it fell into the tinder—though it was a very tiny one—we watched it eagerly, we blew upon it softly, and we were zealous to increase it, so that we might kindle our match thereby. When our Lord Jesus sees a tiny speck of faith in a man's heart, though it be quite insufficient of itself for salvation, yet he regards it with hope, and watches over it, if, haply, this little faith may grow to something more. It is the way of our compassionate Lord not to quench the smoking flax, nor break the bruised reed."[1]

While Jesus does not disparage small faith, neither does he praise it. Jesus speaks to these who have believed with the head only, but he does so by leading off with a conditional sentence. "If. . . ," he says, "*if* you hold to my teaching." True, he does not send them away. But neither does he promise the blessings of the Christian life outright. Rather, there is a task to do, a word to be learned. "You believe something," he seems to say, "believe more; continue in my word until you come at last to rest in me as your Savior."

It often has seemed to me that in these words Jesus was saying something similar to what he was saying in that oft-quoted challenge from the Sermon on the Mount—"Enter through the narrow gate. For wide is the gate and broad is the road that leads to destruction, and many enter through it" (Matt. 7:13). Many have taken this verse to mean that salvation is something to be worked for or else something to be carefully guarded lest through some slip of sin the Christian wanders off the path of salvation and is lost eternally. But it does not mean that. The point of the verse is seen rather in its historical context. Here, early in his ministry, Jesus was speaking to people who as yet had no knowledge of his coming death and resurrection and, of course, were not saved. They believed him (as did those about whom John is writing), but the events upon which salvation depended were yet three years away. In between were years of discouragement in which the early enthusiasm of the Galilean ministry would give way to hostility and eventual persecution. What was to happen to these people during the intervening years? Were they, too, to become discouraged? Were they to drop away? Clearly, Jesus was encouraging them to keep on the narrow way of his teaching until at last, with the cross behind them, they could pass through himself, the narrow door, into salvation.

In precisely the same manner Jesus is also, here in John, encouraging his listeners not to become discouraged by the difficulty of attending to his words or to be offended by what they hear him say. Rather, they are to continue on until, being encouraged by God's grace, they are enabled to embrace Jesus personally as their Savior. Perhaps Jesus is speaking in this manner to you. If so, remember that today you do not have to wait three years to believe or even a moment. Believe now. Commit yourself to Jesus Christ and start on that road of true discipleship that you will follow to your life's end.

Encouragements to Keep On

Are you hesitating? If so, notice that Jesus does not stop speaking to those who had merely believed him after he had encouraged them to continue in his word. He encouraged them to continue; that is true. But he also goes on to provide them with inducements in order that this might surely come about. There are three of them.

First, Jesus said to those Jews who had believed him, "If you hold to my teaching, you are really my disciples." That is, he promised them a *verified discipleship*. They would not be disciples in word only, as so many are who are in our churches today, but they would be true disciples. Some who are in our churches profess to be disciples of Christ, but you never know it until they tell you. You can know them for years and never observe a decision or an action that is distinctly Christian or never hear a distinctly Christian word. This is not being a disciple. Do not be a part-time, hit-or-miss believer. Be a thoroughbred. The first inducement is that by continuing in Christ's Word you will be such a disciple.

The second inducement is that you will know the truth. It is the promise that you will have *certain knowledge* in spiritual things. You will not know all things, of course. Only God knows all things. But what you do know will be certain. I am sorry for those for whom all things are in flux. They think that they believe so-and-so; but then, if conditions change, they might not believe it. Or again, if they are challenged, they change their mind. This is a particularly common situation in our day, because we live in an age in which most people consider truth to be relative. This means that there are no absolutes in this or any other area. You may think you have a certain truth, but that is only truth for you, not necessarily truth for me. Or it may only be truth for now, but not for days to come. What a sad situation! What a pathetic condition! This is not what Christ promises. Jesus promises truth and the certainty of it.

Finally, Jesus promises that *you will be set free*. "The truth will set you free." Jesus himself will set you free; and therefore your freedom will be on a higher and greater level than that which men can offer.

For one thing, it will not be freedom in name only. Once I was told of an interview that some Christians in Hong Kong had conducted with an eighty-two-year-old woman who had shortly before been released from China. She was a Christian, but her vocabulary was filled with much of the terminology of Communism. "When you were back in China, were you free to gather together with other Christians to worship?" they asked her.

"Oh, no," she answered. "Since the liberation no one is permitted to gather together for Christian services."

"But surely you were able to get together in small groups and discuss the Christian faith?"

"No, we were not," the woman replied. "Since the liberation all such meetings are forbidden."

"Were you free to read your Bible?"

"Since the liberation no one is free to read the Bible."

The point of this story is obvious. Freedom does not consist in the word "freedom" (liberation) alone, but in the reality that only the truth of God brings. Moreover, it is a positive freedom. In Christ we are set free from three terrible masters: sin, self, and Satan. We are set free from them to serve Jesus. Have you experienced such freedom? You can, if you will continue in Christ's Word and come to believe *on* him.

106

Free Indeed!

John 8:33–36

They answered him, "We are Abraham's descendants and have never been slaves of anyone. How can you say that we shall be set free?"

Jesus replied, "I tell you the truth, everyone who sins is a slave to sin. Now a slave has no permanent place in the family, but a son belongs to it forever. So if the Son sets you free, you will be free indeed."

Ever since the early Anglo-Saxon dialects gave their formative influence to the English language, the words "free" and "freedom" have been important to the Western world and its culture. Unfortunately, there has not always been agreement on what freedom means. In his speech on the four freedoms, given on January 6, 1941, Franklin Delano Roosevelt spoke largely of human rights: "Freedom of speech and expression—everywhere in the world . . . freedom of every person to worship God in his own way—everywhere in the world . . . freedom from want . . . and freedom from fear—everywhere in the world." William Murray, the first Earl of Mansfield, England, wrote in the eighteenth century, "To be free is to live under a government by law." Others of a more rebellious disposition have spoken of freedom as an escape from law. In American culture, the predominant idea associated with the concept of freedom is freedom from unjust

643

oppression. This significant idea is captured in that well-known inscription found on the Statue of Liberty in New York harbor:

Give me your tired, your poor,
Your huddled masses, yearning to breathe free.

What is freedom? Or, more particularly, what does the Bible mean by freedom? At this point we can hardly escape either this question or the answer, for our text in the eighth chapter of John's Gospel involves a statement in which Jesus claimed to be able to set men free. His exact words were, "So if the Son sets you free, you will be free indeed" (v. 36). In this context two answers are given to the question, "What is freedom?"—first, freedom from ignorance, and second, freedom from sin. Moreover, we are told that a person becomes free only through Christ, through the truth that he brings and through the redemption that he achieved at Calvary.

Freedom from Ignorance

In the first place, the freedom of which the Bible speaks is a freedom from ignorance, by which is meant primarily an ignorance of spiritual things. This is clear from the verse that immediately precedes our section. In that verse Jesus had said to his opponents, "If you hold to my teaching, you are really my disciples. Then you will know the truth, and the truth will set you free" (vv. 31–32).

We are all aware of bondage where natural ignorance is concerned. Someone who does not know is limited. An individual with no education has certain doors barred. The professions are closed. Such a person can do manual, but not white collar, work. An illiterate person faces even more closed doors and will have difficulty obtaining any but the most menial forms of employment. Our country recognizes the truth of these things and therefore, as a general rule, stresses education.

But if this is true on the purely natural level, it is at least equally true or even more true spiritually. A man who does not know the teachings of the Word of God cannot thrive spiritually. A man who does not know the fundamental truths of the Christian faith cannot come to Jesus Christ for salvation.

The really upsetting thing about this situation, however, is that many persons who are not knowledgeable about Christian truth and who are therefore bound by their ignorance are nonetheless unaware that they are ignorant and so resist any attempt to help them to become free. They are like stubborn children. No one blames a child for not knowing all that an adult knows, but at least one expects a child to be willing to learn. If he is not willing, something is wrong. Many persons are like this spiritually.

We do not have to go far for an example either, for one is found in the verses we are studying. Jesus had spoken of freedom to those who were listening to him. But no sooner had he mentioned the word "free" than they reacted violently. Jesus said, "You will know the truth, and the truth will set you free."

But when he said that, they immediately responded, "We are Abraham's descendants and have never been slaves of anyone. How can you say that we shall be set free?" (v. 33). This was patently ridiculous, of course. For years the Jews had been slaves in Egypt. During the period of the Judges there were at least seven occasions when the nation fell under foreign rule. Later there was the seventy-year-long Babylonian captivity. Even as they were talking to Jesus, these men carried coins in their pockets that bore the image of the Roman emperors and thereby testified to Rome's dominion. Yet they said, "We have always been free."

We smile at this kind of self-delusion. But it is no more ridiculous than the self-delusion of people who today are slaves to ignorance in spiritual matters but who will not acknowledge their slavery. They do not know God. Yet they think they know all there is to know and so will not learn about Jesus or come to him.

Truth Saves

Thus far we have looked at two reasons why freedom from ignorance is important: first, because knowledge itself is important—a lack of it limits an individual; and second, because we *are* ignorant. There is a third reason also. Freedom from ignorance is important because it is through a knowledge of spiritual truth that God saves people from sin, from themselves, and from Satan.

Let me give you a typical example. Here is a man who, let us say, lives in your city. He is an average sort of person. He has a normal, nine-to-five job. He has a family. On Friday night he bowls with the league. He likes to golf on Sunday. When he is not out doing something else he watches television. It is a normal life, and he is quite happy with it. He seldom thinks of God, and he would not really know what to think about God even if he did think about him. God just does not enter into his thinking.

Someone begins to talk to him about spiritual things, and in the course of time he comes into a situation in which he begins to learn something of what the Bible teaches. It may be in church. It may be in a home Bible study. It may be through listening to the radio or through reading Christian books. He begins to learn a few basic truths. The first thing he learns is that he is a sinner. Before this he had always thought he was all right because he had never cheated on his wife or robbed anyone. Now he learns that sin is being less perfect than God and that it is seen in such things as pride, selfishness, anger, and worry. For the first time in his life he begins to be disturbed. He learns that God is a God of judgment and that there is a judgment day coming. This really disturbs him. He had never thought of the fact that one day he might have to give an account of what he has done in this life. Now he finds himself lying awake at night thinking about death and what lies beyond it. Finally, this man hears about the death of the Lord Jesus Christ—how he died for his people and how he loves them. These truths now grip him as forcefully as the thought of judgment had gripped him before, and he finds himself calling on Christ in order that he might be saved. The truth of Christianity, made meaningful to him and applied to his heart by the Holy Spirit, saves him. The truth has set him free.

This can be your experience. Are you one who has heard the truths of Christianity and who needs to come to Jesus Christ as your Savior? You can come now. You do not need to do anything but commit your life to him. Believe these truths: you are a sinner; there is a judgment day coming; Jesus died for your sin. Stand firm upon these truths! Do not linger any longer in the bondage of spiritual ignorance!

Freedom from Sin

Second, the Lord Jesus Christ spoke of a freedom from sin. This is involved in verse 34, where Jesus declares, "I tell you the truth, everyone who sins is a slave to sin." Notice that Jesus is not talking about the penalty of sin in this verse. It is not that we are to be set free from sin's penalty. Jesus is talking about sin's power, about the hold that sin has over us, about a defeated Christian life. His point is that he can set a person free from this bondage also.

Are you one who desires such freedom? Probably you have a measure of freedom now. Since coming to Christ you have been free of the fear of judgment. You do not fear death. The guilt of sin does not weigh heavily upon you. You feel that you are free to grow in the knowledge of Christ almost indefinitely. And yet, there is a sin that you cannot seem to shake. You have a temper; you cannot control it. You offend people by your thoughtlessness. You are caught in some sexual sin and cannot escape it. I do not know what the particular point of defeat is in your life, but I do know that Jesus is himself the answer to that defeat. Allow him to free you. Come to him! Learn about him! Call upon him! Claim his promises! He said, "If the Son sets you free, you will be free indeed."

Moreover, there is a role that Christians have in helping others to achieve this freedom. Beyond any doubt, there are some things that God does alone. Bringing new life into a dead soul is one of them. None of us can cause a person to be born again. God alone must do it. But once God has made a person alive, then there is work that God gives us so that we might share in the other's full salvation.

Let me give some biblical examples. When the Lord Jesus Christ brought his friend Lazarus back from the dead, it was the Lord himself who called him: "Lazarus, come out." But after he had brought Lazarus forth, still wrapped in grave clothes, his next words were to those who stood about, by which he invited them to have a hand in Lazarus's full liberation: "Loose him, and let him go." When God called the apostle Paul on the road to Damascus, it was God alone who called him and who brought forth new life in Paul. The others who were with Paul did not even hear the words God spoke. Nevertheless, when Paul had been brought into Damascus, Ananias was then used to visit and baptize Paul that he might receive his sight. God used Philip to bring the light of the gospel to the Ethiopian. He used Priscilla and Aquila to bring a fuller understanding of the truth to Apollos. In the same way, each Christian has a ministry in the life of a person or persons.

Are you saying, as many do, "But I do not have the gift of helping"? If you are, I cannot believe you. Every Christian can do something, for God has given every Christian at least one gift. Most can do much more than they are doing, including some things that they did not think they could do.

Howard G. Hendricks of Dallas Theological Seminary tells in a recent book of a conversation he once had with a man whom he wanted to involve in Christian work. He wanted him to conduct a home Bible class. "Wow," the man objected, "I don't have the gift of teaching."

"How do you know, Bill?" Hendricks replied. "Did God let down a sheet from heaven one night and tell you that?"

"No," he acknowledged, "I just don't have it."

"Have you ever taught?"

"No, I've never taught."

"Then don't tell me you don't have the gift of teaching, my friend, because you don't know that," Hendricks answered. The man thought a bit and eventually agreed to teach. "Today," says the author, "if I want to send my students to see a man who knows how to communicate a lot better than most professionals, I send them out to hear Bill!"[1]

Perhaps you are saying, "But that was Bill. I know I don't have the gift of teaching. I really do know it! What can I do?" Let me take you to another New Testament story. Do you remember the prodigal son?

When the prodigal came home, it was the father who met him. He did not say to the servants, "Go and meet him." The father himself went, and threw his arms about his son's neck and kissed him. The father personally forgave him and restored him to his home. Nevertheless, after he had done this the father then turned to the servants who stood by and said to them, "Bring the best robe and put it on him. Put a ring on his finger and sandals on his feet. Bring the fattened calf and kill it. Let's have a feast and celebrate." My point is that the servants had work in each of these four areas.

First, they were to bring the best robe and put it on the young man. That makes an illustration of good Christian teaching. Robes in Scripture often speak of Christ's righteousness. So we have a role in actually helping to put Christ's righteousness upon the sinner. We are not content merely to preach Christ. We want men to put him on, and we want to help them do it. God uses many, like Bill, in this work of teaching and evangelism.

Second, they were to put a ring on his hand. This speaks of fellowship. Many who cannot teach nevertheless can do this work simply by getting to know others who have become Christians, becoming friends with them, and including them in Christian activities.

Third, the servants were to put shoes on the prodigal's feet. There were roads to be walked, and shoes were necessary. In a similar way some can help others to prepare for life's journey. And as for the preparation of the fatted calf and the rejoicing, well, there are babes in Christ to be fed and many to be cheered and made welcome. There is plenty to be done. Each Christian has a responsibility to help others in God's service.

For Saints and Sinners

If you are not a Christian, then you must respond to Christ's offer of freedom at once without delaying. There is a verse in this section of John that is for you. It is the verse in which Jesus says, somewhat enigmatically, "Now a slave has no permanent place in the house; but a son belongs to it forever" (v. 35). The contrast is between a son, who is the inheritor of the father's property and whose rights cannot be denied or taken away, and a slave who, although he may enjoy some of the privileges of being in the same house as the son, nevertheless can be sold at any time and thus lose his privileges. Obviously this applied to Christ's hearers, who were Jews but who were not God's sons by the new birth. They had all the privileges of being Jews, but unless they came to Christ for salvation the privileges would not last forever. The day would come when even Jerusalem would be destroyed and the Jews would be scattered.

Opportunity does not last forever for anyone. It will not last forever for you if you are not yet a Christian. Christ offers you freedom now—freedom from ignorance and freedom from sin's power. You are in a place where you can hear the gospel, question Christian friends, observe Christianity. Who knows when such things may change? You may have to move to another city. You may get sick. Eventually you will die. Now is the time to believe.

Finally, there is also an application for those who have already received Christ as Savior. Have you been set free from ignorance and from sin? If so, there is work to do, for you have not been set free to be idle. You are set free to serve God. If you are a Christian, God wants you to follow him in Christian service. For this *is* freedom. It is freedom indeed!

107

Sons of Abraham

John 8:37–40

"I know you are Abraham's descendants. Yet you are ready to kill me, because you have no room for my word. I am telling you what I have seen in the Father's presence, and you do what you have heard from your father."

"Abraham is our father," they answered.

"If you were Abraham's children," said Jesus, "then you would do the things Abraham did. As it is, you are determined to kill me, a man who has told you the truth that I heard from God. Abraham did not do such things."

That a personal commitment to Jesus Christ is necessary in order to become a Christian is an idea totally alien to the thinking of many people. Yet it is true, and it needs to be stressed in our day.

A number of years ago my wife and I were dealing with an English woman who had been raised in a religious home. She was not a Christian, but she thought she was. Her father had been a vestryman in the Church of England. From the earliest years she had been brought to Sunday school. She once sang in the choir. In one sense, she even believed all that the Church of England taught, for—although she did not know much—she would never have thought of disagreeing with the Thirty-Nine Articles or with anything in the Prayer Book. For her, to be an English woman was to be a member of the

Church of England, and to be a member of the church was to be a Christian. It was a matter of tradition. It was not until we had spoken to her for some time that she discovered the reality of Christianity and committed her life to Jesus Christ personally.

That story is not an unusual one, of course. But it is an important one, if only because the experience I have described is so common. People consider themselves Christians largely because they have had a Christian father or mother, or because they were raised in a Christian church, or just because there has never been any other religious tradition in their background. If you are one for whom the Christian faith consists largely of such things, you should look closely at these very important verses from John's Gospel.

An Inconsistency

The verses are found in the eighth chapter, and they concern the reaction of certain leaders of the Jewish people to Jesus. Jesus had been talking to these men about spiritual things. But whenever he suggested that there might be a lack in their lives (which he could fill), they reacted violently and defensively. Toward the end of the chapter we find that they went so far as to attempt to stone him. It is a pity that they reacted in this way, of course. It is an even greater pity that men and women often act this way today. Yet it is human nature. Even the most miserable people will react defensively at any suggestion that their lives could be made better.

These men countered Christ's suggestion that they needed something by the claim that they had all they needed through their religious traditions. They traced their ancestry to Abraham claiming that they were all right because "we are Abraham's descendants." God's promises were made to Abraham and to his descendants (Gen. 17:7; 22:16–18). They had descended from Abraham physically. Therefore, they reasoned, we are blessed in Abraham, and there is nothing for us to worry about spiritually.

What did Jesus do when faced by this reply? He made a number of penetrating statements that should have helped these men to understand the true state of affairs and that should help us today.

The first statement was that *there was a strange inconsistency in their lives.* It was an inconsistency between what they professed to be and what they actually were. On the one hand, they were professing to be religious people. Abraham was a man approved by God. He walked with God. He was praised by God. They claimed that this was true of them. Yet, as Jesus pointed out, they sought "to kill him" and thus demonstrated that his "word had no place" in them. Neither of these facts was true of Abraham.

Let us apply this observation of the Lord Jesus Christ to our day. Here is a man or woman—perhaps it is you—who thinks that he is a Christian but to whose way of life Christianity makes little difference. I will not say, though it might be more true than we realize, that, if Christ were actually on the earth physically, you would try to "kill" him. But perhaps you try to kill him where you individually are concerned—by keeping him out of your life. You say you are a Christian, but you have no room in your life for the One who founded Christianity. You believe he lived and died. Perhaps you even believe that he rose again. But it makes no difference to you. Nothing about your life is changed because of him.

It also is true that his word does not abide in you. I do not mean by this that you have never heard or even been able to memorize some of Christ's teachings, though if you think the words "God helps those who help themselves" are in the Bible, you know less of his teachings than you think. But I do mean to say that they are not enough a part of you to affect your decisions. Someone plays a dirty trick on you, and you play one back. "'It is mine to avenge; I will repay,' says the Lord" means nothing to you. When you come home you insult your wife and snap at the children. Christ's commandment that you "love one another" does not enter into your thinking. What of this? Is it not a strange inconsistency? Does it not trouble you? This is not the way of Christ or of those who follow him.

What Is Your Ancestry?

Second, Jesus went on to explain the cause of this inconsistency. It was explained by the true ancestry of these religious leaders. They claimed a natural or physical descent from Abraham, and on this level their claim was quite valid. The difficulty was that their descent from Abraham was only physical; that is, it was external rather than internal, natural rather than spiritual. On the spiritual level (about which Jesus was concerned), their ancestry was something quite different. It was—we must be bold enough to say it—demonic. Spiritually *they were children of their true father, the devil.*

Let me say at once that in its full sense this is not true of most people. Sometimes preachers speak of there being two families in this world—the family of God and the family of the devil—and they imply that if one does not serve God he serves Satan. This is not true in the full sense, but (I must repeat) only in the full sense. Actually, most people serve themselves and are no more interested in serving Satan than they are in serving God. These men were apparently Satan's tools in a way that most people would not be. They proved it by their concerted and vicious efforts to kill God.

On the other hand, there is a sense in which all that is not of God can be traced to Satan, for it was through Satan that sin first entered the universe. Do you sin? Do you find yourself flashing out in anger against someone else? Do you ever exploit someone else? Do you put yourself first in business or in your marriage and allow others to come second? If this is so, then in one sense at least you are demonstrating a demonic ancestry. Such things do not come from the Father of the Lord Jesus Christ.

Jesus taught this truth in a parable once, pointing out that good fruit does not come from a bad tree. It takes a good tree to produce it. Similarly, bad fruit does not come from a good tree. A bad tree creates it. In the same way, you can come to know the true nature of your spiritual family tree by the fruit found on it. What is the fruit in your life? How about your speech? How about your actions? It is interesting that Jesus called attention to both these areas in speaking to the Jewish rulers. For he said, making the contrast between what is of God and what is of Satan, "I am telling you what I have seen in the Father's presence, and you do what you have heard from your father" (v. 38).

Born Again

The obvious conclusion to this study is that, if a person is to be taken out of the family of Satan and into the family of God, he must experience what he would have to experience if this were true physically. What would you have to do to get out of one family and into another? The answer is that you would have to die to the one family and be born again into another. This cannot be done physically, of course. It is only a theoretical argument. But the glory of the Christian gospel is that it can be done spiritually. It is possible to be born again through the work of God's Holy Spirit and on the basis of Christ's death on the cross.

Before we can make this point, however—before we can say that a man *can* be born again—we must make the equally important point that a man *must* be born again and that this is true because no mere physical birth can save him.

This point is made at two other very important places in the Bible. First, it was made by John the Baptist. John had been preaching in the wilderness of Judea and many had come to him for baptism. Some of them had not repented. So John said to these, "And do not think you can say to yourselves, 'We have Abraham as our father.' I tell you that out of these stones God can raise up children for Abraham. The ax is already at the root of the trees, and every tree that does not produce good fruit will be cut down and thrown into the fire" (Matt. 3:9–10). John was telling these men that only an act of God, by which they would become reborn and begin to bring forth good fruit, would save them.

The second important statement of this same point is in the letter of Paul to the Galatians. In one sense the whole letter is a statement of it. Teachers had come to the Galatian churches from Jerusalem saying that one could be saved only by first becoming a Jew, a child of Abraham. It was all right to have Christ, but there must be Abraham too. Faith was all right, but there must also be law. There must be a physical ancestry. In this case, Paul replied to the doctrine so strongly that he actually said, "If you let yourselves be circumcised [that is, become a Jew in order to acquire Jewish ancestry], Christ will be of no value to you at all" (Gal. 5:2). Nothing matters but becoming "a new creation" in Christ (Gal. 6:15).

Are you a new creation in Christ? Have you been born again into God's family? On one occasion Jesus spoke to a man who had every advantage that ancestry and religious tradition could bring. His name was Nicodemus. He was a Jew, a teacher, a man of influence and prestige. Yet Jesus said, "You must be born again" (John 3:7). This is God's work, but it comes about as a man or woman begins to turn his or her back on any advantage supposedly derived from man and instead begins to draw near to Christ, trusting him for salvation. True children of God are not those with an impeccable religious ancestry, but rather those who believe as Abraham believed and who obey as Abraham obeyed.

The Example of Abraham

The final point of Jesus' reply to these religious leaders was that in spite of all he had said, it was still possible for them to learn from their ancestry if they would only do it. To be sure, this is not said directly. But it seems to be implied in Christ's final reference to Abraham. Jesus pointed out that it was because they did not like what he said that they were trying to kill him. Then he added, "Abraham did not do such things" (v. 40). Granted that Abraham did not seek to have Christ killed and did not reject him, what, then, did he do? The answer seems to be that he received the word of God readily and trusted God for his salvation.

I am not sure of this next point, but it seems to me that Jesus probably was thinking of a specific incident from Abraham's life as he said this. Do you remember the story in which three supernatural beings came to Abraham to warn him of the pending destruction of Sodom (Genesis 18)? These messengers are described in a strange way. Sometimes they are described as three beings. Sometimes they are described as one. Their words sometimes are prefaced with the statement, "The Lord said." Who were these beings? Who was this person? At the least we are dealing with angels, but they are not called angels. Some, therefore, have speculated that this was a preincarnate manifestation of the Lord Jesus Christ himself and that Abraham, therefore, literally saw the Lord Jesus.

If this is true—and I believe it may well be—then Abraham literally did the opposite of what these religious leaders were doing and many persons do today. The leaders were rejecting Jesus. Abraham, on the other hand, ran to him and entreated him to come into his tent. Let me make it personal. Do you have an ancestor who was a genuine believer in the Lord Jesus? Do you trace your religious feelings to some genuine experience by one who is or was close to you? If you do, this is not entirely bad. But you must not trust to the relationship only. You must do as he or she did. You must do as Abraham. Do you have a godly father? Then do as he did and follow Jesus. Do you have a praying mother? Then do as she does and pray to Jesus that your sins might be forgiven and that you might become his follower. No one wants to be a hypocrite. You do not want to be one. See to it that you make what you have been professing to be actually true in your experience.

Run to Jesus! Welcome Jesus! Invite him in, and not just into your tent or house but into your life as well. You will find that he will bless you and that he will teach you wonderful things about his will and ways, just as the heavenly messenger taught Abraham.

A Word for Christians

There is a final word for Christians. This study has dealt largely with the strange inconsistency of someone professing to be a believer while he or she is not and, actually, betrays that fact by conduct. But another and even stranger inconsistency exists when those who really are Christians do not display Christlike conduct. This is often true, of course. There is a reason for it. Christians do not lose their old nature merely by becoming Christians. The old nature will assert itself; but while it is true that it happens, it still should not be characteristic of the Christian's behavior. The Christian should reveal the hand of Christ in his life.

Years ago a young dental student studied in Philadelphia under a dentist who was known for the perfect way in which he made amalgam fillings. He made them so well they looked like inlays, which are normally much harder to make and more expensive. The fillings were so good that the dentist was known as "the amalgam king." Well, the time came when the young student finished his course and was drafted into the army. In the army he did dental work and eventually ended up on the west coast, three thousand miles from his home city of Philadelphia. One day a draftee came into his office for some work, and the young man who had studied in Philadelphia began to examine the fillings. Suddenly he straightened up and asked, "Do you come from Philadelphia?"

"Yes," he was told.

"I thought so," the young dentist said. "Your work has been done by Dr. Ward C. Miller, the amalgam king."

I am sure you can see the application. In this life it will never be true that every aspect of our lives will reveal the touch of the Lord Jesus Christ, but there must be some areas that can be identified as his workmanship. Others should be able to point to you and say, "It is the work of Jesus Christ, the great physician. It is the work of the King."

108

That Other Family

John 8:41-50

"You are doing the things your own father does."

"We are not illegitimate children," they protested. "The only Father we have is God himself."

Jesus said to them, "If God were your Father, you would love me, for I came from God and now am here. I have not come on my own; but he sent me. Why is my language not clear to you? Because you are unable to hear what I say. You belong to your father, the devil, and you want to carry out your father's desire. He was a murderer from the beginning, not holding to the truth, for there is no truth in him. When he lies, he speaks his native language, for he is a liar and the father of lies. Yet because I tell the truth, you do not believe me! Can any of you prove me guilty of sin? If I am telling the truth, why don't you believe me? He who belongs to God hears what God says. The reason you do not hear is that you do not belong to God."

The Jews answered him, "Aren't we right in saying that you are a Samaritan and demon-possessed?"

"I am not possessed by a demon," said Jesus, "but I honor my Father and you dishonor me. I am not seeking glory for myself; but there is one who seeks it, and he is the judge."

I do not know who first originated the popular phrase "the universal fatherhood of God and the universal brotherhood of man," but I suspect that it is a product of nineteenth-century liberalism. I know that it is not a proper expression of true Christianity. The phrase sounds good. It suggests that all men are really brothers despite their differences and that all worship the same God regardless of the different

655

names they give to him. But that is just not true, and both the Word of God and history refute it. The true picture is presented in the verses to which we come in this study.

A Heightened Debate

We can recall from previous studies that the debate between Jesus and the religious leaders had been growing more and more intense. This has already been seen in the actions of these men, as well as in their speech. Now, even their speech becomes more strident. They had begun by claiming to be Abraham's seed; that is, descendents of the man whom God had promised to bless as the father of a special people and who was to be a blessing to many. But after Jesus had disputed their claim, they intensified it, saying then that they were actually the children of God (v. 41). On his part, Jesus also intensified his denial. He had begun by denying that they were Abraham's seed spiritually. He adds to that a denial that they are God's children. Finally, he says openly that they actually are children of their true father, the devil.

The reaction to this last statement must have been intense. So we are not surprised to find these leaders taking up stones to try to kill him just a few verses later. These words stirred their indignation, as Christ knew they would. But they were the truth. They had to be said whether or not the men were offended.

It is the same today, of course. For if a desire not to offend men were the measure of what could be taught, little of the teaching of the Word of God could be communicated. Years ago an evangelist went to a little town in Nevada to hold meetings. When he met the minister of the church in which the meetings were to be held, he was told, "Now, my friend, I want to tell you that there are certain things you must not say here and certain sins about which you must not speak. For instance, it would never do for you to talk about divorce; this is the divorce capital of America, and many of our people have been married and divorced several times. They are sensitive on that issue. You cannot talk about drinking, for that is a big business here. Don't mention gambling."

The poor evangelist looked at the minister and asked, "Well, of whose sins may I speak?"

"Go for the sins of the Piute Indians," he was told. "They never go to church anyway."

There are truths that need to be stated whether or not men and women are offended. Since Jesus knew this, he spoke the truth here. From our point of view it is good that he did, for as a result of it we have in these verses the clearest teachings about Satan and of the truth that God is not the father of all men and that all are not brothers that is to be found in John's Gospel. Actually, there is only one other place in the Gospel where Satan is even mentioned, and that does not tell us much about him. It is where we are told that the devil entered into Judas Iscariot (13:2, 27).

A Personal Devil

What do these verses tell us about Satan? First of all, they tell us that there is a devil—a real one because he is not a figment of human imagination, and a personal one because he is not merely some vague, abstract idea of evil. Jesus indicates this when he speaks of the devil by name and refers to him with the personal pronoun "he."

The idea of a personal devil has been denied by large segments of the Christian church, of course, and has become almost a laughing matter in current society. Due to the revival of witchcraft and Satanism in recent years, it is perhaps not so much a laughing matter as previously. Still many would regard thoughts about there being a real devil as hardly serious. In the popular mind the devil is a funny little man dressed up in long red underwear, with horns and a tail. And "since I could never believe in a funny little man in red underwear, with horns and a tail," so the argument goes, "I could never believe in a devil." Few who think this way see that this is quite a different image of Satan from that portrayed in the Bible, and even fewer (including Christians) recognize the picture of a little man with horns as Satan's stratagem.

In writing to the Corinthians on one occasion the apostle Paul noted that we are not ignorant of Satan's schemes (2 Cor. 2:11). The word "scheme" means a trick, plot, contrivance, or stratagem. So the point is that Christians know, or should know, about Satan's tricks for seeking to blind men's minds and secure them for himself. One of these, which he uses at some points of history, but not at all points, is to make people believe that he does not exist.

The idea of a funny little man with horns has had an interesting development that is connected at one point (wrongly, or course) with the Bible. In the Middle Ages, when most of the people were illiterate and the church used miracle plays to teach basic Bible stories and doctrine, there was a need to make whatever character represented the devil immediately recognizable on the stage. This could not be done by writing; but there was a pagan idea in vogue according to which Satan was somewhat of a monster, with horns, and this form was used. Moreover, this idea of Satan's appearance was assumed to be supported by the Bible. For back in Isaiah, in a prophecy against Babylon, there is mention of a creature that would one day, it is said, roam about over the fallen and deserted city. The Hebrew word for this animal or creature is *sair*—it means a wild goat—but few knew what it meant. Thus, in some early translations of the Bible it was called a "satyr," one of the half-human, half-bestial figures of mythology. The Bible was thereby assumed to have described a creature like that of the popular Satan figure, and the medieval practice seemed vindicated. In modern times, with an equal lack of support, the devil has been conceived as the sophisticated tempter of the Faust legend or of the popular American stage play and movie *Damn Yankees*.

Since the devil of fiction is so unbelievable as to be almost pathetic, it is no wonder that millions—knowing nothing more than this fiction—discount him. But this is a mistake about which we should be warned. According to Jesus, there is a devil and there are people who follow him. In fact, he warned his disciples to pray, "And lead us not into temptation, but deliver us from the evil one" (Matt. 6:13).

A Fallen Being

Second, Jesus teaches that the devil is a fallen being. He does this in two ways: first, by showing the height from which he fell ("not holding to the truth") and, second, by showing the depths to which he descended ("he is a liar and the father of lies"). It goes along with both points that "he was a murderer from the beginning."

Unfortunately, this point too is rejected by many, assuming that they even believe in a devil. Rather than believing that Satan is a depraved form of what he once was, they prefer to think of him as heroic and more or less as the champion of fallen man. On this point John Milton is probably the biggest offender. For while it is true that in the opening pages of his great epic *Paradise Lost* he does describe the fall of Satan from heaven, it also is true that the greater part of those pages and the first book of the epic describe Lucifer's heroic efforts to rise from the depths of hell and make something of his supposed new kingdom. In Milton's hands he does this brilliantly, so brilliantly, in fact, that some commentators have termed Satan rather than Jesus the book's hero. This is not what Scripture says.

To begin with, Satan has never been in hell and does not control hell. The Bible tells us that God has created hell, preparing it in part for the devil and his angels, and that Satan will one day end up there—although he is not there yet. For another, the Bible describes Satan as at one time being "full of wisdom and perfect in beauty." It says that he was once "in Eden the garden of God," that he was "the anointed cherub," that he was "perfect" in all his ways from the day he was created, until sin was found in him (Ezek. 28:12–15). In Isaiah we are told of his fall through pride and through the arrogant desire to replace God. In that passage Satan says, "I will ascend to heaven; I will raise my throne above the stars of God; I will sit enthroned on the mount of assembly, on the utmost heights of the sacred mountain. I will ascend above the tops of the clouds; I will make myself like the Most High." God replies that as a result of his sin he will actually be "brought down to the grave, to the depths of the pit" (Isa. 14:13–15). This is not the portrait of a heroic being but of a fallen being. It is of one from whom a person should turn in horror.

Moreover, Satan has brought great havoc on the human race. He is a murderer and the author of murder, as Jesus told his listeners. The first crime following the fall of Adam and Eve was a murder, for as a result of the fall Cain slew his brother. Five chapters farther on in John we read that Satan entered into Judas to betray Christ into the hands of his enemies, so that they might kill him. Satan's history is written in blood.

It also is written in deceit, for he is a liar, as Christ said. Satan lied to Eve— "You will not surely die!" (Gen. 3:4). But she did die spiritually and thus lost communion with God. In 1 Kings we read that lying spirits (presumably demons) went forth into the prophets of Ahab so that he would go into battle against the Syrians and be slain at Ramoth-gilead (1 Kings 22:21–23). In Acts we are told that Satan entered into Ananias to cause him to lie about the price of his property, as the result of which he died (Acts 5:3). Satan lies today. Consequently, we are to regard him as dangerous, deceitful, and malicious, but above all as a sinful being and as a failure. He sinned when he failed to remain in his high calling.

A Limited Being

Third, Jesus indicates that Satan is a limited being. That is, he is not omniscient, as God is; he is not omnipotent, as God is; he is not omnipresent, as God is. This is not so explicitly stated in these verses as in other portions of the Bible, but it is implied. For if Satan is a murderer from the beginning, he is limited in the area of the ethical life. If he is a liar and the father of it, he is limited in understanding. If he is to face judgment, as Jesus says next, he obviously is limited in power; for he cannot avoid it. Thus, although we should be aware of Satan and warned about him, we should nevertheless not get into the habit of thinking of the tempter as anything like an evil equivalent of God.

This is worth thinking about in detail. To begin with, Satan is not omniscient. God knows all things, but Satan does not. Above all he does not know the future. No doubt Satan can make shrewd guesses, for he knows the nature of man and the tendencies of history well. The so-called revelations of mediums and fortune-tellers—when they are not outright deceits—fall in this category. But this is not true knowledge of what is to come. Thus, the predictions are vague and generally do not hold water. At one point God stated this in the form of a challenge to all false gods, saying, "'Present your case,' says the Lord. 'Set forth your arguments,' says Jacob's King. 'Bring in your idols to tell us what is going to happen. . . . tell us what the future holds, so we may know that you are gods. Do something, whether good or bad, so that we will be dismayed and filled with fear.'" (Isa. 41:21–24).

Neither is Satan omnipotent. Thus, he cannot do everything he wants to do, and, in the case of believers, he can only do what God will permit. The great example here is the case of Job, who was safe until God had first lowered the hedge that he had thrown up about him. Even then God did this for his own worthwhile purposes and kept Job from sinning.[1]

Finally, Satan is not omnipresent, which means that he cannot be everywhere at the same time tempting everyone. God is omnipresent. He can help all who call upon him, all at one time. But Satan must tempt one individual at a time or else operate through one or more of those angels, now demons, who fell with him. The interesting consequence of this fact is that Satan has probably never tempted you or any Christian you know. Even in the Bible we find very few who were tempted by Satan directly. Whom can you think of who was so tempted? There was Eve, of course. Christ was tempted. Peter was tempted. We are told that the devil entered into Ananias to cause him to lie about the price of his land, and into Judas. But that is about all. On one occasion Paul may have been hindered in his plans by Satan (1 Thess. 2:18), but on another it was only a messenger of Satan who buffeted him (2 Cor. 12:7). Similarly, it was only lesser demons who opposed an angel bringing a revelation to Daniel (Dan. 10:13, 20). And, although 2 Kings 6:16 may mean to suggest that a great host of devils, as well as soldiers, surrounded Elisha at Dothan—outnumbered by the Lord's host, however—Satan himself is not said to have been among them.

This simply means that while the Christian must never ignore or underestimate Satan and his stratagems, neither must he overestimate him. And, above all, he must never do this to the point of taking his eyes away from God. God is our strength and our tower. He limits Satan. Thus, he will never permit a Christian to be tempted above that which he is able and, indeed, will always provide the way of escape that he may be able to bear it (1 Cor. 10:13). As for Satan, his end is in the lake of fire (Matt. 25:41).

Two Ways

There are two ways open before us. "There is a way that seems right to a man, but in the end it leads to death" (Prov. 14:12). This is Satan's way. And there is a "road that leads to life" (Matt. 7:14), which is God's way. The two paths lie before each individual.

On the one path Satan makes his promises. But he is the father of lies, and his words cannot be trusted. He is offering wisdom, as he did to Eve in the garden—"You will be like God, knowing good and evil"—but the wisdom of Satan leads to folly in spiritual things. He is offering love, but the end is hate. He is offering that which is pleasant—"all the kingdoms of the world and their glory"—but the end is torment for those who follow him.

On the other path stands Jesus with his promises. In one sense they are the reversal of Satan's promises. He says. "You are blind!" But he gives sight, and wisdom follows. He has a message of hate. "I hate sin," he declares. But he will turn you from sin and draw you to himself with a great love. Finally, he warns about torment. He has more to say about hell than anyone else in the Bible. But he offers pleasantness to those who follow him. All his ways are "pleasant" and all his "paths are peace" (Prov. 3:17). Will you follow him? Will you commit yourself to him as your Savior?

109

The Last Enemy

John 8:51

"I tell you the truth, if anyone keeps my word, he will never see death."

Some time ago I received a letter from an eighty-one-year old woman who was afraid to die. She was a Christian and probably should have been less fearful as she drew near the end of her earthly life. But she was still afraid and so expressed openly what many others feel but will not speak of. In view of her fear it was a privilege to show her that spiritual death is conquered and that even physical death may be totally transformed for Christians.

Fear of death lies deep in the heart of many persons, and sometimes it is not so deep. The Bible says, "Dust you are, and to dust you will return" (Gen. 3:19). It calls death an enemy. "The last enemy to be destroyed is death," according to Paul's comments on the subject in his first letter to the Corinthians. Poets may make light of death, as did James Russell Lowell, who called death as "beautiful as the feet of a friend, coming to welcome us at our journey's end." But Francis Bacon was closer to the truth when he acknowledged that "men fear death as children fear the dark." Dr. Samuel Johnson, the maker of the dictionary, expressed what many feel when he was confronted by a friend's final illness. "At the sight of this last conflict I felt a sensation never known to me

661

before: a confusion of passions, an awful stillness of sorrow, a gloomy terror without a name."

How comforting in the light of our fears is the promise of Jesus that is the basis of our study. His exact words are, "I tell you the truth, if anyone keeps my word, he will never see death" (John 8:51). It is a great promise and may be considered in three parts: first, the condition upon which the promise is based; second, the promise itself; third, the assurance that the promise can be trusted.

The Conditions

The first item is the condition upon which the promise is based—"if anyone keeps my word." It is a condition, for when Jesus began the phrase by the word "if" he indicated that there is something we must do after which the promise will follow.

We should be glad that he put it as he did, of course. For the offer "if anyone keeps my word" opens the promise to all sorts of people. Next to the terms of this condition other characteristics of a man or woman fade into relative unimportance. A person may be quite weak in faith so that he often is doubting the reality of spiritual things, but if he keeps Christ's saying he will never see death. He may be timid or shy so that he is afraid to express what he actually believes in his heart, but if he keeps Christ's saying he will never see death. He may have been a great sinner before he was found by Christ and saved by him. He may have been a very upright man, even to the degree of being filled with pride at his own high attainments; if he has kept Christ's saying, he will never see death. This is the important point, and it is for this reason that I have repeated it. The condition is: "If anyone keeps my word." Have you kept it? Are you keeping it? If you do, you shall never see death.

I can imagine that someone may be asking, "But what does it mean to keep Christ's word?" It is a good question, and the answer is worth exploring. It means several things.

First, it means that you must *hear Christ's word;* that is, you must hear with understanding. Indeed, how else can a person keep it unless he hears it in the sense of understanding what it means? It is clear that this is involved in Christ's thought because it is expressly stated in the fifth chapter in a verse that is almost an exact parallel of the one here. In that verse Jesus says, "I tell you the truth, whoever *hears* my word and believes him who sent me has eternal life and will not be condemned; he has crossed over from death to life" (v. 24).

Let me illustrate what is involved in hearing Christ's word. A number of years ago Dennis Cochrane, a missionary to the Duna Indian tribe of New Guinea, was looking for a word in the Duna language that would convey what the Bible means by faith. The Dunas had a word for faith, but it did not imply the necessary action. Faith is believing God and acting upon that belief. Besides, there did not seem to be any other word that implied action either. Finally, while putting a number of Duna folk tales into written form in order to become better acquainted with the language, Cochrane came across a story in which a small animal, like a squirrel, was chased up a tree by a dog. "I'm going to get you," the dog said. This did not bother the squirrel, however, because it knew that a dog cannot climb trees. The story acknowledged that the squirrel heard the threat, but it was the kind of hearing that allowed the words to go into one ear and out the other. After several more threats and some growling, the dog finally said, "All right, I'm going to get my friend, the. . . ." Here he mentioned an animal that could climb trees. At this point in the story it was said that the squirrel heard the saying in another sense. This time the verb literally meant, "The saying went down into his ears." It got through. As a result, the squirrel started for another area of the forest as soon as the dog left to find the friend who could climb. The last word was the word that Cochrane later used to translate the word "faith," for it means "to hear with understanding and act on it."

It is in this manner that we also are to keep Christ's word. We are to hear it and allow it to sink into our understanding.

Second, to keep Christ's word also means to commit oneself to Christ or to *believe him*. This is involved in the verse from John 5 also, for Jesus said, "I tell you the truth, anyone who hears my word and *believes* him who sent me has eternal life." To believe *on* Christ is not just to hear him in the sense that I have been explaining: to understand what he says and to acknowledge that what he says is true. This is good. We must do it. But it is not enough. Even the devils believe in this sense, for the Bible tells us that they believe and tremble. What is needed is a step beyond this—first to believe him and then to believe in the sense of actually committing oneself to him for salvation. To put this in the form of an illustration, we can say that it is the type of belief exercised by a girl who, in addition to believing the word of a young man, agrees to marry him.

Finally, to keep Christ's word obviously also means to *obey him*. Indeed, this is one of the primary meanings of the word "keep" in this sentence. The other related meaning is that of guarding a prisoner. So the whole idea is to keep Christ's word (and obey it) as carefully as one would guard a criminal entrusted to one's care. Do you keep Christ's word in that sense? Do you hear his word, believe him, and obey his instructions? If not, you need to stop here and examine your relationship to him. For it is to those who do that and only to them that the promise applies.

The Promise

This brings us to the promise itself—"he will never see death." What does this mean? It is obvious that it does not refer to physical death primarily. For Jesus himself died, and since that time all his followers have died. It is true that some may not see death even in this sense; for those who are living at the return of Christ will not die. Still, those are few in number compared with the many others and regardless of that number it is clear that Jesus is not talking primarily of physical death in this saying. Here again, the parallel verse in John 5 is a help to our understanding. There the phrase "will not see death" is paralleled by "has eternal life, and will not be condemned; he has crossed over from death to life." In other words, the primary reference is to spiritual death, and the promise is that the one who keeps Christ's word will never experience that final death that is the result of God's judgment.

This becomes clearer when we recognize that death is separation. In physical death the soul and spirit are separated from the body. They go. The body remains behind. In spiritual death the soul and spirit are separated from God. It is the second that is most frightening.

But this is what Jesus removed for all who believe on him. Apart from his death, all would need to experience death in this sense. The Bible says, "The soul who sins is the one who will die" (Ezek. 18:4, 20). It says, "For the wages of sin is death" (Rom. 6:23). This death is separation from God. It is the direct and inevitable consequence of our sin. But when the Lord Jesus Christ took that separation for us during the hours of darkness when he hung on the cross, he removed this death forever for those who trust him. Now those who trust Christ do not live in fear of it. On the contrary, no longer facing death as separation from God, they sing with Paul, "Where, O death, is your victory? Where, O death, is your sting?" (1 Cor. 15:55).

Let us say, too, that the reality of escape from the second (or spiritual) death also transforms the way in which we look at the first (or physical) death. Why? For this reason: If the grave does not hold terror of judgment, of a judicial separation from God for eternity, then it holds the prospect of a full union with him. And this means that death is a gain, as Paul says in Philippians. To be absent from this life is to be present with God. Thus, although an actual physical death may be accompanied by pain, it always has overtones of glory and is a homecoming. As D. L. Moody died he said, "Is this death? This is not bad; there is no valley. This is bliss. This is glorious." Others have had a similar testimony. Because of Christ's death it is only the shadow of death, rather than the reality, that touches Christians.

Assurance

Finally, I want you to consider the assurance Jesus gives that his words can be trusted. He gives it at the beginning of the verse. The King James Version uses the words "verily, verily." In the Greek the words are "Amen, amen."

"Amen" is a word that is found in nearly every language of the world, one of the few in that category, though it comes from an original Hebrew verb meaning "to support with the arm" or "carry." In its intransitive form the verb meant "that which is supported" or "that which is shored up." Hence, it came to mean "firm" or "unshakable." The word occurs in this original sense in Isaiah 22:23 in reference to a firm place in a wall, where a nail can be driven.

In time, particularly in biblical language, "amen" took on two uses that have since become dominant. First, the word was used of God, as one of his attributes. This is not surprising, of course; for if the word means "that which is unshakable," the reference to God is quite natural. Thus, we find God spoken of as the Amen, or, as some versions have it, as the God of truth. Isaiah quotes God as saying, in the context of a prophecy of judgment and of faithfulness toward his own, "Whoever invokes a blessing in the land will do so by the God of truth; he who takes an oath in the land will swear by the God of truth. For the past troubles will be forgotten and hidden from my eyes" (Isa. 65:16). Being the Amen, or being faithful, is one of God's great characteristics.

The second use of the word is most common. It is the use of the word by men to and women express agreement with what God is saying. Thus, when the law was read in formal convocation to Israel upon the sides of Mount Gerazim and Mount Ebal shortly after the conquest of Canaan, all the people, we are told, responded by saying, "Amen." Thus, too, do we end our prayers; for we thereby express agreement with what is said and reaffirm our faith in God's promises.

When we come to the use of "amen" in the New Testament, we find all these characteristics present, but we find something more. This something more is of great importance for Jesus' words in John. In the New Testament the word is found in 127 verses, in some of them more than once since Jesus frequently repeated the word in his use of it. In seventy-six of these, "amen" comes at the beginning of the sentence, and in each case—this is the new point—it is God who is speaking. In forty-eight other verses "amen" occurs at the end of the sentence, and in these cases man is speaking. This thought is tremendous, for it means that when God speaks, God prefaces his remarks with the affirmation that what he says is truthful. "I do solemnly affirm that what I am about to say is true," says God. After he says it his people then use the word as an echo ("Amen"), by which they mean, "We acknowledge and believe that God is faithful."

The truth of God is the foundation of all truth and of all life. The superstructure is our faith in his reliability. He says, "Amen." We echo, "Amen, amen."

"I tell you the truth [the Greek words are literally, "Amen, amen"], everyone who sins is a slave to sin," Jesus says just a few verses earlier in the chapter (8:34). We hear his statement, and our hearts sadly echo, "Amen, amen." Jesus says, "I tell you the truth [amen, amen], unless you eat the flesh of the Son of Man and drink his blood, you have no life in you" (6:53). We say, "Amen, amen." "I tell you the truth, I am the gate for the sheep" (10:7). "I tell you the truth, whoever hears my word and believes him who sent me has eternal life and will not be condemned; he has crossed over from death to life" (5:24). "I tell you the truth, if anyone keeps my word, he will never see death" (8:51). To these great sayings our hearts echo, "Amen."

One final verse suggests the result of this great Amen that begins with God and is answered by our hearts. In Isaiah 28:16 there is a verse which says, "See, I lay a stone in Zion, a tested stone . . . the one who trusts will never be dismayed." The last phrase, "will never be dismayed," really means "will not be confused and thereby make run away." The promise is that the one who believes in Christ will not do this. You say, "But what does that have to do with the theme we are studying?" It has this to do with it: the word translated "trust" is actually the word "amen" in its verbal form. So God is actually saying that the one who puts his amen to God's declaration of truth will not fall into confusion and flight.[1]

"Amen," says God, as he lays the foundation. "Amen," say his people, as we build upon him. This is the secret of assurance and confidence in all things of the Christian life, including the confrontation of death, the last enemy. "I tell you the truth, whoever keeps my word, he will never see death." Amen and amen.

110

Christ and Abraham

John 8:52–56

At this the Jews exclaimed, "Now we know that you are demon-possessed! Abraham died and so did the prophets, yet you say that if anyone keeps your word, he will never taste death. Are you greater than our father Abraham? He died, and so did the prophets. Who do you think you are?"

Jesus replied, "If I glorify myself, my glory means nothing. My Father, whom you claim as your God, is the one who glorifies me. Though you do not know him, I know him. If I said I did not, I would be a liar like you, but I do know him and keep his word. Your father Abraham rejoiced at the thought of seeing my day; he saw it and was glad."

We are coming to the end of the conversation that took place between Jesus and the religious leaders of his day, as recorded in John 8. Consequently, we are coming to the end of a very important section of John's Gospel.

The early chapters of John (chapters 1–4) have served mainly to introduce the Lord Jesus Christ. In those chapters the reception of Jesus by the people of his day was for the most part favorable; at least, there was no hostile reaction. In the present section (chapters 5–8), this initially open reception turns to one of increasing hatred on the part of the leaders, as we have seen. Thus, these chapters begin with the controversy over the sabbath and end with the conversation, recorded in John 8, which we have been studying.

In this conversation the leaders have increasingly expressed their hostility toward Jesus. For his part, Jesus has been increasingly clear about their

667

true ancestry. In both cases, the conversation has centered around the personality and example of Abraham, so much so, that Abraham is mentioned either by the religious leaders or by Jesus eleven times in the chapter. This is doubly remarkable in that he is mentioned nowhere else in John's Gospel.

The example of Abraham was originally raised in verse 33. The leaders had made a claim. They said, "We are Abraham's descendants," meaning that they based their confidence in the matter of salvation on their relationship to Abraham. God had promised to bless Abraham and his seed, and they were Abraham's seed physically. "Therefore," they reasoned, "we are blessed, and there is nothing for us to worry about." Against this kind of fallacious spiritual reasoning, Jesus went on to point out that what matters with God is not physical but spiritual descent. The question that he asked was, "Are you descended from Abraham spiritually? Do you do as Abraham did?"

This point is particularly prominent in the verses to which we come now. They thus especially lead us to consider Abraham's example. Granted that physical descent is not the important thing! Granted that God is not impressed with family trees! But what is he impressed with? Or, to put it in better language, what did Abraham do that pleased God? On the basis of this and other passages we may answer: (1) Abraham put the calling of God above earthly honors; (2) Abraham believed God in spite of circumstances; and (3) Abraham placed his ultimate hope in the coming of the Lord Jesus Christ, and he rejoiced in his coming.

The Calling of God

First of all, then, Abraham put the calling of God above earthly honors. There were honors to be obtained in this life, for Abraham was rich and undoubtedly prominent, first, in Ur of the Chaldees and, second, in Haran. But these did not detain him. When God called he immediately left the past behind and set out for the land God was showing him.

The story is told in the twelfth chapter of Genesis in these words: "The LORD had said to Abram, 'Leave your country, your people and your father's household and go to the land I will show you. I will make you into a great nation and I will bless you; I will make your name great, and you will be a blessing. I will bless those who bless you, and whoever curses you I will curse; and all peoples on earth will be blessed through you.'" (Gen. 12:1–4).

This is very appropriate to the theme of John 8, as also to the bigger problem of why so many people are unwilling to accept Jesus Christ as their Savior. Here were prominent religious figures who were anxious to retain their own honor. And here was Jesus, who was honored by God in such a way that their little earthly honors seemed tawdry by comparison. They had honor, but he spoke the truth. They had power, but he was able to make the blind see and the lame walk. Moreover, he honored God by knowing and obeying him (v. 55).

"Who do you think you are?" they asked. The question must have been asked in an insulting way, for they were implying that he wrongly was making himself greater than Abraham, their patriarch, or the prophets who had followed him.

Jesus replied, "If I glorify myself, my glory is nothing. My Father, whom you claim as your God, is the one who glorifies me. Though you do not know him, I know him. If I said I did not, I would be a liar like you, but I do know him and keep his word" (vv. 54–55).

These men were concerned with earthly honors. So against this background Abraham becomes an example of a man who sought the honor that comes from God only. How wise this is! All true honor must come from God; all other honor is meaningless and passing. On this point Barclay writes perceptively, "It is not difficult to honor oneself. One can quite easily surround oneself with a kind of synthetic halo. It is easy enough—in fact, it is fatally easy—to bask in the sunshine of one's own approval. It is not overly difficult to win honor from men. The world honors the successful and the ambitious man. But the real honor is the honor which only eternity can reveal; and the verdicts of eternity are not the verdicts of time."[1]

How does this apply to us? In this way. When a Christian sets out to follow the call of God in his life, as Abraham did, he will certainly hear discouraging words from the world. "What do you want to do that for?" he will be asked. "Don't you know that you might have to become a missionary? Think of all the good times you'll have to give up. Don't you know that you will never get ahead in this life like that?" The comments are endless. But the Christian must simply say, "That may be true or not. I do not know. What I do know is that I have determined to place the calling of God above earthly honors."

This was the example of Abraham. For this he was commended by God. "By faith Abraham, when called to go to a place he would later receive as his inheritance, obeyed and went, even though he did not know where he was going. By faith he made his home in the promised land like a stranger in a foreign country; he lived in tents, as did Isaac and Jacob, who were heirs with him of the same promise. For he was looking forward to the city with foundations, whose architect and builder is God" (Heb. 11:8–10).

Faith over Circumstances

Second, Abraham believed God in spite of circumstances, and they were difficult circumstances too. For one thing, there were famines in Abraham's new land. The Bible says that one famine was "grievous." At this point Abraham did not do so well, for he left the land of promise to go to Egypt. But he gradually learned to trust God through such experiences. There were also family problems in one of which Lot, his nephew, separated from Abraham and took all the good land for himself. Abraham remained in the less attractive, mountainous region, but he kept closer to God. There was constant danger from marauding desert bands. On one occasion four of these combined to attack the cities of the valley of Sodom and succeeded in carrying off Lot and his family. Abraham pursued these kings and recovered both the family and the spoils. In all these trials Abraham's faith grew in spite of circumstances.

By far the greatest trial of Abraham's faith, and the one in which his faith shines brightest at this period, was God's challenge to him to believe that he could give him a son. At first this did not seem to be a promise calling for great faith, for Abraham expected to have children. But as the years went by and the child did not come, it became increasingly problematic. There was the problem of succession, of course. Who was to inherit Abraham's great wealth? For a time Abraham thought that his fortune would go to his steward, Eliezer of Damascus; but God showed him that Eliezer was not to be the one. For a time Abraham's faith slipped and he began to place his hope in Ishmael, a son he had engendered through a concubine when he was eighty-six years old. He even prayed that God would accept Ishmael as the heir—"If only Ishmael might live under your blessing." But God replied that it was not to be Ishmael. The son in whom the promise was to come would be born of the aged patriarch and Sarah.

Finally, Abraham reached the age of ninety-nine, Sarah being about ninety, and by this time the promise that they could have a child seemed preposterous. Still there was the promise. God *had* promised. Abraham believed God. God changed his name from Abram (which means "father of many") to Abraham (which means "father of a great multitude"). Within a year after he had done this, Isaac, the son of the promise and an ancestor of the Lord Jesus Christ, was born miraculously.

The Bible speaks of Abraham's example at this point when it says, "Without weakening in his faith, he faced the fact that his body was as good as dead—since he was about a hundred years old—and that Sarah's womb was also dead. Yet he did not waver through unbelief regarding the promise of God, but was strengthened in his faith and gave glory to God, being fully persuaded that God had power to do what he had promised" (Rom. 4:19–21).

If you are a believer in the Lord Jesus Christ, you and I share faith in a sovereign God. He is in control of all things. He could make your circumstances more pleasing if he thought it best. He can remove barriers. He can eliminate difficulties. If he does not do this, however, then he acts as he does for a purpose; and you should trust him. One of those purposes is undoubtedly to *teach* you to trust him, which you would not do at all if everything that ever came into your life was pleasant and the journey of life was always easy.

Christ's Day

Finally, Abraham placed his hope in the coming of Jesus Christ and rejoiced in that coming. Jesus indicates this when he says, "Your father Abraham rejoiced at the thought of seeing my day; he saw it and was glad" (v. 56).

I must admit that this is a difficult verse to understand and that there have been many ways of interpreting it. One popular way is to suppose that Jesus merely meant that Abraham was living in paradise at the time and that he rejoiced in Christ's ministry. The difficulty with this view is that the subject of dispute is not Abraham's continued consciousness beyond the grave but rather Christ's preexistence. The next verses say, "Before Abraham was born, I am." Besides, if Christ had wanted to say that Abraham was still living and rejoiced in his birth and ministry, it would have been far more natural for him to have used present tenses for the verbs ("Abraham is rejoicing to see my day; and he sees it, and is glad"). It seems proper, then, to refer the saying to something that happened to Abraham back in Abraham's day rather than to something contemporary with Christ's ministry.

To place the vision back in Abraham's own time does not in itself solve the problem, however. For most of the rabbis did this—that is, spoke of a vision of the Messiah that Abraham was supposed to have had—and yet disagreed on how it happened. Some of them began with the initial promise of God to Abraham as recorded in Genesis 12:3. This said, "All peoples of the earth will be blessed through you." They taught that when this was given, Abraham knew that it referred to the coming of the Messiah and so rejoiced in God's promise.

Another view began with the vision of the future history of Israel recorded in Genesis 15:8–12, supposed to have been extended to include the coming of the Messiah. Two further views were based on misinterpretations of Scripture. One interpreted the laughter of Genesis 17:17, when God promised the son to the aged Abraham and Sarah, not as an expression of incredulity but as happiness that the birth of Isaac would lead on to the birth of Israel's deliverer. The other used a literal reading of Genesis 24:1—"Abraham was . . . well advanced in years," literally, "gone into the days"—to suggest that he saw into the future. These views seem strange to us, as indeed they should. They are hardly convincing, as Leon Morris, who records much of this material in his commentary on John, acknowledges.

Is this all, however? Can no more be said? I believe that more can be said; for the occasion of the vision of Abraham of Christ's day is to be found, I feel, in the story of the near sacrifice of Isaac on Mount Moriah in which Abraham learned in a new way that "the Lord will provide." God came to Abraham and told him to take his son, the heir of the promise, and sacrifice him on a mountain three day's journey away. It must have been a terrible struggle for the old man that evening as he wrestled with God's command, but sometime during the night he hit upon the solution. He knew that he must obey God, however wrong it seemed, but he also knew that God was a God of his word and that he had committed himself to produce a great nation through Isaac. Isaac had no children at this point. So if God was telling Abraham to kill Isaac, then the God who had done a miracle in Isaac's birth was just going to have to do a miracle in his death. In other words, there was going to have to be a resurrection.

This sounds novel, of course, for not many persons are used to hearing the story taught in this way. Yet it is biblical teaching, for the story indicates that

Abraham fully expected to bring Isaac back down the mountain with him after the sacrifice (Gen. 22:5). Moreover, the author of Hebrews states explicitly, "By faith Abraham, when God tested him, offered Isaac as a sacrifice. He who had received the promises was about to sacrifice his one and only son, even though God had said to him, 'It is through Isaac that your offspring will be reckoned.' Abraham reasoned that God could raise the dead, and figuratively speaking, he did receive Isaac back from death" (Heb. 11:17–19). Abraham believed that God was going to do a miracle in bringing Isaac back from the dead—precisely the miracle that God the Father did with Jesus Christ the Son, as the special language of those verses from Hebrews indicates.

But even this is not all. For when the trial was over and God had intervened to save Isaac and provided a ram for the sacrifice in place of the boy, Abraham rejoiced and called the name of the place Jehovah Jireh, which means "the Lord will provide" (Gen. 22:14). Earlier, as they had gone up the mountain and Abraham had said this to the servants, it could have meant "the Lord will provide a resurrection of Isaac." Now it could only mean that the same God who provided a ram in substitution for the death of Isaac would one day provide his own Son as the perfect substitute and sacrifice for our salvation.

At this moment, I believe, Abraham saw the coming of Jesus clearly, including the meaning of his death and resurrection, and he rejoiced in that coming.[2]

An Example

Abraham can be an example for you, just as any godly person can be an example. So the question is: Do you do as Abraham did? More specifically: (1) Do you put the calling of God above earthly honors? (2) Do you believe God in spite of circumstances? (3) Do you place your hope in the fact that Jesus came to earth to die for you and rejoice in that coming? No physical relationship to Abraham or to any other godly person will save you, but you will be saved if you do as Abraham did. The God of Abraham should become your God.

111

Is Jesus God?

John 8:57–59

"You are not yet fifty years old," the Jews said to him, "and you have seen Abraham!"

"I tell you the truth," Jesus answered, "before Abraham was born, I am!" At this, they picked up stones to stone him, but Jesus hid himself, slipping away from the temple grounds.

Several years ago I heard a psychiatrist, who was also an existentialist, say, "There are only two great questions in this world: Who am I? and, Where am I going?" I heard the statement and agreed in part that these are great questions. But though I agreed in part, it was only in part. For, although these are great questions, they are not the greatest questions that should be asked and for which we should seek answers. One greater question forms the title of this study: Who is Jesus Christ? Is Jesus Christ God? On the answer to that question hangs our destiny.

A Timely Issue

Who is Jesus Christ? This is the question of questions in John's Gospel. Indeed, as we have seen, the Gospel was written almost entirely to provide an answer to it. The Gospel begins with a full statement of Christ's divinity—"In

673

the beginning was the Word [that is, Jesus], and the Word was with God, and the Word was God" (1:1). It ends with the statement, "Jesus did many other miraculous signs in the presence of his disciples, which are not recorded in this book. But these are written that you may believe that Jesus is the Christ, the Son of God, and that by believing you may have life in his name" (20:30–31). In between these verses much evidence is given in support of Christ's claim.

What is the issue in this central portion of John's Gospel? Is the issue the distinct nature of his teachings? Is it the sabbath question itself? Is it Christ's good deeds or lack of them? It is none of these things. Rather, the issue is: Who is Jesus Christ? Is Jesus God?

Is Jesus God? If he is not, then let us say so—but only after having considered the evidence. If he is God, then he has a right to our allegiance and loyalty. We must follow him. You cannot honestly be indifferent to Jesus Christ. He did not leave you that option. Thus, you must either follow him as your God and Lord, or you must seek to eradicate his presence from your life, as the religious leaders of his day did. Which will it be? This is the great question of John. It is the great question raised by Christianity. It is a question for you. Will it be Christ, God in the flesh? Or will you be your own "God"? It must be Christ if he is who he declared himself to be.

Christ's Claim

The verse that we are going to study is one in which Jesus claimed to be God explicitly. He was not always so explicit; but he was in this case, and this produced startling consequences. The leaders of the people had been challenging everything he said, and they had just challenged his statement that Abraham had rejoiced to see his day and that he saw it and was glad. They said, "You are not yet fifty years old, and you have seen Abraham?"

He replied, using his most solemn form of introducing a saying, "I tell you the truth, before Abraham was born, I am" (vv. 57–58). This so infuriated them that they immediately took up stones to stone him.

To our way of thinking, at least at first sight, it is a bit hard to see why this particular saying would have provoked such a radical response. Stoning was the penalty for blasphemy, for making oneself out to be God. So this is what they understood him to be doing. But how does one get that from these words? And in what sense was he saying it? It is obvious from the saying itself that Jesus was claiming to have existed before Abraham was born. It also is obvious from the tense of the verb—"Before Abraham was born, *I am*"—that he was claiming an eternal preexistence. But this alone, we might think, would not be sufficient cause for stoning. The real reason for their violent reaction is found in the fact that when Jesus said, "I am," he actually was using the divine name by which God had revealed himself to Moses at the burning bush. When Moses had asked, "Suppose I go to the Israelites and say to them, 'The God of your fathers has sent me to you,' and they ask me, 'What is his name?' Then what shall I tell them?" God said to Moses, "I am who I am. This is what you are to say to the

Israelites: 'I AM has sent me to you'" (Exod. 3:13–14). In Hebrew this is the word "Jehovah," and it is this word that Jesus so easily takes to himself in this saying. He claimed to be Jehovah, using the very word "Jehovah." So it was because of this that the Jews, who immediately recognized his claim for what it was, reached out to kill him.

Many Claims

We have said that this was an unusually direct and overpowering claim, and it was. But we must not overlook the fact that it was only one of many claims both direct and indirect by which Jesus declared himself to be God's equal.

Practically everything that Jesus had to say was an indirect claim to divinity. His first preaching is an example. When John the Baptist had come preaching the imminent arrival of God's kingdom, he pointed to One who would himself embody that kingdom. Jesus came, and Jesus' first preaching was the announcement of the kingdom's arrival: "The time has come, . . . the kingdom of God is near. Repent and believe the good news!" (Mark 1:15). Later, speaking of himself, he said to the Pharisees, "The kingdom of God is within you" (Luke 17:21). This was a claim that the prophecies of the Old Testament were about him and were fulfilled in him.

All Christ's words about the Old Testament fall into this category also, for the summation of his teaching was, "Do not think that I have come to abolish the Law or the Prophets; I have not come to abolish them but to fulfill them" (Matt. 5:17). When he invited people to follow him—"Follow me, and I will make you fishers of men" (Matt 4:19)—he implied that he was of sufficient stature to be worth following. When he forgave sins, he did it knowing that he was doing what only God can do. Toward the end of his life he promised to send God's Holy Spirit to be with the disciples after his departure, which again implies divinity.

Remarkable among his claims was his unique reference to God as his Father. This was by no means a common form of expression in Judaism, as it is in the English language. No Jew ever spoke of God directly as "my Father." Yet, not only was this the form of address that Jesus used, particularly in his prayers, it was also his only mode of addressing God and it referred to his relationship to the Father exclusively. Jesus said, "I and the Father are one" (John 10:30). He said, "Father, the time has come. Glorify your Son, that your Son may glorify you. . . . Righteous Father, though the world does not know you; I know you" (17:1, 25).

Eventually Jesus taught his disciples to address God as Father also, as a result of their relationship to himself. But even in this case his relationship to God as Father and their relationship to God as Father were different. Thus, he spoke to Mary Magdalene, saying, "Go to my brothers and tell them I am returning to my Father and your Father, to my God and your God" (20:17). He did not say "to *our* Father" or "to *our* God."

"So close was His connection with God," writes John Stott, "that he equated a man's attitude to himself with his attitude to God. Thus, to know Him was to know God (John 8:19; 14:17); to see Him was to see God (John 12:45; 14:9); to believe in Him was to believe in God (John 12:44; 14:1); to receive Him was to receive God (Mark 9:37); to hate Him was to hate God (John 15:23); and to honor Him was to honor God (John 5:23)."[1]

Jesus' "I am" sayings are worthy of special notice also, for he claimed to be all that men need for a full spiritual life. Only God can rightly make such claims. "I am the bread of life" (6:35). "I am the light of the world" (8:12; 9:5). "I am the gate" (10:7, 9). "I am the good shepherd" (10:11, 14). "I am the resurrection and the life" (11:25). "I am the way and the truth and the life" (14:6). "I am the true vine" (15:1, 5).

One great and final example of Christ's unique conception of himself occurred shortly after the resurrection on the day Jesus appeared among the disciples, Thomas being present. Jesus had appeared to the disciples earlier when Thomas was absent. But when Thomas was told about the appearance, he had replied, "Unless I see the nail marks in his hands and put my finger where the nails were, and put my hand into his side, I will not believe it" (20:25). Now the Lord appeared to them all once more, this time including Thomas, and he asked Thomas to make the test he had wanted to make: "Put your finger here . . . and reach out your hand" (v. 27). Thomas, who was overcome by Christ's presence, immediately fell to the ground and worshiped him saying, "My Lord and my God" (v. 28). Think of it: "Lord and God!" *Adonai! Elohim! Jehovah!* And Jesus accepted the designation! He did not deny it! It is no wonder, in light of this testimony, that this is the story John chooses to end all but the postscript of his Gospel.

These, then, are a few of Christ's claims. Thus, whatever we may think of the claims themselves, there can at least be no doubt that Christ made them. Moreover, they remain unchanged. History has not eradicated Christ's claim to be God. Time has not changed it. The Jesus who made the claim then is the same Jesus who is our living contemporary, and the Scriptures tell us that he is the same "yesterday and today and forever." He calls on you to follow him. Will you do it, forsaking all else? If he is not God, then you can safely ignore him. But if he is God, then anything less than a total surrender to him is folly and any other loyalty is idolatrous.

The Rock of Ages

There are three parts to the verses we are considering. The first is the claim of Christ, ("Before Abraham was born, I am"). This has taken most of our space and is important, but the others deserve space also. The second is the reaction of the leaders to that claim ("At this, they picked up stones to stone him"). The third is the sad result ("Jesus hid himself, slipping away from the temple guards").

Stoning can mean different things, all the way from simple displeasure to the desire to have someone killed. As such it can stand for any degree of reaction to Christ by men and women who reject him. I remember, years ago when I was in Jordan and was trying to take a picture of a man who was winnowing grain, how the man picked up stones to stone me. He was not trying to kill me. But he did not like me to be trying to take his picture. He was showing displeasure in that way. Sometimes, as in the case of beggars or animals, stoning was used to drive a person or an animal away. At other times, as in this story, it was used as a means of execution. To put it in contemporary terms, then, some merely express displeasure at Jesus while others (expressing the same basic reaction) try to eliminate his presence from their lives.

The strange thing about this is its folly. For Jesus Christ cannot be so easily gotten rid of. If he is God, he is eternal. He is the Ancient of Days. How can one eliminate the Ancient of Days from one's days? He is the Lord of life. How can one exclude the Lord of life from one's life? Imagine trying to dislodge the Rock of Ages with a handful of stones!

The Lord Jesus Christ is the Rock of Ages yet, and you will not get rid of him by throwing things at him. He is inescapable. He is planted in life. Thus, you must either come to terms with him now, or you must do so on the day of judgment. You have one of two choices. You may destroy yourself by pounding yourself against him, just as you can destroy a piece of wood by pounding it upon an anvil. Or you may build upon him. Why not build upon him? The Rock of Ages makes a great foundation. Jesus said that the one who builds upon him will be like a house founded upon a rock upon which the rains descended and the floods came but which fell not. Why not try him? Why not put him to the test?

Jesus Hid Himself

Finally, the verses also indicate the sad result of the action of those who try to get rid of him. We read, "Jesus hid himself, slipping away from the temple guards" (v. 59). These are sad words, and they are doubly sad because in closing this section of the Gospel they have the added effect of permanence.

What does it mean when we are told that Jesus hid himself? First, it means that although these men could not harm Jesus, nevertheless, they could not benefit from him either. It will be the same for you if you try to keep him out of your life. If you do not allow Jesus to be God in your life, you will not harm him. You cannot harm the invincible and omnipotent God. But you will not benefit from him either. The Lord Jesus Christ came to bring those divine benefits to you. He is the life. He came to give you life, abundant life. He is the light. He wants to shine upon you, to illuminate your darkness and guide you. He is the bread upon whom you may feed and grow. He is the living water who can quench your spiritual thirst. You forfeit these benefits if you refuse him his rightful place in your life.

Second, the verse tells us that there are some from whom Jesus does slip away or "pass by" as the King James Version states it. We live in a day when men and women are won over to ego-tickling dogmas of universalism, the idea that all will be saved. But there is nothing in the Word of God to justify that conclusion. You say, "But why doesn't God save all men?" I don't know, but he doesn't. And here is a case. Notice that throughout this entire conversation Jesus has not even been trying to convert these religious leaders. He has merely been exposing their sin. Moreover, we are told that Jesus eventually passed by and went his way. There are some people whom God gives up (Rom. 1:24, 26, 28). God gives up nations, if they will not live by righteous standards. God gives up churches, when they depart from their first love. God gives up individuals. Woe be to the person whom the Lord Jesus Christ passes by!

Finally, the verse leads us to see that there are some whom God saves anyway. I say "anyway" because I recognize that all of us, even those who become Christians, deserve to be passed by.

Notice this. In the King James text of John 8, the last words are "passed by." It is a tragic note, a tragic end to the contacts of Christ with these religious leaders. But in the opening verse of the very next chapter, just four and five words later, the words occur again in a story that tells us that "*as Jesus passed by,* he saw a man who was blind from his birth" and saved him. Here was a man who in his blindness could not even see the Lord Jesus. Yet Jesus saw him and gave him both physical and spiritual sight. He could not seek Christ, yet he was found by him. How wonderful! What a great hope for the sinner! "Jesus passed by." Yes. But "as he passed by" he saw this one and saved him. With people such as these he began to build his church. Are you such a one? Why should you not be? Why should you not be one who finds Jesus?

Notes

Chapter 57: Christ and Judaism

1. Of the several suggested rearrangements of the text of John's Gospel, none has been better argued than the transposition of chapters 5 and 6. In the judgment of the present author the case for rearrangement has been overstated, however. So in the absence of any manuscript evidence and any otherwise compelling reasons, the traditional order has been retained. A good discussion of the problem, plus a defense of the traditional order, may be found in Leon Morris, *The Gospel According to John* (Grand Rapids: Eerdmans, 1971), 297–98.

2. Ben Zion Bokser, *Judaism and the Christian Predicament* (New York: Knopf Press, 1967), 17.

3. Samuel Sandmel, *We Jews and You Christians* (Philadelphia: Lippincott, 1967), 20.

4. A. Roy Eckhardt, *Elder and Younger Brothers* (New York: Charles Scribner's Sons, 1967), 126.

5. Quoted in a report by *Christianity Today*, 10 May 1968, 40.

6. Bokser, *Judaism and the Christian Predicament*, vii.

Chapter 59: Lord of the Sabbath

1. Lewis Sperry Chafer, *Grace* (Grand Rapids: Zondervan, 1950), 244.

2. Donald Grey Barnhouse, "The Christian and the Sabbath," *Commentary on Romans 14:5–6* (Philadelphia: The Bible Study Hour, 1958), 18–19. This material is omitted from the final book version of the Roman studies.

Chapter 60: The History of the Sabbath

1. Chafer, *Grace*, 251–52.
2. Ibid., 260.
3. Barnhouse, "The Christian and the Sabbath," 11.

Chapter 61: The Day of the Resurrection

1. Chafer, *Grace*, 273–74.

Chapter 62: How to Celebrate Sunday

1. Gerald R. Cragg, "Exposition of the Epistle to the Romans," *The Interpreter's Bible,* vol. 9 (New York: Abingdon, 1954), 620.

2. Chafer, *Grace,* 284–85.

3. D. Martyn Lloyd-Jones in *Preaching and Preachers* (Grand Rapids: Zondervan, 1971), 157–58 speaks of the same thing from his experience.

4. Chafer, *Grace,* 290–91.

5. John R. W. Stott, *Christ the Controversialist* (London: Tyndale Press, 1970), 165.

Chapter 63: Is God Silent?

1. Robert Anderson, *The Silence of God* (Grand Rapids: Kregel, 1965), 1.

2. Stott, *Christ the Controversialist,* 210.

Chapter 65: A Matter of Life or Death

1. J. A. Motyer, *After Death: A Sure and Certain Hope?* (New York: Curtis Brown Ltd., n.d.), 20.

Chatper 67: Why Miracles?

1. C. S. Lewis, *Miracles: A Preliminary Study* (New York: Macmillan, 1947), 11.

2. Arthur W. Pink, *Exposition of the Gospel of John,* vol. 1 (Grand Rapids: Zondervan, 1970), 278.

Chapter 68: The Witness of the Scriptures

1. Reported in *The Christian Century,* 27 October 1971, 1257–63.

2. Dean M. Kelley, *Why Conservative Churches Are Growing* (New York: Harper & Row, 1972).

Chapter 69: The Purpose of the Scriptures

1. Martin Luther, *What Luther Says,* vol. 1, comp. Ewald M. Plass (St. Louis: Concordia, 1959), 69–70. Used by permission.

Chatper 71: The Accusation of the Scriptures

1. William Barclay, *The Gospel of John,* vol. 1 (Philadelphia: Westminster Press, 1956), 201.

2. Donald Grey Barnhouse, "How God Saves Men" (Philadelphia: The Evangelical Foundation, 1955), 28.

3. The illustration is found in a slightly different form in Donald Grey Barnhouse, "How God Saves Men," 31–34.

Chapter 72: The Fourth Miracle

1. Pink, *Exposition of the Gospel of John,* vol. 1, 299–300.

Chapter 74: Who's in Charge?

1. From Barclay, *The Gospel of John*, vol. 1, 209.

Chapter 75: The Fifth Miracle

1. Donald Grey Barnhouse, *Let Me Illustrate* (Westwood, N. J.: Revell, 1967), 119.

Chapter 76: The Search

1. Quoted by A. W. Tozer in *The Pursuit of God* (Harrisburg: Christian Publications, 1948), 18–19.

2. The story of Abraham and Isaac is told at greater length in volume 1 ("God's Greatest Gift" a study of John 3:16) and in the book *How God Can Use Nobodies* (Wheaton: Victor, 1974), 41–51 by the author.

3. A. W. Tozer, *The Pursuit of God* (Harrisburg, Pa.: Christian Publications, 1948), 27.

Chapter 77: A Golden Sentence

1. Pink, *Exposition of the Gospel of John*, vol. 1, 320.

2. The story of Philemon is told in this way by H. A. Ironside, *Charge That to My Account and Other Gospel Messages* (New York: Loizeaux Brothers, 1931), 5–15.

Chapter 79: Those Who Shall Come

1. *Select Works of Jonathan Edwards*, vol. 2 (London: Banner of Truth Trust, 1959), 192, 198.

Chapter 80: The Certainty of Divine Grace

1. The texts relating to rebirth are also discussed in volume 1 in the chapters on John 1:13 and 3:3–5.

Chapter 81: No One Driven Away

1. Charles Haddon Spurgeon, *All of Grace* (Chicago: Moody Press, n.d.), 46–47.

2. Charles Haddon Spurgeon, "High Doctrine and Broad Doctrine," *Metropolitan Tabernacle Pulpit*, vol. 30 (Pasadena, Tex.: Pilgrim Publications, 1971), 57–58.

Chapter 82: The Keeping Power of God

1. *Luther's Works*, vol. 23, trans. Martin H. Bertram (St. Louis: Concordia, n.d.), 66.

Chapter 83: God's Will Confirmed by Jesus

1. Charles Haddon Spurgeon, "The Father's Will," *Metropolitan Tabernacle Pulpit*, vol. 19 (Pasadena, Tex.: Pilgrim Publications, 1971), 340.

Chapter 84: Murmurs of Disbelief

1. See the discussion on John 6:10–15 in this volume.

2. Martin Luther, *The Bondage of the Will,* ed. by J. I. Packer and O. R. Johnston (Westwood, N.J.: Revell, 1957), 311.

3. Leon Morris, *The Gospel According to John* (Grand Rapids: Eerdmans, 1971), 371.

Chapter 88: Nowhere to Go but Forward

1. Charles Haddon Spurgeon, "A Home Question and a Right Answer," *Metropolitan Tabernacle Pulpit,* vol. 28 (London: Banner of Truth Trust, 1971), 116–17.

Chapter 89: A Disturbing Revelation

1. Pink, *Exposition of the Gospel of John,* vol. 1, 364. The entire discussion of Judas by Pink is found on pp. 362–65.

2. Ibid., 365.

Chapter 90: What Time Is It?

1. However, see the discussion of the dating of all the events of Passover week (volume 3, "The King Is Coming," John 12:12–19) for the most plausible day and year of the crucifixion.

2. This is the implication of the word translated as "time" in John 7:6, the word *kairos.*

Chapter 91: What Do You Think of Jesus?

1. John R. W. Stott, *Basic Christianity* (Grand Rapids: Eerdmans, 1959), 32.

2. C. S. Lewis, *Mere Christianity* (New York: Macmillan, 1958), 41.

Chapter 93: Judging by Right Judgment

1. Morris, *The Gospel According to John,* 409.

Chapter 95: "Where I Am, You Cannot Come"

1. From *Luther's Works,* vol. 23, 254.

2. The story of Job is told in a similar manner by Donald Grey Barnhouse, *God's River* (Grand Rapids: Eerdmans, 1959), 87–90.

Chapter 97: Christ, A Divider of Men

1. Charles Haddon Spurgeon, *Sermons on the Gospel of John* (Grand Rapids: Zondervan, 1966), 59.

2. For a fuller discussion of the geneaologies of Jesus see volume 1, "I Am He" (John 4:25–26).

Chapter 99: The Woman Taken in Adultery

1. J. Duncan M. Derrett, *New Testament Studies,* vol. 10 (1963–64), 4–5.

Chapter 100: Never a "Thing"

1. Paul Tournier, *A Place for You* (New York and Evanston: Harper & Row, 1966), 13.

2. Paul Tournier, *A Doctor's Casebook in the Light of the Bible* (New York, Evanston, and London: Harper & Row, 1960), 123–24.

3. Ibid., 124.

Chapter 101: "I Am the Light of the World"

1. Alexander Maclaren, "The Gospel of St. John" in *Expositions of Holy Scripture*, vol. 7 (Grand Rapids: Eerdmans, 1959), part 1, 325.

2. Ibid.

Chapter 104: The Uplifted Christ

1. R. A. Torrey, *The Uplifted Christ* (Grand Rapids: Zondervan, 1965), 24–30.

Chapter 105: Believing on Jesus

1. Charles Haddon Spurgeon, "Believing on Jesus and Its Counterfeits," *Metropolitan Tabernacle Pulpit*, vol. 37 (London: Banner of Truth Trust, 1970), 112–13.

Chapter 106: Free Indeed!

1. Howard G. Hendricks, *Say It with Love* (Wheaton: Victor Books, 1972), 112–13.

Chapter 108: That Other Family

1. See Chapter 39, "Where I Am, You Cannot Come" (John 7:32–36).

Chapter 109: The Last Enemy

1. This material is adapted from a study of the word "amen" by Donald Grey Barnhouse, *God's Glory* (Grand Rapids: Eerdmans, 1964), 116–21.

Chapter 110: Christ and Abraham

1. Barclay, *The Gospel of John*, vol. 2, 39.

2. For more on the Abraham story see on 6:22–27. The story also is told at greater length in volume 1 ("God's Greatest Gift," a study of John 3:16) and in *Ordinary Men Called by God*, 39–48, by the author.

Chapter 111: Is Jesus God?

1. Stott, *Basic Christianity*, 26.

Subject Index

Abba, 554

Abraham, 393, 423, 424, 576; and Sodom, 653; calling of, 668, 669; name of, changed, 670; death of, 398; descendants of, 393–95, 556, 649–54; descent from, 668; example of, 653, 672; pleads for Sodom, 401, 442; sacrifice of Isaac, 466, 467, 671, 672; saw Christ's day, 670–72; trust in God of, 669, 670; walk of, with God, 650

Absalom, 364

Achan, 466

Adam, 400, 460, 491; and Eve, 424, 658

Adultery, 603; evidence proving, 603, 604

Afterlife, 398

Agnosticism, 538

Agnostics, 621

American Book of Days, 373

American Standard Version, 357

American way of life, 455

Amos, 475

Ananias and Satan, 660

Ananias, 647

Ancestry, spiritual, 651, 652

Ancient of Days, 677

Anderson, Robert, 551

Andrew, 449

Angels, 653

Anna, 423, 432

Annas, market of, 351

Anti-Semitism, 352–54

Apostolic Constitutions, 602

Archeological evidence, 419, 420

Aristophenes, 512

Ark of the Covenant, 569

Assurance, 664

Augustine, 463, 496, 516; and Pelagius, 513

Authorized Version, 428, 430, 638

Bacon, Francis, 661

Balak, 424

Baptism, ix, 471, 533

Barclay, William, 434, 447, 453, 460, 514

Barley bread, 447, 448

Barnhouse, Donald Grey, 437, 450, 461, 515, 531

Bauer, Bruno, 429

Belief, 494, 495, 638, 639

Believer, satisfied, 587, 588

Believers, 592, 593, 594

Believing is seeing, 542

Believing on Christ, 663

Berger, Peter L., 417

Bergman, Ingmar, 386

Berkouwer, 482

Bethesda, pool of, 356, 357, 361

Bethlehem, 591

Bethsaida, 446

Beveridge, William, 359, 360

Bible Study Hour, 520

Bible, reading of, 533; superstitious reverence for, 430; as witness to Christ, 416, 431, 438. *See also* Scripture, Word of God

Birth from above, 490, 491

Bitterness, 351–54

Blasphemy, 674

Blessing, flood of, 588; God's, 581; to others, 599

Blind, lame, paralyzed, 358

Body, soul, and spirit, 399, 400

Bonar, Horatius, 576

Bondage, spiritual, 575

Bonhoeffer, Dietrich, 611

Born again, 652

Bokser, Rabbi Ben Zion, 352

Brazen serpent, 518

Bread, daily, 478, 479; necessary for life, 477; produces growth, 479; suited for everyone, 477; true, 480

Brotherhood of man, 655

Brown, Raymond E., 524
Bucer, 482
Buddhism, 634
Building on the Amen, 666
Bullinger, 482
Bunyan, John 354, 538

Caesar, Julius, 349, 469
Cain, 591, 658
Calvin, 482, 516, 525; and Arminus, 513
Calvinism, ix
Calvinistic faith, 482
Calvinistic Methodists, 482
Cana of Galilee, 410
Canaan, 616
Capernaum, 464, 476, 482, 512, 535
Certainties, spiritual, 505
Chafer, Lewis Sperry, 362, 370, 371, 375, 380, 382
Challenge, 612
"Cheap grace," 611
Children, of believers, 581; protected by Christianity, 574
Christ Jesus, and Abraham, 667–72; and Judaism, 349–54; and the Scriptures, 554, 555, 572, 573; and the woman caught in adultery, 610–12; appearances of, 376, 377; ascension of, 376; believing on, 637–42; bore our sin, 611; bound to, 539, 540; as "bread of life," 475–80, 518, 519; coming to, 495–500; compassion of, 576, 604, 610; cross of, 519; death of, 486, 562, 563, 632, 633; disciples of, commissioned, 377; as divider of men, 589–94; as emancipator, 574, 575; feeding on, 442, 520–22, 525–27; finding, 678; following, 617, 618; forgiveness from, 555; glory of, revealed, 410, 412; as God, 555, 573, 673–78; God's plan for, 549, 550; great attraction of, 634, 635; as healer of broken hearts, 575, 576; hid himself, 677, 688; as Holy One of God, 542; identity of, 553–58; incarnation of, 530; inescapable, 558; in the Old Testament, 422–26; as judge, 401; none like, 595–600; not a deceiver, 557; not insane, 556, 557; not just a good man, 554–56; obeyed the Father, 388, 389; one with the Father, 387, 388; prayers of, 612; as prophet, priest and king, 452, 453; rejected, 591; resurrection of, 375; satisfies, 413, 599; seeking, 464; seeking God in, 468; sees us, 460; sent from God, 596, 597; sinless, 622;

as Son of God, 675; sufficiency of, 441–43; teachings of, 560; trusting in, 623; understanding, 610; union with, 527; way to the Father, 390; words of, 533, 534, 662, 663; work of, 571–76
Christian, becoming a, 461, 462
Christianity, anemic, 481
Christmas story, 431, 432
Christs, billions of, 456, 509
Church, 417, 482, 678
Churchill, Winston, 469
Circumcision, 410, 568
Circumstances, God of, 604, 605
Cleopas and Mary, 425
Cloud in the desert, 614–18
Cloud of Unknowing, 465
Cochrane, Dennis, 662, 663
Codex Bezae, 602
Codex Sinaiticus, 602
Codex Vaticanus, 602
Commitment, 408, 558
Committee, to kill Jesus, 365, 366
Common sense, 628
Communion, 533
Condemnation, 400
Confession of sin, 432
Confidence, misplaced, 433
Consultation on Church Union, 417
Contempt for others, 599, 600
Council of Trent, 417
Cross, 530, 531, 546
Crucifixion, 633
Cynicism, 610
Cyrus, 609

Dabney, 482
Damnation, 397, 400
Daniel, predicted the time of Jesus, 551
David, 363, 364, 423, 448, 460, 468, 567, 576
Day of Atonement, 569
Day of Pentecost, 470
Death, 400, 423, 611, 632, 633, 661–66
Decisions, 549
Decline and Fall of the Roman Empire, 387
Deposits, capital, 502, 503
Depravity, 483, 511
Desert, temperatures in, 616
Despair, 443
Destinies, two, 399, 400
Devil, 520, 578–81, 651; fallen being, 658, 659; images of, 657; liar, 659; limited being, 659; murderer, 658, 659; personal, 657, 658. *See also* Satan

Devils, 639
Disbelief, murmurs of, 511–16
Disciples in a storm on Galilee, 458–61
Discipleship, 529–34, 641
Dividends, God's, 504
Doctrine, 511, 512, 560, 561, 562
Dying in one's sin, 629

Eating, involves appropriation, 521; necessary for life, 520; personal, 521; response to a felt need, 521
Eckhardt, A. Roy, 352, 353
Edwards, Jonathan, 484
Einstein, 349, 484–86, 507, 513
Elisha, at Dothan, 660; provided for by a widow, 450
Elite, Jewish, 350, 351
Elizabeth, 394
Emancipation, 574, 575
Emmaus disciples, 425
Emmaus, road to, 376
Encouragement, 641
Enemy, last enemy, 661–66
Episcopal Church in America, 482
Epistemology, 403
Esau, 394
Eternal life, 385, 386, 527
Eternity, possessing it in time, 391–96
Eusebius, 602
Evangelism, 516
Eve, tempted by Satan, 660
Evidence for Christ's teaching, 514, 515

Faith, 412; defined, 494; growth of, 459–61; in Jesus, 462; kept by God, 502; eye for, 639
False religions, 539
Family, devil's, 655–60
Famine, 669; for the Word of God, 475, 476
Faust legend, 657
Feast of Tabernacles, 548, 578, 584, 586, 614
Feeding of the five thousand, 412, 413, 439–56
Feeding on Christ, not the Lord's Supper, 524, 525; results of, 527, 528
Fellini, 574
Fellowship, 647
Forgiveness, 606; not easy, 611
Formalism, 364, 365
"Four freedoms," 643
Freedman, Noel, 352
Freedom, 538, 641; from sin, self and Satan, 642; true, 643–48
Frustration, 443

Gaius, 593, 594
Galilee, despised, 591; storm on, 458, 459
Garden of Gethsemanae, 596
Genealogies, 609
Ghosts, believing in, 409
Gibbon, Edward, 387
Gladitorial contests abolished by Christianity, 573, 574
God the Father, alpha and omega, 488; believing, 543; call of, 393–95, 668, 669; determined, 508; forgotten by?, 443, 444; gave them up, 627, 628; grace of, 372, 481, 486; guards our deposits, 501, 502; has spoken, 387; helps the helpless, 356; immanence of, 460; judgment of, 397, 398; names of, 597; promised a Redeemer, 424; redeems sinners, 424; scales of, 436–38; separation from, 629, 630; silence of, 385–90; sovereign, 481, 670; testimony of, 404, 405; uses little things, 448; will confirmed by Jesus, 505–10; witness of, 622, 623; words from, 598; wrath of, 401
God's doctrine, satisfies, 563, 564
God's hedge, 579, 580
God's time and our time, 548, 549
Golden Rule, 436
Good works will not save, 471
Goodspeed translation, 357
Gospel, free offer of, 481
Grace, 357–59, 372, 588; certainty of divine, 487–92; day of God's, 628, 629; doctrines of, ix; electing, 481, 483; free offer of God's, 486; irresistible, 487; not under law, 378; or regulations, 362; prevenient, 463
Grant, Frederick C., 352
Guinness, Os, 386

Halley, Edmund, 551
Haran, 668
Hard sayings, 530, 531
Healing, of the nobleman's son, 412; of the paralyzed man, 412
Hearts, restless, 463
Hell, 629, 630; controlled by God, 658
Hendricks, Howard G., 647
Herod, 351, 432
Higgins, George G., 417
Holy of Holies, 569, 616
Holy Spirit, 377, 418, 463, 464, 587, 646, 652
Honor, comes from God, 669; concern for earthly, 669
Hostility, x, 351, 451, 452, 577, 667
Human needs, focus on, 465

Human resources, failure of, 441
Humanity, needs of, 356, 357
Hunger and thirst, 598, 599
Hymns, "Arise, my soul, arise!", 474; "Grace! 'Tis a charming sound," 493; "I am an empty vessel," 442, 443; "I have no help but thine," 576; "Jesus shall reign where'er the sun," 453; "Long my imprisoned spirit lay," 575; "Not the labors of my hands," 570; "Round each habitation hov'ring," 616; "There was no other good enough," 632; "What can wash away my sin?", 569;
Hypocrites, 545, 567, 568

"I am," 674, 675
"I am with you," 578
"I am" sayings, 477, 518, 554, 614, 676
Ignorance, 600; freedom from, 644, 645
Illustrations, amalgam king, 654; "C and E" Christian, 494, 495; carnivores and herbivores, 483; change in the bride's status, 527; child's felt needs, 519; continental drift, 509, 510; cowboy who searched the Bible, 563, 564; crossing Niagra Falls, 639; death of D. L. Moody, 664; debate declining into invective, 625, 626; deciding the case on its merits, 622; doctor's diagnosis, 423; Duna word for "faith," 662, 663; "Egypt, the gift of the Nile," 498; ending of Romans, 593, 594; execution of Latimer and Ridley, 540; filled with God's fullness, 528; fireplace with no base, 561; floated by the tide, 588; focusing on our own problems, 465; fully surrendered, 450; getting on the train or being picked up, 491, 492; Halley's comet, 551, 552; helpless survivor, 359; house of the Egyptian farmer, 387, 388; "I don't have the gift," 647; inscriptions on the cross, 507, 508; Johnson's definition of oats, 448; judge paying the fine, 550; Lincoln's pardon of the condemned soldier, 576; man traveling on a river, 549; message from the boss, 404; mirror, 568; multiple traffic violations, 562; murmuring, 454; "my case is very peculiar," 623, 624; *ne plus ultra*, 399; no armor for the back, 538; no freedom since the liberation, 641; "of whose sins may I speak?", 656; "old man Klein," 493, 494; onomatopoeia, 512; ordination vows, 523; oriental silversmiths, 457, 458; palimpsest, 629; penny in the bank, 504; physical conception, 491; play called "time," 492; pointing a finger, 567; real "re-Bible," 592; reluctant student convert, 496, 497; scales of God, 437, 438; Scotsman on the ocean liner, 517; sea lion that spit fish, 531, 532; servant in *King Lear*, 492; signpost, 407, 408; soldiers who have life, 515; "standing on the rock," 420; surety for a star witness, 506, 507; *The Silence*, 386; throwing off the scent, 570; time lapse photography, 552; *Titanic*, 433; two natures in Christ, 418; view from the Empire State Building, 562; walking toward the light, 354; watch in the sawdust, 461; "we could be doing with that chap Jesus," 460, 461; wedding service, 526; "Why do you love me?", 611; witnesses for the prosecution, 415, 416; won by the uplifted Christ, 635, 636; work of Andrew done for me, 450; "you ate my Jell-O," 489
Impossibilities, categorical, 357
Inability, man's 482–84; natural and moral, 483
Incarnation, hard doctrine, 530
Inconsistency, 650, 651
Invitation, a great, 584–86; and a promise, 583–88
Invitations, 583
Ironside, Harry A., 359, 563, 592
Isaac, 394, 423, 467; death of, 398
Ishmael, 394
Israel, x

Jacob, 394, 423, 424; cared for by God, 444; death of, 398
Jacob's ladder, 518
Jairus, faith of, 598
James, William, 547
Jason, 593, 594
Jehovah Jireh, 672
Jericho, 466
Jerome, 602
Jerusalem, fall of, 362
Jesus, see Christ Jesus
Jew, advantages of being, 353
"Jews," the, 350
Job, believed in the resurrection, 399; story of, 578–81
John the Baptist, 350, 394, 412, 422, 423, 572, 597, 652, 675; arrest of, 351; prophet, 405, 406; witness of, 415, 416; witness to Jesus, 404–7
Johnson, Samuel, 448, 661
Jonah, 600; sign of, 410

Joseph, 398
Joy, 381, 382
Judaism, Christ and, 349–54
Judas, 536, 638, 659; why Jesus chose,
    544–46
Judgment, 397, 398, 563; day of, 629; God's
    prerogative, 389; judging by right,
    565–70; must not trust our own, 623
Just and the justifier, 605
Justice, will send us to hell, 401, 402

Keeping power of God, 499–504
Kelley, Dean M., 417
King James Version, 398, 400, 502, 512, 664,
    677, 678
King Lear, 492
Knowing God, 385–87
Knowledge, certain, 641; Christ's superior,
    621, 622; gaining spiritual, 645; little,
    452, 453; pride in, 446; source of, 633
Kuyper, Abraham, 482

L'Abri Fellowship, 386
Lad with bread and fish, 447–49
Lamps, two great, 615
Latimer, Hugh, 540
Latin Vulgate, 602
Law of God, 565; condemns, 437, 566–68;
    use of the, 568–70
Laws of nature, 413
Lazarus, 489, 598, 605, 646; resurrection of,
    413
Legalism, 363
Leper, faith of a, 598
Let Me Illustrate, 461
Lewis, C. S., 409, 496, 555, 556
Liberalism, 632
Life, abundant, 395, 677; and death, 397–402;
    before conversion, 537, 538; before faith,
    515, 516; gift of God, 389, 392, 393; new
    quality of, 508; or death, 522; resurrection,
    395, 396;
Light, coming of the, x; kindled, 406; of the
    world, 613–18
Loneliness, 443
Lord's Day, 375, 379
Lord's Prayer, 478
Lord's Supper, three views of, 524, 525
Lot, 402
Love, cords of, 488, 489; drawn by, 635, 636;
    inexplicable, 611; of things, 479
Lowell, James Russell, 661
Lucius, 593, 594

Luther, Martin, 421, 482, 500, 516; and
    Erasmus, 513, 514

Macbeth, 547
Maclaren, Alexander, 617, 618
Man born blind, 413, 428, 678
Man's doctrine, God's doctrine, 559–64
Man, a trinity, 399, 400; fall of, 423; funda-
    mental need of, 634; sin and inability of,
    481
Management defined, 445
Manipulation, 476, 477
Manna, 615; miracle of, 476
Mannas, two, 517–22
Mariology, 417
Mary Magdalene, 376, 675
Mary, Virgin, 394, 418, 448
Men, words of, 599, 600
Mercy, 485; or God's justice, 400–2
Messiah, 364, 405, 452, 476, 591, 614
Middle Ages, 657
Milton, John, 658
Miracle, third, 355–60; fourth, 439–44; fifth,
    457–62
Miracles, 409–14; witness of Jesus', 404, 406,
    415, 416
Mishnah, 567
Mohammedanism, 634
Money, trust in, 446, 447
Monotheism, 573
Moody Institute of Science, 552
Moody, Dwight L., 450, 664
Moralism, dead, 539
Morris, Leon, 514, 671
Moses, 370, 394, 422, 428, 448, 452, 476, 477,
    480, 508, 518, 590, 609, 676; accusation of,
    435; and Aaron, 568; no Sabbath before,
    368; prophesied Christ's coming, 424;
    wrote the pentateuch, 419
Mount Gerazim and Mount Ebal, 665
Mount Moriah, 671
Mount of Olives, 612
Murray, William, 643

Naaman, 389, 450
Naivete, 610
National Council of Churches, 417
Nazarite, 406
New American Standard Version, 430
New English Bible, 638
New International Version, 638
Nicodemus, 392, 431, 578, 600, 652
No escape, 630
Nowhere to go but forward, 535–40

Obedience, 388, 389
Obeying Christ, 663
Offerings, received on Sunday, 377
Old Testament, great themes of, 423, 424
Onesimus, Paul and, 471–74
Open book, open mind, 425, 426
Opportunity, 648; day of, 540
Ovid, 547

Pageant of salvation, 474
Papias, 602
Paradise Lost, 658
Passover, 440, 441, 548, 596
Paul, 371, 482; and Judaism, 353; and
    Philemon, 471–74; and Silas, 514;
    conversion of, 646, 647; increasingly aware
    of his sin, 509
Pentecost, 550, 586
People, needy, 440
Perfection, 434
Perseverance of the saints, 499–504
Personalism of the Bible, 609
Peter, 425, 536, 537, 539–44, 550, 586, 639;
    appealing, 541; or Judas, 546; tempted by
    Satan, 660
Pharisees, attempt to arrest Jesus, 596; desired
    human honor, 434; scorn of, 626, 627
Philadelphia Conference on Reformed
    Theology, ix
Philemon, Paul and, 471–74
Philip, 440, 443, 446, 447
Philippian jailer, 470
Phillips translation, 357
Phillips, J. B., 561
Pilate, 351
Pilgrim's Progress, 538
Pink, Arthur W., 411, 442, 470, 544, 545
Plot to trap Jesus, 601
Poe, Edgar Allan, 512
Politics, 455
Pompeii, 478
Pool of Siloam, 614
Possessions, 466, 467
Powers, supernatural, 503
Prayer, 533
Preaching, encouragement in, 485
Prejudice, justifying, 455
Preservation by God, 508
Pride, 432, 574, 599, 600
Priscilla and Aquila, 647
Prodigal son, 522, 647
Progressive revelation of Christ, 519
Promise, great, 587, 588

Prophet, the, 590
Prophetic word, 408
Propitiation, 634
Psalms, prophecies of Christ, 425
Purpose, firm, 349, 350

Quartus, 593, 594
Quest for the "historical Jesus," 429
Question, relevant, 536, 537
Questions, three important, 572; three
    insulting, 625–27

Rationalism, age of, 417
Reaction, selfish, 453, 454
Rebirth, 489–91
Redeemer, trust in, 423
Reformation, Protestant, 416
Reformation, social conscience of, 574
Reformed faith, 482; hard doctrine, 531
Reimarus, Hermann Samuel, 429
Religious language, 386
Religious leaders, hated Jesus, 566
Resurrection, day of, 373–78; lifted up by, 633;
    of believers and unbelievers, 399
Revelation, demanding, 408; disturbing,
    541–46
Revised Standard Version, 430, 638
Revolution, social, 573, 574
Rich man and Lazarus, 410
Ridley, Master, 540
Righteousness of Christ, 647
Robert the Bruce, 570
Rock of Ages, 676, 677
Roman Catholic church, 416, 417
Roman Catholic Confraternity translation,
    357
Roosevelt, Franklin Delano, 643
Ryle, John Charles, 420

Sabbaterianism, 368
Sabbath day's journey, 363
Sabbath, 566, 626; end of the, 371; for Israel
    only, 367–71; history of, 367–72; Lord of,
    361–66; observance, ix; origin of, 368–71;
    regulations, 363
Sabbath-Sunday question, 361–84
Sacrifices, point to Christ, 569
Sadducees, question about the resurrection,
    604
Saints and sinners, 648
Salvation, not of man, 490; sure, 507
Samaritans, 350
Samson, 406, 448

Samuel, 406

San Andreas fault, 510

Sandmel, Rabbi Samuel, 352

Sanhedrin, 351, 578

Satan, 424, 578–81, 645, 651; assaults of, 580, 581; his schemes, 657. *See also* Devil

Satanism, 657

Saying "no" to self, 454

Scribes, careful work of, 430

Scripture, accusation of, 433–38; decline of faith in its authority, 416, 417; doctrine of, ix, 561; Jesus fulfills, 572, 573; misuse of, 427–32; Old Testament, 404; one subject, 422–25; one author of, 422; opened by Jesus, 425; purpose of, 407, 421–26; validated by prophecy, 552; witness of, 407, 415–20; wrongly made an end in itself, 429, 430. *See also* Bible, Word of God

Search for Jesus, 463–68

Secular idealogies, 538

Seeing and believing, 409

Seeking, halfhearted, 467, 468

Sejanus, 351

Self, dying to, 454

Self-delusion, 645

Sentence, a golden, 469–74

Sermon on the Mount, 435, 640

Sermon outlines, 449

Servicemaster Corporation, 445

Shakespeare, William, 492, 547

Shekleton, Mary, 442

Sheol, 398

Shepherds, 432

Signs, 406; and wonders, 410, 411; seven major, 411–13

Simeon, 423, 432

Simon Magus, 638

Sin, 414, 423, 502; cleansed from, 570; freedom from, 646; horror of, 603, 604; rejected because of, 634; source of our problems, 599

Sinner, words to the, 605

"Sinners in the Hands of an Angry God," 484

Slavery, 573, 574, 645

Sodom, 669; and Gomorrah, 401

Solomon, 460

Sosipater, 593, 594

Spirit, not flesh, 532, 533

Spurgeon, Charles Haddon, ix, 482, 494, 497, 506, 588, 589, 640

Standards, God's, 434; internal, 436

Statue of Liberty, 644

"Stone the builders rejected," 374, 375

Stoning, 676, 677

Stott, John R. W., 383, 390, 407, 554, 556, 676

Strauss, David Friedrich, 429

Success, 450, 451

Suffering, 386, 502

Sunday, 373–78; eleven important events on, 375–77; for Christians only, 380; how to celebrate, 379, 384; to be active, 382, 383; to be expectant, 383, 384; to be joyful, 381, 382

Susanna, story of, 608

Talmud, 560

Taste and see, 413, 414

Taxes, question about, 604

Ten Commandments, 362, 435

Tenth Presbyterian Church, 373, 625

Tertius, 593, 594

Testimony, impartial, 622

Textual problems, 602, 603

Theophany, 615

Thirty-Nine Articles, 482, 649

Thomas, 675; Christ's appearance to, 556

Tiglath-pileser, 419

Time, to believe, 581, 582; what is the?, 547–52

Timothy, 593, 594

Titus, 351

Torrey, Reuben A., 623, 624, 634, 635

Tournier, Paul, 608, 609

Tozer, A. W., 466

Transformation of water into wine, 412

Translations, various, 430

Treating people as things, 608

Troubled by God, 627

Truth saves, 645, 646

"Tulip" acrostic, 482

Two or three witnesses, 606, 620, 621

Two ways, 660

Unity, 593, 594

Universal fatherhood of God, 655

Universalism, 677

Ur of the Chaldees, 393, 668

Walking on the water, 413

Warfield, B. B., 482

Wesley, Charles, 575

Westminster Shorter Catechism, 381

Will of God, absolute and self-determined, 506

Williams translation, 357

Wise men, 431

Witchcraft, 657

Witness, 383; character of a, 621

Witnesses, agree, 619–24; discrediting, 619; to Christ, 403–8

Witnessing, ix

Woman of Samaria, 392, 450

Woman taken in adultery, 601–12

Word of God, 610, 644; Bible images for, 491; brings life, 533; details of, 597; different from human books, 418. *See also* Bible, Scripture

Word studies, "again" *(palin* and *anothen),* 490, 491; "Amen" *(amen),* 664, 665; "daily" *(epiousios),* 478; "hard" *(skleros),* 530; "lifted up" *(airo* and *hupsoo),* 633; "sign" *(semeia),* 410, 411; "tribulation" *(thlepsis),* 502, 503

Words, and works, 411; from God, 598; of life, 533, 534

Workmanship, Christ's, 654; God's, 503

Works, human, 471

World peace, 538

Worship, active, 383; pattern for, 377, 378

Written word, 408

Wycliffe, 482

Yoke, Roman, 455, 456

Your God Is Too Small, 561

Zacchaeus, 496

Zadok, Rabbi, 351

Zakkai, Rabbi Johanan Ben, 351

Zwingli, 482

Scripture Index

Genesis

2:2–3—368
2:17—400
3:4—659
3:15—424
3:19—661
12:1–4—668
12:3—424, 671
15:8–12—671
17:7—650
17:11—410
17:17—671
18—653
22:2—467
22:5—672
22:14—672
22:16–18—650
22:18—424
24:1—671
25:8—398
35:29—398
37:35—398
49:10—424

Exodus

3:13–14—675
3:14—556
13:21–22—615
16:23, 29, 30—370
16:29—363
20:8–10—362, 566
20:10–12—369
31:12–17—369
33:17—609

Leviticus

12:3—567
16:22—569
23:15—370

Numbers

9:17–23—617
10:35–26—616
16:33—398
24:17, 19—424
35:30—620

Deuteronomy

1:17—389
6:4—573
6:5—435
16:9—370
17:6—620
18:15—405, 424
18:18—424, 452
19:15—620
22:23–24—608
27:26—435, 567
32:2—431
32:39—389

Joshua

24:2—393

1 Samuel

2:6—389
16:7—544

1 Kings

8:27—460
22:21–23—659

2 Kings

5:7—389
6:16—660
15:29—419

2 Chronicles

36:21—353

Nehemiah

9:13–14—369

Job

1:1—579
1:8—579
1:9–10—579
1:11—579
1:20–21—580
2:1–5—581
19:25–26—399
42:10—581

Psalms

16:10—425
16:11—585
22:26—442
23:1—470
27:8—468
27:13—542
37:5—461
40:7–8—507
44:22—502
49:15—399
51:1–3, 5—423
77:3—627
110:1—425
114:7–8—614
118:22–24—374, 375
132:15—452
139:7–10—460, 539

Proverbs

3:5, 6—623
3:17—660
7:27—398
14:12—660

Isaiah

1:19—441
12:3—614

14:9–15—398
14:13–15—658
22:23—664
28:16—665
41:21–24—659
45:3—609
54:13—515
55:1–2—442
55:6—582
55:8—560
61:1–2—555

Jeremiah

17:13—605
17:21–22, 27—363

Ezekiel

18:4, 20—664
28:12–15—658

Daniel

9:25–26—551
10:13, 20—660

Amos

8:11–12—476

Micah

5:2—591

Malachi

3:1—406
3:16—506
4:5–6—590

Matthew

3:9–10—652
4:19—675
5:6—468, 585
5:17—572, 675
6:13—658
7:1–5—603
7:12—435
7:13—640
7:14—660
8:23–27—459
9:1–2—358
10:29–31—460
10:34–36—589
11:4–6—573

11:10—406
11:28—604
12:3–8—364
12:9–13—365
14:15–21—440
16:16—541, 573
18:19—505
22:21—366
23:27—436
25:41—660
26:35—537
26:52–54—425
27:4—545
28:9—376, 381
28:20—460

Mark

1:2—406
1:15—675
2:1–5—358
2:5—555
4:35–41—459
6:32–44—440
6:45—458
6:48—460
9:37—676
10:45—390, 453

Luke

1:15—406
1:35—418
2:12—410
4:18–19—575
4:21—555, 575
5:17—21—358
7:27—406
7:48—555
8:22–25—459
9:12–17—440
11:27–28—533
11:29–30—410
15:19—470
16:31—410
17:21—675
18:18—470
19:10—359
21:38—602
24:27—555
24:31, 32—425
24:39—376
24:45—426
24:45–47, 48—377

John

1—518
1–4—x, 667
1:1—674
1:3—412
1:4—392, 614
1:6—406
1:11—577
1:13—490
1:14—616
1:15–18—595
1:18—597
1:20–21—405
1:21—452
2–11—411, 412
2:1–11—412
2:24–25—610
3:3—358, 431, 490
3:5—491
3:7—653
3:14—632
3:14–15—631, 632
3:16—470, 635
3:18—400
3:19—614
3:24—351
3:28—406
4:10—470
4:22—350
4:24—383
4:46–54—412
5—349, 350, 447, 452
5–8—x, 626
5:1—349
5:1–16—365
5:1–18—412
5:2–9—355
5:9–16—361, 367, 373, 379
5:16—366
5:17–23—385
5:17–30—387
5:17–47—385
5:19—387
5:19–20—404
5:20—388, 389
5:21—389
5:23—390, 676
5:24—662, 665
5:24–27—391
5:24–29—392
5:25–26—395
5:28–29—395, 397

5:28–30—398
5:30–32—422
5:31–32—405
5:31–47—387, 403
5:33–34—622
5:33–35—351, 422
5:35—406
5:36—406, 409, 410, 523
5:36–38—405
5:37–38—415, 416
5:37–40—407
5:37–42, 44—428
5:37–47—407, 422
5:39—421, 428
5:39–44—427
5:39–47—623
5:44—434
5:45–47—407, 422, 433
5:46—554
6—ix, 350, 447, 452, 615
6–8—667
6:1–4—439
6:1–14—412
6:1–15—440
6:2—485
6:5–9—445
6:6—485
6:9—485
6:10–15—451
6:14—452
6:16–21—413, 457
6:18—458
6:21—461
6:22–27—463
6:24—485
6:26–27—464
6:27—470
6:28–29—469
6:29—470, 525
6:30–35—475
6:32—519
6:33, 38, 51—530
6:35—413, 442, 477, 525, 676
6:35–40—512
6:36—484
6:36–37—468, 481, 513
6:37—484–88, 493–95, 500,
    507, 531
6:38–39—499, 500
6:39—485, 508
6:39–40—508
6:40—505, 525
6:41–42—512

6:41–47—511
6:44—358, 393, 482, 531
6:44–47—513
6:45—515, 525
6:47—515
6:48–51—517, 518
6:51—519, 524, 530
6:52—524
6:52–59—523
6:53—665
6:55–58—524
6:56—527
6:57—528
6:60, 67—530
6:60–61—530
6:60–65—529
6:61–62—531
6:66–68—535
6:68—536
6:69—542
6:69–71—541
7—543, 615
7:1—548
7:1–10—547
7:6—551, 597
7:6–8—548
7:11–13—553
7:12—554, 557
7:14–18—559, 560
7:16–17—598
7:17—558, 563
7:19—566
7:19–24—565
7:20—614
7:24—566
7:25—572
7:25–31—571
7:26—572
7:28–29—597
7:31—572
7:32—626
7:32–36—577
7:33–34—578
7:35—582
7:37–38—598, 615
7:37–39—583
7:38—599
7:40—452, 590
7:40–44—589
7:41—590
7:41–42—591
7:43—590
7:44—592

7:45–52—595
7:46—596
7:47–48—599
7:49—599
7:51—600
7:53–8:11—601, 607
8—349, 615, 667
8:3–11—626
8:7—605
8:9—605
8:10–11—605
8:12—477, 602, 513, 518,
    614, 676
8:13—621, 626
8:13–18—619
8:14–15—621
8:15–16—621, 622
8:17—621
8:17–18—622
8:19—676
8:19–27—625
8:21—628
8:21, 24—629
8:22—626
8:25—627
8:28—633
8:28–29—631
8:29—638
8:30—638
8:30–32—637
8:31–32—638, 644
8:33—645, 668
8:33–36—643
8:34—646, 665
8:35—648
8:37–40—649
8:38—652
8:41—626, 656
8:41–50—655
8:51—661, 662, 665
8:52–56—667
8:54–55—669
8:55—668
8:56—555, 670
8:57–58—674
8:57–59—673
8:59—677
9–12—x
9:1–41—413
9:5—477, 518, 676
9:22—350
9:29—428
9:33—429

9:38—358
9:41—358
10:7—665
10:7, 9—477, 518, 614, 676
10:11, 14—477, 518, 614, 676
10:27–28—502
10:30—675
10:37–38—406
11:1–46—413
11:25—413, 477, 518, 676
11:35—614
11:40—542
12:18—413
12:32—632
12:33—632
12:44—676
12:45—676
12:46—618
13–17—x
13:2, 27—657
14:1—676
14:6—390, 468, 477, 518
14:9—676
14:10—411
14:17—676
15:1, 5—477, 518, 614, 676
15:22–24—411
15:23—676
17:1, 25—675
18–21—x
18:10—514
20:7—676
20:17—376, 675
20:21—377
20:22—377
20:25—676
20:28—573, 676
20:29—556
20:30–31—392, 411
21:6, 11—514

Acts

1:12—371
2:2—418
2:22–23—550
2:31—425
2:37—470
2:42, 46–47—382
4—425
4:11–12—375
4:12—422
5:3—659
7:2—393

8:42, 44—393
13:14, 27, 42, 44—371
14:15—556
15:21—371
16:13—371
16:19—514
16:30—470
16:31—471
17:2—371
17:27–28—460
17:30–31—397, 563
18:4—371
20:7—377
27:15, 17—418

Romans

1:4—573
1:24, 26, 27—628, 678
3:1–2—353
3:10–11—463, 483
3:22–23—634
3:23—437, 562
3:26—605
4:11—410
4:19–21—670
5:8—635
6:4—454
6:6—454
6:23—611, 629, 664
7:18—358
8:17—585
8:28–29—508
8:35, 37–39—502
8:36—502
9–11—354
9:4–5—353
9:6–13—394
11:29—396
14:5–6—372
16—593, 594

1 Corinthians

1:30—618
2:14—464, 490
6:20—592
10:13—443, 504, 579, 660
10:31—384
11:26—525
15:3—550
15:9—509
15:55—664
15:58—384, 496
16:2—377

2 Corinthians

2:11—657
5:21—569
6:2—582, 629
10:5—623
12:7—660

Galatians

1:8—381
2:20—528
3:10—435, 567
3:13—635
3:13–16—424
3:28—593
4:4–5—549
4:9–11—371
4:10—374
5:2—652
5:22–23—509
6:14—454
6:15—652

Ephesians

1:4—485
2:1–10—592
2:8—491, 494
2:10—503
3:8—509
3:19—528
6:12—503

Philippians

1:6—508
3:8—539
3:13–14—593
4:6–7—504
4:19—443, 470

Colossians

2:14—371
2:15—503
2:16–17—371

1 Thessalonians

2:18—660
5:16–17—384

1 Timothy

1:15—509

2 Timothy

1:12—501

Hebrews

4:15–16—443
10:7—507, 544
11:3—542
11:6—494
11:8–10—669
11:17–19—467, 672
12:2—354
12:6—458

James

1:17—506
1:18—489
2:10—435

1 Peter

1:18–20—550
1:23—491

2 Peter

1:4—395
1:21—418

1 John

3:16—635
5:8, 16—389
5:9–10—543

Revelation

3:20—468
13:8—550
14:13—629

James Montgomery Boice is president and cofounder of the Alliance of Confessing Evangelicals, the parent organization of *The Bible Study Hour,* on which he has been the speaker since 1969. He is the senior pastor of Philadelphia's historic Tenth Presbyterian Church.